'In his sweeping survey of the damage do
predominant modern interpretation of natur
outlines a radically nonmodern "speculative
examines the shortcomings of numerous modern philosophical movements
that have proved to be impotent in the face of destructive socio-economic
doctrines – such as a voracious and parasitic form of capitalism. Maintaining
that a genuinely comprehensive philosophy of nature may yet result in more
responsible attitudes towards Nature and all its creatures, Gare holds out some
hope for a self-destructive civilization on the verge of immanent collapse.'

Murray Code, Guelph University, Canada

'Gare's Manifesto is a clarion sounding against nihilism. Prevailing technoscience
is a monism built upon minimalist models that yields only heat death in the
long term and human extirpation in the more immediate future. Gare posits
instead a "speculative naturalism" that explores a dialectical worldview in terms
of those feedbacks among social and material processes that provide meaning
and "happiness" in terms of a life fulfilled. A philosophical and ecological guide
to survival in necrophilic times!'

Robert E. Ulanowicz, University of Florida, USA

'From a scientific perspective, Arran Gare in this work struggles with problems
raised by the mutually reinforcing practices of Newtonian science and analytical
philosophy, which have motivated the ascendency of "technoscience" and the
eclipse of a more holistic "ecological science". His own perspective on science-
in-society emerges from a generally phenomenological viewpoint. Taking a
dialectical stance, he urges that our conceptual world needs to get beyond focus
on Analysis and some timid tentative Synopses. Intellectual work needs instead
to go all the way toward forming working Syntheses which can serve as guiding
frameworks for scientific investigations. He urges Speculative Naturalism, in
the form founded by Schelling, which transcends both British analytical
philosophy and French structuralism as being suitable for guiding scientific
inquiry. This would place scientific investigations in a generally developmental
framework, which would be accessible as well to perspectives in the humanities
as a philosophy of science. Then, as well, importantly, such an approach
potentially presents a framework informative for environmentalism. This latter
connection points toward the goal of creating an "ecological civilization".'

Stanley Salthe, Brooklyn College of the City University of New York, USA

'Widely and deeply researched, this book is a challenge and a wake-up call for
philosophers and non-philosophers alike. He joins theory and practice to show
the inadequacy of most contemporary philosophies and economic/political
policies for creating "an ecologically sustainable civilization".'

William S. Hamrick, Professor Emeritus of Philosophy,
Southern Illinois University Edwardsville;
author of Kindness and the Good Society *and co-author of* Nature and Logos

'In the modern value free research university, history of any kind is reduced to information about this or that past event. The effort to understand what is happening by describing the way the present has come to be has been largely excluded at a time when such understanding is essential for wise response to unprecedented global crises. When universities awaken from their dogmatic slumber, Gare's account of the history of thought will become the classic basis for building new institutions responding to urgent needs.'

John Cobb Jr., Professor Emeritus of Theology, Claremont School of Theology, Claremont, California, USA

The Philosophical Foundations of Ecological Civilization

The global ecological crisis is the greatest challenge humanity has ever had to confront, and humanity is failing. The triumph of the neo-liberal agenda, together with a debauched 'scientism', has reduced nature and people to nothing but raw materials, instruments and consumers to be efficiently managed in a global market dominated by corporate managers, media moguls and technocrats. The arts and the humanities have been devalued, genuine science has been crippled, and the quest for autonomy and democracy undermined. The resultant trajectory towards global ecological destruction appears inexorable, and neither governments nor environmental movements have significantly altered this, or indeed, seem able to. *The Philosophical Foundations of Ecological Civilization* is a wide-ranging and scholarly analysis of this failure.

This book reframes the dynamics of the debate beyond the discourses of economics, politics and techno-science. Reviving natural philosophy to align science with the humanities, it offers the categories required to reform our modes of existence and our institutions so that we augment, rather than undermine, the life of the ecosystems of which we are part. From this philosophical foundation, the author puts forth a manifesto for transforming our culture into one which could provide an effective global environmental movement and provide the foundations for a global ecological civilization.

Arran Gare is Associate Professor of Philosophy and Cultural Inquiry at Swinburne University of Technology, Australia.

Routledge Environmental Humanities

Series editors: Iain McCalman and Libby Robin

A full list of titles in this series is available at: www.routledge.com/series/REH.

The *Routledge Environmental Humanities* series is an original and inspiring venture recognising that today's world agricultural and water crises, ocean pollution and resource depletion, global warming from greenhouse gases, urban sprawl, overpopulation, food insecurity and environmental justice are all *crises of culture*.

The reality of understanding and finding adaptive solutions to our present and future environmental challenges has shifted the epicenter of environmental studies away from an exclusively scientific and technological framework to one that depends on the human-focused disciplines and ideas of the humanities and allied social sciences.

We thus welcome book proposals from all humanities and social sciences disciplines for an inclusive and interdisciplinary series. We favour manuscripts aimed at an international readership and written in a lively and accessible style. The readership comprises scholars and students from the humanities and social sciences and thoughtful readers concerned about the human dimensions of environmental change.

The Philosophical Foundations of Ecological Civilization

A manifesto for the future

Arran Gare

Routledge
Taylor & Francis Group

LONDON AND NEW YORK

earthscan
publishing for a sustainable future

First published 2017
by Routledge
2 Park Square, Milton Park, Abingdon, Oxon OX14 4RN

and by Routledge
711 Third Avenue, New York, NY 10017

First issued in paperback 2018

Routledge is an imprint of the Taylor & Francis Group, an informa business

British Library Cataloguing-in-Publication Data
A catalogue record for this book is available from the British Library

Library of Congress Cataloging-in-Publication Data
Names: Gare, Arran, 1948- author.Title: The philosophical foundations of
ecological civilization : a manifesto for the future / Arran Gare.
Description: New York, NY : Routledge, 2016. | Includes bibliographical
references and index.
Identifiers: LCCN 2016006617 | ISBN 9781138685765 (hardback) |
ISBN 9781315543031 (ebook)
Subjects: LCSH: Environmental ethics. | Human ecology--Philosophy. |
Environmentalism--Philosophy.
Classification: LCC GF80 .G44 2016 | DDC 179/.1--dc23
LC record available at HYPERLINK "https://protect-us.mimecast.
com/s/1drmB5uRr3eOtZ." https://lccn.loc.gov/2016006617

ISBN 13: 978-1-138-59739-6 (pbk)
ISBN 13: 978-1-138-68576-5 (hbk)

Typeset in Bembo
by Saxon Graphics Ltd, Derby

Contents

Preface

Working as an historian and philosopher of science and mathematics and a social and environmental philosopher in one of the most environmentally destructive, anti-intellectual and nihilistic nations on Earth, research on this book has involved continual struggle just to defend the conditions for independent research. It has involved a struggle against the corruption of universities and other public institutions, and against the paralyzing intellectual fragmentation promoted by government policies. However, the advantage of working in this environment has been that the inter-connections between passive nihilism, the marginalization of genuine philosophy, the fragmentation of intellectual culture, the corruption of public institutions – most importantly, universities and research institutions, subversion of democracy, depoliticization of the population, domination by transnational corporations, plundering of public assets and ecological destruction, that is, the forces driving the whole of humanity to ecocide, have been far easier to see. Concomitantly, it has also been easier to see the immense importance of developing fully fledged philosophy to overcome people's disorientation, to free their minds to understand the world in all its complexity, to appreciate the meaning of life and its history and to face up to the problems confronting them, and to envisage new and realistic possibilities for the future. And it has been far easier to appreciate immense importance and the value of solidarity of those challenging power elites and the corruption of intellectual life, both locally and internationally.

Locally, I owe an immense debt of gratitude to Alan Roberts, Glenn McLaren and other members of the Complex Processes Research Group at Swinburne University; internationally, to John Cobb Jr., Murray Code, David Ray Griffin, Michel Weber, James O'Connor, Joel Kovel, Michael Zimmerman, Takis Fotopoulos, Stan Salthe, Jesper Hoffmeyer, Kalevi Kull, Plamen Simeonov, Stuart Kauffman, Sasa Josifovic, Iain McGilchrist, Zhihe Wang, Xu Chun and Shuji Ozeki, among others. I am indebted to Juliet Bennett, Andrew Dawson and Stan Salthe for comments on various drafts of this work. I would also like to pay tribute to Pan Yue who has vigorously promoted the goal of ecological civilization in China.

Introduction

If the world's leading climate scientists are right, and there is no reason to believe they are not, unless very drastic action is taken to stop greenhouse gas emissions, we are in danger of producing a runaway greenhouse effect that will be unstoppable. It will transform the global ecosystem so radically that billions of people will die and civilization might not survive. Even without a runaway greenhouse effect, the melting of Greenland and Antarctic ice will flood river deltas and coastal plains, which grow much of our food and where many of world's major cities are located. There will be more extreme weather events and more precipitation, but this will be over the oceans and the polar regions. In the tropics, also where much food is grown, it will be hotter and much drier. The die off of species occurring at present matches the great die offs that marked the end of past geological eras. It is predicted that by mid-century the Amazon rainforest will have been destroyed, along with all ocean fisheries. European honey bees, which have co-evolved with flowering plants and humans and are responsible for the fertilization of plants that produce up to a third of our food, are dying off in huge numbers. In Asian cities such as Beijing the air is often barely breathable, with 4000 people dying each day in China from the effects of air pollution. These are only some of the most obvious signs of a looming global ecological catastrophe. Yet as George Monbiot (2006) has shown, action to address this situation is obscenely inadequate. As Ulrich Beck summed up our predicament:

> The transformation of the unseen side-effects of industrial production into global ecological trouble spots is ... not at all a problem of the world surrounding us – not a so-called 'environmental problem' – but a far-reaching institutional crisis of industrial society itself. ... What previously appeared 'functional' and 'rational' now becomes and appears to be a threat to life, and therefore produces and legitimates dysfunctionality and irrationality. ... Just as earlier generations lived in the age of the stagecoach, so we now and in future are living in the hazardous age of creeping catastrophe. What generations before us discovered despite resistance, and had to shout out loud at the world, we have come to take for granted: the impending 'suicide of the species'.
>
> (Beck 1996, p.32, 34, 40)

Notwithstanding the agreements reached at the 2015 conference in Paris on reducing greenhouse emissions, it appears that governments are more preoccupied with economic growth than the survival of humanity. Concern with growth is often justified as the only way to overcome unemployment, a threat that nowadays hangs over almost everyone. But governments are more preoccupied with technological advances that will throw people out of work, supposedly in order to improve productivity, than employment. Perhaps this is their real concern. But the evidence is that apart from the manufacture of computer chips, since the 1970s these technological advances have reduced labour productivity (although this varies between countries), while new technologies are, on aggregate, producing more greenhouse gases and putting greater stress on ecosystems (Friedman 2005, p.91). Still, it is held to be obvious that economies have flourished over the last forty years through the liberation of markets from bureaucracies and parochial national self-interest. However, quite apart from recurring financial crises that threaten to cripple the global and many national economies, the underlying causes of which have not begun to be addressed, studies by Perelman (2007, 3ff.) and Piketty (2014, p.571ff.) reveal that the vast majority of working people in the advanced Western countries have become worse off since 1973 (although this also varies between countries). They have to spend more time in education to get work and then, when they are properly employed, have to work longer hours for the same or less income. Also, most work has been transformed by the McDonaldization of the economy, making it soul destroying rather than fulfilling. And employment is not guaranteed, with young people now facing permanent precarious employment and precarious economic futures, forming a new class, the precariat, just above the growing class of permanently unemployed.

Perhaps our altruistic ruling elites have concluded that the welfare of people in affluent countries had to be sacrificed so that the rest of the world could develop their economies and share the benefits of economic growth. But the vast majority of people in these developing economies are also worse off. As Vandana Shiva and others have shown, they have been and continue to be pushed off their land by agribusinesses which are replacing sustainable agriculture by unsustainable agriculture. Rural populations have moved and are being moved into the slums of cities, creating what Mike Davis (2006) characterized as a planet of slums. To survive, they are then forced to work in ecologically inefficient factories in conditions reminiscent of early nineteenth century Britain, or join criminal gangs. Either way they are contributing to expanding the ecological footprint of humanity which is already unsustainable, although not contributing as much as the obscenely wealthy elites in these developing countries, among the true beneficiaries of these policies, at least in the short term.

One would expect under these circumstances that political movements and political leaders would emerge, charting new directions for their societies. However, most radical political movements now appear only interested in protesting; they have no alternative visions for the future and appear uninterested in developing them. Even when they gain power, political radicals squander their opportunities. It seems that whichever politicians gain power, whether they call themselves conservatives, liberals, social democrats or communists, with minor variations they pursue the same policies, freeing markets, promoting managerialism, selling public assets, undermining work security and replacing workers with new forms of technology, further empowering the super-wealthy and adding to the ecological footprint of humanity. Alternatively, they become corrupt, ingratiating themselves to the rich and attempting to buy support from the poor with handouts, usually at the expense of productive workers. With very few exceptions, the only real alternatives are offered by religious fundamentalists and paranoid nationalists, who are hostile to environmentalists. The few other alternatives that have been offered have been derided or dismissed, whether justly or not, as efforts to return to the past, or as being totally unrealistic.

Understanding all this is impossible through the received interpretative schemes of common sense. And if common sense is inadequate, then unless people accept their depoliticization, as many have, they have to turn to academics to provide better interpretative schemes. What they find here is a multiplicity of perspectives associated with an increasing number of schools of thought and a growing number of disciplines and sub-disciplines, coming into and going out of fashion at faster and faster rates, sometimes supporting each other, sometimes opposing each other, fragmenting further people's capacity to understand the world. Even Marxism has fragmented. The credibility of the humanities has been almost completely destroyed by such fragmentation, but the situation is little better in the human sciences, or even in the natural sciences. Radical economists argue that mainstream economics legitimating neoliberal agendas has been totally discredited, but they are divided among themselves. They are ignored by the mainstream economists who maintain their control over economics departments and leading journals and have exclusive access to politicians and government officials. The natural scientists have been wrong so often on simple matters such as what is a good diet that they have lost credibility. Some supposed experts, claiming to be skeptical environmentalists, still claim there is no environmental crisis. If in quest of more solid foundations for our beliefs, we fall back to the physical sciences, and finally to physics as the most successful science in history, and for reductionists, the ultimate science which must explain the findings of all other sciences, we find incompatibilities between the major theories and no progress in dealing with these. Some physicists claim that the dominant research program, designed to overcome this situation, is not really science at all. As Peter Woit (2007) put it, it is not even wrong. If we ignore such critics of the state of physics and accept the mainstream view we are told that nature can only be understood through mathematics which now cannot be interpreted in non-mathematical language, and the mathematics used in advanced physics requires at least a doctorate in theoretical physics or mathematics. In other words, we are being told to forget about trying to understand the cosmos and our place within it, and to leave this to the experts, who can't even agree on what science is.

It is only natural under these circumstances to turn to philosophy and philosophers, which apparently, at least some young people are doing. What they find is the increasing dominance of analytic philosophers who have fragmented philosophy itself, either defending scientism, handing over to the floundering scientists (and the experts) the power to define reality, or in the case of those opposing scientism, defending commonsense, despite its obvious inability to comprehend the complexity of the world in which we now live. If young people turn to 'continental' philosophers they find French philosophers have embraced structuralism, which is another form of scientism, or poststructuralism, with poststructuralists deconstructing the humanities, claiming that even the quest for a comprehensive understanding of the world is oppressive. It is somehow seen as radical chic to debunk the assumptions on which democracy is based. There remains the alternative of some form of Idealism still defended by German philosophers, but Idealism is hardly the best philosophy for grappling with ecological problems, and in the light of the apparent progress of the sciences and skeptical attacks on Idealism by deconstructive postmodernists, young people have good reasons for seeing Idealism as implausible and irrelevant to facing up to global ecological destruction. Just when philosophers are desperately needed, it seems most have decided to redefine philosophy to render it irrelevant to the challenges facing civilization, except perhaps to contribute to the development of information technology and the entertainment industry.

The argument presented here is that there are alternative ideas that have been and are being developed that are adequate to the crises we are facing, but to be effective, they need to be identified, integrated and further developed. Such ideas are marginalized for the very good reason that they really do challenge the current structures of power and its power elites, and more fundamentally, the culture through which most people define themselves and their goals. What is required is the means to achieve this integration in order to mobilize humanity to redefine its place in the cosmos and its destiny, and then on this foundation, to create a society that augments life and the current regime of the global ecosystem. This will require a reorientation of philosophy to overcome fragmentation and replace the defective philosophical assumptions that have dominated modernity, including mainstream science. It will require a revival of speculative philosophy and the philosophy of nature. It is to this end that this book is a manifesto for ecological civilization; but it is also a manifesto for the philosophy of nature and for speculative philosophy. It is a manifesto for 'speculative naturalism' along with 'speculative dialectics' as a condition for creating an ecological civilization.

There is a further problem that, in the current intellectual and cultural environment, philosophy has been so discredited that to lay claim to being philosophical, and more than that, to invite people into the quagmire of arguments over which philosophy to embrace, is still to invite dismissal as being of no practical relevance. The eminent Spanish/Argentinian/Canadian philosopher of science (my own base discipline) Mario Bunge observed, 'academic philosophy has become rather stale. It is obsessed with its own past, suspicious of radically new insights, inward-looking, largely removed from worldly concerns, and therefore of hardly any help in tackling most of the issues faced by ordinary people' (Bunge 2001, p.9). This is how most people now see academic philosophy, at least in Anglophone countries. Philosophy is an intellectual labyrinth that philosophers themselves have demonstrated leads nowhere. But this is to identify philosophy with what most academic philosophers now do, ignoring the tendency, noted by George Orwell, for words to be used to signify the exact opposite of what they originally meant. Much of what presently purports to be 'philosophy' is really anti-philosophy, if one understands what philosophy was in the past.

Philosophy in the past has been central to the formation of civilizations. It is, as Alfred North Whitehead (1932, p.x) argued, 'the most effective of all the intellectual pursuits.... It is the architect of the buildings of the spirit, and it is also their solvent: and the spiritual precedes the material'. Philosophy underpins civilizations, whether done well or badly, taken seriously or ignored. As Whitehead observed:

> [A] philosophic outlook is the very foundation of thought and of life. The sort of ideas we attend to, and the sort of ideas which we push into the negligible background, govern our hopes, our fears, our control of behaviour. As we think, we live. This is why the assemblage of philosophic ideas is more than a specialist study. It moulds our type of civilization.
>
> (Whitehead 1938, p.63)

The argument running through this manifesto is that philosophy, along with the humanities generally, has a crucial and indispensable role to play in revealing the deficiencies of our culture, and in doing so, laying the foundations for the cultural transformations required to overcome the problems engendered by these deficiencies, and that work on this is being greatly hindered not only by governments, but also by academics, including those dominating the discourse of philosophy. They are locking in place the deficient assumptions of modernity while smothering efforts to develop radically new ways of thinking. This work is a protest against the gap between what philosophy should be and what it has become in Anglophone countries: the abstruse argumentation about minor issues characteristic of much of analytic philosophy (although there are prominent exceptions to this) or the quest to keep abreast of the latest intellectual fashions emerging from Paris characteristic of many devotees of 'continental philosophy', and consequently, withdrawal from the broader ambitions that defined philosophy in the past. Without such ambitious philosophy to relate all domains of culture, other disciplines inevitably fragment into a multiplicity of sub- and sub-sub-disciplines, corrupting the whole of academia and intellectual and cultural life generally. We need new concepts to overcome this fragmentation through which the problems of culture, society and civilization can be understood and effectively addressed, along with the means to develop and defend them. However, more than this is involved. These problems need to be addressed in such a way that these concepts are appropriated and embodied in practices, institutions and in people's orientation to life. It is in this way that the foundations for a future civilization can be put in place.

To create a viable future, it will be necessary to open the way for questioning and replacing the prevailing reductionist form of naturalism, along with the scientism engendered by and supporting it; and correspondingly, for questioning and replacing the debased notions of life and humanity promoted by orthodox biologists, economists and psychologists. These are being insulated from such questioning by philosophers. What is wrong? C.D. Broad pointed out that, traditionally, philosophers utilized three 'methods': analysis, synopsis (that is, 'viewing together') and synthesis. Analytic philosophers privilege analysis, but have limited its role, in most cases now excluding any place for the analysis of experience. With the exception of Scandinavian analytic philosophers, most have also radically reduced the role accorded to synopses, narrowing their perspectives and blinding them to the incoherencies of culture and their complicity in its problems. Often, although not always, this is associated with a disdain for the history of philosophy, resulting in the contexts needed to make sense of the more important philosophical questions and arguments having been lost. Such analytic philosophers have acquiesced in the fragmentation of intellectual inquiry and culture. Most importantly, these analytic philosophers have excluded almost entirely any role for the synthetic thought to overcome such fragmentation and to develop new ways of thinking and new concepts to replace prevailing defective thinking and defective concepts.

When philosophy has utilized all three methods to the full, its contributions to other disciplines, to the broader culture and to civilization have been immense. Again, as Whitehead proclaimed:

> Philosophy is the welding of the imagination and common sense into a restraint upon specialists, and also into an enlargement of their imaginations. By providing the generic notions philosophy should make it easier to conceive the infinite variety of specific instances which rest unrealized in the womb of nature.
>
> (Whitehead 1978, p.17)

Such philosophy transforms culture, thereby creating new subjectivities with the strength of character and solidarity to change the direction of history. A work that explicitly aspires to do this, is a manifesto. As Mikhail Epstein pointed out:

> [M]anifestos proclaim new ... cultural epochs, and they trigger these movements by the very act of their proclamation. Manifestos are performative rather than descriptive speech acts; they implement what they pronounce. ... Manifestos are neither factual nor fictional – they are formative.
>
> (Epstein 2012, p.14)

While there are profound intellectual and cultural reasons for promoting speculative naturalism, the most important is that it is required to challenge the reduction of science to techno-science, challenge the radical devaluation of the arts, humanities and 'humanistic' human sciences, and challenge the subsequent nihilism and the consequences of this nihilism. Overcoming nihilism, it will be argued, is necessary to revive the struggle for genuine democracy to liberate people from the imperatives of the global market, from corporate managers and from technocrats, and this is essential for effectively confronting and overcoming the threat of global ecological destruction. Post-nihilistic philosophy is required to lay the foundations for and to set humanity on the path to a new, ecologically sustainable civilization; or as the Chinese environmentalists have called for, an 'ecological civilization'.

With this in mind, some guidance on how to read this book is in order. Philosophers, philosophy students and those who already have a strong interest in philosophy, particularly those who have come to realize the enormity of the environmental crisis and the significance of the failure to deal with it, can usefully read the book straight through, although I would expect such people to read the pieces that most interest them before doing so. They will see that the aim of the book is to describe, defend and deploy a speculative dialectical approach to provide a synoptic overview of the development of modern philosophy and science, particularly after Kant, showing the relationship and the differences between rival philosophical traditions, and to defend and develop a new philosophical synthesis that can replace current orthodoxies. It is an attempt to explain the current marginal state of philosophy while showing that philosophy is far more important and has far more potential than is presently recognized. The book defends one largely overlooked tradition of philosophy, speculative naturalism, against others, through this speculative dialectical form of thinking. Finally, this highlights the challenges philosophy now faces and shows how philosophy should be advanced in the future, not only to deal with philosophical and theoretical issues and to advance the natural and human sciences, but to guide people in the present to deal with practical problems, to formulate policies, to engage in political struggle and to do so in a way that involves laying the philosophical foundations on which the future can be built.

For those grappling with environmental problems, such as academics, scientists and students in diverse disciplines other than philosophy, green activists, civil servants, members of green political parties and political leaders previously uninterested in philosophy, reading this book is not so straightforward. Although I wrote this book with this readership in mind, I would discourage such readers from reading the book from beginning to end in the order that it is written. Without a prior interest in philosophy it is difficult to see why any time should be taken examining and critiquing leading analytic philosophers, or examining the history of French philosophy and its relation to Marxism. While it might not seem so irrelevant, such practically oriented people are unlikely to see why they should examine the crippling influence of logical positivism, not only on the arts and the humanities, but also on science, and why speculative natural philosophy is essential to the progress of all of these. These readers, after reading this introduction, would be better off reading the conclusion first, then Chapter One, followed by Chapter Five and Chapter Six. Chapter Five identifies the 'Radical Enlightenment' (as opposed to the mainstream 'Moderate Enlightenment') as the suppressed tradition upholding the social imaginary of autonomy, liberty and democracy. Chapter Six offers a new world-orientation and vision of the future to aim at, utilizing developments in ecology and human ecology to rethink the Radical Enlightenment. It is shown how this world-orientation could enable environmentalists to be more effective, how it could unite them into a global movement to transform civilization. These chapters suggest that without such a world-orientation and without such a vision of the future, encapsulated in the notion of ecological civilization, environmentalists, including green political parties, will have only a marginal impact, even if they gain some power, and a global ecological catastrophe will be unavoidable. At the same time these chapters point to the significance of work being undertaken in diverse disciplines, work which is having far less impact than it should because of the failure to link it with other work, and make some effort to make these links, for instance linking political philosophy and ethics with work in ecology.

However, if the perspective offered here is not to be seen as just another point of view which can be dismissed by power elites and ignored by the rest of the population, it is necessary to ground and defend the claims being made in these chapters. It should then be evident why it is necessary to read Chapter Three and Chapter Four to understand the failures of Marxism and the importance of natural philosophy to defend and advance genuine science, as opposed to technoscience. Finally, to understand and to challenge philosophical doctrines that have been crippling the advance of philosophy, undermining the humanities, legitimating defective economic, ethical and political philosophies, supporting outmoded ideas in science and undermining any solidarity among those oppressed by power elites, it is necessary to read the Chapter Two. Here the work of the most influential American philosopher of the twentieth century, W.V. Quine, characterized by Hilary Putnam as 'The Greatest Logical Positivist' (1990, pp.268–277), is placed in historical context, revealing its limitations, its fundamentally defective assumptions and its paralyzing effects. These deficiencies are highlighted by a brief description of the work of rival analytic philosophers, most importantly, Jaakko Hintikka, and of the tradition of Idealism, but are shown to be more fundamentally challenged by Friedrich Schelling's conception of philosophy. Schelling is defended as the philosopher who successfully overcame the dualisms of Kant's philosophy, reconciling natural philosophy, history and art. His work exemplifies a form of speculative dialectics. It offered the path that modern philosophy should have taken, the path taken by process metaphysicians. This is the philosophy being revived by philosophically oriented scientists and mathematicians and is being defended throughout this work.

1 The ultimate crisis of civilization

Why turn to philosophy

This book supports, further articulates and advances a new vision of the future that, I believe, has the potential to unite humanity to overcome the greatest crisis it has ever had to confront, the immanent destruction of the current regime of the global ecosystem. This is the regime of which humanity is part, in which it has co-evolved with other species and produced a stable interglacial period that, for 10,000 years, has been ideal for humans. This is the period in which civilizations have emerged and flourished, and which maintains the conditions for their existence. It has become clear that to continue on our present path will accelerate ecological destruction until massive environmental changes, for instance a runaway greenhouse effect, will bring about a switch from one global ecosystem regime to another that will render human life in most of the presently populated world all but impossible, just as overfishing of cod around Newfoundland produced a switch that has all but eliminated cod (Holling, 2010). Such regime changes are increasingly common, with an almost total collapse of ocean ecosystems expected over the next 50 years. It can and is likely to happen to the global ecosystem unless there is a drastic change of direction of civilization (Gare 2014a). The possibility of such regime changes are conceptualized in complexity theory as bifurcations, or more dramatically, as catastrophes. Conceived as 'tipping points', this is the main focus of research of Germany's leading climate scientist, Hans Joachim Schellnhuber, who on the basis of his research published a paper titled 'Global Warming: Stop Worrying, Start Panicking?' (2008). It is inconceivable that ruling elites do not know that failing to deal with greenhouse gas emissions poses a threat to the lives of billions of people. It appears that many members of the new global ruling class who dominate the politics of nations tacitly accept climate destabilization as a Darwinian mechanism for culling excess human population, possibly serving as a weapon of mass destruction against Asians, with other vulnerable regions such as much of Africa, the Arabian Peninsula, Brazil and Australia being collateral damage. Spencer Weart in *The Discovery of Global Warming* (2016), has provided a continually updated hypertext explaining the advances in climate science showing why we face this threat.

If in two hundred years there has not been a catastrophic collapse of the current global ecosystem with all the complexity of its life, along with most of the world's human population, and people are living civilized lives, living in ways that augment rather than undermine the resilience of their ecosystems, it will be because there will have been a major cultural, social and economic transformation of the whole of humanity (Klein 2014; Kovel, 2007). The destructive dynamics of globalized capitalism with its intensive and extensive expansion of commodification, its managerialism, its consumerism, its debasement of culture, its corruption of public institutions, pulverization of communities and subversion of democratic processes, its plundering of public assets, concentration of wealth, income and power in the hands of the global corporatocracy, and the domination of people and nations by transnational corporations imposing and then manipulating market forces, will have been overcome. For this to have been achieved, a new vision of the future will have captured people's imaginations and inspired them to struggle for and achieve what two centuries earlier had appeared so unimaginable, where as one person observed, 'it is easier to imagine the end of the world than to imagine the end of capitalism' (Jameson 2003, p.76). While there are several contenders for this, the only vision at present to have this potential is the vision put forward by radical Chinese environmentalists and embraced at least in principle by the Chinese government, first as a goal of government policy in 2007, and in 2012, written into their constitution, the vision of an ecological civilization (Gare 2012a).

It is also becoming clear that what is standing in the way of articulating this vision and effecting this transformation are deep assumptions about humanity, its place in nature and its destiny inimical to such a future. These assumptions are embedded in and are continually reproduced not only by proponents of neoliberalism, neoconservatism and scientism, but by our institutions and forms of life, and are placed beyond questioning by the fragmentation of intellectual culture, making it almost impossible to comprehend the forces at work in modern societies and how their oppressive and destructive dynamics could be overcome. Only instrumental knowledge, the categories of economics, power politics, Darwinism and social Darwinism, are taken seriously. We live in a culture where, as Ulrich Beck aptly put it: 'Concepts are empty: they no longer grip, illuminate or inflame. The greyness lying over the world ... may also come from a kind of verbal mildew' (Beck 2000, p.8).

Individuals from all spheres of life and from a variety of academic disciplines are beginning to question these assumptions and are struggling against this intellectual fragmentation. Fighting this verbal mildew, some are turning to philosophy. This includes ecologists. As David Abram observed almost twenty years ago:

> The ecological crisis may be the result of a recent and collective perceptual disorder in our species, a unique form of myopia which it now forces us to correct. For many ... the only possible course of action is to begin planning and working on behalf of the ecological world which they now discern. And yet ecological thinking is having a great deal of trouble taking root in the human world – it is still viewed by most as just another ideology;

meanwhile, ecological science remains a highly specialized discipline circumscribed with a mostly mechanistic biology. Without the concerted attention of philosophers, ecology lacks a coherent common language adequate to its aims; it thus remains little more than a growing bundle of disparate facts, resentments, and incommunicable visions.

(Abram 1996, p.82)

Traditionally, philosophers concerned themselves with the major problems confronting their civilizations, struggling to overcome one-sided, fragmented forms of thinking that had led to disasters, enabling people to find meaning in their lives whatever the circumstances while providing them with the means to orient themselves to create the future. Philosophers are (or were) the 'physicians of culture', as Nietzsche observed. Philosophy was not just one discipline among others. It was the transdiscipline that questioned the assumptions and interrogated the values and claims to knowledge of all other disciplines, revealing their significance in relation to each other, integrating their insights, asking new questions and opening up new paths of inquiry and action. In accordance with its origins in Ancient Greece, the goal of philosophy was to provide the foundations for an integrated understanding of the cosmos and the place of humanity within it through which people could define their ultimate ends. It had the responsibility for engaging with the broader culture and its problems and contradictions, for investigating the relationship between culture, society and civilization, and for working out how people could and should live and how society could and should be organized. It was also an end in itself, the culmination and affirmation of the spirit of free inquiry urged by curiosity to question all received methods, beliefs and institutions in its passionate quest to understand the universe and achieve wisdom. For such reasons, as Karl Jaspers (1993, 144) interpreted Friedrich Schelling: 'Philosophy must enter into life. That applies not only to the individual but also to the condition of the time, to history and to humanity. The power of philosophy must penetrate everything, because one cannot live without it'. Philosophy was central to the formation of individuals and society, and it was the core of the university.

The crisis of philosophy and the humanities

What those who turn to philosophy looking for guidance find, however, is that except in rare instances, philosophers who have the privileged conditions provided by universities to address this greatest of all challenges, have redefined philosophy. In Anglophone countries in particular they have transformed it into a multiplicity of subdisciplines and specializations that exclude the questions that challenged the greatest philosophers of the past and exclude engagement with the greatest challenges of the present as unscholarly. Environmental philosophy, usually characterized as environmental ethics, has been channeled into a minor sub- sub-discipline where, even if radical positions are adopted, they are impotent. Philosophy as a whole has continued its trajectory from the early Twentieth Century, where Robin Collingwood (1939) lamented, philosophers were producing 'a philosophy so scientific that no-one whose life was not a life of pure research could appreciate it, and so abstruse that only a whole-time student, and a very clever man at that, could understand it' (p.51) while at the same time they were claiming philosophy as 'a preserve for professional philosophers, and were loud in their contempt of philosophical utterances by historians, natural scientists, theologians, and other amateurs' (p.50). Turning their backs on ethics, political philosophy and even epistemology, they reveled in the uselessness of philosophy. The consequences of this are with us in the present. As John Cottingham observed:

> Philosophy is among the fastest-growing A-level subjects in Britain. This suggests that despite the pressure from governments to increase the teaching of technical, career oriented subjects, a lot of sixth-formers have a stubborn interest in more traditional enquiries about the meaning of life. ... But frustration often ensues as the aspiring philosophy student climbs higher. The university study of philosophy in the anglophone world now offers little by way of a grand synoptic vision of human life and our place in the scheme of things. Instead, the subject has fragmented into a host of highly technical specialisms, whose practitioners increasingly model themselves on the methods of the natural sciences. By the time they reach graduate studies, most students will be resigned to working within intricate, introverted 'research' programmes, whose wider significance they might be hard pressed to explain to anyone outside their special area.
>
> (Cottingham 2011, p.25)

Effectively, mainstream academic philosophers in Anglophone countries are proselytizing a debilitating, passive nihilism while denigrating and censuring any questioning of this nihilism, either from professional philosophers or anyone else, undermining not only philosophy but the humanities, the arts, universities, education, democracy and civilization, and the capacity of humanity to deal with the threats that are now facing it. Perversely, professional philosophers have aligned philosophy with anti-intellectualism and anti-intellectuals.

The contention of this manifesto is that the resurrection of philosophy, and along with it the humanities, the liberal arts and genuine science, will only be achieved by reviving natural philosophy. So, as well as being a manifesto for ecological civilization, this is also a manifesto for natural philosophy, or more precisely (distinguishing it from the naturalism of analytic philosophers), for speculative naturalism. This is the philosophy required to redefine the nature of humanity and its place in nature and the cosmos, to support, integrate and further develop disciplines and professions which have defied the fragmentation, overspecialization and dogmatism of current intellectual inquiry, to open the way to a post-nihilist culture. Only in this way can we achieve a comprehensive understanding of our current situation, open new horizons and enable people to envisage a future in which they will not be in a permanent state of economic insecurity and will have the liberty to augment rather than undermine the conditions for life, and to orient them to battle successfully for this future.

Speculative naturalism is distinguished both from the kind of philosophy that eschews speculation and focuses entirely on critical analysis, and from Idealism. Idealism developed largely as a reaction to the Cartesian/Hobbesian/Newtonian cosmology forged in the scientific revolution of the Seventeenth Century, while critical analysis developed as a reaction against Idealism. While eschewing speculation does not imply support for Newtonian cosmology, or support for speculative philosophy imply support for Idealism, in recent decades there has been a strong tendency to assume these linkages. The dominant figures in the tradition of critical analysis, or analytic philosophy as it is now called, particularly in the USA and other Anglophone countries, have vigorously upheld a reductionist naturalism based on largely Newtonian assumptions (without being aware of this), and defended the claims of mainstream science to be able to extend its methods to explain every aspect of reality, including human consciousness. That is, in the tradition of positivism and logical positivism, they have defended 'scientism', the view that science has a monopoly on the methods required to acquire and accumulate genuine knowledge, including defining what is genuine knowledge. Despite analytic philosophy itself originating in Austria and Germany, philosophy that is not analytic and naturalist tends to be labeled 'continental philosophy', with the usually tacit assumption that 'continental' philosophers (many of them in Anglophone countries) are continuing a tradition of philosophical thinking that upholds intuitions, claims to knowledge or forms of reasoning that transcend any naturalistic or scientific explanation. In doing so, it is upholding some form of Idealism. This is evident in the recent histories of continental philosophy by Braver (2007) and Redding (2009), both of which characterize continental philosophy as Idealist. At its worst, Idealism is seen to be speculative. Speculative naturalism not only brings into question the correlation between these oppositions but rejects this categorization as the root cause of the paralysis, trivialization and marginalization of philosophy, and along with this, the undermining of the arts and the humanities and the entrenchment of nihilistic assumptions of mainstream reductionist science in the broader culture and society. Acting on these nihilistic assumptions is now producing effects that threaten the future of democracy, civilization, humanity and the current regime of the global eco-system. Alive to these threats, speculative naturalists, many of them eminent scientists and mathematicians, are concerned to revive and reinstate 'philosophy' as the quest for a comprehensive understanding of humanity and its place in nature to challenge and replace the prevailing world-view, to overcome this nihilism and to avoid a global eco-catastrophe.[1]

On the surface of it, the generality of the categories defining these oppositions and the difficulty of categorizing all philosophers in terms of these opposition would make such strong claims, and such a strong agenda, highly questionable. World-wide, philosophy in recent decades has been characterized by an immense diversity of ideas and approaches (Habermas1992b). It is possible to point to a whole range of philosophers who cannot be pigeonholed by these categories. This is particularly true of philosophies and philosophers lumped together as 'continental philosophy'. Paul M. Livingston (2012) argues that poststructuralism has converged with the metalogic of analytic philosophy, while James Bradley (2012) has argued that 'continental philosophy' is an Anglo-American invention, and in fact French 'continental philosophy' has converged with analytic philosophy in denying any status to subjects. The structuralist reaction led by Claude Lévi-Strauss against neo-Hegelians, phenomenologists and proponents of hermeneutics have almost completely swept aside such Idealist and humanist philosophies, most importantly, the existentialism of Jean-Paul Sartre. According to orthodox structuralism and poststructuralism, the world and human subjects are nothing more than the effects of those functional structures that define their behaviour. While structuralism was a form of reductionism, it was antithetical to the kind of naturalism promoted by Anglophone philosophers. Under the influence of Peirce, Scandinavian analytic philosophy has converged with phenomenology, hermeneutics and semiotics. Marxist philosophers are generally opposed to reductionist naturalism and to speculative Idealism and have developed a range of philosophical positions. Promising developments have included the dialectical critical realism of Roy Bhaskar which has been applied to the problems of dealing with climate change and achieving sustainability (Bhaskar 2010). The recent proponents of 'speculative realism' or 'speculative materialism' do claim to promote speculative thought while being anti-Idealist, although what they mean by 'speculative' is by no means clear (Bryant 2011; Johnston, 2014). This is an anti-Kantian philosophy very different from speculative naturalism. There is also an assertive group of philosophers promoting revolutionary developments within science who are influenced by process metaphysics, complexity theory and Peircian semiotics who do value speculation, although such philosophers are barely tolerated and have only a marginal influence. (Hooker 2011). However, from the perspective defended here, this diversity is symptomatic of the marginalization of philosophy and simply serves to disguise which ideas really dominate, and how speculative naturalism which could effectively challenge the dominant ideas, has been marginalized.

The two cultures and the triumph of scientism

It is not just the overt and explicitly defended views that are the problem, (although these certainly are a major part of the problem), but tacitly held assumptions that constrain the way people think and the way debates are framed, the way disciplines, universities and research institutions are organized, and the way some views are taken seriously by academics, people in power and the broader public, while other, often better defended views, are ignored and then forgotten. The tacitly assumed polar oppositions manifest the deep rooted Cartesian dualism that permeates our culture (Mathews 2003, p.173ff.) This is manifest in the disjunction between mainstream science, as defended by positivists, and the humanities and the arts as defended by Idealists. These are evident in the recurring debates between what C.P. Snow referred to as the two cultures, that of scientists and that of literary intellectuals, Snow's debate with F.R. Leavis echoing the earlier debate between T.H. Huxley promoting scientific materialism and Mathew Arnold, who was aligned with the British Idealists, which in turn resonated with debates in Germany, France and Italy and the earlier critique by Idealists of Newton and of Goethe by Helmholtz. This opposition is manifest also in the opposition between neo-classical and institutionalist economics, mainstream and humanistic psychology and physical and human geography. It is also manifest in the opposition between orthodox, structuralist and analytical Marxism and Hegelian, phenomenological and humanist Marxism. The tendency to misrepresent philosophies as either analytic, naturalist and aligned with science or 'continental', Idealist and aligned with the humanities and the arts is a manifestation of these deeply held assumptions. Philosophies that do not fall on one side or the other of this divide tend to be ignored and marginalized. In all cases, this opposition has upheld a fundamentally flawed understanding of humanity's place in nature. Because more recent philosophers questioning this divide, such as the speculative realists, are insufficiently radical in their thinking, they have not succeeded in overcoming such tacitly held assumptions and thereby escaping what has become an intellectual ghetto. Only other philosophers read their works.

The outcome of the struggle between these polar oppositions has been the triumph of mainstream reductionist science over the humanities, particularly in Anglophone countries. This is evident in the virtual self-destruction of the humanities in these Anglophone countries in the last decades of the Twentieth Century, legitimated and helped along by both proponents of the American form of analytic philosophy and of French structuralism and post-structuralism. In all cases, despite the differences between them, these developments were really the triumph of scientism. The triumph of analytical and structuralist Marxism over humanist Marxism was also a triumph of scientism over the humanities. While the humanities have not been so completely defeated in France, Germany, Italy and other European countries as in North America, Britain and Australia, the trend towards marginalization of the humanities is clear in these countries also, a situation well analysed by Jerome Kagan (2009). The consequence has been the collapse of career prospects for those educated in the humanities in the civil service, institutions of education, media and politics. The marginalization of the humanities has been associated with the almost complete triumph in status accorded to algorithmic thinking (which can be performed by computers) along with claims to specialist expertise, particularly in economics, over imagination, understanding, insight, comprehension, wisdom and good judgment and the education required to foster these. The breaking up of non-analytic philosophy into multiple schools and directions characterized by a rapid succession of fashions is really a manifestation of its marginalization. This is also evident in the dissolution of the Humboldtian model of the university where the Arts and Science faculties were regarded as central because of their commitment to truth, the transformation of science into nothing but techno-science, the decline of democracy, the rise of managerialism, the unprecedented authority of neo-classical economists and the revival of social Darwinism.

To reveal what is tacitly assumed, how these oppositions have played out and why, and how these assumptions have structured culture and society and have influenced the trajectory of civilization, it is necessary to provide a schematic historical perspective on how they originated and co-evolved. To do so, it is first necessary to examine the form of analytic philosophy and scientism that triumphed in USA. It is here that the influence of this philosophy with its destructive impact on the humanities has taken its most extreme form. At the same time, this has revealed most clearly the threat posed by this trivialization of philosophy.

Alasdair MacIntyre (1987) in an address to the American Philosophical Association noted that philosophy is now seen to be:

> … a harmless, decorative activity, education in which is widely believed to benefit by exercising and extending the capacities for orderly argument, so qualifying those who study it to join the line of lemmings entering law school or business school. The professor of philosophy, on this view, stands to the contemporary bourgeoisie much as the dancing master stood to the nobility of the *ancien regime*. The dancing master taught the eighteenth-century expensively brought up young how to have supple limbs, the philosophy professor teaches their twentieth-century successors how to have supple minds.
>
> (p.85)

John McCumber published an account of the development of philosophy in USA, titled *Time in the Ditch* (2001), in which he tried to account for the apparent marginalization of philosophy. It is almost universally accepted that philosophy has been marginalized in USA and is of little significance in the modern world.

While this is true if one considers philosophy as originally understood, in another sense, nothing could be further from the truth. To begin with, as Paul Livingston (2012) pointed out, the form of life in the modern world is the outcome of 'the technicization of *information* made possible by the logical-mathematical *formalization* of language' achieved by philosophers. The consequences of 'the material and technological *realization* of some of these very same formal structures *on* the actual organization of contemporary politics' have been enormous. 'This includes, for instance, the actual communicational and computational technologies that today increasingly determine social, political, and economic institutions and modes of action around the globe' (p.4). This has not brought about a diminution of the role of intellectuals in society, but a massive expansion of their role, but in a completely new form.

This has been well described by Carl Boggs who also pointed out the effects of this on universities:

> The ideological influence of intellectuals has grown enormously during the past century, especially in the industrialized world, where modernity has meant the eclipse of isolated strata of traditional elites and the rise of an expanding stratum of rationalizing intellectuals attached to Enlightenment values of reason, secularism, scientific and technological progress, and control of nature. … [N]owhere has the impact of modernization been felt more than in the structure of higher education, where the traditional intellectual as classical scholar, philosopher, cleric, or literary figure has been replaced by the technocratic intellectual whose work is organically connected to the knowledge industry, to the economy, state, and military.
> (Boggs 1993, p.97)

This transformation is carried out under the banner of scientism, claiming that only scientific knowledge based on empirical evidence and deductive logic deserves to be taken seriously as knowledge.

However, while crippling the humanities in the name of scientism, this is not the triumph of science. What we are seeing is nothing like the science of the past in which great scientists challenged received assumptions to advance whole new ways of understanding the world, revealing unity in diversity and enabling people to better understand themselves and their place in the cosmos. What we now have is 'techno-science', science as portrayed and defended by analytic philosophers and directed by markets and human resource managers. It is the form of science that Norbert Wiener (1993) warned would be the outcome of 'Megabuck Science' dominated by people with well-defined missions, ultra-specialisation, short-term perspectives and indifference to science for its own sake. What has been the outcome of this? Bruce Charlton, a medical researcher, recently published a book *Not Even Trying: The Corruption of Real Science* (2012) decrying the current state of scientific research. He compared it to a factory in Poland before the collapse of communism: 'The factory was producing vast quantities of defective drinking glasses *which nobody wanted*. Nobody wanted to even use them. So the glasses were simply piling-up in gigantic stacks around the factory building – using-up resources, getting in everybody's way, and taking-up all the useful space' (p.14). Evidence in support of this claim is provided by Philip Mirowski in *Science-Mart: Privatising American Science* (2011). Charlton suggested that science now is so bad it would be better to pay researchers to do nothing than to continue with what they are doing. This is not the worst of it. Publishers Springer and IEEE have removed more than 120 refereed papers from their subscription services after it was discovered that they were computer generated nonsense by SCIgen (Noorden, 2014). Such science has not produced any deeper understanding of the world but the mass production of fragmented knowledge and pseudo-knowledge, providing corporations with the means to make profits, governments with the means to make weapons, and power elites generally with the means to control or confuse people. It has been complemented by the almost complete domination of public policy by the revived pre-Keynesian form of neo-classical economics that has been used to justify imposing markets on every facet of life. Science that implies limits to the quest for domination and profits, such as ecology, human ecology, climate science, institutional and ecological economics, has been undermined and marginalized.

As Boggs argued in a later work, *The End of Politics: Corporate Power and the Decline of the Public Sphere* (2000) this new techno-science has facilitated corporate colonization that 'has achieved qualitatively new levels of power, accelerated by growing economies of scale, mergers among corporations, the great resilience of the permanent war economy, massive corporate entry into media and popular culture, and … the process of globalization' (p.68). At the same time, this technology has created a media centred world with its decentred subjects, fragmented culture, the transformation of everything possible into commodified spectacles, an increasingly fragmented public life, fragmentation of the public sphere, depoliticization and paralysis of transformative politics, and the hollowing out of democracy. In short, '[g]rowing corporate power has been accompanied (and legitimated) by a return to Nineteenth Century laissez-faire principles of material self-interest, extreme individualism, and social Darwinism' (p.257) and '[t]he sad reality is that progressive movements in the United States have been able to sustain only the most feeble ideological and organizational presence … [and] no national coalition or party has emerged that is capable of making political inroads or framing durable visions or strategies of change' (p.256). Boggs summed up the consequence of this:

> As the world system becomes more rationalized at the top owing to the enhanced fluidity and mobility of capital – and to the integrative power of the technological and informational revolutions – transforming it seems more and more impossible. The centers of power have become more remote and inaccessible, seemingly beyond the scope of tangible political opposition. The splintering of meaning, so celebrated in the postmodern age, is also splintering the public sphere, and only serves to aggravate this historical impasse, helping to account for deep cynicism and pessimism among intellectuals and ordinary citizens alike.
>
> (Boggs 2000, p.212)

What Boggs is describing is the triumph of neoliberalism with its agenda of creating one global market, or *One Market Under God* (2000) as Robert Frank described it, dominated by transnational corporations and their managers, the corporatocracy, most importantly, the financial sector of this, defining the rest of the population as consumers rather than citizens of democratically organized communities. They have succeeded by manufacturing consent, eliminating the economic security required for citizenship, while subverting by coöpting potential opposition and marginalizing and undermining those who they have not been able to coöpt. That is, they have embraced the arguments of Walter Lippmann from 1920s who argued, in opposition to John Dewey, that democracy is impossible and that ruling elites must 'manufacture consent' of the masses through public relations while disempowering them.

This points to a second way in which philosophy is far from a harmless activity. By withdrawing from the quest for a comprehensive understanding of the world (which is essential to the quest for wisdom) and censuring philosophers who still strive for this, philosophers have left the broader population without the means to orient themselves in this new world order, to identify the agenda of those in the centres of power, to resist and overcome the splintering of meaning or to work towards the creation of a better future, and to govern themselves. While overtly postmodernist cultural theorists promoting bowdlerized versions of French philosophy are the visible defenders of this splintering of meaning and of the public sphere, a far more potent force has been Anglophone analytic philosophy. Philosophers have left people powerless in the face of the mind-control industries of advertising and public relations, and effectively rendered democracy impossible.

While in reality, neoliberalism, along with neoliberal strategies, are complex with many divisions and conflicts, only the willfully blind cannot see that this has been the most powerful driving ideological force in the world since the 1970s (Plehwe 2006). The 'incredulity towards metanarratives' proclaimed by postmodernists is an expression of the defeat of any alternative hegemonic discourse. Without a new master discourse opposing neoliberalism able to replace those that have lost their credibility, a discourse which can unite people into a major political force, opposing actions fizzle out without having any lasting effect. Examining one oppositional event, Boggs noted it resulted in 'nothing of a political legacy – "politics" referring here to far more than simple electoral activity. With no articulated vision or program, no organizational strategy, no perspective on issues of power or governance, the catharsis of rebellion quickly vanished' (Boggs 2000). The only real challenge to all this, Boggs observes, is the Green movement. As he noted in *Ecology and Revolution*:

> [T]he Greens have for three decades embodied the closest thing the world has seen to a mature, strategically defined ecological radicalism. Despite limits and flaws, they seem to constitute the only political force, with some global presence, dedicated to reversing the modern crisis – and the only force with a coherent strategy for change.
>
> (Boggs 2012, p.149)

In fact, though, Green activists attempting to grapple with global ecological destruction wrought by this global neoliberal regime and corporate power have been almost totally ineffectual, as Michael Shellenberger and Ted Nordhaus in *The Death of Environmentalism* (2004), Christine MacDonald in *Green, Inc.* and myself in 'Colliding with Reality' (Gare 2014a) have argued.

Continuing the struggle against nihilism

The rise of neoliberalism and the consequent paralyzing of efforts to grapple with the ecological crisis manifest the deeply rooted nihilism of the civilization of modernity, and the present work continues the quest of my earlier works to understand and overcome this nihilism. In *Nihilism Incorporated: European Civilization and Environmental Destruction* (1993a) and *Beyond European Civilization: Marxism, Process Philosophy and the Environment* (1993b) (later combined in *Nihilism Inc.* (1996)) I traced and attempted to explain the evolution, triumph, world domination and ecological destructiveness of European civilization, engendering, embodying and reproducing a nihilistic culture indifferent to the prospect of ecocide. These books were written when two branches of European civilization, one led by USA, the other by the Soviet Union, were vying for total world control. The first volume, drawing upon Marx, Nietzsche, Whitehead, Heidegger, the Frankfurt School philosophers, Joseph Needham, Robert Young and Pierre Bourdieu, was a genealogy of this nihilism. The second volume was a study of Marxism and its implementation, together with a defence of process philosophy. Despite the Soviet Union purporting to be influenced by Marx, the triumph of Marxist-Leninism over other, more radical forms of Marxism, was shown to have produced a culture surprisingly similar to that dominating the West. Only if Marx's insights are situated in the broader philosophy of some form of process metaphysics, it was argued, could a genuinely different path into the future be charted. Process metaphysics, influenced by Chinese thought, was shown to be the philosophy required to transcend European civilization to create an environmentally sustainable global civilization. A version of this, building on the work of earlier process philosophers, was elaborated, defended, and its implications revealed.

My third book, *Postmodernism and the Environmental Crisis* (1995), was a response to what appeared to be the final crisis of the civilization of modernity, a crisis engendered, it was argued, by the looming global ecological crisis, accentuated by the growth of transnational corporations and the globalization of the economy destroying the middle class dream in affluent countries. The incredulity towards metanarratives, taken to define postmodernity, was shown to equate to the collapse of belief in progress which, as Nietzsche pointed out, had taken the place of God in the modern world. 'Postmodernists' responded to this crisis in two different ways. Deconstructive postmodernists embraced the fragmentation of culture as liberating, the constructive postmodernists argued that we now have to rebuild the sciences, overcome the division between science and the humanities, and redefine progress through process metaphysics. The most influential philosophers embraced by deconstructive postmodernists were Foucault and Derrida, who were strongly influenced by Nietzsche and Heidegger, philosophers devoted to diagnosing the nihilism of modernity. Their diagnoses, that modernity is characterized by the will to power turned against itself, or that through enframing the world to reveal it only as standing reserve to be exploited, offered some direction for overcoming this nihilism. However, the development of their ideas by Foucault and Derrida, at least as appropriated by deconstructive postmodernists in USA, amounted to an assault on the humanities. Deconstructive postmodernists helped cripple opposition to the nihilistic implications of mainstream science. To defend the humanities and support the constructive postmodernists, a synthesis of the work of Pierre Bourdieu and Paul Ricoeur, influenced by the same philosophers who influenced Foucault and Derrida, was shown to provide an alternative and more creative and more defensible response to the disorientation generated by the postmodern condition. Drawing on work of Mikhail Bakhtin, Alasdair MacIntyre and David Carr to further develop Ricoeur's work on narratives, a new, dialogic environmentalist grand narrative was proposed and defended.

Despite success in predicting the future, there was a certain naivety in the conclusions of each of these books. It was assumed that if it could be shown that nihilism is not objectively valid but follows only from highly questionable and ultimately defective assumptions, if it could be shown that major thinkers of the past had been misinterpreted and their ideas were far more profound, critical and illuminating than their followers appreciated, if attention were drawn to great thinkers and the implications of their work spelt out, then as people became more aware of the precarious situation humanity is now in, these arguments would be welcomed as part of a struggle to create a less belligerent and more ecologically sustainable global civilization. This optimism was not justified by the arguments of these books, however, which pointed out that orthodox Marxists and deconstructive postmodernists were not really challenging the assumptions of the dominant culture of modernity. In this regard, there was a peculiar affinity between orthodox Marxists and deconstructive postmodernists that only became fully apparent as neoliberalism increased its stranglehold on countries and the world's dominant institutions. The proponents of each, despite the claims of the philosophers they purported to be inspired by, were not only aligned with, but shared the same assumptions as neoliberals, and in fact, in furthering their own interests were strengthening the dominant order. So, it should not have been surprising that, as Alain Supiot noted, in the European Union, former Eastern European communists and many Western Marxists allied themselves with neoliberals against social democrats, social liberals and traditional conservatives in their efforts to impose markets on every facet of life (Supiot, 2012). And Theodore Dalrymple noted in *Our Culture, What's Left of It* (2005), 'there has been an unholy alliance between those on the left, who believe that man is endowed with rights but no duties, and libertarians on the right, who believe that consumer choice is the answer to all social questions' (p.14).

Castoriadis and the challenge of the radical enlightenment

Why are communists, purported radical intellectuals and right-wing neoliberals aligned with each other? The key lies in their attitudes to democracy. In complex modern societies, there are three ways of coordinating large numbers of people: through bureaucracies, through markets, and through democratic institutions and processes. Neoliberalism is really a fusion of bureaucracies and markets against democracy. Managers of transnational corporations, the new globalized corporatocracy dominated by its financial sector, with the assistance of technocrats, have taken power from the institutions of democratic governments. Subverting democracy has been promoted by transferring the site of freedom for the masses from the political realm and the realm of work, to the realm of consumption, effectively enslaving them to the corporatocracy. At the same time the corporatocracy gained the freedom to control politicians, plunder public assets and redistribute wealth and income to the super-wealthy, and if they so choose, to destroy the global ecosystem. The figure who displayed the deepest insight into this transformation was Cornelius Castoriadis, a former Marxist who, influenced to some extent by Heidegger, became highly critical of Marxism. Castoriadis (1987) identified two opposing social imaginaries dominating modern civilization, one, the emancipatory project of autonomy whereby people put into question and take responsibility for their institutions and beliefs, a project begun in Ancient Greece; the other, pseudo-rational mastery of the world. As he put it in 'The Pulverisation of Marxism–Leninism':

> Contrary to a confused prejudice still dominant today – and which is at the basis of the contemporary version of classical 'liberalism' – the capitalist imaginary stands in direct contradiction to the project of emancipation and autonomy. Back in 1906, Max Weber derided the idea that capitalism might have anything at all to do with democracy… Capitalism subordinates everything to the 'development of the forces of production': people as producers, and then consumers, are to be made completely subordinate to it. The unlimited expansion of rational mastery – pseudomastery and pseudorationality – as is abundantly clear today – thus became the other great imaginary signification of the modern world, powerfully embodied in the realms of technique and organization.
>
> (Castoriadis 1997b, p.61)

Communists, as opposed to Marx who often said that all he knew was that he was not a Marxist, have simply embraced the capitalist imaginary of (pseudo-) rational mastery of nature and people. People are evaluated as producers. What communists created in the Soviet Union, Castoriadis argued, was bureaucratic capitalism. Consequently, former communists are entirely at home in a world dominated by neoliberals who have created a new form of bureaucratic capitalism run by corporate managers promising rational mastery of the world by intensifying competition, applying scientific (Taylorist) management principles, quantifying all work activities and forcing workers to compete with each other for employment while heavily in debt and without a security net. Supposedly radical postmodernist intellectuals who have no interest in promoting democracy are tacitly supporting this same imaginary, looking at it from the perspective of consumers rather than producers. They cannot see any role for an education in the humanities, the education designed to cultivate the virtues of people so that they can take their place in and uphold the liberty of self-governing communities, taking responsibility for themselves, their communities and the future. Consequently, they condemn those who attempt to foster such virtues as elitists who transgress the freedom of individuals to have their own preferences, consume what they like and live lives of self-indulgence.

By invoking the Ancient Greeks, Castoriadis was really calling for a new renaissance, that is, a 'rebirth' of the quest for autonomy. But his is only the latest of a whole series of such quests, of which the Florentine Renaissance, which gave birth to the humanities and civic humanism, was only one. In modernity, there is a suppressed tradition, the 'Radical Enlightenment' that has struggled to uphold this quest against the atomism, utilitarianism and instrumentalists thinking of the dominant 'Moderate Enlightenment', and it has not been powerless. It has effected a sequence of renaissances. Currently, each of these has attracted historians concerned to rescue democracy as the very meaning of this term is being destroyed by misuse of the term. These renaissances are required because from the very beginning, the quest for autonomy had powerful opponents who were very often successful in suppressing it. This is one reason why history is so important to the emancipatory social imaginary; as a means to recover and inspire the suppressed quest for autonomy, and also to expose the illusions and decadence that follows its suppression. Its opponents are hostile to or contemptuous of history, or try to neutralize it, along with the humanities and arts generally, for the very same reason. In 'The Greek *Polis* and the Creation of Democracy', Castoriadis (1997a, pp.267–289) showed that philosophy itself is a product of the quest for autonomy. It is when people question and take responsibility for their beliefs and institutions that philosophy emerges, and it becomes indispensible to a democratic society. Democracy requires notions of justice and truth, and the quest to define and advance them and to reach consensus is a condition of the possibility of effective collective decision-making and solidarity in action. Science itself, when it is understood as more than instrumental technological knowledge, is a byproduct of this search for truth. The quests for justice and truth have always been a threat to tyrants and oligarchs, although they still want the payoffs generated by these quests.

Once the social imaginary of rational mastery is understood, its sinister side soon becomes apparent. People themselves become objects to be manipulated and controlled. Effectively, they are to be conceived of as, and then rendered, totally predictable, devoid of real life, and with the quest for rational mastery, this is how not only humans but the whole of nature generally is understood. This social imaginary of rational mastery cannot acknowledge real life, and insofar as there appears to be life, it is committed to transforming it into something lifeless, for instance, transforming animals into machines for converting low priced grass into high priced flesh, or if possible, carrying out this process without living animals as intermediaries. This explains the peculiar ambiguities in the policies of neoliberal (or neoconservative) governments, their commitment to reducing producers into efficient, low cost transformers of low priced materials into high priced products, and then if possible, replacing them altogether through advanced technologies. Even as consumers, people are to be made into predictable instruments of the economy; their preferences and decisions are controlled by advertisers. In the most recent form of capitalism, advertising is important for goading consumers into accumulating debt, which effectively enslaves them and makes them far more controllable (Lazzarato, 2015). And they are expendable. If developments in robotics replace people while advances in medical technology extend the lives of the ruling elites indefinitely, people who reproduce themselves will no longer be needed.

Understanding this, another feature of this social imaginary of rational mastery becomes intelligible. While opposed to the social imaginary of the quest for autonomy, it has co-evolved with it. Since the quest for rational mastery cannot present itself in its naked form without revealing its sinister side, it advances by appropriating the language of the quest for autonomy, disguising itself while neutralizing the language it has appropriated. Those moved by the social imaginary of autonomy are not totally disempowered by this strategy as they can then attempt to recover and further develop the original meaning of this language. Such a dialectic was evident in communist countries where opponents of managerialism, legitimating their claims through Marx's philosophy, could point to Marx's work, particularly to Marx's *1844 Manuscripts* and the *Grundrisse,* to show that technological mastery of the world was not Marx's main preoccupation; it was with emancipation and autonomy. Similarly, with the destruction of democracy by corporate powers with the complicity of liberals in USA promoted as the advance of freedom enshrined in the American Declaration of Independence. Michael Sandel (2005) and more rigorously, J.G.A. Pocock (1975) have pointed to the influence on the founding fathers of the republican philosophy of Renaissance civic humanism and what liberty meant to them – it meant freedom from slavery, and self-governance. However, those concerned with rational mastery deploy a range of other strategies to achieve their ends. The quest for truth is transformed and undermined, not by attacking it, but by equating it with scientific knowledge gained by applying the scientific method, elevating techno-scientists, including economists, into a priesthood whose claims to knowledge are placed beyond questioning by the general public, while simultaneously promoting extreme skepticism about all other claims to knowledge. While the social imaginary quest for technological mastery has had its committed defenders (most importantly, Friedrich Hayek, Milton Friedman and Herman Kahn), it often serves its proponents better to simply get rid of or cripple the work of those who effectively criticize their beliefs, while simultaneously allowing those whose ideas serve their interests to flourish. This is particularly effective when those augmenting the power of the power elites portray their work as radical, such as vulgar Marxists who promote a Hobbesian view of humans and the deconstructive postmodernists who, promoting skepticism about ideals, undermined the humanities.

Neither Marxism nor postmodernism are now at the centre of intellectual debates. Nihilism (or the claim that all values are equal, which is nihilism in disguise) and cultural fragmentation are being actively promoted to free privileged elites from ethical claims and to subvert efforts to challenge the current state of society and its ecologically destructive tendencies. However, the success of the global corporatocracy has revealed the extent that proponents of the social imaginary of autonomy had advanced their cause, evident in the greater humanity and greater appreciation of all life achieved by European civilization, notwithstanding the advance of the mechanistic view of the world. Despite the subordinate position of this social imaginary, there had been an irregular, but slow advance of the quest for justice, liberty and democracy. Herder and Hegel had been right to identify this tendency to progress in freedom and humanity. With neoliberalism, these advances are being demolished faster than they can be put on the endangered list. Institutions such as universities that upheld higher values, that in the past educated the people who constrained markets and bureaucracies to serve the common good, are being subverted by transforming them into transnational business corporations, acknowledging no other ends than maximizing profitability and maintaining the conditions for this end. Institutions of government are being transformed into instruments to extend the global market and augment the wealth and power of transnational corporations, financial institutions and their managers. The redefining and marginalization of philosophy is part of the process by which not only philosophy, but the humanities and genuine science are being sabotaged. The niches where the broad intellectual work required to counter the fragmentation of culture and replace defective assumptions could be carried out, where people could assert themselves without fear of retribution, expose corruption and oppression and reveal new possibilities for the future, are disappearing. Without powerful public institutions strongly committed to truth, justice and liberty, the market is concentrating wealth and power, and is becoming a machine for destroying local and global ecosystems, on land, in the oceans, and in the air.

Defending speculative naturalism is therefore not merely a matter of presenting arguments in terms of the quest for truth. There is the deeper problem of defending the practice of pursuing the truth; that is, the practice of questioning received beliefs to reveal their deficiencies and then developing better alternatives. It is necessary also to defend the niches (or cultural fields) in society where truth can be pursued. This involves defending the autonomy of cultural fields from economic and political fields, defending the Humboldtian form of the university, defending the humanities and defending genuine science and its institutions as more than means to develop profitable or military technology to serve power elites. Defending the quest for truth and its conditions is central to defending genuine democracy and the public institutions required for its functioning, to maintaining control over national economies against efforts by transnational corporations and the global corporatocracy to subvert such control, and to defending civilization. It involves defending the social forms required for people to participate in the adventures of ideas and the political actions necessary to create and sustain an ecological sustainable world–order. Opposing nihilism is not just an intellectual exercise; it is itself political action and involves political struggle.

Reconfiguring the history of philosophy after Kant

With this in mind, the present work continues the search to understand the civilization of modernity and to reveal what is blocking efforts to transform culture to confront the problems we face. The argument of the second, third and fourth chapters of this work is that the main traditions of modern philosophy should be understood as divergent responses to the philosophy of Immanuel Kant, and when examined in this way, speculative naturalism can be shown to be the most defensible of these traditions. Chapter Two, 'From analytic philosophy to speculative naturalism' examines analytic philosophy, its roots, and the naturalistic turn it took in USA under the influence of Willard van Ormand Quine. Really a development of logical positivism, this form of analytic philosophy originated as a form of neo-Kantianism that radically downgraded the role of synopsis and eliminated the role accorded to synthesis by Kant, then attempted to develop a formal language which it claimed to be universal, identifying this universal language with the language of mainstream science. In doing so it has locked in the assumptions of current reductionist science, and of the broader culture insofar as it is influenced by scientism. It has eliminated any place in the world for subjective experience or consciousness, or even life, and eliminated any values apart from efficient calculation in the service of the struggle for survival and domination by 'gene machines', machines by which strings of DNA reproduce themselves, along with 'pleasures' which are the byproduct of this struggle. It has produced one of the most nihilistic cultures that has ever existed.

Understanding the dominance of this philosophy reveals why any effort to defend the humanities through any form of Idealism, whether neo-Kantian, neo-Hegelian, hermeneutical or phenomenological, is bound to fail. However, by tracing analytic philosophy back to Kant and, drawing on Jaakko Hintikka's work to bring into question the claim to being able to provide a universal language, the questionability of assumptions these US analytic philosophers had placed beyond questioning is revealed. Also revealed is the existence of a very different philosophical program, also deriving from Kant that, while giving a place to analysis, does not eschew synopsis or synthetic thought. It makes speculation central to philosophy, and is naturalist rather than Idealist. This challenges the nihilism of reductionist science and analytic philosophers at its roots and provides the basis for defending the status of the humanities and the ideals they stand for. Speculative philosophy, associated with the revival of dialectics, took both Idealist and naturalist forms. Most commonly, it is the Idealist forms that people associate with speculation, but here it is argued that the naturalistic form of speculative philosophy, defended by Friedrich Schelling in his effort to forge a new synthesis of natural philosophy, art and history, is far more promising than Idealism for achieving a comprehensive understanding of the world and our place and significance within it.

The third chapter, 'Dialectics: from Marxism to post-Marxism', examines the career of Marxist dialectics as traditionally the most influential alternative to Anglophone analytic philosophy. It is also an analysis of the failure of Western Marxism and the failure of French philosophy, despite promising development. Dialectics was embraced by Marx, Marxists and post-Marxists; consequently, we would expect a defense of speculative naturalism from these thinkers that could have served to liberate humanity from its nihilistic culture. However, it is shown that dialectics was embraced by Marxists in a truncated, problematic form (with a few exceptions, notably Aleksandr Bogdanov, Joseph Needham, Ernst Bloch, Richard Levins, and then later, eco-Marxists such as André Gorz, James O'Connor and Joel Kovel) that generally eschewed speculation, equating this with Idealism, and even Marxists' materialism is problematic. Marx's own dialectics was essentially critical, and efforts by his followers to go beyond this resulted in fierce debates, with some Marxists following Engels and assimilating dialectics to scientism and treating its principles as universal laws of development, while others, turning to Hegel and then phenomenology and giving a central place to subjects and agency, aligned Marxism with the humanities and treated 'nature' as merely a social category.

While originally these debates took place in the Germanic world, the most important debates on Marxism occurred in France, and France is usually seen to be the centre of opposition to Anglophone analytic philosophy and to the scientistic naturalism of the US variety. Examining these debates, it is shown that Marxist dialectics and French philosophy produced their own opposition between defenders of the humanities associated with existential phenomenology, notably Jean-Paul Sartre, and scientism associated with the structuralism of Claude Lévi-Strauss, Louis Althusser and, to a lesser extent, Maurice Godelier. The dialectic between these opposing positions generated major advances in dialectics, with the development of the genetic structuralism of Jean Piaget, Lucien Goldmann and Pierre Bourdieu, and with advances in hermeneutics in Paul Ricoeur's work on metaphors and narratives. The synthesis of these could be even more promising. However, while highlighting the deficiencies of Germanic and Anglophone analytic philosophy, these thinkers were ambivalent toward naturalism (even when they claimed to be materialists). They did give a limited place to speculative thinking, but no French philosopher, with the partial exceptions of Gaston Bachelard and Maurice Merleau-Ponty (who died before he could fully develop his ideas) succeeded in formulating a fully non-reductionist naturalism that could transcend the opposition between science and the humanities and provide the foundations for a new social order. It is suggested that for this reason neither Marxism nor French philosophy has been able to combat the influence of analytic philosophy and reductionist scientism, overcome the destructive dynamics of a reinvigorated global market, or, most importantly, effectively combat the now prevailing nihilism and its ecologically destructive consequences.

After assessing the achievements and limitations of the best Marxist and post-Marxist work on dialectics, the following chapter examines the efforts of three speculative naturalists, Robin Collingwood, C.S. Peirce and Alfred North Whitehead to characterize philosophy. While none of these identified their characterization of philosophical thinking as dialectical, it is argued that this is the best way to understand their philosophical work, and it is argued that, influenced by the tradition of thought that goes back to Schelling, these philosophers, developing radically new conceptual frameworks to understand the world, were advancing dialectical thinking. With their insights revived and further developed by post–positivist philosophers of science, they have provided a far better understanding of the reasoning required to genuinely advance science and mathematics than analytic philosophers. Also, they have provided many of the concepts required to transcend the limitations of current science. The naturalism of analytic philosophy is compared to speculative naturalism, showing just how crippling analytic philosophers have been to intellectual and practical life, particularly to science and the arts. Speculative naturalism, particularly as this was developed by the theoretical biologist, mathematician and natural philosopher Robert Rosen, is also compared to the speculative materialism of Badiou, the leading figure to emerge from the French tradition of structuralist Marxism and the leading proponent of speculative materialism. It is argued on this basis that the speculative naturalists not only provide a better basis for understanding the greatness and achievements of mathematics, which Badiou argues should be at the centre of philosophy, but open the way to further advances in mathematics and science that align these with the humanities. For this reason, they provide a much stronger basis for transcending the deficiencies of Marxism. And they provide the basis for the revival of genuinely democratic politics. Speculative naturalism, focusing on the nature of life, enables humans to be understood as conscious, reflective and creative beings emergent from other life forms, participating in the dynamics of ecosystems, nature and history. This involves conceiving both nature and humans as complex processes of creative becoming.

Speculative naturalism, the radical enlightenment and ecological civilization

This defence of speculative naturalism provides the basis for the fifth and sixth chapters, 'Reviving the radical enlightenment through speculative naturalism' and 'From the radical enlightenment to ecological civilization: creating the future'. These provide a broader perspective to understand and advance the debates examined in the first three chapters. It has become evident that there were two, antithetical Enlightenments. While the Moderate Enlightenment, inspired by John Locke and Isaac Newton and committed to the technological domination of nature and possessive individualism, that is, rational mastery of the world, to use Castoriadis' characterization of this, claimed to break with the past and to inaugurate a new era based on a new notion of reason, the Radical Enlightenment, based in the humanities rather than science, sought to uphold and advance the Renaissance quest for liberty as self-governance inspired by the Ancient Greeks and the republican Romans. In Castoriadis' terminology, it was a struggle to revive the social imaginary of autonomy. The importance of Kant for the Radical Enlightenment is that he defended and gave a central place to freedom in his philosophy, thereby upholding the humanities. This brings us back to the humanities and claim of this work to be a manifesto. It also brings us back to Epstein's claim, quoted in the introduction of this book, that manifestos are performative rather than descriptive, proclaiming new eras. There are two eras being proclaimed in this work: within philosophy, an era of speculative naturalism, reinstating philosophy in particular and the humanities in general to their proper position in intellectual and cultural life, encompassing and transforming the sciences and reviving the Radical Enlightenment and the quest for liberty (the focus of Chapter Five), and following this, an era in which humanity will begin to create an ecologically sustainable civilization; an ecological civilization (the focus of Chapter Six).

Epstein pointed out that while the practical outcome of the natural sciences is technology through which nature is transformed, and the practical outcome of the human sciences is the transformation of society through politics, the practical outcome of the humanities is the transformation of culture. With culture, the object and the subject are one, and to transform culture is to transform ourselves, to create new subjectivities. Transforming culture can and will involve transforming our conceptions of natural science and technology, social science and politics, the humanities and culture, and how we conceive our relationship to the rest of nature. This puts political philosophy and ethics at the centre of philosophy and the centre of the humanities, as not merely concerned with how we should organize society and how we should live, but with what we should be striving to become and what kind of civilization we should be striving to create. It is necessary for philosophy to provide people, who are always situated and acting within institutions, cultural forms and naturally and socially created physical environments, with the conceptual frameworks to orient or re-orient themselves in the world, to define their goals and to act and live well and effectively. Chapter Five promotes a dialectical synthesis of Aristotelian thought and the republican ideas of Rome as revived in the Florentine Renaissance with the communitarian ideas of neo-Hegelian philosophy of the German Renaissance, defended on naturalist foundations. Chapter Six utilizes advanced work in ecology, largely inspired by speculative naturalists, to reformulate the Radical Enlightenment. It provides a unifying conceptual framework through process relational theoretical ecology for an ecological political philosophy and an ethics of virtues able to produce the subjectivities with the virtues and character necessary to defend current institutions from corruption (for instance, universities), to develop these in new directions, and to create and sustain new institutions embodying a commitment to liberty and to augmenting the conditions for life. This is presented as the politics and ethics of 'eco-poiesis' or 'home-making' which can serve as the foundation for creating an ecological civilization, and inspiring people to realize this.

This manifesto is partly (although not only) a work in metaphilosophy, showing how philosophy has lost its way and defining what it should be. It is also a work in philosophy concerned to orient people to create the future. It is a rejection of scientism, a defense of the humanities, and a defense of the location of philosophy in the humanities, providing the humanities embrace natural philosophy and engages with and encompasses the sciences. In arguing for speculative naturalism I have deployed all the methods available to philosophers: analysis, synopsis and synthesis, to show how recent philosophers, by refusing to acknowledge a role for synthesis and by devaluing synopses, have not only crippled themselves, but have crippled science and the humanities and damaged culture and society. Not only analytic philosophers (who clearly, are the most culpable) are responsible for this, but also many 'continental' philosophers. Marxists, for instance, in promoting dialectics tend to be skeptical of speculative thought. To highlight these deficiencies, I have described the work of some philosophers who did avail themselves of all these methods, notably Schelling, Collingwood, Peirce and Whitehead, while Bogdanov, Needham, Bloch and Merleau-Ponty are also alluded to. However, this manifesto is not a defense of their work as such, nor a total rejection of analytic philosophy or of the dialectical philosophy of the Western Marxist and post-Marxist 'continental' philosophers I have explicated and criticized. Both analysis and critical dialectics are defended dialectically as components of philosophy that should include analysis, synopses and synthetic thinking as essential to speculative philosophy.

That is, far from being a rejection of critical dialectics, an expanded form of dialectics that makes speculation central has been defended, and it has been deployed. The whole manifesto is a work in dialectics, involving synopses to 'view together' different philosophers and philosophical traditions, in this way defending, deploying and developing dialectical thought. From being defined in opposition to analysis and speculation, dialectics as deployed and defended in this work encompasses analysis, synopsis and synthesis and is essentially speculative. The work begins with the approach to philosophy exemplified by Quine that is most abstract and therefore most one-sided. However, the critique of this is not meant to deny completely the value of Quine's work. While the equation of naturalism with scientism is attacked, the promotion of naturalism is taken to be an advance in philosophy. Furthermore, there is value in analysis, but it is argued that Hintikka's form of analytic philosophy is superior, overcoming much of Quine's one-sidedness. While Hintikka is an analytic philosopher, his work opens the way for and even embraces some aspects of dialectics and speculative philosophy. After showing the promising start to speculative dialectical philosophy by the post-Kantians, Fichte and Hegel, and to the naturalist version of this developed by Schelling, it is shown in the following chapter how most Marxists again truncated the potential of both dialectics and philosophy by excluding any role for speculation in the creation of the future. The dialectical philosophers Georg Lukács and Sartre, the structuralists Lévi-Strauss, Althusser and Godelier, the genetic structuralists,

Piaget, Goldmann and Bourdieu and the hermeneutic narratologists Ricoeur, David Carr and Mikhail Bakhtin, are examined and criticised, again, not to reject them, but to draw attention to their achievements while showing that their thinking also is one-sided. Their insights also need to be incorporated into a broader perspective. It is to address this one-sidedness that the speculative naturalists, carrying on the tradition that originated with Schelling, are defended, but in a way that is designed not to idolatrize them but to require that speculative naturalists incorporate the advances of analytic, phenomenological, structuralist and hermeneutic philosophy, contributing to an ongoing quest for comprehensive understanding of ourselves and the world. This should be seen as the process of humanity's (and nature's) self-creation that can never be complete and can never be finalized. Recognizing this is in itself wisdom.

So long as the importance of such speculative philosophy and wisdom are acknowledged, then the Marxist point that philosophy should not be just contemplation but should also orient people to live and to change the world; that is, to create the future, should be embraced. The failure to appreciate the importance of ideas to orient people manifests the residual Cartesian dualism of orthodox Marxism. To change one's understanding of the world is to participate in the transformation of culture, which is to change the world, and is the condition for social and political action to create new social forms and to develop new forms of technology. On this assumption alone the work of Robert Rosen must be judged not only more profound and more defensible than the work of the French Marxist philosopher, Alain Badiou, but also more relevant to praxis. This leads on to the humanities, including political philosophy and ethics, which are specifically concerned with our self-creation through the transformation of culture.

The introduction to this book, this chapter and the last two chapters highlight the crises facing us in our everyday lives and as participants in history. The last chapter identifies major work underway in theoretical ecology, eco-semiotics, human ecology, eco-Marxism, ecological economics and political ecology. While this chapter is designed to point to the most promising work in specific disciplines, it is also designed to show why philosophy, including metaphysics, natural philosophy, philosophical biology, philosophical anthropology, social and political philosophy and ethics, is required to overcome the isolation and marginalization of such work, to link it together and integrate it with the humanities so that it can effectively challenge current orthodoxies and their proponents and constitute a new grand narrative of emancipation. It also shows that philosophy is required to transform culture and produce new subjectivities. It is shown how a naturalistic form of speculative dialectics can orient those engaged in specialist work and in political action and provide an alternative hegemonic culture, a culture that can challenge, overcome and replace, not only intellectually but in practice, the hegemonic 'anti-culture' that has locked us onto a path of decadence and enslavement to powers that are driving us to a global ecological disaster. Chapter Six and the conclusion set forth the basic ideas required to create an ecological civilization.

Note

1 Because the term 'philosophy' is claimed by members of philosophy departments who have redefined it to match their preoccupations, scientists and mathematicians who are engaged in this project often do not characterize their work as philosophy, although it would have been recognized as such by the great philosophers of the past. Many academics who call themselves philosophers, which after all means 'lovers of wisdom', bring to mind what was called the Ministry of Love in George Orwell's *1984*, the place where people showing any sign of dissidence were taken to be tortured and then vaporized.

2   From analytic philosophy to speculative naturalism

Where did philosophy go wrong? How, within a century, at a time when there has never been more need for philosophical ideas that could challenge the *status quo*, offer new ways of understanding the world and new visions of the future, has philosophy degenerated from its central place in education and culture into a marginal discipline consisting of developing formal languages to serve the information technology industry, apologetics for mainstream science, fragments of abstruse arguments within specialized sub-disciplines addressed only to other academics, or efforts to keep abreast of the latest intellectual fashions coming out of Paris? To comprehend the parlous state of philosophy in the modern world it is necessary to understand the triumph of analytic philosophy that now not only dominates philosophy departments in Anglophone countries, but is invading countries that traditionally have offered alternatives, even France. In doing so, it is necessary to look at the opposition between analytic and speculative philosophy.

The opposition between analytic philosophy and speculative philosophy was characterized by C.D. Broad (1887–1971), a leading British philosopher whose career coincided with the eclipse of speculative philosophy, in two famous papers, the first published in 1924, the second in 1947. In 'Critical and Speculative Philosophy' (1924), Broad characterized critical philosophy (which evolved into analytic philosophy) as analysis and clarification of the basic concepts and presuppositions of ordinary life and of science. It was assumed by its proponents that philosophical problems could be treated and dealt with in isolation from each other, and that philosophy, like science, could accumulate indubitable knowledge. On the other hand, speculative philosophers attempt to arrive at an overall conception of the nature of the universe and the position within it of human beings by taking into account the whole range of human experience—scientific, social, ethical, aesthetic, and religious: 'Its business is to take over all aspects of human experience, to reflect upon them, and to try to think out a view of Reality as a whole which shall do justice to all of them' (1924, p.96). Returning to the problem of the eclipse of speculative philosophy in 'Some Methods of Speculative Philosophy', Broad characterized three methods used by philosophers generally that define philosophy as such. These are 'analysis' (which had come to completely dominate, and which he did not bother to describe any further), 'synopsis' (whereby the inconsistencies between various normally separate domains of experience are confronted – 'synopsis' means 'view together') and most importantly and uniquely to speculative philosophers, 'synthesis', which aims to 'supply a set of concepts and principles which shall cover satisfactorily all the various regions of fact which are being viewed synoptically' (1947, p.22).

It is important to note that speculative philosophers must use all three methods, analytic philosophers only the first two, with a greatly reduced role accorded to synopsis, although there are exceptions to this, particularly among Scandinavian analytic philosophers. Analytic philosophers even limit what can be analysed, with most analytic philosophers now excluding the analysis of experience, while granting no place to the analysis of basic assumptions and how they influence action and thinking. Some analytic philosophers have even excluded analysis of concepts from philosophy, focusing entirely on analysis of the logical form of propositions or sentences and inferences from them. However, it is also possible to analyse the process of enquiry, concepts and experiences. Much of phenomenology is devoted to the analysis of experience and could be regarded as a form of analytic philosophy, although it seldom is. Analytic philosophers tend to ignore or downplay the significance of the contradictory assumptions of different domains of life and experience because they ignore the synoptic overviews (often involving narratives that are themselves a form of synthetic thinking) that are required to reveal these contradictions and expose deeply rooted taken-for-granted assumptions that generated these contradictions. Then they disallow or dismiss the synthetic forms of reasoning required to develop new conceptual frameworks that could transcend these contradictions. Because they have no way of dealing with contradictions between diverse domains of experience or discourses they either accept these as unavoidable (the neo-Kantian solution), or more commonly, privilege one domain at the expense of all others, focusing their efforts on explaining away phenomena associated with other domains (characteristic of both the proponents of scientism and the proponents of 'ordinary language').

The eclipse of speculative philosophy: from Bolzano and Frege to Quine

Mainstream analytic philosophy has its roots in Austria and Germany in the philosophies of Bernard Bolzano (1781–1848), Rudolf Hermann Lotze (1817–1881) and Gottlob Frege (1848–1925), in each case criticizing and severely modifying the philosophy of Immanuel Kant (1724–1804). Robert Hanna in *Kant and the Foundations of Analytic Philosophy* (2001) argues that 'Bolzano and Helmholtz are the advance guard of analytic philosophy … [and] Frege is the first of its two Founding Fathers' (p.6) (the other was Bertrand Russell). This historical background had been examined from a different, pro-analytic philosophy perspective in J. Alberto Coffa in *The Semantic Tradition from Kant to Carnap: To the Vienna Station* (1991), and has been examined more recently by Hans-Johann Glock in *What is Analytic Philosophy* (2008).

It is important to understand the pivotal position of Kant's philosophy in the history of philosophy. It was the culmination of efforts to deal with the epistemological problems engendered by the scientific revolution of the Seventeenth Century. The main figures in the scientific revolution were Galileo (1564–1642), Descartes (1596–1650), Newton (1643–1727) and Leibniz (1646–1716). They were all philosophers, and had had to combat opposition to natural philosophy by skeptics. While they appeared to have succeeded, the dualism between mind and body engendered a new form of skepticism, articulated most fully in the work of David Hume (1711–1776). How could the mind, spatially enclosed within the body, gain any knowledge of the external world? Hume concluded that we cannot. All there are, are sense impressions and faded copies of these succeeding each other, and passions, on the basis of which we experience regularities of succession enabling us to make predictions, although we have no grounds for assuming any rational necessity in these regularities, and no basis for assuming a mind apart from these series of sense impressions, their faded copies and passions. Reacting against both this skepticism, and more fundamentally, to the Copernican revolution that had relegated humanity to an insignificant place in an infinite universe, Kant effected a second Copernican revolution that not only claimed to have overcome this skepticism, but returned humanity to the centre of the cosmos. The infinite universe of matter in motion is largely a product of the forms of intuition (space and time), the imagination and categories of the understanding contributed by the mind by means of which it organizes its sense impressions. The scientific world-view is in some sense a human construction, and the experienced world has to be constructed the way it is to be intelligible. Knowledge has a 'synthetic' aspect to it. While claiming to put science on a secure epistemological foundation, Kant's philosophy simultaneously delimited what scientific knowledge could claim. It could only make claims about the phenomenal realm. Kant showed that it could not invalidate our assumption that we, as part of the noumenal realm, have a free will, resurrecting the significance accorded to humanity and along with this, providing a place for ethics and aesthetics. At the same time Kant established philosophy as the foundational discipline on which metaphysics, science and all other domains of enquiry had to be based; or so it seemed to those who embraced Kant's work. As we will see later on, this was a major revival and advance of the Radical Enlightenment in opposition to the mechanistic thinking, atomism and debased view of life and humanity of the Moderate Enlightenment.

Bolzano criticized Kant for failing to distinguish subjective representations and objective representations, and in the latter, between representations and objects of representations (Coffa, p.29f.). Focusing on objective representations in his case involved redefining and privileging the notion of analysis and focusing philosophy on 'objective meaning', while eliminating any positive role for synthesis. Lotze defended and further developed this argument. So, while Kant had argued that synthesis is involved in both empirical knowledge (synthetic *a posteriori* knowledge) and mathematical and metaphysical knowledge (synthetic *a priori* knowledge), Bolzano, and following him Lotze and then Frege, developed a philosophy that eliminated any role for mental processes, whether ideas, images or imaginative projections, in characterizing the meaning relations between signs. Frege argued that concepts are objective and subject only to the laws of logic, and the focus on logic should be distinguished from epistemological issues. Criticising Kant, he proclaimed: 'The concept has a power of collecting together far superior to the unifying power of synthetic apperception' (Frege 1950, §47), although as Hanna (2001, p.182) has pointed out, Frege endorsed Kant's notion of synthetic *apriori* knowledge. Following Lotze, Frege held that validity pertains to propositions, not concepts, and can be affirmed or denied regardless of the objects they refer to (Gabriel, 2002). Propositions were treated as Platonic entities, having a status independent of consciousness and not locatable in space and time. Frege's philosophy, along with all those neo-Kantian philosophies influenced by Lotze, has been characterized as 'Transcendental Platonism' (Gabriel 2002, p.41).

Michael Dummett (1981), who characterized analytic philosophy as post-Fregean philosophy, wrote, 'it was almost certainly a historical necessity that the revolution which made the theory of meaning the foundation of philosophy should be accomplished by someone like Frege who had for idealism not an iota of sympathy' (p.684). Frege wanted a purely 'objectivist semantics' based on generalizing the mathematical function to analyse the logical structure of propositions (Johnson 1987, p.xxxf.). This involved translating statements into algebraic formulae, delimiting thereby what statements could make any meaningful claims and what they could make their claims about, while making explicit the operations that could be performed on these formulae. In this way the validity of inferences drawn from these statements could be tested and evaluated, and the algebraic formulae could then be translated back into non-algebraic statements. Philosophy was refocused on developing adequate means to encode statements algebraically and adequate means for interpreting the permutations of these algebraic representations, and then dealing with the paradoxes generated by this project. This has defined the trajectory of most analytic philosophy ever since.

However, there was more to Frege's project than this. It involved severely delimiting the realm of what could be studied through logic and thereby what could be taken as meaningful discourse, redefining philosophy accordingly. The only existence claims that can be made through Frege's logic are that for a class or kind *x,* there exist objects of that kind; or as Quine (1961, p.15) famously put it, 'to be is to be the value of a variable'. P.F. Strawson (1992) clarified what this meant: 'our ontology comprises just the things which the variables of quantification must range over, or take as values, if our beliefs are to be true' (p.42). Such a claim excludes the fundamental question traditionally asked by philosophers – whether whatever is claimed to exist, 'is' in the most fundamental sense as *self-explanatory*, thereby not being further demonstrable or derivable, since, as James Bradley (2004) put it: 'it carries all the reasons for itself in its own nature' (p.209). Finding this self-explanatory being (or beings) is the ultimate goal of the synthetic thinking of speculative philosophy, with the aim of accounting for, understanding and explaining all else through it (or them) in a coherent way. Frege and those who followed him ruled out the possibility of even asking the question: What is the ultimate self-explanatory being?

Frege's ideas were taken up in England by Bertrand Russell (1872–1970), G.E. Moore (1873–1958) and the young Ludwig Wittgenstein (1889–1951), in Austria by Rudolf Carnap (1891–1970) and the Vienna Circle, by Hans Reichenbach (1891–1953) and Carl Hempel (1905–1997) in Germany, and then in USA by Willard van Orman Quine (1908–2000). Frege had attempted to reduce arithmetic to logic, and this project was taken up by Bertrand Russell and then Russell and Whitehead, with the intention of explaining all mathematics through logic, and then logic and set theory. While Frege had rejected Kant's claim that arithmetical knowledge is *synthetic a priori* but still accepted that geometrical knowledge is *synthetic a priori*, Russell argued that no mathematical knowledge is *synthetic a priori*. All mathematical knowledge, he claimed, is analytic. While Frege had granted a place to sense as well as reference in characterizing the meaning of terms in propositions (so that the meaning of 'the morning star' was granted a status along with the reference to the planet Venus), Russell narrowed logic further (and along with it, philosophy) by acknowledging only reference, and in this he was followed by most subsequent analytic philosophers. Combining Hilbert's formalism with the logicism of Frege and Russell, Carnap attempted to show through the painstaking analysis of language, most importantly the language used in science, that theories could be expressed as a set of 'protocol sentences' in which all the terms would have a clear semantic denotation. The early Wittgenstein, arguing that what exists are 'states of affairs' that can be analysed into atomic facts, brought this argument to its apotheosis. The task of the scientist was to analyse sentences into atomic propositions and map these logical atoms onto atomic facts. This project, essentially a project of mechanizing reasoning, was supported in USA during the cold war in order to enhance human performance before the Russians found the means to do so. The proponents of this project, the logical atomists and logical positivists, succeeded in transforming the core of philosophy from metaphysics to the study of language, bringing about what later came to be known as the 'linguistic turn' in philosophy.

Analytic philosophers then divided over the relationship between the role accorded to mathematical logic and its interpretation, and the significance accorded to the language of science in relation to ordinary language. The later Wittgenstein, John Austin, Gilbert Ryle, P.F. Strawson, Stanley Cavell, John Searle and the later work of John McDowell exemplify a tradition that, rejecting the domination of philosophy by symbolic logic, has placed its faith in ordinary language and its careful analysis of concepts and everyday reasoning to reveal subtle distinctions, misleading inferences, the complexity of rationality and irrationality, necessary assumptions, and the value of informal argument, defending these against the imperialism of mathematical logic and the language of science. Generally, this involved appreciating the practical context of language and reasoning. Ludwig Wittgenstein in *Philosophical Investigations* (1968) in particular made this point forcefully: "'So you are saying that human agreement decides what is true and what is false?' – It is what human beings say that is true and that is false; and they agree in the *language* they use. That is no agreement in opinions, but in forms of life' (p.241). In making such claims, ordinary language analytic philosophers have drawn on Kantian philosophy and often utilized a form of transcendental deduction to show the necessity of accepting the validity of assumptions accepted in everyday life, despite being inconsistent with purportedly scientific accounts of human behavior. McDowell has explicitly related his work to Kant's philosophy. The focus on ordinary language offered some support for the humanities and the values they have traditionally promoted, but ruled out speculative thought and synthesis whereby the humanities could challenge the assumptions of mainstream science, requiring a radical modification of what is taken to be logic and science. Ordinary language analytic philosophy came to dominate in Britain, although it also had its adherents in USA, most notably, Cavell and Searle, and in Scandinavia, Georg von Wright. Scandinavian analytic philosophers generally are far less dogmatic and far more open to different schools of thought, as is evident in Dagfinn Føllesdal's characterization of analytic philosophy in, 'Analytic Philosophy: What is it and Why Should one Engage in It?' (1996). Føllesdal defines it as a commitment to argument and justification as opposed to using rhetoric, and on this basis he includes hermeneuticists and phenomenologists as analytic philosophers. Recently, philosophers have revived interest in John Dewey and William James and a longer tradition of philosophy going back to Kant and Hegel. Richard Rorty and Robert Brandom exemplify this development. And there are crossovers with what has come to be known as 'continental philosophy'.

However, analytic philosophy had been closely associated with the development of symbolic logic, and ordinary language analytic philosophy was really a belated reaction to the logical atomism and logical positivism of enthusiastic proponents of symbolic logic and the quest to interpret, defend and extend mathematics and mainstream science through it. While this reaction succeeded in showing that human reasoning cannot be reduced to the kind of manipulation of symbols characteristic of artificial intelligence as claimed by many mainstream analytic philosophers (where artificial intelligence incorporated their characterization of reasoning), ordinary language analytic philosophy only slowed down the advance of efforts to develop mathematical logic as an alternative to the reasoning based on ordinary language. The efforts to shore up this tradition by going back to the pragmatism of James and Dewey, and further back to Hegel, have failed to strengthen this holding operation. The most influential analytic philosophers, particularly in USA, followed Carnap, Reichenbach and Hempel. Carnap privileged mathematical logic and stipulated that statements are meaningful only when they are syntactically well-formed, with non-logical terms being reducible to terms occurring in the basic observational evidence statements of science. While analytic philosophers influenced by Peirce and Scandinavian analytic philosophers focused on mathematical logic without dismissing the insights of the humanities or ignoring 'continental philosophy' and maintained broader interests, in USA, despite the influence of Peirce and Dewey, philosophers continued the tradition of logical positivism, upholding the cognitive claims of mainstream science and its ambition to explain everything, including all aspects of human existence. With a few notable exceptions, these philosophers regarded ethics, politics and aesthetics as irrelevant to tough minded philosophers, many of whom concluded that these domains were beyond the realm of rational discourse.

Where analytic philosophers have continued to grapple with ethics, politics and aesthetics, again with rare exceptions, they have accepted their marginalization as denizens of minor sub-disciplines, rendering what they say insignificant. This is true of most environmental ethics, a sub-discipline of a sub-discipline. As Ulrich Beck argued, in the face of the global ecological crisis, trying to constrain technocracy through ethics would be 'like a bicycle brake on an international jet' (Beck 1992, p.106). Analytic philosophy is characterized by an implicit respect for argument, clarity (a notion left crucially unclear) and precision (left crucially imprecise) that, its proponents believe, can be achieved only by focusing on narrow topics, philosophizing 'piecemeal and in fragments', while avoiding the 'big questions' that traditionally characterized philosophy. 'Vague' concepts, recognized as of central importance by C.S. Peirce among others (including Nicholas Georgeşçu-Roegen (1971, p.44ff,), Murray Code (1995, pp.160–167 and Cornelius Castoriadis (1997a, p.290–318) as essential for grasping the creativity of life and of central importance to the humanities, are ignored, thereby upholding a conception of the world that renders life unintelligible and eliminates any thought of creating a better future apart from improving algorithms for reasoning, advancing technology and achieving rational mastery of the world. Questions about what is the good life, traditionally central to philosophy, have been largely excluded from such analytic philosophy as not being amenable to rigorous argument or to scientific treatment, with those who have engaged with such issues suspected of liaising with disreputable continental philosophers.[1] This quest for rigour has been taken to such extremes that analytic philosophy is now in a state of crisis because in their quest for precision they 'now question the defensibility and ultimate intelligibility of the very idea of analysis' (Hanna 2001, p.11).

The most influential American analytic philosophers (notably Quine and Donald Davidson) further narrowed philosophy by rejecting Frege's transcendental Platonism and downplaying or even denying any significance to concepts and conceptual frameworks. While Quine is sometimes labeled a conceptual pragmatist, he accorded little significance to the development of concepts, focusing instead on the truth or otherwise of sentences (Quine, 1960). Davidson (1984, pp.183–198) went on to question the very idea of conceptual schemes. Committed to allowing only the first order predicate calculus in logic as valid form of reasoning, Quine acknowledged theoretical networks, theories, theoretical terms and theoretical sentences, but privileged observation sentences over theoretical sentences as the cornerstone of semantics and knowledge. 'Semantics', however, was given a very restricted meaning by him and allied analytic philosophers, with 'meaning' characterized not as a 'psychic existence' but as 'a property of behavior' (Quine 1969, p.29). Other US analytic philosophers embraced the Polish philosopher Alfred Tarski's 'semantic definition of truth' according to which meaning could be reduced to specifications of truth conditions of sentences. Explicating what became the common view on the connection between the definition of truth and the concept of meaning among such analytic philosophers, Davidson wrote in 'Truth and Meaning' (1984), 'the definition works by giving the necessary and sufficient conditions for the truth of every sentence, and to give truth conditions is a way of giving the meaning of a sentence' (p.24). Effectively, this is an effort to eliminate 'meaning' by reducing it to something else: truth conditions. This removed from philosophy a whole domain of analysis that had been and continues to be fruitful: conceptual analysis.

Led by Quine, analytic philosophers then redefined philosophy again, arguing that it is part of, or continuous with, science, differing from the rest of science only in degree of generality. Quine claimed that the core of philosophy is logic, and characterized this as part of science. It should be emphasized that not all analytic philosophers in USA who have focused on mathematical logic have followed Quine in this; Davidson, for instance, was a proponent of humanism rather than scientism (Pearson, 2011), while Saul Kripke and Hilary Putnam have dissociated themselves from naturalism. However, in a recent history of analytic philosophy since Quine, Berto and Plebani (2015) showed that Quine's work has generated vigorous debates on the question of what is ontology, that is, debates on 'metaontology'. This has resulted in the emergence of a number of divergent philosophical positions, and most Anglophone analytic philosophy has been focused on conflicts between the proponents of these positions, revealing the crucial role Quine's philosophy has played in the subsequent development of analytic philosophy. Following Quine, José Benardete in *Metaphysics: The Logical Approach* (1989) simply characterized the work of logicians as metaphysics, entrenching this form of analytic philosophy by eliminating any place for natural philosophy. Most analytic philosophers work within the limits of the assumptions Quine put in place, and it is Quine's work that is the key to understanding and evaluating the project of mainstream analytic philosophy and to understanding how it differs from other philosophy.

Central to Quine's philosophical position was his attack on the place that had been accorded to 'meaning' in language, and even more fundamentally, to 'subjects of consciousness', however conceived. Reviewing his work on this, George Romanos (1983) concluded that 'Quine has come to regard the various concepts of linguistic meaning as totally lacking in systematic theoretical significance and therefore of no use as explanatory concepts' (p.111), an assessment endorsed by Quine. In 'Two Dogmas of Empiricism' published in *From a Logical Point of View* (1961),[2] he had attacked the neo-Kantian claim to have justified synthetic *a priori* knowledge because it assumes such linguistic meaning. If successful, his argument would invalidate not only much of neo-Kantian philosophy and the arguments of ordinary language analytic philosophers, that is, the 'linguistic Kantians', it would deny much of the significance, claimed by Frege and Russell, for philosophical knowledge revealed through analyzing the logical forms of propositions or sentences and the relationship between concepts.

It was through this rejection of synthetic *a priori* knowledge that Quine initiated the 'naturalistic turn' in philosophy that has since come to dominate analytic philosophy. Usually, this naturalism is assumed to be 'scientism', the view that, as Quine put it in *Theories and Things,* 'it is within science itself, and not in some prior philosophy, that reality is to be identified and described' (Quine 1981, p.21). With Quine and his followers, this implied a support for reductionism, allowing that only physical and chemical processes are real, although he was not always consistent on this.[3] Extending his alliance with science, in a famous paper 'Epistemology Naturalized' published in Quine (1969, pp.69–90), Quine defended the 'naturalization' of epistemology, by which he meant that scientific knowledge itself is part of nature and could and should be treated as an object of scientific investigation. As he put it:

> Epistemology, or something like it, simply falls into place as a chapter of psychology and hence of natural science. It studies a natural phenomenon, viz., a physical human subject. This human subject is accorded a certain experimentally controlled input – certain patterns of irradiation in assorted frequencies, for instance – and in the fullness of time the subject delivers as output a description of the three dimensional external world and its history.
> (Quine 1969, p.82f)

Quine also endorsed the effort by Donald Campbell, a psychologist, to base evolutionary epistemology on the notion of blind variation and selective retention, which Campbell believed would account for the development of instincts and our cognitive abilities generally.

Having excluded any role for *a priori* knowledge, let alone synthesis, Quine endorsed the autonomy of science, which meant endorsing mainstream science, limiting any criticisms to issues of clarity and logical rigor, reducing the role of philosophers to science's under-laborers. As he put it (revealing a very strange view of what science is): 'Logic, like any science, has as its business the pursuit of truth. What is true are certain statements; and the pursuit of truth is the endeavor to sort out the true statements from the others, which are false' (Quine 1959, p.xi). Presumably, a good scientist then is someone who has memorized the true statements recorded in text books, the view of science held by Brazilians in 1950 when the nuclear physicist Richard Feynman proclaimed in a public lecture to them on Brazillian science after a year of teaching physics in Rio de Janeiro, 'the main purpose of my talk is to demonstrate to you that *no science* is being taught in Brazil' (Feynman 1986, p.216). Students had no ability to ask questions or perform experiments and were merely memorizing sentences which had no meaning for them.

Quine's naturalism was embraced and extended by, among others, Ronald Giere, Richard Boyd, Arthur Fine and David Lewis. Philip Kitcher (1984) attempted to explain mathematics and its development naturalistically, while various efforts to characterize mind in accordance with reductionist naturalism, either explaining away consciousness, claiming either that consciousness does not exist, or that the phenomena of consciousness are not what they appear to be but are something that is part of the natural order that can be explained by science. Such work has been well described by Paul Livingston in *Philosophical History and the Problem of Consciousness* (2004). The first option included behaviorism favored by Quine and Paul Churchland's 'eliminative naturalism', while Jaegwon Kim has argued for epiphenomenalism and the former student of Quine, Daniel Dennett, has attempted to explain away subjective states and qualia as nothing but dispositions, which, he argued, can be explained through neo-Darwinian evolutionary theory (Dennett 1991). Dennett allowed that we could refer to intention, design and function in nature, but argued that these are shorthand for purely physical processes as described by physics, which alone grasps the world the way it really is. Another position that looks more radical has been put forward recently by the British philosopher Galen Strawson, son of the eminent British analytic philosopher P.F. Strawson, but now working in America. Strawson immediately laid claim to being an authentic naturalist. 'I'm a naturalist, when it comes to concrete reality. I'm an out-and-out naturalist, a philosophical or metaphysical naturalist. ... I'm a physicalist or materialism naturalist. I don't believe there is any non-physical concrete reality' (Strawson 2013, p.101, 102) he claimed, revealing what is required to be taken seriously by mainstream American philosophers. He then went on to argue that since it is indubitable that we do have experience, a genuine physicalist naturalism must acknowledge this and accept panpsychism along with the conception of nature promulgated by mathematical physicists. However, this is still scientism (although with some appreciation of the ignorance of physicists), with panpsychism simply added on as an additional property of physical existence. And true to the tradition of analytic philosophy, Strawson makes no effort to work out how experience which is part of nature takes the form of human consciousness. (This contrasts with the speculative paper by the theoretical physicist Lee Smolin, 'Temporal Naturalism' (2015), where he argues that to account for qualia, it is necessary to rethink physics to take time as succession of present moments as real.)

In *Understanding Naturalism* Jack Ritchie questioned whether in light of this diversity of views put forward by proponents of naturalism, the term 'naturalism' is empty. He concluded that it is not, summing up what they have in common: 'Descartes, Kant and Carnap all called for a new philosophy to ground the sciences. Naturalists take the view that we should start with our well-developed science and build our philosophy from there' (Richie 2013, p.196). Effectively, under the banner of naturalism, Quine and his allies have been defending three separate doctrines: metaphilosophical naturalism according to which philosophy is a branch of science, epistemological naturalism according to which there is no genuine knowledge outside science as Quine characterized it, and ontological naturalism according to which there is no realm other than the world of matter, energy, spatio-temporal objects or events as characterized by mainstream science. Not all of those who have been influenced by Quine have accepted all three of these doctrines. Some versions of naturalism exemplified by Brian Ellis (2010) and Alexander Bird (2010) differ in accepting modal logic and defending a form of essentialism and do acknowledge a place for natural philosophy. They grant a place to dispositional properties, producing a 'scientific metaphysics' rather than an anti-metaphysical scientism. In doing so, however, they seldom depart from the commitment to an objectivist semantics, assuming the actual world, along with any possible world, consists of entities and sets built out of those entities which have properties and stand in definite relation to one another at each instant, and that meaning consists in the relationship between abstract symbols and elements in models of the real world or possible worlds that consist of these entities. All other forms of reasoning are denied any validity. Correct reasoning is nothing more than manipulating symbols in accordance with the set-theoretical logic of the model. There is no place in this conception of meaning for synthesis associated with understanding.

Philosophers inspired by Quine tend to be contemptuous of synoptic thinking, including historical work. Any effort to summarize the central doctrines of any philosophical position or to examine the state of philosophy, central to achieving synopsis, is dismissed for failing to acknowledge the full diversity and complexity of what is being summarized. This has served to insulate from scrutiny a variety of assumptions these analytic philosophers have managed to put in place, including their contraction of the scope of philosophy. Through control of academic appointments, Quine and his allies dominated the direction of American philosophy (McCumber 2001, p.46). Philosophy is not only reduced to analysis, it is reduced to analysis of the syntactical relations between symbols and their relation to observations, with very little place for the analysis of experience, language or concepts and no place for syntheses. Without giving a place to synopses and therefore regarding the history of philosophy as of no significance, these philosophers have developed a form of philosophy that denies the historical perspective required to reveal how impoverished this conception of philosophy is, or the deleterious effects the domination of such philosophy has had on the broader culture, including science.

Major criticisms have been leveled against this form of naturalism, not only from ordinary language analytic philosophers but also from analytic philosophers whose focus is on mathematical logic. These include Saul Kripke, Nicholas Rescher, Hilary Putnam, Mario De Caro, Jerry Fodor and the Finnish philosopher Jaakko Hintikka. There have been criticisms of Quine among such analytic philosophers for identifying naturalism with a scientific world-view, and a call for a more liberal form of naturalism (Caro and McArthur 2004). Through this form of naturalism, efforts are underway to bridge the gap between naturalism and norms or values (Caro and McArthur 2010). Concern by analytic philosophers to free philosophy from the Quinean straightjacket has led to a revival of interest in past traditions of thought. Both Richard Rorty in *Philosophy and the Mirror of Nature* (1980) and Hilary Putnam in *Renewing Philosophy* (1992), in very different ways, called for a return to Dewey. Sami Pihlström in *Pragmatism and Philosophical Anthropology: Understanding Our Human Life in a Human World* (1998) and more recent books has aligned himself with the broader tradition of pragmatism, focusing more on William James. Robert Hanna and Michael Friedman have called for a return to Kant and neo-Kantianism, with Ernst Cassirer promoted as providing a philosophy that could transcend the analytic – continental philosophy divide. Even Philip Kitcher (2011) has complained that excessive concern with rigorous argument has resulted in scholastic self-indulgence for the few which has totally marginalized philosophy. Kitcher, like Richard Rorty and Hilary Putnam, calls for a return to John Dewey's program for philosophy. However, analytic philosophers who do call for a more liberal naturalism and aspire to give a place to normativity are in the awkward position of having no means to develop an alternative world-view because they have excluded any place for the synthetic thought required to do so, and do not take seriously the work of those who have provided such synthetic thought, even when as in the case of Peirce and Whitehead, they made major contributions to logic and analysis. As a rigorously worked through position, Quine's work is the outstanding representative of and reference point for the form analytic philosophy takes when it is committed to replacing common sense with mathematical logic (Davidson and Hintikka 1975). It is the culmination of logical positivism as it developed under the influence of Frege. So, despite the work of his critics in analytic philosophy, Quine's naturalism remains the reference point for defining this tradition of analytic philosophy.

Hintikka's critique of Quine

Why this should be so is illuminated most fully by the work of Hintikka (although Hintikka can be seen as aligned with Saul Kripke, and to a lesser extent, Hilary Putnam), a strong critic of Quine who has argued against Quine's dismissal of concepts and concomitantly, of *a priori* knowledge and of the narrow focus of Quine's work (Hintikka 2007). Unlike Quine, Hintikka has made original contributions to logic and has a very wide range of interests apart from logic, science and the philosophy of mathematics, having engaged with 'continental' philosophers and written major studies in the history of philosophy (Hintikka 1974). Hintikka often discusses the work of Kant, Husserl and Heidegger and also the work of Collingwood and Peirce, and is acknowledged by Martin Kusch as the most important influence on his book *Language as Calculus VS. Language as Universal Medium* (1989), a study of Husserl, Heidegger and Gadamer. Having used Quine's philosophy as a foil in developing his own ideas and conception of philosophy, Hintikka has pinpointed what differentiates his own work (and allied analytic philosophers) from mainstream analytic philosophers from Frege, Russell, Wittgenstein, the Vienna Circle through to Quine and Alonzo Church. This is the assumption of these philosophers, following Frege (although already assumed by Bolzano), that language is a *lingua universalis* – a universal medium whose symbolic structure reflects directly the structure of our world of concepts. In other words, Frege and the logicians who followed him, aspired through their work in mathematical logic to create a perfect universal language. Echoing Leibniz as interpreted by Friedrich Trendelenburg, in response to criticisms by Schröder of his *Begriffsschrift*, Frege claimed to be developing a *lingua characterica*, not merely a *calculus ratiocinator* (Heijennoort 1967).

Hintikka (1997) rejected this, arguing that his concern has been to create a *calculus ratiocinator*, a method of symbolic calculation which would mirror and refine the processes of human reasoning (which, Hintikka cautioned, 'cannot be exhaustively formulated as a calculus' (p.115). In doing so he has aligned himself with a different tradition running from De Morgan, Boole, Jevons and Schröder to Peirce, and so is aligned with American analytic philosophers influenced by Peirce, such as Putnam. On the basis of this commitment Hintikka has developed a version of a 'model-theoretic view of language' in which the prime function of formal language is to identify and decide between possibilities or scenarios. This, he argued, requires 'game theoretic semantics' to interpret models. In *Socratic Epistemology: Explorations of Knowledge-Seeking by Questioning* (2007) he has developed an 'epistemic logic', a logic of knowledge and belief (although Hintikka argues that 'information' properly understood would be a more appropriate term than knowledge or belief), and an interrogative logic, a logic of discovery based on asking and seeking answers to questions. This is a development of Robin Collingwood's logic of question and answer according to which propositions are not Platonic entities and their meaning can only understood in relation the questions for which they are proposed answers, a dialectical form of logic developed in opposition to the symbolic logic of Russell and Whitehead. On this view, inferences should not be understood in relation to the meaning and reference of propositions, but from what is meant by them, undermining Frege's (and Quine's) efforts to eliminate any place for the subject in logic. Hintikka argues that the quest for a *Lingua Universalis,* and the assumption that language could be understood as such, justifies Collingwood's claim that eras are dominated by deep assumptions that have been placed beyond questioning. This particular assumption has produced a cluster of 'symptoms' that need to be cured. Since those who assume the idea of *lingua universalis* see language as an iron curtain between reality and us, since everything we say is in language, there is a fascination with ineffability, a rejection of metaphysics as nonsense, a tendency to focus on syntax and ignore semantics, and in the case of Quine, hostility to modal logic and a failure to recognize the usefulness of model theoretic techniques (which are based on modal logic and, as Hintikka argues, require a more powerful semantics of interpretation than Quine, and some proponents of modal logic, are willing to countenance).[4]

Hintikka's analysis of this opposition might not be entirely correct; Quine and Co. are more sinister than he portrays them because they want both a *lingua universalis* and a *calculus ratiocinator,* with the only language acknowledged as valid being one facilitating calculation. Not only has this effort undermined the humanities; it has helped cripple science and mathematics and reduced much of philosophy to an endless engagement with the inevitable paradoxes generated by striving to work within the framework of such impoverished languages. Despite their commitment to accumulating conclusive arguments, it appears that analytic philosophers cannot agree on anything, and have great difficulty even understanding each other, a state most of them are blind to and are incapable of overcoming because, having dismissed any role for synopses, most of them have no interest in the history of philosophy or hermeneutics.

By striving only for a *calculus ratiocinator,* and acknowledging limits to formulating reasoning as a calculus, Hintikka's work reveals the value of analysis when it is used in conjunction with synopses and is not being used to exclude all claims to knowledge not based on analysis or inconsistent with reductionist science. However, despite his undeniable achievements, except in Scandinavia Hintikka has not had the same impact on philosophy as Quine. The reason appears to be that while Quine had a program to impose and develop an entire philosophy, Hintikka offered only a diversity of insights and investigations into how to develop formal languages and reasoning procedures to facilitate better 'calculations' or decisions; that is, to improve our powers of reasoning (although in his historical studies, particularly his studies of Aristotle, he recognized that there is far more to philosophy than this). As the editors of an anthology on Hintikka's philosophy wrote in their conclusion:

> Most readers recognize that Quine's philosophy is shaped by his commitment to the all-encompassing metaphysical framework of philosophical naturalism. By contrast, if there is an all-encompassing framework that future readers will associated with Hintikka's work, they will find it as one of the conclusions, rather than as a premise of his many investigations. Hintikka's philosophy is driven principally by what he can prove.
>
> (Kolak and Symons 2004, p.209)

Basically, Hintikka as an analytic philosopher and logician par excellence (despite his interest in Collingwood, Heidegger and Gadamer and the history of philosophy), has not offered a philosophy in the traditional sense, whereas, surreptitiously, Quine was doing so. Quine was defending a desiccated form of the world-view of orthodox, reductionist science as a total philosophy. By contrast, Hintikka has offered nothing for those who want a world-view and a grand research program. However, Hintikka offers no reason to confine philosophy to analyses and synopses, and in fact he has synthesized ideas in developing more adequate forms of reasoning. Despite his alignment with analytic philosophy, he has paved the way to go beyond it, and Scandinavian philosophers influenced by him have embraced the work of Peirce and are beginning to develop philosophy in this direction. Stjernfelt's *Diagrammatology: An Investigation on the Borderlines of Phenomenology, Ontology, and Semiotics* (2007) is an example of this.

Because Hintikka himself did not propose or defend a synthetic philosophy, the major deficiencies in Quine's philosophy exposed by Hintikka were ignored by Quine's disciples who continued with business as usual. Consequently, the defining goal of mainstream analytic philosophers is still the defense of a form of 'naturalism' that is identified with scientism based on their understanding of science as ascertaining which sentences are true. Their success in imposing their agenda was summed up by Glock:

> In the wake of Quine, few analytic philosophers these days would dare to publish a book on the philosophy of mind, without at least professing allegiance to some form of naturalism in the preface. Thus Jackson states: 'Most analytic philosophers describe themselves as naturalists' …. Kim confines the point to the present: 'If current analytic philosophy can be said to have a philosophical ideology, it is, unquestionably, naturalism' …. And Leiter … diagnoses a 'naturalistic turn' in philosophy that rivals the earlier linguistic turn in importance.
>
> (Glock 2008, p.137)

And this has meant that, as Hanna put, 'all serious metaphysical, epistemological, and methodological questions in philosophy can be answered only by direct appeal to the natural sciences'. Quine's transformation of the analytic tradition can appropriately be dubbed the 'scientific turn'. After Quine 'analytic philosophy is *scientific philosophy*' (Hanna, p.10). Frederick Olafson in *Naturalism and the Human Condition* described the outcomes of this 'hard' scientistic naturalism:

> [W]ithin American philosophy … naturalism has become an all purpose philosophy for those who think that the natural sciences can provide answers to all the problems with which philosophers have traditionally tormented themselves or at least to the ones that do not simply dissolve on closer inspection. So convinced of its truth are the supporters of this thesis that they have great difficulty crediting the idea that there is any alternative to it that deserves to be taken seriously and is not just a shameless reversion to the superstitions of the past.
>
> (Olafson 2001, p.7)

Quinean naturalism remains the reference point for developing philosophy. The extent to which his philosophy dominates is evident not only in the triumph of his way of understanding philosophy in Anglophone countries, but the identification of naturalism with scientism, the decline of the humanities, and the spread of this form of analytic philosophy to Europe, despite growing dissent from within analytic philosophy itself. As Glock noted:

Analytic philosophy is roughly 100 years old, and it is now the dominant force within Western philosophy. … It has prevailed for several decades in the English-speaking world; it is in the ascendancy in Germanophone countries; and it has made significant inroads even in places once regarded as hostile, such as France.

(Glock 2008, p.1)

Those like Martha Nussbaum who continue to defend the humanities by drawing on their knowledge of classical literature and ideas while ignoring the triumph of scientism, are respected, but have very little influence. The most well known opponents of Quinean analytic philosophy also reject naturalism as such in order to affirm humanity, all dimensions of human experience, and the human condition in all its richness and diversity, taking it for granted that these are inconsistent with naturalism. This was the case with some of the ordinary language analytic philosophers, but more resolutely through the phenomenology movement inspired by Husserl, whether orthodox, hermeneutic or existentialist, and it was the case with Olafson who was carrying on the tradition of existential phenomenology. More recently, German philosophers have vigorously defended the humanities have done so by opposing it to the naturalism of contemporary Anglo-Saxon thinking (Freundlieb 2003). With the exception of some analytic philosophers who have embraced process metaphysics such as Nicholas Rescher and Mark Bickhard (who therefore are not opposed to synthetic thinking, even if they do not practice it), naturalism as promoted by analytic philosophers has come to be almost synonymous with scientism, reductionism and denigration of the humanities.

The 'continental' alternative to analytic philosophy: neo-Kantianism and idealism

Usually, those reacting to the perceived sterility and nihilistic implications of such analytic philosophy, particularly 'ordinary language' analytic philosophers, have turned to German, French, or occasionally Italian or Spanish philosophers and traditions for inspiration, often categorized pejoratively as 'continental philosophy', forgetting the origins of analytic philosophy in Germany and Austria. Neo-Kantianism, Hegelianism, hermeneutics, phenomenology, hermeneutic phenomenology, existentialism, critical theory, structuralism and poststructuralism have all been embraced or promoted as antidotes. Marx and Husserl are not so much reference points for defining philosophical positions but sites where proponents of different philosophies have confronted each other to claim these thinkers as their own. While this has involved studying a vast range of thinkers, Kant, Hegel, Marx, Nietzsche, Dilthey, Husserl, Heidegger and Habermas have served as the main reference points for these traditions, and it is impossible to understand these thinkers except in relation to Kant and his second Copernican Revolution. This revolution made consciousness, individual or social (along with epistemology), the reference point for philosophy in place of being, and it was this (rather than the arguments of Berkeley) that inspired the Idealist tradition of thought. While efforts to revive Hegel, Marx and Nietzsche are common, the return to Neo-Kantianism (Makkreel and Luft 2010) appears to be a more serious challenge to analytic philosophy, and all such work of revival highlights the extent of the influence of Kant on subsequent philosophy.

Most continental philosophers appear to have accepted Kant's skeptical arguments against a facile acceptance of appearances as reality in view of the role of synthesis in empirical judgments. Lee Braver has argued in *A Thing of This World: A History of Continental Anti-Realism* (2007) that Kant's Copernican Revolution has suffused the thought of the greatest philosophers of continental Europe, including Hegel, Nietzsche, Heidegger, Foucault and Derrida, who are examined, and Kierkegaard, Husserl, Gadamer, the Frankfurt school, Deleuze and the structuralists, who are not. Kant is portrayed as having engendered an enduring focus on the nature and complexity of experience and the role of concepts (etymologically, 'to take to oneself, to take and hold') and conceptual frameworks in the organization of experience, and a consequent antipathy to realism. The notion of concept (*Begriff*) had been incorporated into philosophy by Leibniz to replace 'ideas' and 'notions' in order to avoid the duality between noesis and aesthesis, or thinking and perceiving, and Kant took the term from Leibniz. Even the structuralism and post-structuralism of more recent French philosophy can trace one of its roots back to Ernst Cassirer, the most influential neo-Kantian in Germany before the rise of Naziism. While speculative realists such as Alain Badiou have set out to free philosophy from this Kantian influence, their Pythagoreanism is really a different form of Idealism. A manifestation of this Idealism is that there has been a lack of engagement by the most of the philosophers in the traditions of continental philosophy with the problem of explaining how sentient, self-conscious humans could have evolved from and within nature. Given the almost universal acceptance that humans evolved from other species and life evolved from inanimate nature, only academics now take Idealism seriously.

This might appear a gross oversimplification, since Kant himself was opposed to Idealism. Certainly Hegel was an Idealist, but Frederick Beiser (2005, p.9) in an influential work on Hegel has argued that the influence of Kant on Hegel has been grossly overstated; Hegel was an Idealist in the sense that he was upholding the Platonic notion of ideas. Marx is usually characterized as a materialist and Nietzsche was hostile to Idealism. Following Brentano, Husserl, the founder of phenomenology, began by calling on philosophers to go back to Aristotle rather than back to Kant, and initially upheld a form of realism on this basis. Heidegger and those influenced by him aligned themselves with phenomenology, but rejected Husserl's idealist turn. Habermas in an essay titled 'Metaphysics After Kant' published in *Postmetaphysical Thinking: Philosophical Essays* (1992b) has defined the problem for philosophy as how to continue after the discrediting of metaphysics, which he equated with Idealism, and has rejected the central role accorded by philosophers to consciousness.

However, Beiser's claims are questionable, Marx's materialism really meant following Fichte (an Idealist) and arguing for the primacy of praxis over contemplative knowledge, and Nietzsche's perspectivism manifests the influence on him of Kant. Research has shown that right from the beginning Husserl was corresponding regularly with Paul Natorp of the Marburg School of neo-Kantian philosophy, and increasingly came under the influence of neo-Kantianism generally. In doing so he developed phenomenology in a more Idealist direction (Luft 2010), although later he moved away from Idealism again, foreshadowing more recent efforts to 'naturalize' phenomenology (Thompson 2007). Michael Friedman (2000, 39ff.) has shown that Heidegger's turn to Husserl and then to hermeneutics were taken to overcome problems in neo-Kantianism, which was his real point of departure. Western Marxists, with the exception of Ernst Bloch, Joseph Needham, the later Merleau-Ponty and the eco-Marxists, treated 'nature' as a social category. And Habermas's philosophy, rejecting the focus of Idealism on consciousness and arguing for the centrality of communicative action instead, is really a development of Wittgenstein's later philosophy, which in turn was a development of neo-Kantianism, focusing on language in place of the categories as the transcendental condition for the intelligibility of experience for knowledge and rational action.

While phenomenologists inspired by Husserl attempted to enthrone the presuppositionless description of experience as the method of philosophy, allowing little or no place to speculation, members of these 'continental' traditions have not been so uniformly hostile to speculative thought as analytic philosophers. Kant had argued against speculative theology, and many neo-Kantians were unsympathetic to speculative thought. Kant had argued that there are *a priori* assumptions that are the condition for organizing the sensory manifold into an intelligible world and had revived the notion of dialectic to characterize debates that led to opposing positions (thesis and antithesis) without any basis for judging between them; that is, the 'antinomies of pure reason'. His successors embraced his notion of 'concepts', but in doing so, argued that these have changed through history. They were inspired by this to examine the evolution of concepts and to develop through speculation more adequate conceptual frameworks to understand the world. Beginning with Hegel, they characterized such thinking as dialectics, returning to Plato for guidance on how to think dialectically, and embraced the notion of speculative philosophy. This was the post-Kantian tradition of 'speculative Idealism', the most notable philosophers identified with this (some mistakenly, I will later argue) being Solomon Maimon, J.G. Fichte, Schelling, Hegel, F.H. Jacobi and Friedrich Schleiermacher.

These German philosophers helped inspire British and American Idealism, which gave a central place to speculation and also came to be known as speculative Idealism, the most eminent proponents of which were T.H. Green (1836–1882) and F.H. Bradley (1846–1924) in Britain and Josiah Royce (1855–1916) in USA (Mander 2001). Speculative Idealism came to be identified with a coherence theory of truth and a view of reality as an organism comprising a Self, Mind or Spiritual principle. These Idealists were seen by their opponents as the epigone of the German speculative Idealists. The British Idealists in particular were the target of the early British analytic philosophers (notably by Moore), who often characterized their own position as a defense of realism against Idealism. Defenders of this Idealist tradition still exist, although they have been marginalized. Consequently, there has been a strong tendency by analytic philosophers to identify speculative philosophy with speculative Idealism, a contamination of Anglophone philosophy by continental traditions, and then to define this as the ultimate polar opposite of first, realism, and then later, particularly in USA, naturalism. Reacting to this, in Germany Dieter Henrich has argued that the inescapable reality of the subject cannot be explained through naturalism and again has defended a form of Idealism, and along with this, speculative metaphysics (Freundlieb 2003). French philosophers are also strongly influenced by these German philosophers, although they have their own distinctive traditions. As we shall see in the following chapter, they have not succeeded in providing an alternative to the increasingly dominant tradition of Anglophone analytic philosophy.

This sketch of 'continental philosophy' clearly confuses criteria (or shows the confusion) over what counts as Idealism, and also can easily be challenged on details. However, as far as the present argument is concerned, what is at issue here is not so much the explicitly argued views of various philosophers, but more deeply held assumptions that have framed intellectual debates and the organization of educational institutions, constraining the thought of diverse philosophers for two centuries. It is not only the diverse views expressed that are important here, views which for the purpose of this argument I have greatly simplified, but the unexpressed and institutionalized assumptions and tendency to categorize philosophers on one side or the other of this divide and to be blind to or to misinterpret views that do not fit into one or the other of these opposing sides. There has been a tendency to categorize philosophy as either analytic or continental, and then more recently, as either analytic and naturalist, or Idealist and possibly speculative, and to conflate these oppositions. This has had the effect of blinding people to, or at least facilitating the marginalization of a tradition that is naturalistic, humanistic and speculative at the same time, a tradition I have characterized as speculative naturalism.

Recovering the tradition of speculative naturalism: from Schelling to process metaphysics

Speculative naturalism is a far more potent opposition than any form of Idealism, speculative or otherwise, to the creeping dominance of analytic philosophers promoting scientism and claiming a monopoly on naturalism and the prestige of science and mathematics. This is a tradition that could be characterized as effecting a third Copernican Revolution. It is a post-Kantian tradition, accepting Kant's second Copernican Revolution that had focused on human consciousness and agency, but then naturalizing Idealism to conceive nature in such a way that living beings, subjects and humanity, with all their cognitive and creative powers, can be seen as having evolved within, as part of and as participating in a creative nature. As Alfred North Whitehead (1861–1847) wrote in *Process and Reality* (1978, p.88), characterizing his own version of this, '[f]or Kant, the world emerges from the subject; for the philosophy of organism, the subject emerges from the world'. This is a tradition that accepts that all that we know is related to human consciousness – since to deny this is self-contradictory as Collingwood (1939, p.44) pointed out, but by rejecting a pervasive and often tacitly assumed Cartesian dualism, defends realism and naturalism. It avoids Bolzano's argument against Kant by holding that nature, which preceded the existence of humans, is achieving its highest consciousness of itself (so far as we know) through human consciousness.

The blindness to such speculative naturalism is evident in the marginalization of naturalists such as Whitehead, John Dewey and the process metaphysicians in USA, and Rom Harré and Roy Bhaskar in Britain, the philosophers who opposed reductionist naturalism and gave some place to speculation (even if not referred to as such), but more importantly, through the misinterpretation of major philosophers and a failure to acknowledge their achievements and influence. The most blatant misrepresentation of a major philosopher, a philosopher who should be recognized as a principal founder (along with Herder and Goethe) and one of the most important figures in the modern tradition of speculative naturalism, is F.W.J. Schelling (1775–1854). As noted, Schelling is generally categorized as an Idealist (Redding 2009). Schelling figures prominently as an Idealist in a recent major work on the history of German philosophy by one of the leading American historians of German philosophy, Frederick Beiser, titled *German Idealism* (Beiser 2002). Yet Schelling in his break with Fichte, rejected Idealism. In his *System of Transcendental Idealism* devoted to deducing categories to grasp the whole of reality, Schelling clearly states that transcendental philosophy, which takes the subjective as primary, is only one part of philosophy, the other being nature-philosophy (*Naturphilosophie*) which takes the objective as primary (Schelling 1978, p.7). For nature-philosophy, 'The concept of *nature* does not entail that there should also be an intelligence that is aware of it. Nature, it seems, would exist, even if there were nothing that was aware of it. Hence the problem can also be formulated *thus:* how does intelligence come to be added to nature, or how does nature come to be presented?' (1978, p.5). Soon after, in *Universal Deduction of the Dynamical Processes* (1856–61, I/4, pp.1–78) where he attempted a 'dynamic construction of matter', Schelling argued that the Philosophy of Nature is more fundamental than Idealism. In 1809 in *Of Human Freedom* Schelling argued that idealism is inadequate for characterizing human freedom, being only capable of a formal conception, 'not the real and vital conception of freedom … that … is a possibility of good and evil' (1936, p.26), and in the third version of *The Ages of the World* written circa 1815 he characterized Idealism as the philosophy of people who had dissociated themselves from the forces that are the basis of their existence and become 'nothing but images, just dreams of shadows' (2000, p.106).

Accepting Kant's arguments for the creativity of the mind, he was effecting a third Copernican revolution, demanding that nature be conceived in such a way that such creative minds could have evolved from and within it. Many years later, circa 1835, in his lectures *On the History of Modern Philosophy*, Schelling argued that his philosophy transcended the opposition between materialism and spiritualism, realism and Idealism (1994, p.120). In his 1842 lectures in which he set out to attack Hegel's Idealism, Schelling clarified the difference between naturalism and Idealism that has defined the difference between Idealism and speculative naturalism ever since. While Hegel had argued that Being is the most empty concept, Schelling argued that philosophers must accept that there is an unprethinkable Being (*unvordenkliche Sein*) that precedes all thought, including scientific and philosophical thought. Even if Bolzano were right in criticizing Kant for failing to distinguish between subjective representations and objective representations, and between representations and objects of representations, and Hanna (2001) has shown that this is very doubtful, this was not the case with Schelling, and this did not preclude acknowledging creativity in cognition and giving a central place to speculative thought. It was in his *First Outline of a System of the Philosophy of Nature* that Schelling defended speculation as 'Speculative Physics' (2004, p.193ff.). Acknowledging the central place of concepts in cognition, Schelling went on to question the concepts of Newtonian science and to argue that these have to be transcended to make intelligible the emergence of life, humanity and the development of consciousness, both through history and in individuals.

Another case illustrating how dualistic categorizations lead to misrepresentation is the way R.G. Collingwood has been described. A major opponent of analytic philosophy, Collingwood is almost always portrayed as an Idealist. However, he himself pointed out that his own views had been misrepresented because only two philosophical positions were recognized, realism (defended for the most part by analytic philosophers) and Idealism. As he wrote in his autobiography, 'any one opposing the "realists" was automatically classified as an "idealist"' (1939, p.56). Collingwood is most well known as a philosopher of history and as an historian, but he also wrote a book, *The Idea of Nature* (1945), essentially a history of the philosophy of nature, and offered his own speculative philosophy of nature very much in the Schellingian tradition, although Schelling was not acknowledged. As Guido Vanheeswijck (1998) argued, Collingwood, like Whitehead, was a process philosopher. Collingwood also developed the logic of question and answer which became an important method for exposing hierarchies of assumptions to reveal the ultimate metaphysical presuppositions of an era, including assumptions about nature, thereby exposing the illusions of philosophers dismissive of metaphysics.

Schelling's Nature Philosophy had an enormous influence on other philosophers, who also have tended to be misinterpreted. C.S. Peirce, for instance, who is usually categorized with the pragmatists who are generally defined by their support for the pragmatist theory of truth, wrote to William James:

My views were probably influenced by Schelling ... by all stages of Schelling, but especially by the *Philosophie der Natur.* I consider Schelling enormous ... If you were to call my philosophy Schellingianism transformed in the light of modern physics, I should not take it hard.

(Esposito 1977, p.203)

While philosophers paid attention to Peirce's work in logic and epistemology, until the recent revival of interest in his work by biosemioticians his speculative cosmology was largely ignored. Like Schelling, Peirce was a speculative naturalist concerned to conceive physical existence in a way that would enable humans to be understood as products of and creative participants within nature, with metaphysics, aesthetics and ethics accorded a place in his philosophy along with logic and science. This was also true of other philosophers categorized as pragmatists, including William James, John Dewey, George Herbert Mead and Roy Wood Sellars. Along with these, Friedrich Engels, the proponents of *Lebensphilosophie,* philosophical biology and philosophical anthropology, Henri Bergson, Aleksandr Bogdanov (the founder of 'tektology'– the general theory of organization), Alfred North Whitehead, Ernst Bloch, the later Merleau-Ponty, the later Castoriadis (Adams 2011, pp.137–144), Gilles Deleuze and other proponents of process metaphysics were also directly or indirectly influenced by Schelling, and each has advanced the tradition of speculative naturalism. This synoptic history of the background to the development of speculative naturalism is designed to provide some idea of what it entails, preliminary to defending it.

From transcendental deductions to dialectics: from Kant to Hegel

The defense of speculation by post-Kantian philosophers was in response to the perceived limitations of Kant's transcendental deductions while, unlike the anti-Kantians, accepting Kant's arguments that experience is organized by imagination, forms of intuition and categories of the understanding, and that empirical research always involves posing questions to nature assuming these forms and categories, or 'concepts'. The notion of 'concept' had been taken up and developed a philosophical notion by Leibniz as an alternative to 'idea' and 'notion', and was embraced by Kant. To overcome the degenerate state of metaphysics, and to put it on solid foundation to provide apodictic knowledge as the Ancient Greeks had succeeded in doing for logic and mathematics and Bacon and Galileo had succeeded in doing for science, Kant in the preface to *Critique of Pure Reason* had argued for a new dimension of philosophy, 'transcendental philosophy' (Kant 1996, B viii – B xxiv). This, Kant claimed, has its own distinctive method, transcendental deduction, involving the analysis of judgements by which the forms of intuition and the categories of the understanding, that is, the basic concepts which are the condition for any possible judgment, can be discovered and justified as necessarily presupposed for judgements to be possible. Like mathematical knowledge, this would be synthetic *a priori* knowledge, but of a different kind than mathematical synthetic *a priori* knowledge. To understand what Kant was doing, it is necessary to appreciate the central place he accorded the synthetic component of knowledge, that is, *synthesis*. Kant argued that we can only know what we have in some sense created, defending a constructivist theory of both empirical knowledge, which always involves imagination and the deployment of concepts to organize the sensory manifold, and mathematics where cognition occurs through the construction of concepts, expressing a universal validity in an individual case, for instance, in the construction of a triangle, whether in imagination or with a diagram (1996, pp. A 713, B 741, p.668f.). In both cases, such construction involves synthesis, which requires imagination. He characterized synthesis as 'the act of putting various presentations with one another and comprising their manifoldness in one cognition', this being 'the mere effect produced by the imagination, which is a blind but indispensible function of the soul without which we should have no cognition whatsoever, but of which we are conscious only rarely' (Kant 1996, A 77–78, B 103, p.130).

Kant failed to demonstrate the necessity of his forms of intuition and categories of the understanding through transcendental deductions. While he specified what transcendental deductions are not, he failed to specify what they are (Breazeale 2010, p.42ff.; Bar-On 1987, 74ff.). This was a major source of dissatisfaction with his work among both his opponents and supporters. It would appear that transcendental philosophy aiming at synthetic knowledge of the forms of intuition and the categories of the understanding that is not *a posteriori* but *a priori* would require 'intellectual intuition' and speculative imagination, a notoriously difficult aspect of Kant's philosophy (Makkreel 1994, 28f.). Kant did consider the possibility of 'intellectual intuition' as a direct experience of the 'I' and the Absolute, but rejected it as a form of noumenal knowledge, which he had deemed impossible. And he characterized speculation as a fruitless theoretical exercise in which cognition aims at an object, or concepts of an object, of which one cannot gain any experience (1996, A635f. and B663f., p.612). First Fichte, and then following him, Hegel, Schleiermacher and Schelling regarded their work as speculative because they gave a place to a third kind of experience along with sensible objects and the concepts required to cognize them as such – experience of reflection on the nature and development of experience and on the generation of concepts, and on the adequacy of concepts used to interpret experience. As we have noted, this gave rise to a post-Kantian tradition of philosophy which embraced Kant's notion of forms of intuition and categories of the understanding as conceptual frameworks and developed Kant's concept of synthesis, but went beyond Kant to treat synthesis as central to such speculative knowledge. Speculation, by which old concepts could be brought into question and new concepts and conceptual frameworks elaborated, that is, 'synthetic' thinking as Broad characterized it, was made central to philosophy, and along with synthetic thinking, synoptic thinking.

The philosopher who made the crucial break that began this post-Kantian tradition of speculative philosophy was J.G. Fichte (1762–1814). Fichte was the first philosopher to embrace and defend intellectual intuition[5] and to accord extended powers of synthesis to it, and to claim that Kant's notion of construction could be extended from mathematics to cognitive development. Kant had argued that some debates in philosophy are irresolvable. These are the antinomies of pure reason; for instance, the claim that all composite substances are made of simple parts (thesis) and no composite thing consists of mere simple parts (antithesis), and that to explain appearances there must be a causality through freedom (thesis) and all that happens is determined by the laws of nature (antithesis). Fichte set out to show that through synthetic thinking it is possible to reconcile these antinomies, and in doing so, achieve higher syntheses.[6] Allowing this form of synthetic thinking provided him with a way to construct the concepts required to organize experience, achieving self-comprehension in the process. All of this is made possible, Fichte argued, by 'the wonderful power of productive imagination in ourselves' (Fichte 1982, p.112, 185, 187). Through such thinking Fichte attempted to establish and justify the forms of intuition and the categories of the understanding without postulating an unknowable thing-in-itself. For Fichte, intellectual intuition is not a faculty of the subject, but is the subject knowing itself and thereby constituting itself in a non-objective manner through mediation of what can be known objectively. He argued for the priority of praxis, taking theoretical knowledge as derivative (1982, p.61, 256). It is through action that the sensible world (which Fichte characterized as first and foremost, feeling, including the feeling of resistance to our striving) is constituted as objects, and it is only on reflection that we develop concepts of these objects. However, Fichte later concluded that self-consciousness and free agency are further dependent upon being recognized by and recognizing other finite rational beings as free and ascribing efficacy to them. 'No Thou, no I: no I, no Thou' he proclaimed (1982, p.172f.).

There were two 'methods' involved in this speculative philosophizing, although these should not be seen as completely separate. The first, which to some extent anticipated Husserlian phenomenology and which Daniel Breazeale (2010) characterized as the 'phenomenological synthetic method', consists of a 'genetic description of experience itself' whereby 'the necessary acts of the I demonstrates that consciousness, in order to posit itself, must also posit a "world" with a certain necessary structure' (p.48). The conscious act associated with this has a synthetic function, differentiating and connecting at the same time. The second and more important method was characterized by Breazeale as the 'dialectical synthetic method', the essence of which involves revealing in what respect opposites (thesis and antithesis) are alike, thereby discovering the unity in opposites, generating new determinations. Breazeale explicated what this method involved on the basis of diverse comments by Fichte over a range of texts:

This method … proceeds by making explicit a contradiction (or, alternatively, a vicious circularity) implicit in a previously derived set of propositions, and then actively 'seeking out' [*aufsuchen*] some new, 'higher principle' that allows one to avoid the objectionable contradiction (or circularity) and is *therefore* declared to be 'necessary'. Unlike conceptual analysis, logical inference, or syllogistic reasoning, this 'dialectical' method of derivation is thoroughly *synthetic*, in the sense that the new principle that 'hebt' oder 'aufhebt' the contradiction in question is not 'contained in' and thus cannot be analytically derived from the problematic set of concepts and propositions that it resolves. Furthermore, since it is not derived from experience, but is instead a product of pure thinking, this new principle is '*a priori*' and represents a synthetic *a priori* extension of our cognition.

(Breazeale 2010, p.55)

Clarifying this further, Breazeale continued:

What is essential to note about this method of dialectical-synthetic thinking is that no algorithm is available for solving such problems. At each stage of such a derivation one encounters new *contradictions* that cannot be analytically resolved, fresh *problems* to be solved and novel *challenges* to be met. To say, with Fichte, that an appropriate solution to such problems is something we have to 'aufsuchen' is to recognize that every such problem must be dealt with in its own terms and that each requires a fresh exercise in *creative problem solving*. Neither past nor present experience can offer us any guidance in such cases, for here we remain within the realm of pure reason – or, if one prefers, of pure 'reasons' – and must therefore seek our solution in the pure realm of *imaginative thinking*.

(Breazeale 2010, p.56f.)

This new conception of philosophizing had an enormous influence on Hegel (who downplayed the role of synthetic thinking), Schleiermacher and Schelling (who was closer to Fichte).

This 'method' of speculation was characterized and developed by G.W.F. Hegel (1770–1831) as dialectical thinking (Hegel 1975 §81, p.117). However, Hegel modified Fichte's 'method' by introducing Reason as a transcendent power beyond mere understanding (Hegel 1977b, 110ff, 130ff.). To do this he drew on Kant's discussion of dialectics in the antinomies of pure reason, but greatly modified Kant's concept of dialectics by drawing on and developing the notion of dialectics as it had been characterized and defended by Plato (whereas Kant's reference to dialectics had been resolutely Aristotelian, according it a much lower status). Plato had characterized dialectics in Book VI of the *Republic,* but all his dialogues were exercises in dialectics – as enquiry based on posing and seeking answers to questions whereby people could come to survey a subject as a whole, enabling them to avoid the disasters that followed from partial understanding of ideas and situations and ignoring all relevant factors required for good decisions (Lamprecht 1946). While Socrates had used questioning to arrive at ethical truths, Plato developed this as a general approach to achieving comprehensive knowledge. He argued that dialectic goes beyond mathematics by using hypotheses not as principles, but as Collingwood (2005) put it, 'as the hypotheses that they are, employing them as stepping stones to reach something which is not an hypothesis but the principle of everything' (p.13). Conceiving dialectics as the way to expose one-sidedness of abstract propositions of understanding and how these necessarily veer into their opposites as the 'negative' side of dialectics, Hegel followed Fichte in rejecting Kant's pessimism about resolving these antinomies and defended speculative philosophy as the 'positive' or speculative side of dialectics, understood as the process of overcoming contradiction, one-sidedness, and differences to achieve more comprehensive knowledge (Hegel 1975, §81, p.115ff.).[7] Following Plato, dialectics was characterized by him as posing a series of questions to reveal and overcome such one-sided concepts to arrive at the unconditioned categories through which the Absolute is comprehended as a self-conscious totality that includes the philosopher and the philosopher's consciousness of the Absolute. This was characterized by him as the development of Reason.

In his first major work to deploy and elaborate on the notion of dialectics, the Preface to his *Phenomenology of Spirit,* Hegel introduced the notion of the 'speculative proposition' or 'speculative sentence' (Hegel 1977a, §61, p.38). This is built on the Socratic question that allows us to bring any aspect of experience before the mind and consider its being and meaning. Hegel argued that the mind is made dialectical by formulating questions, allowing it to move from one question to another. The speculative sentence according to Hegel 'is merely the dialectical movement, this course that generates itself, going forth from, and returning to, itself' (1977a, §65, p.40). As Donald Verene explicated this notion: 'The speculative sentence turns this series of perspectives back upon itself, revealing the pattern of self-development. The ancient pursuit of the question, joined with the power of expression framed in the speculative sentence, gives philosophy its fullest range of thought' (Verene 2009, p.ix). Embracing this idea of philosophy, Verene noted that 'speculation excludes neither reflection nor analysis' but it is the 'logic of question and answer that is the key to philosophy, far more than argument. Anyone can argue, but few can ask the right questions' (p.ix). While reflection and argument operate at a distance from the object, '[t]o speculate … is … to narrate the inner life of the object' (p.3).

Hegel's dialectic involves three steps: taking a view, belief, concept or category as fixed, then reflecting on this to reveal what is implicit within it, but also, to reveal its abstractness and one-sidedness and one or more contradictions, followed by a speculative step of positive reason in which a higher stage is reached which embraces earlier beliefs, concepts or categories and contains the contradictions within them (without necessarily eliminating them) to achieve a more concrete, because less one-sided perspective. The dialectics of Hegel's *Phenomenology of Spirit* was simultaneously an effort to achieve a comprehensive knowledge of the Absolute, to show through this comprehensive knowledge that achieving this was the *telos* of human history, at the same time revealing the intelligibility of human history as a stepwise development not only of knowledge, but of tools developing through the dialectic of labour and institutions developing through the dialectic of recognition (Williams 1992, 1997). These have provided the conditions for the dialectic of representation to unfold to achieve this comprehensive knowledge. After the initial engagement with highly abstract approaches to attaining knowledge, questions were formulated to show how a succession of forms of Spirit had extended recognition of people's freedom, creating the objective conditions where people could control nature and achieve higher and higher levels of consciousness of their destiny and of the place of Reason in history, culminating in consciousness of the Absolute as Absolute self-consciousness. The dialectic begins by examining the claim to be able to ground knowledge on a foundation of sense-certainty, revealing the one-sidedness of this claim, leading to successively less one-sided efforts to provide a foundation for knowledge (perception, understanding, research traditions etc.), eventually showing that it is only from the perspective of the self-conscious totality that includes an account of the development of humanity through history and all the defective (because one-sided) approaches to comprehending the world, that true knowledge, which includes the self-knowledge of the individual and of humanity, is achieved and recognized as such.

This dialectic, operative in Hegel's history of philosophy, political philosophy and aesthetics, was more open than the geometrized dialectic of his *Science of Logic* (1990) and *Logic* (1975), which, unfolding the inner relations between categories (the 'movement of concepts'), beginning with the most empty category, Being, moved on (often in triads) to eventually grasp the Absolute in all its diversity as a self-creating World-Spirit, including consciousness of this, in the 'Concept' or 'Notion'. On the basis of dialectics so conceived, Hegel took nature to be of necessity posited by Spirit as its other and projected dialectics from thought and culture to the entire cosmos, treating the categories as the ground-plan of reality and of the structure of the cosmos prior to its creation, in place of his earlier work focusing on the development of cognition through human history. This Idealist dialectic short-circuited and avoided the major problem confronting naturalist proponents of dialectics of developing a conceptual scheme which could account for the emergence of cognitive processes from an originally non-conscious nature in which humans did not exist.

Defending speculative naturalism through dialectics: from Hegel to Schelling

The notion of dialectics, which had long history from the Greeks onwards (McKinney 1983) was embraced and developed by other post-Kantian philosophers who developed the idea of dialectics differently. The most sustained effort at the time to characterize dialectical thought explicitly was made by Friedrich Schleiermacher (1768–1834) in his lectures on philosophy, published as *Dialectic or, The Art of Doing Philosophy*. Referring to the work of Plato on dialectics, Schleiermacher related dialectic to speculation, proclaiming that 'mathematics is more closely allied to the empirical form, dialectic more allied to the speculative form. ... [S]peculative natural science can be set forth only according to dialectical principles...' (Schleiermacher 1996, p.73). What is clear from this work is the complexity of dialectical thinking compared to the characterization of reasoning by mainstream analytic philosophers, anticipating conceptions of rationality developed by the post-positivist philosophers of science in the second half of the Twentieth Century.[8] However, Schleiermacher saw himself as aligned with Schelling and it is speculative philosophy as developed by Schelling (who only later used the terms 'dialectics') that is the most important for understanding speculative naturalism, particularly his much later work where he was reacting to Hegel's philosophy (Beach 1990; Beach 1994, p.84ff.; Gare 2013a).

In developing his own conception of philosophy as speculative thinking Schelling took Fichte's work as his point of departure and focused on and developed the notions of synthesis and construction to forge a synthesis of natural philosophy, art and history. He took over from Fichte the view that the subject is activity that can be appreciated as such through intellectual intuition, that objects of the sensible world can only be understood in relation to the activity of the subject, that conceptual knowledge is derivative from practical engagement in the sensible world, that there can be and is also an appreciation of other subjects as activities rather than objects, and that the formation of the self-conscious self is the outcome of the limiting of its activity by the world and other subjects. Schelling also took over and further developed Fichte's defense of construction and his genetic, dialectical approach to construction. He defended an even stronger thesis against Kant's effort in 'The Discipline of Pure Reason' in *The Critique of Pure Reason* to limit construction to mathematics (Kant 1996, A725/B753ff., p.677ff.), arguing that 'the philosopher looks solely to the act of construction itself, which is an absolutely internal thing' (Schelling 1978, §4, p.13).[9] Thought is inherently synthetic, Schelling argued, and begins with genuine opposition either between thought and something opposing it, or other factors within thought. This necessitates a new synthetic moment that can be treated as a product or factor in the next level of development.

Building on Kant's and Fichte's ascription of a central place to imagination in such synthesis and developing Kant's concept of construction and extending Fichte's genetic approach from the development of cognition to the development of the whole of nature, Schelling characterized 'intellectual intuition' as a form of knowledge gained through a reflective and imaginative experimentation and construction by the productive imagination of the sequence of forms produced by the procreative causality of the 'Absolute' (i.e. the unconditioned). In his explication of Schelling's constructivist form of philosophy Bruce Matthews wrote of the relation between intellectual intuition and the productive imagination:

> '[I]ntellectual intuition' and the 'productive imagination; ... are used by [Schelling] to describe different aspects of the same productive power. Intellectual intuition is the *window through which we see into* the productive

imagination. Conversely, intellectual intuition is the *screen* onto which the productive imagination projects its visions. But it is the power of *Einbildung* that allows us to mediate and *make one* the dualities of the universal and particular *in concreto*.

(Matthews 2011, p.195)

Intellectual intuition reproduces in imagination the process by which nature, through limiting its activity, has constructed itself as a diversity of processes and products, self-construction in which the philosopher in his or her particular situation is participating. In this way, Schelling embraced and further radicalized Kant's more radical conjectures: his dynamism according to which matter is defined by forces of attraction and repulsion and his conception of living organisms put forward in the *Critique of Judgment* as unities in which the parts are both causes and effects of their forms. Referring to this dialectic as the 'standpoint of production' in contrast to the Kantian 'standpoint of reflection', Schelling was concerned not only to show the social conditions for objective knowledge, but the nature of the world that enables it to be known objectively and explained at least partially through Newtonian physics while at the same time producing subjects that can achieve knowledge of it and of themselves. This in essence is the whole project of speculative naturalism. Later, the process of developing such comprehensive knowledge of nature and humanity was also characterized by Schelling as dialectics.

As opposed to Hegel, particularly Hegel's geometricised dialectic of his *Science of Logic* 1990), Schelling's version of dialectics was infused with willing. The production of truth goes beyond abstract logic and is guided by volition. The advance of the dialectic adds something new; it does not simply sublate earlier phases of the dialectic as in Hegel. As Beach (1994) translated Schelling: 'The dialectical method is, like the dialogical method, not demonstrative but productive; it is that in which truth becomes produced' (p.269n:50). That is, it embraces and extends Kant's constructivist account of mathematics to knowledge generally. Dialectical construction assumes a generative order of nature that is ontologically prior to this dialectical production of truth, and is reproduced by this dialectical production. This construction (or reconstruction) enables the universal and the particular, the ideal and the real, to be grasped together. Through such construction, Schelling characterized the whole of nature as a self-organizing process, showing how it had successively generated opposing forces, apparently inert matter (in which stability is achieved through a balance of opposing forces), extension, causation, space and time, organisms, inner sense and sensory objects, humanity and our present consciousness. Nature on this view is the activity of opposing forces of attraction and repulsion generating one form after another. Inverting Kant's characterization of causation, Schelling argued that mechanical cause-effect relations are abstractions from the reciprocal causation of self-organizing processes. Matter is itself a self-organizing process. While 'matter' emerges through a static balance of opposing forces, living organisms were characterized by Schelling as responding to changes in their environments to maintain their internal equilibrium by forming and reforming themselves, a process in which they resist the dynamics of the rest of nature and impose their own organization. In doing so, they constitute their environments as their worlds and react to these accordingly.

Schelling did not believe that this dialectical reconstruction of nature by itself would guarantee the truth of his system of philosophy, however. Philosophers should develop their own systems, knowing that no system could be final. Dialectics extends from thoughts of individuals to the thoughts of others and to the relationship between philosophies and philosophical systems and also the findings of empirical and experimental research guided by these systems. Philosophy advances as less perfect forms of philosophy are discarded and their valuable contents assimilated to more perfect forms. A philosophical system should be judged according to its coherence and comprehensiveness, and its capacity to surpass by including more limited philosophical stances. Here, Schelling fully embraces the Platonic notion of dialectics as developed by Hegel in the *Phenomenology of Spirit* that it is a way of overcoming limited, one-sided ways of thinking, and through this, continually moving towards a more comprehensive knowledge of the Absolute. It is only through providing a history of philosophy that defines its claim to truth in contrast to the work of other philosophers that a system can be properly defended, and then only provisionally, a history that Schelling provided in *On the History of Modern Philosophy* (1994). It was in critiquing Hegel's *Science of Logic* (1990) that Schelling pointed to the unprethinkable Being that precedes all thought and is always more than can be grasped in thought, and the role of volition in producing truth. While undermining Hegel's panlogism and the basis for assuming that the quest for comprehensive understanding of the whole could ever be finally successful, Schelling held that it is a necessary regulative principle to strive for this.

Notes

1 Political philosophers in the tradition of analytic philosophy such as John Rawls and Robert Nozick steered clear of the question, What is the good life? Charles Taylor and Alasdair MacIntyre who have touched on this question are really opponents of analytic philosophy working in an environment dominated by analytic philosophers.

2 Along with *Word & Object* (1960), *From a Logical Point of View* (1961) contains the core of Quine's whole philosophy, although his mature doctrine is best found in his essay 'Ontological Relativity' in *Ontological Relativity and Other Essays*, (1969).

3 On this, and its somewhat confused nature, see David MacArthur, 'Quinean Naturalism in Question' (2008).

4 It would appear that Hintikka believes that analytic philosophers who embrace modal logic and accept model theoretic techniques while still striving for a *Lingua Universalis* have not faced up to the incompatibility of these ideas. David Lewis's argument that all possible worlds are actual or real (modal realism) can be interpreted as an effort to overcome this incompatibility. See *The Possible and the Actual: Readings in the Metaphysics of Modality* (Loux 1979) for some of the arguments surrounding the interpretation of modal logic.

5 There has been much dispute over the meaning of 'intellectual intuition' in Kant, Fichte and Schelling and over whether there was any continuity in the development of this

concept in these three thinkers. See (Estes 2010, 164–177). Estes argues against claims that there was no continuity in the use of this concept.

6 This departure by Fichte and the effect it had on Hegel is described by Violetta L. Waibel (2010, pp.300–326).

7 Thorough and clear analyses of Hegel's notion of dialectics is provided by Finocchiaro (2002, Ch.7) 'Hegel and the theory and practice of dialectic', Gadamer (1976) and Limnatis (2008). The complexity and different dimensions of Hegel's dialectics and the difficulties in interpreting what Hegel meant by it are discussed in the essays in *The Dimensions of Hegel's Dialectic* (Limnatis 2010).

8 Scheiermacher's dialectics and recent thought on reasoning are compared in Andrew Bowie (2005, 73–90).

9 The central role of construction in Schelling is examined by Toscano (2004) and Radu (2000, p.8ff.).

3 Dialectics

From Marx to post-Marxism

Subsequent philosophers building on the work of Fichte, Hegel, Schleiermacher and Schelling have further advanced both the practice and our understanding of dialectics, although not always characterizing it as such. Much of the work on dialectics has been undertaken by Marxists, almost all of whom claim to be materialists in one form or another. While some Marxists have made original contributions to dialectics, much of their work has been philosophically crude and confused. To avoid getting bogged down in the morass of disputes over Marxism it is tempting to simply ignore Marxists, and even to abjure the use of the term 'dialectics' because of its association with Marxism. However, as we have seen, dialectics has a far longer history than Marxism and has been central to defenses of both speculation and synthetic thinking. Furthermore, ideas on dialectics of Marx himself and some unorthodox Marxists are so important to the development of this broader tradition of dialectical thinking that they cannot be ignored without significant loss to efforts to revive this tradition. Marxism has been one of the most important intellectual movements to have questioned and to have claimed to provide an alternative to the dominant world-view of reductionist scientific materialism.

Furthermore, Marxist dialectics is still being actively promoted. In 2008 a major anthology was published, *Dialectics for the New Century* edited by Bertell Ollman and Tony Smith, with contributions from most of the world's leading proponents of Marxist dialectics, defending dialectics over a range of disciplines and in relation to major practical issues. While there were differences between the contributors, these were not the focus of the anthology which was designed to present Marxist dialectical thought as the living alternative to the positivist and reductionist thinking that currently prevails. To this end, in the second chapter 'Why Dialectics? Why Now?' Ollman succinctly summed up his understanding of Marxist dialectics as consisting of six moments:

> There is an ontological one having to do with what the world really is (an infinite number of mutually dependent processes that coalesce to form a structured whole or totality). There is the epistemological moment that deals with how to organize our thinking in order to understand such a world (as indicated, this involves opting for a philosophy of internal

relations and abstracting out the main patterns in which change and interaction occur). There is the moment of inquiry (where, based on an assumption of internal relations among all parts, one uses the categories that convey these patterns as aids to investigation). There is the moment of intellectual reconstruction or self-clarification (where one puts together the results of such research for oneself). This is followed by the moment of exposition (where, using a strategy that takes account of how others think as well as what they know, one tries to explain this dialectical grasp of the 'facts' to a particular audience). And, finally, there is the moment of praxis (where, based on whatever clarification has been reached, one consciously acts in the world, changing it and testing it and deepening one's understanding of it all at the same time). These six moments are not traversed once and for all, but again and again, as every attempt to understand and expound dialectical truths and to act upon them improves one's ability to organize one's thinking dialectically and to inquire further and deeper into the mutually dependent processes to which we also belong. In writing about dialectics, therefore, one must be very careful not to single out any one moment – as so many thinkers do – at the expense of the others. Only in their internal relations do these six moments constitute a workable and immensely valuable dialectical method.

(Ollman 2008, p.10f.)

It is here that one might expect a defense of speculative naturalism. However, even when defending dialectics, most Marxists show little interest in speculative thought, and have an ambiguous relation to naturalism. What should be evident from Ollman is that, like Quinean naturalism, an ontology is assumed and then an epistemology together with a method of inquiry are proposed that virtually exclude the possibility that this ontology might be found defective. While this ontology might be (and in my view, is) superior to Quine's reductionist ontology, dialectics is characterized here in such a way that no alternatives can be taken seriously, and therefore no defense of it can be offered for it either. Furthermore, it leaves out one of the most important features of dialectics emphasized in particular by Schelling (and later by Lucian Goldmann, who identified himself as a Marxist), the need to constantly engage with different philosophical systems, research programs and even other cultures in the quest to develop ever more adequate conceptual frameworks for understanding the world. One of the most important consequences of this, is that while offering the basis for a radical critique of global capitalism, no alternative ways of conceptualizing social relations that could be deployed to transform existing relations between people and between humans and nature are offered (as Aleksandr Bogdanov, another Marxist, offered with his 'tektology').

While Ollman's characterization of dialectics does appear to represent the views of most current Marxist dialecticians, it could be argued that he has not done justice to the tradition of Marxist dialectics. Rather than rest content with received views, to properly evaluate Marxist dialectics it is necessary to examine the history of its development from Marx and Engels onwards. At the same time, a study of the history of Marxist dialectics can reveal how the emancipatory potential of Marxism has been weakened by the failure to appreciate the importance of speculation in dialectics. Marxism had an enormous influence on French philosophy from the Second World War onwards. It is impossible to understand the development of French philosophy except in relation to Marxism, and correspondingly, the most important philosophical work on dialectics was undertaken in France. It is French philosophy more than the philosophy of any other European country that people turn to when looking for alternatives to Anglophone, and particularly US analytic philosophy. A study of Marxist dialectics, particularly as it was taken up and debated in French philosophy, is required to explain why speculative naturalism continued to be marginalized even by those who have embraced dialectics. In accordance with dialectics, it is better to examine and critically appropriate the contributions to dialectics by Marxists along with the French thinkers influenced by them, indicate what they have achieved and where they are defective and where they can be augmented, and assimilate these ideas to the broader tradition of speculative naturalism.

Marx's dialectics

In developing his ideas on dialectics, Marx (1818–1883) was influenced by Fichte, Schelling and Hegel, along with some of the Young Hegelians. Following Fichte, Schelling and the Young Hegelians, he embraced the notion that we are first of all active in the world and develop our concepts in action before we reflect upon these concepts. Humanity is in a process of self-creation through the transformation of nature through history. Reflection should never be allowed to mislead people into thinking that they are somehow outside or above the world they are becoming conscious of in reflection; they are always active participants within the world, and even their reflective consciousness is a development within and of the world. Following Schelling, Marx believed that it is because we are participants within the world that we are able to reconstruct the constructive stages of its development. In the 'Economic and Philosophic Manuscripts of 1844', Marx confined himself to reconstructing the development of humanity, denying even the possibility of understanding nature except in relation to the development of humanity (Marx 1978, p.92). Through history, humanity is seen to develop its productive powers, however doing so in an alienated form. With class society culminating in the domination of workers by the bourgeoisie who own the means of production, humanity is alienated from both their labour and the products of their labour. Consequently, as their productive powers increase, the more powerful the alien, objective world becomes, and the poorer they and their inner worlds become. Humanity's species-being becomes alien to it, estranging people from their own bodies, from nature and from their spiritual or human essence, thereby estranging them from each other and from themselves. The dialectical unfolding of this logic entails humanity recovering this alienated essence by re-appropriating their productive powers in a communist society.

Marx then rejected this notion of humanity as the subject-object of history and focused instead on the development of people as individuals being formed by and forming their relationships to each other in their productive activities. In his mature work, he confined himself almost entirely to reconstructing and thereby comprehending the development of the 'bourgeois mode of production', or what came to be called capitalism, enabling him and those who read his work to understand themselves as the products of this socio-economic formation, constrained by it, but also having the potential in conjunction with other oppressed people to liberate themselves from its oppressive tendencies and participate in creating a new socio-economic formation. He continued to study pre-capitalist socio-economic formations, but his work on this, much of it in the *Grundrisse,* was not published. In his later years he even questioned the possibility of developing a general theory of history, and appeared to be charting a path whereby through building on the *mir* (agricultural communes), Russians might be able to avoid capitalism on the path to communism (White 1996).

Marx's major achievement was to have grasped the dynamics of the bourgeois mode of production as an emergent, unfolding process, recognizing that it was unique with its own dynamics that cannot be understood as simply a further development of processes that preceded it (Gare 1996, Ch.9). This involved grasping in reflective consciousness the categories of economics, the 'forms of existence' through which people define and are defined in their social practices, and in relation to which every other social practice has to be understood. To analyze these categories, Marx studied carefully and utilized the dialectical form of investigation and presentation of categories Hegel had developed in his *Science of Logic.*[1] He was also influenced by the form of dialectics Hegel developed in the *Phenomenology of Spirit* whereby the shapes of consciousness, practical and theoretical, were not grasped statically but dynamically in their development and transformation. The categories of economics can be reflected upon as a coherent framework of concepts, but to be properly understood they have to be grasped as having emerged to articulate a self-reproducing socio-economic formation. This continually reproduces instantiations of these categories: commodities, money, labour-power, capital, interest, rent etc., along with the relations of production, that is, proletarians, the bourgeoisie and the relationship between them. In this socio-economic formation, the proletariat, deprived of access to the means of production and therefore obliged to sell their creative potential as a commodity (as labour-power), and the bourgeoisie struggling to maintain their privileged position in society and committed to the illusion of accumulating 'capital' (as though it were a substance rather than an aspect of a social relation), are produced and reproduced as such, a reproductive process that is inherently unstable and extremely dynamic. This instability is accentuated because the categories reify social relations, treating them as things and blind people to the real nature of these social relations and processes of which they are part. To exist, members of this social formation must constantly revolutionize the forces of production and expand its sphere of activities, extending the commodity form both intensively, commodifying more and more of society and nature, and extensively, encompassing the globe. It must grow until it destroys the conditions of its existence, whatever these might be. Both members of the proletariat and the bourgeoisie are enslaved by this dynamic, albeit in different ways. Comprehending these dynamics involved engaging with the work of economists who in the past had, in representing economic processes, uncritically accepted the categories embodied in the practices of these economic processes, therefore conceiving capitalism as a natural order, oblivious to the historically unique nature of these categories and their articulation in this mode of production. Effectively, they have bought into the illusion that social reality is a quantitative relation between objects and ignored the processes that produce this objectified social reality. Insights into the limitations of these economists and the categories they presupposed as natural, provided a major argument for the superiority of his own characterization of industrial capitalism and the implicit categories on which his critique was based, which at the same time revealed the possibility of overcoming and replacing capitalism and the categories articulating it.

Marx's understanding of dialectics as expressed in the *Theses on Feuerbach* is also important because it demands appreciation that we are part of the world we are trying to understand, and to be engaged in dialectical thinking is to be participating in the formation or transformation of oneself as well as one's society and nature. This was the side of Marx that Bogdanov, Lukács, Karl Korsch and Antonio Gramsci rediscovered. While heavily influenced by Hegel, this aspect of Marx's dialectics was really closer to Schelling's, being directly influenced by it and by others who were influenced by him, notably Ludwig Feuerbach and August von Cieszkowski. The relation of the categories of economics is not a bloodless relation of a timeless logical structure unfolding by logical necessity to overcome contradictions. While the development of society could not be understood except in relation to the categories and their logical interconnectedness, the evolution of these categories within society requires volition. Also, there are emergent dynamics to capitalism that could not be understood through the categories that constitute it, and it is these emergent dynamics with their instability, dynamism and vulnerability to being overcome that manifest the deficient, one-sided nature of these abstract categories. Most importantly, these categories blind those who objectify others as instruments to be exploited and reify social relations, to the internal relations between these others and themselves, and between humanity and nature. They are blinded also to the processes that produce and reproduce these reified relations. Because of these deficiencies, actions based on defining relations between people, their societies and nature through these categories continually produce effects that contradict what is intended, undermining the processes and formations of which they are components and which are the conditions of these actions being successful. Even if actors within this system become aware of these contradictions, because the categories are embodied in practices as forms of existence, these contradictions cannot be dealt with – except by replacing these forms of existence. Essentially, this must involve creating a different socio-economic formation embodying different categories.

Taking Schelling's insights on the relationship between categories and will further than Schelling, Marx abandoned the commitment to determinism, if he ever believed in this. There is no necessity for contradictions to lead to the replacement of deficient categories by categories that do not lead to such contradictions. The dynamics of history is not the dynamics of a subject–object moving dialectically from one defective conceptual structure to another that is more adequate. Social and cultural forms emerge that transcend such dialectical logic and confront people as a second nature to which they must adapt. Marx pointed out that contradictions in society in fact frequently do not impel any development. As he argued in Volume I of *Capital* in relation to the contradictory conditions associated with the exchange of commodities, these develop 'a *modus vivendi*, a form in which they can exist side by side'. And he went on: 'This is generally the way in which real contradictions are reconciled' (Marx 1962, p.106). Marx castigated the 'dialectical' account of economic categories and development in his critique of Proudhon in *The Poverty of Philosophy* (Marx 1973, Ch.2). He never portrayed the overcoming of capitalism as anything more than a possibility. Success requires those who are oppressed to become conscious of their situation and to have the vision and will to overcome their oppression when the inevitable crises occur.[2] It is not a logical necessity, dialectical or otherwise.

Despite the profundity of Marx's study of political economy and the dynamics of capitalism, by abandoning of his earlier notion of humanity and the stress he placed on changing the world rather than merely interpreting it, he misled most of his followers, including Engels, leading them to underestimate how important interpreting the world is if it is to be changed. The original title of *Capital* was *Das Capital: Kritik der politischen Oekonomie*. It was a work exposing the illusions of the economists, not a work of political economy as it was treated by his followers. Without the concept of humanity presupposed in 'The 1844 Manuscripts', Marx could not promote a vision of the future that would inspire people to free themselves to realize their full humanity and express themselves in their work without being exploited as instruments (Marx 1978, pp.66–125). His later work implied, despite his intentions and efforts to correct his followers, as in his 'Critique of the Gotha Programme' where Marx derided the labour theory of value (Marx 1978, pp.525–541), that the problem with a capitalist economy is that people are not paid the full value of their labour-power and do not develop the forces of production as rapidly as they could if the economy were centrally planned, that consciousness of these deficiencies will be produced as the forces of production come into conflict with the relations of production, and that inevitably this will lead to the replacement of the market system. The real problem is that people's creative potential is being reduced to 'labour-power' and nature is being treated purely instrumentally as nothing but a factor of production.

Marx offered some penetrating insights (later developed by Marxist historians of science, most importantly, Aleksandr Bogdanov, Joseph Needham and following them, Robert Young (1985), into how capitalism had engendered a conception of nature that reveals only how it can be controlled, and then a conception of evolution as the product of the struggle for survival through projecting the struggle for survival in Victorian society onto nature, thereby legitimating this brutal society as natural and irreformable. He also noted that Romantic ideas about nature accompanying such ideas disguise rather than challenge this world-view. However, he offered nothing to replace either the mechanistic view of nature or Darwinian evolutionary theory. He did not entirely exclude nature from his analysis of the development of capitalism, criticizing his followers for embracing the labour theory of value and ignoring the contribution of nature to production, and in the third volume of *Capital,* pointing to the destructive effect on land of the 'metabolic rift' generated by the separation of the city from its countryside; but these were more asides than a central component of his critique of capitalism. Marxists, most of whom embraced the labour theory of value, tended to ignore this aspect of Marx's work until very recently (with eco-Marxists being notable exceptions). The consequence of this has been that orthodox Marxists, believing they were following Marx, embraced the categories and values of a capitalist economy and in the Soviet Union produced a bureaucratic capitalism, and following the collapse of the Soviet Union, have gone on to embrace neoliberalism as the most effective means to develop the forces of production (Supiot 2012).

Engels (1820–1895) was right to see that Marx's work required a general theory of history and an alternative conception of nature to properly situate and then further advance both his insights and the orientation required for effective action. As James White (1996) has shown, in a work that preceded *Capital* but was never published, *The Critique of Political Economy,* Marx had utilized categories deriving from Schelling. Having abandoned these, the analyses of *Capital* were left without the broader framework required to justify them. The problem with Engels' work is that he defended the 'orthodox Marxist' view of history with its 'base-superstructure' model driven by the quest to develop the forces of production that Marx had abandoned. As Marx wrote in *A Contribution to the Critique of Political Economy* 'What is called historical evolution depends in general on the fact that the latest form regards earlier ones as stages in the development of itself and conceives them always in a one-sided manner…'. (Marx 1970, p.211) And it was in response to French socialists who embraced the base-superstructure model of society and called themselves Marxists that Marx famously said to Engels: 'All I know is that I am not a Marxist'. This base-supestructure dichotomy echoes Descartes' dualism, and implies that the superstructure, including thought, is not part of the material world and therefore cannot be causally efficacious.

In *Anti-Dühring* and *Dialectics of Nature* Engels did offer an alternative conception of nature drawing upon both Schelling and Hegel and synthesizing their ideas with more recent developments in the sciences (the discovery of the cell, the idea that all natural processes are transformations of energy, and Darwin's theory of evolution) that gave a place to creativity and emergence. And his philosophy of nature has proved fruitful in many branches of science. The work of Richard Levins and Richard Lewontin (Levins and Lewontin 1985; Lewontin and Levins 2007) in biology illustrates this, but there were also major advances in Soviet science inspired by Engels, particularly in the 1920s (Graham 1971; Weiner 1988). But Engels developed his natural philosophy in a way that confused Idealism with materialism, identified speculative philosophy with Idealism and science with positivism, and thereby confused the very idea of dialectics. The three 'laws of dialectics', the transformation of quantity into quality, the identity of opposites, and the negation of the negation, in no way did justice to Marx's notion of dialectics which sought to uphold the ability of people to transform the world of which they are a conscious part, the central theme of the *Theses on Feuerbach*. Although Engels did refer to our capacity to produce things as demonstrating that we could know the Kantian 'thing-in-itself', he generally characterized thought as 'the more or less abstract pictures of actual things and processes' (as though thought itself is not actual), simply reflecting the dialectical laws supposedly discovered in nature and human history (Engels 1962, p.133). Using the dialectical analysis of concepts and their transformations as a metaphor for, or rather, confused with the causal processes of nature, these were not presented and defended as a speculative account of nature orienting people as participants within nature and society for action to change the world, but were objectified as scientific laws found in nature and society. As George Lichtheim wrote in his classic study of Marxism:

> Of this complex dialectic Engels retained only the outer shell. Not that he formally abandoned a single element of the Marxian canon. He merely upset its equilibrium by making it appear that the purpose of the whole operation was to bring the old materialism up to date. The heart of the doctrine – the constitutive role of conscious activity – was replaced by a faith in *science* as the correct description of the determinate processes; matter was invested with a capacity for giving birth to mankind; and Kant was rebuked for having dared to suggest that the world is partly our creation.
> (Lichtheim 1961, p.252f.)

This confusion was entrenched through the work of Giorgi Plekhanov who coined the term 'dialectical materialism' and promoted this as the true Marxist view of nature and history. Plekhanov defended a totally determinist theory of history, arguing (following Spinoza) that freedom is only the recognition of necessity, that is, submission to the laws of nature and socio-historical development (Lichtheim 1961, p.258, n.2). This confusion has been analysed by James White in his book *Karl Marx and the Intellectual Origins of Dialectical Materialism*:

> According to Engels, Nature had been thought immutable because it had been studied 'metaphysically', not 'dialectically'. People had fallen into the

habit of: 'Observing Natural objects and Natural processes in their isolation, detached from the whole vast interconnection of things; and therefore not in their motion, but in repose; not as essentially changing, but as fixed constants; not in their life, but in their death'. This idea is easily recognizable as being derived from Schelling's conception of the Speculative, as opposed to the Reflective point of view. Where Schelling would have used the term 'Speculative', Engels employed the term 'dialectical'. In the same way, 'Reflective' had been replaced by 'metaphysical'.

(White 1996, p.285f.)

Dialectics for Engels was 'nothing more than the science of the general laws of motion and development of Nature, human society and thought' (Engels 1975, p.162). As White wrote of Engels' 'dialectics': 'the dialectical laws of motion, in fact, consisted of the principles of the Speculative method, common to Schelling and Hegel, presented as a series of individual maxims' (White 1996, p.286).

Dialectics after Marx and Engels: Hegelian Marxism, existential phenomenology and Jean-Paul Sartre

The more philosophically aware Marxists, interpreting Marx as reworking Hegel's philosophy by following Fichte and Schelling and defending the primacy of praxis over theory, dismissed Engels' claim to have discovered the general laws of motion operating through nature, human history and thought as confused and unjustified (Lukács 1971, p.3ff.). While Engels claimed to be a materialist, the only way he could justify his projection onto nature of his dialectical laws would have been to have embraced speculative Idealism and to have portrayed the evolution of nature as a development of the World-Spirit. Portraying his work as the discovery of the laws of nature amounted to a synthesis of Absolute Idealism and positivism which left no place for human volition, the view embraced and promulgated by Plekhanov. Building on Marx's work, Marxist critics of Engels clarified important aspects of dialectics and how dialectics differs from reasoning characteristic of both pre-Kantian rationalists and empiricists, and from positivists and pragmatists (Kolakowski 1971). They have greatly clarified the relationship between reason and praxis, revealing the relationship between the categories defining and mediating relations between people, the tendency for social relations to be reified and fetishised, the role of consciousness in both blinding people to the true nature of their relations (false consciousness produced by ideology, cultural hegemony and the culture industry), and revealing their potential to overcome illusions and take action to transform societies. The rejection of the objectifying tendencies of scientistic Marxism were best characterized by Georg Lukács in *History and Class Consciousness,* the spirit of which was summed up in his proclamation:

As long as man concentrates his interest contemplatively upon the past *or* future, both ossify into an alien existence. And between the subject and the object lies the unbridgeable 'pernicious chasm' of the present. Man must be able to comprehend the present as a becoming. He can do this by seeing in it the tendencies out of whose dialectical opposition he can *make* the future. Only when he does this will the present be a process of becoming, that belongs to *him*. Only he who is willing and whose mission it is to create the future can see the present in its concrete truth.

(Lukács 1971, p.204)

However, with the exception of Ernst Bloch and Marxist historians and philosophers of science (beginning with the Russian Aleksandr Bogdanov and advancing in the work of Joseph Needham and Robert Young) and some eco-Marxists, these 'Western' Marxists have almost completely ignored nature, or treated 'nature' as merely a social category, and generally have made no effort to justify or explain their conception of humans as capable of dialectical thinking and of creating a better, more humane form of society.

While there have been a number of Marxists inspired by Hegel who have clarified and made important contributions to dialectics, including Bloch, Lukács, Gramsci, Lucian Goldmann, Henri Lefebvre and Fredrick Jameson, among others, the works that most clearly illustrate the contribution to and deficiencies of dialectical thinking of these 'Hegelian' Marxists are Jean-Paul Sartre's *Search for a Method* (1968) and his unfinished two volume *Critique of Dialectical Reason* (Sartre 1960; Sartre 1991). These were written largely in response to criticisms of his philosophy by Maurice Merleau-Ponty, who in *Adventures of the Dialectic* (1973), repudiated his earlier alignment with Hegelian Marxism. Defending himself and dialectics against Merleau-Ponty's criticisms, no other works of Marxism have been so focused on revealing the relationship between dialectics and praxis, or have been more fully aligned with the humanities or more critical of 'scientism'. Sartre was influenced by the phenomenology of Husserl and Heidegger, as well as Marx and Hegel, and was a central figure in the development of existentialist philosophy. The existentialists were continuing the critique of Hegel that began with Schelling's critique of him in 1842, amplified by those who attended his lectures, most famously, Søren Kierkegaard, and also by Nietzsche who was indirectly influenced by Schelling through the work of Schopenhauer. Phenomenology provided a rigorous method of examining experience through which the insights of these philosophers could be defended and further developed. Sartre embraced Heidegger's focus on Being, but did not accord it any meaning, focusing instead on the call by Heidegger in his early work for resolute action.

Sartre not only embraced Lukács critique of orthodox Marxism for dissolving people into the laws of nature and history, but extended his critique to Lukács himself, charging him with imposing *a priori* or preformed concepts on experience, forcing 'the events, the persons, or the acts considered into prefabricated molds' (Sartre 1968, p.37). Characterizing the proletariat as the subject-object of history, Lukács gave a place to agency while explaining the failure of the proletariat to realize their potential as the effect of reification engendered by commodification, but he could not acknowledge the uniqueness of each individual or the particular situations in which they were engaged. Sartre argued that that human beings, and ultimately, particular individuals in their unique situations, are the source of the human world, and that no matter how oppressive and hopeless things appear, people can change this world. To comprehend history it is necessary to comprehend people in their particular situations, their relation to broader historical developments mediated by a whole range of collectivities, using a 'progressive-regressive method' whereby people's projects are grasped in relation to past actions which created the present material conditions and the existing field of possibilities (Sartre 1968, Part II and III). The project, by which humans define themselves, must be understood as the negation of these conditions in the name of that which is to be produced. While acknowledging a place for analytic thought, Sartre held such thought, along with the anti-dialectical 'practico-inert', to be a 'permanent threat to the human' (Sartre 1976, p.710). It can be made into an intellectual principle and ideology of a society separating people, objectifying them in order to dominate and oppress them. However, as Sartre argued, 'analytic Reason is a synthetic transformation to which thought intentionally subjects itself' in order to 'control itself in exteriority'; that is, 'it is a particular moment of dialectical Reason' (Sartre 1976, p.58f.), and presupposes synthetic thought.

Dialectical reason, Sartre argued, is always situated. It is praxis, requiring of us that we appreciate that knowledge of dialectics itself is a specific praxis situated in history, contrasting this notion of dialectics with the 'transcendental' dialectic of orthodox Marxism which imposes an *a priori* logic on humans. Developing this notion of dialectic, Sartre examined and sought to make intelligible 'from the inside' the French revolution, the revolution in Russia that created the Soviet Union, the subsequent rise of Stalin and the oppression that resulted from Stalinism, and consequently, the failure of the Soviet Union to realize its promise. In doing so, Sartre strove to show the intelligibility of human history, although he argued that achieving full intelligibility would never be possible. Sartre dealt with a vast range of events, forms and relations in articulating this notion of dialectics, examining all forms and levels of human interaction from chance collections of individuals to the highly integrated social institutions and the relationship between sub-groups and broader groups while studying a great diversity of concrete situations. In doing so he presented a succinct summary of his core notion of dialectics:

> [T]he *constituent dialectic* (as it grasps itself in its abstract translucidity in individual *praxis*) finds its limit within its own work and is transformed into an *anti-dialectic*. This anti-dialectic, or dialectic against the dialectic (dialectic of *passivity*), must reveal *series* to us as a type of human gathering and alien action as a mediated relation to the other and to the objects of labour in the element of seriality and as a serial mode of co-existence. At this level we will discover an equivalence between alienated praxis and worked inertia, and we shall call the domain of this equivalence the *practico-inert*. And we

shall see the group emerge as a second type of dialectical gathering, in opposition both to the *practico-inert* and to impotence. But I shall distinguish … between the constituted dialectic and the constituent dialectic to the extent that the group has to constitute its common *praxis* through the individual *praxis* of the agents of whom it is composed.

(Sartre 1972, p.66f.)

Using this complex notion of dialectics based on the praxis of individuals, Sartre described how people who are 'serialized' and opposed to each other as isolated individuals and thereby oppressed by the practico-inert ensemble that defines the situations they have to deal with, can come to appreciate that others who appear as competitors, are in similar situations. This can generate a 'group in fusion' as people come to appreciate the perspectives of others, which can lead to joint praxis as the group becomes an effective collective actor rebelling against their serialization, alienation and passivity. The joint or collective praxis of the group develops through a sequence of totalizations, detotalizations and retotalizations to constitute an increasingly powerful and complex movement (consisting of a diversity of subgroups with complex inter-relations between them) and a political force, eventually being able to overthrow the old order and create new institutions and a new social form. However, through his study of the Bolshevik revolution in Russia and the Soviet Union, Sartre showed how in the quest to protect the new social order, this in turn can produce a new practico–inert ensemble and new forms of serialization.

Sartre's work on dialectics was published just as the popularity of existential phenomenology in general and his own work in particular went into decline. There were a number of reasons for this. One is that this work did not provide the orientation required for effective action by the New Left struggling to overcome what they saw as the oppressive tendencies of the post-WWII world order. A major reason for this is that he did not differentiate the dialectics of representation, recognition and labour found explicitly in Hegel's early work (Habermas 1974, Ch.4) but assumed and further developed throughout his work and therefore did not examine how these can, or can fail to be, coordinated, or understand the importance of the struggle for recognition and how this is inseparable from the communities and their histories to which people belong. As Alasdair MacIntyre pointed out in *After Virtue*, according to Sartre's conception of humans, 'the self is detachable from its social and historical roles and statuses. … [It is] a self that can have no history' (MacIntyre 2007, p.221). This is despite Sartre's concern with the intelligibility of history. Without recognizing all these dimensions, that is, each of the three dialectical patterns and their interrelationship in communities, he could not explain why people subordinate themselves so willingly to people with power, or the significance of denial of recognition and the promise of granting people proper recognition has in motivating people to action, and thereby the conditions under which they will be willing to take political action.[3] Without appreciating each of these dialectics and their interpenetration it was not really possible for Sartre to understand how effective coordination of activities could be achieved in the very large numbers of people in modern societies, to understand the possibilities for different economic, social and political organization, or what kinds of institutions could genuinely liberate people. Consequently, his work failed to provide the means to comprehend the emerging new world order dominated by transnational corporations, or provide a means to counter the ideology of neoliberalism that served to legitimate this new world order (a far more oppressive political, social and economic order than the social-democratic consensus against which members of the New Left of the 1960s had been protesting). This triumph of neoliberalism was associated with efforts to control the institutions of learning that had fostered student radicalism by transforming them into business corporations to eliminate the niches where such radical ideas could be nurtured and developed, while co-opting New Left protestors against social democracy by claiming that the best way to support individual freedom is to dismantle the welfare state and remove all constraints on markets designed to serve the common good (while at the same time massively increasing expenditure on 'internal security' and surveillance and subsidies to big corporations). The triumph of neoliberalism over the New and Old Left can be partly explained by the deficiencies in the work of radical intellectuals such as Sartre. Essentially, social dynamics were found to have an opacity, inertia and dynamics that could not be accounted for simply as the 'practico-inert', and overcoming oppressive social relations was found to require far more than oppressed people coming to appreciate that others are suffering as themselves and uniting by developing totalizing perspectives to seize political power.

The structuralist reaction to phenomenology

Whether these were reason enough for ignoring Sartre's work, it is now clear that existential phenomenology, Marxist or otherwise, gave way to a new intellectual movement, structuralism. In its initial form this was an almost complete negation of existentialism, although only a partial negation of dialectics. Structuralism developed in a range of disciplines: mathematics, linguistics, anthropology, psychiatry, literature and cultural studies, and in Marxist social theory. Structuralists succeeded partly because they promoted themselves as scientific, challenging those who claimed a form of knowledge that was not scientific. That is, they aligned themselves with scientism against the humanities. However, they succeeded at least partly also because they addressed the deficiencies in existentialist Hegelian Marxism exemplified by Sartre. One of the foremost structuralists and champions of structuralism, Claude Lévi-Strauss, devoted almost all of the last chapter of one of his most important works, *The Savage Mind* (dedicated to the memory of Merleau-Ponty), to criticizing Sartre's *Critique of Dialectical Reason* Lévi-Strauss 1972. Ch.9). Pierre Bourdieu wrote of this debate:

> It is not easy to communicate the social effects that the work of Claude Lévi-Strauss produced in the French intellectual field, or the concrete

mediations through which a whole generation was led to adopt a new way of conceiving intellectual activity that was opposed in a thoroughly dialectical fashion to the figure of the politically committed 'total intellectual' represented by Jean-Paul Sartre.

(Bourdieu 1990, p.1f.)

While most of the structuralists (and 'poststructuralists', although in France those designated as poststructuralists in Anglophone countries were still seen in France as structuralists) were hostile to phenomenology and to the pretensions of the humanities to have knowledge superior to that gained through science, many were not hostile to dialectics as such but only to the form it had taken in the work of the Hegelian Marxists and in Sartre.

Lévi-Strauss is usually seen as building on the work of Saussure as this had been taken up and developed by Russian semioticians based in Prague and Vienna, treating culture as consisting of synchronic systems of signs. Influenced by Troubetskoy's work showing how phonemes gained their 'value' or significance through their difference from other phonemes, forming a system based on binary oppositions, Lévi-Strauss argued that there is a hierarchy of levels in the organization of signs: morphemes, lexemes, etc. all the way up to mythemes, with each level operating as a pattern of binary oppositions. However, Lévi-Strauss's major achievement was based on his alignment with the Bourbarki group of mathematicians, defining kinship relations, beliefs, customs and symbolic systems as theoretical objects that could be examined mathematically. As Jean Piaget noted in his celebrated book, *Structuralism:*

> while [Lévi-Strauss] took his departure from linguistics, and while phonological or, more generally, Sassaurian, structures inspired his search for anthropological structures, the really decisive discovery for him was, as is well known, that kinship systems are instances of algebraic structures – networks, groups, and so on. … And it turned out that not only kinship systems, but all the 'practices' and cognitive products of the societies under study – the passage from one system of classification to another, or from one myth to another – lend themselves to this sort of structural analysis.
>
> (Piaget 1971c, p.110)

At the same time, Lévi-Strauss firmly aligned himself with the sciences, even a form of reductionism, suggesting that it could rescue associational psychology which 'had the great merit of sketching the contours of … elementary logic, which is like the least common denominator of all thought, and its only failure was not to recognize that it was an original logic, a direct expression of the structure of the mind (and behind the mind, probably, of the brain)' (Lévi-Strauss 1969, p.163). Unlike the logical positivism supported by analytic philosophy this concern to develop a scientific understanding of society did not involve a complete rejection of dialectics and synthetic thought. Lévi-Strauss's main objection to Sartre was that he contradicts himself in denigrating analytic reason when his own work pre-supposed it. Essentially, Lévi-Strauss was inverting the status accorded analytic and dialectic reasoning, arguing against the notion that analytic reason is only a component of dialectical reason and arguing instead that dialectical reason is a component of analytic reason. As he put it: 'I do not regard dialectical reason as something other than analytic reason, upon which the absolute originality of the human order would be based, but as something additional in analytic reason' ... 'The term dialectical reason ... covers the perpetual efforts analytic reason must make to reform itself if it aspires to account for language, society and thought' (Lévi-Strauss 1972, p.246). As Piaget re-interpreted this, 'this comes down to a complementarity according to which synthetic reason's inventiveness and progressiveness make up for the lack of these in analytic reason while the job of verification remains reserved for the latter' (Piaget 1971c, p.123). Lévi-Strauss also acknowledged that from Sartre's perspective he was an 'aesthete' who studies men as though they were ants, not as someone who in his work is participating in social praxis in the very process of making society and history intelligible.

Lévi-Strauss suggested various issues which differentiated his own work from that of Sartre's, however the really crucial difference was his commitment to defining theoretical objects that can be studied scientifically, while Sartre was committed to rejecting such an approach for conferring an illusory independence from social praxis to these 'objects'. The construction of theoretical objects could still give a central place to the mental, however, which has always been an embarrassment to logical empiricists. For this reason structuralists could still give a place to dialectics in society and allow that there are contradictions in society. Their disagreement with Hegelian Marxists such as Lukács and Sartre was over how dialectics and these contradictions were to be understood. This issue came to the fore in the work of structuralist Marxists such as Louis Althusser and Maurice Godelier.

Arguing that Marx's notion of contradiction derived from Kant and Fichte rather than Hegel, Althusser claimed that the real breakthrough in Marx's research was to have identified a theoretical object that could be scientifically studied to reveal its dynamics. To justify this he drew upon Gaston Bachelard's philosophy of science. This was anti-positivist and accorded a place to dialectics, including synthetic thinking and granted a central place to the development of concepts and theoretical objects; but Bachelard's dialectics was not Hegel's form of dialectics (Lecourt 1975, p.74ff.). In the case of Althusser, embracing Bachelard was associated with a rejection of the very idea of a dialectic of consciousness which could reach reality by itself, since according to him consciousness only accedes to reality when it discovers what is other than itself (Althusser 1977a, p.143). This 'other', Althusser in 'Contradiction and Overdetermination' argued, is the structure of society consisting of a base (the forces and relations of production) and a superstructure (the state apparatuses) that could contain contradictions (Althusser 1977a, Part III). This theoretical framework enabled Althusser to draw on the work of a range of theorists, both Marxist and non-Marxist. He drew on Gramsci's concept of cultural hegemony and Jacques Lacan's structuralist psychoanalysis (strongly influenced by the work of Lévi-Strauss) to develop a new theory of ideology and the 'ideological state apparatus' as 'the imaginary relationship of individuals to their real conditions of existence' (Althusser 1983, p.36). This involved accepting a radical disjunction between ideology and science. While this notion of ideology was questionable, it highlighted the limitations of Sartre's conception of the subject both in relation to understanding how oppressed and exploited people are dominated and to the problematic nature of assuming free human agents able to take responsibility for themselves and their own, their communities' and others' futures. Without acknowledging them, Althusser also drew on the work of the *Annales* school of historians, most importantly, Fernand Braudel. Braudel argued that there is not one temporal development in history but 'innumerable different rivers of time' (Braudel 1980, p.39) and the need to investigate all these different temporalities and examine how they relate to each other. Following Braudel, Althusser argued that:

> ... [a]s a first approximation, we can argue from the specific structure of the Marxist whole that it is no longer possible to think the process of the development of the different levels of the whole *in the same historical time*... On the contrary, we have to assign to each level a *peculiar time*, relatively autonomous and hence relatively independent, even in its dependence, of the 'times' of the other levels.
>
> (Althusser 1977b, p.99f.)

This pointed to a far more complex history than Sartre had envisaged and highlighted the limitations of his work.

Even more important for highlighting the questionability of the assumptions about human subjects and their capacity for agency of existentialists was the work of Michel Foucault. A onetime student of Althusser originally influenced by Hegelian thought and existentialist psychiatry, Foucault rejected these and allied intellectual movements. With his Ph.D. supervised by the historian of biology Georges Canguilhem, who was strongly influenced by Bachelard, Foucault extended work on the history of science from physics and biology to the human sciences, focusing on 'discursive formations' and the non-discursive practices of social control in which they function and which support them. Aligning himself with Nietzsche against Hegel, his work involved a complete rejection of dialectics, although it could be claimed that there are dialectical elements to his thinking despite this. He argued for historical *a prioris* or *epistemes*: the Renaissance *episteme*, the classical *episteme* and the modern *episteme*, each of which had dominated for a period of time. He saw these as succeeding each other without any rationality in this succession (apart from being advances in the practices of social control). The focus on the body manifest the influence of Merleau-Ponty, while the examination of discourses and their relation to power manifest the influence of Nietzsche, Heidegger and structuralist semiotics (although Foucault denied being a structuralist).

Like Althusser, Foucault also was influenced by Braudel and acknowledged multiple durations of events, and also the spatiality of social life. As he put it in 'Truth and Power':

> It's not a matter of locating everything on one level, that of the event, but of realising that there are actually a whole order of levels of different types of events differing in amplitude, chronological breadth, and capacity to produce effects. The problem is at once to distinguish among events, to differentiate the networks and levels to which they belong, and to reconstitute the lines along which they are connected and engender one another.
>
> (Foucault 1980, p.114)

While Marx showed how people are enslaved by a capitalist economy in such a way that they are constrained to reproduce the system that enslaves them, Foucault showed how this was true of a multiplicity of formations. The human sciences which claim objectivity, as with the political economy critiqued by Marx, are really mystifying social relations, keeping people under surveillance in order to produce predictable, disciplined bodies. These formations, Foucault argued, preceded capitalism and are required by it to make people governable so that a capitalist economy can be sustained.

However, Althusser and Foucault and their followers left so little room for free agency that they rendered the whole idea of liberation from oppressive social formations inconceivable. More problematic, their accounts of social formations simply could not fully account for how people actually live and think or the way societies function and change. Arguments against Althusser came from another structuralist, Maurice Godelier. Influenced by Husserl and Braudel and then by Lévi-Strauss, Godelier argued that in all material activities, human practices and social relations there are mental components, although they are never reducible to thought, and mental components have a diversity of functions. On this basis, he could accept that dialectics has a place in social dynamics, but argued that 'Marx's dialectic has nothing to do with Hegel's, because they do not depend on the same notion of contradiction' (Godelier 1967, p.91). Embracing the concepts of system and structure, he argued that 'there are contradictions internal to a single level of a society's functioning and contradictions between that society's organizational levels' where contradictions are understood as:

> ... relations between properties of relations, and therefore relations of the second degree, which are lacking in purpose, in intentionality. As such, they are not occasioned by any human will. .... To be more precise, they are simply the negative effects of the properties of social relations when the limits of the conditions of their reproduction are reached. ... Thus we have contradictory development, a development of unintentional contradictions within the reproduction process of that society.
>
> (Godelier 1986, 66f.)

In other words, there are contradictions when intentional action by members of a society structured in a particular way produce effects that undermine the conditions for pursuing what is intended. While these unintentional contradictions have an effect on the evolution of societies, 'they do not operate by themselves and are insufficient to explain this evolution' (Godelier 1986, p.67).

This is much clearer than Althusser's notion of contradiction and accords with Marx's study of capitalism. It also reveals what is required to deal with such situations. As Godelier proclaimed: 'the degree of control by humanity over its own destiny therefore depends in the last instance upon its capacity to become aware of and, above all, to take charge of the unintentional part of its existence' (Godelier 1986, p.67). When Godelier engaged with the work of anthropologists and historians he 'found it impossible to adopt the notions of infrastructure and superstructure just as they were' (Godelier 1986, p.16). It was impossible, for instance, to differentiate the institutions forming relations of production from kinship relations, and impossible to explain kinship relations as a mere effect of productive processes. In opposition to Althusser and his disciples, Godelier could only accept that there is a hierarchy of functions, in which social relations that support production processes having more influence (Godelier 1986, p.148), and later he abandoned even this.

Genetic structuralism and dialectics

If Althusser and the structuralist Marxists were striving to save Marxism in France, they failed. The most prominent philosophers of the next generation, Jean-François Lyotard, and more ambiguously, Jacques Derrida, turned against not only Marxism and dialectical thought, but undermined philosophy itself. Alain Badiou, the last holdout against this trend, described their philosophy as postmodern, and characterized it thus:

> [P]ostmodern philosophy proposes to dissolve the great constructions of the nineteenth century to which we remain captive – the idea of the historical subject, the idea of progress, the idea of revolution, the idea of humanity and the ideal of science. Its aim is to show that these great constructions are outdated, that we live in the multiple, that there are no great epics of history or of thought: that there is an irreducible plurality of registers and languages in thought as in action; registers so diverse and heterogeneous that no great idea can totalize or reconcile them. At base, the objective of postmodern philosophy is to deconstruct the idea of totality – to the extent that philosophy itself finds itself destabilized. Consequently ... it installs philosophical thought at the periphery of art, and proposes an untotalizable mixture of the conceptual method of philosophy and the sense-oriented enterprise of art.
>
> (Badiou 2005b, p.32f.)

It is questionable whether Lyotard, Derrida and their epigone should have achieved such prominence, however. After Merleau-Ponty's untimely death in

1961, he was largely forgotten, except by a minority who have either revived interest in his work in recent years, or as in the case of Castoriadis who despite his claims, was strongly influenced by Merleau-Ponty, are themselves now receiving greater attention. Merleau-Ponty had developed a form of phenomenology that was untouched by the criticisms of these postmodernists and was charting a different direction for philosophy in the philosophy of nature, while Castoriadis appears to have been prophetic in characterizing the direction civilization would take, while upholding the ideal of autonomy that is becoming increasingly appealing as people are losing their liberty with the globalization of the market, the corruption of politics and rise of Taylorist managerialism. Furthermore, it could be argued that the most important advances in Francophone philosophy were made by a new movement of thought, genetic structuralism, led by philosophers who had abandoned or distanced themselves from philosophy for the human sciences: psychology, in the case of Jean Piaget, literary theory in the case of Lucian Goldmann, and anthropology and sociology, in the case of Pierre Bourdieu. These were the really important dialectical thinkers of the following generation.

The work of Bourdieu provided a more comprehensive exposure of the limitations of the work of Lévi-Strauss, Althusser and Foucault (while pointing out the limitations of Sartre's philosophy), and also a better framework for interpreting the achievements of Marx while accommodating insights of more recent research, including real insights of Lévi-Strauss, Foucault and Sartre. Originally a philosopher hostile to Sartre, deeply indebted to Bachelard's philosophy of science (which he made abundantly clear in *The Craft of Sociology* (1991)) and sympathetic to the structuralism of Lévi-Strauss, Bourdieu discovered while studying the Kabyle in Algeria that while what people say they were doing concurred with structuralist predictions, for instance, describing kinship relations and stating who should marry whom, what they did, for instance who they actually did marry, was very different. To account for this, Bourdieu defended the primacy of praxis over reflective thought and set about comprehending the logic of practice, in doing so advancing the insights of Merleau-Ponty (who in turn was echoing Fichte, Schelling and Marx). He had come to believe that '[o]f all the oppositions that artificially divide social sciences, the most fundamental, and the most ruinous, is the one that is set up between subjectivism and objectivism' (Bourdieu 1977, p.25), and concluded that through such a study of the logic of practice, this could be overcome. From being unreservedly hostile to Sartre, he argued that:

> Jean-Paul Sartre deserves credit for having given an ultra-consistent formulation of the philosophy of action that is accepted, usually implicitly, by those who describe practices as strategies explicitly oriented to ends explicitly defined by a free project or even, with some interactionists, by reference to the anticipated reactions of other agents.
>
> (Bourdieu 1990, p.42)

While critical of Sartre's inability to acknowledge durable dispositions, Bourdieu also rejected an objectifying approach to social reality that involves unwittingly adopting a scholastic relation to what they are studying. Of this, he wrote:

> Objectivism constitutes the social world as a spectacle offered to an observer who takes up a 'point of view' on the action and who, putting into the object the principles of his relation to the object, proceeds as if it were intended solely for knowledge and as if all the interactions within it were purely symbolic exchanges.
>
> (Bourdieu 1990, p.52)

Lévi-Strauss and Althusser and his followers illustrated this. Of Lévi-Strauss' structuralism, Bourdieu concluded that 'Beneath its air of radical materialism, this philosophy of nature is a philosophy of mind which amounts to a form of idealism' (Bourdieu 1990, p.41). In the case of 'structuralist readers of Marx' (i.e. Althusser and his followers) the consequence was a 'fall into the fetishism of social laws' (Bourdieu 1990, p.41). He criticized the whole idea of components of society as 'apparatuses' since, he argued, it is impossible to reduce people to predictable cogs. In attempting to overcome the subject/object opposition to transcend the opposition between Sartre and the structuralists, Bourdieu developed a form of genetic structuralism and characterized himself as a genetic structuralist (Bourdieu 1993, p.179).

Genetic structuralism is an alternative form of structuralism, with even greater intellectual ambitions. It echoes and supports a form of dialectics closer to that of Fichte and Schelling than Hegel, although there is no evidence of influence. It takes praxis as prior to and the condition for the development of reflective thought, and closely parallels Fichte's effort to reconstruct the stages of development of cognition, as Nectarios Limnatis noted (Limnatis 2008, p.229ff.). As such, as Hans Furth has shown in his examination of 'Piaget's Theory of Knowledge: The Nature of Representation and Interiorization' (1981, pp.68–82), it is radically at odds with logical empiricism and mechanistic conceptions of causation, and although not using the term, takes it for granted that cognition at all levels is synthetic. Jean Piaget was the foremost spokesperson for genetic structuralism. Lucien Goldmann, a Marxist cultural theorist strongly influenced by Lukács who identified himself as a genetic structuralist, characterized Piaget as 'the most authentic dialectician, at least in the West' (Piaget 1976: 126). Although Bourdieu did not refer to Piaget, Omar Lizardo (2004) has demonstrated that there was a strong influence. It is clear from his work in confronting the limitation of Lévi-Strauss's form of structuralism that he was reworking Piaget's concept of cognitive structures to develop his core concept of *habitus,* although in doing so he was also influenced by Merleau-Ponty's phenomenology of embodiment. It was through this concept of *habitus* that Bourdieu attempted to overcome the opposition between approaches to social reality that focused on subjects and those that objectified social reality, and to develop a more subtle notion of dialectic of social structure and agency than had existed hitherto. To properly understand Bourdieu's achievements, and limitations, however, it is first necessary to examine the ideas of Piaget.

Piaget studied philosophy and also mathematics and science before embarking on a career researching the development of cognition. He became increasingly critical of philosophers who objected to his work in psychology, claiming intuitive or *a priori* knowledge that meant that experimental research in psychology was of no value. However, he was even more critical of positivism and defended a constructivist theory of not only mathematics but of cognitive development generally. He referred approvingly in his book *Insights and Illusions of Philosophers* to thinkers who 'have realized that the epistemological significance of a scientific theory only fully shows itself when seen in its historical perspective. This is so because it answers the questions raised by earlier doctrines and prepares the way for its successors by a network of relationships which continue or contradict it' (Piaget 1971a, p.74). He embraced structuralism not through the influence of Saussure and semiotics but through the influence of the Bourbaki school of mathematics. 'Structure' he argued 'is comprised of three key ideas: the idea of wholeness, the idea of transformation, and the idea of self-regulation' (Piaget 1971c, p.5). A structure is a self-regulating system of transformations characterized by wholeness that is both structured and structuring (Piaget 1971c, p.10). Mathematical structures, notably, the 'group', exemplify these properties. Piaget was concerned with how sequences of structures are generated, beginning with the organism in interaction with its environment. The two core ideas of all his research were 'that since every organism has a permanent structure, which can be modified under the influence of the environment but is never destroyed as a structured whole, all knowledge is always assimilation of a datum external to the subject's structure', and 'that the normative factors in thought correspond biologically to a necessity of equilibrium by self-regulation: thus logic would in the subject correspond to a process of equilibrium' (Piaget 1971a, p.8). Development was seen as taking place through a process of assimilation of data from the environment and accommodation of the organism to the environment, achieving new levels of equilibration, developing from a sensori–motor form of intelligence in which cognition and action are inseparable, to concrete operations in which there is some capacity to cognize situations independently of action, to formal operations where people are able to reflect on and develop their own cognitive structures. While Piaget was primarily concerned with the development of cognition in humans, tracing the developments from childhood which eventually enable adults to develop mathematics and science, in *Biology and Knowledge* (1971b) he traced back the development of cognition to the most elementary forms of life, characterizing this cognition as continuous with the differentiation and generation of form in organisms along developmental paths or 'chreods' as characterized by the theoretical biologist, C.H. Waddington.

Looking at the relationship between structuralism and philosophy, the first problem Piaget addressed was the relationship between structuralism and dialectics. Referring to the debate between Lévi-Strauss and Sartre, he noted:

...the antagonists appear to us to have forgotten the fundamental fact that in the domain of the sciences themselves structuralism has always been linked with a constructivism from which the epithet 'dialectical' can hardly be withheld – the emphasis on historical development, opposition between contraries, and '*Aufhebung*' ('*dépassements*') is surly just as characteristic of constructivism as of dialectic, and that the idea of wholeness figures centrally in structuralist as in dialectical modes of thought is obvious.

(Piaget 1971c, p.121)

Piaget defended Sartre against Lévi-Strauss and his static, ahistorical form of structuralism, but criticized Sartre for his positivist view of science which failed to acknowledge that science itself develops dialectically. He also criticized Lévi-Strauss for the very limited place he accorded construction, which requires dialectic, praising Bachelard's book *La Philosophie du non* for pointing out how mathematicians, logicians and scientists advance by negating one of the apparently essential or necessary attributes of a given or completed structure (for instance, rejecting commutativity in algebra, rejecting two values in logic, or accepting the oscillation back and forth between the corpuscular and wave theories of light in physics). Consequently, he argued, 'dialectic over and over again substitutes "spirals" for the linear or "tree" models with which we start, and these famous spirals or non-vicious circles are very much like the genetic circles or interactions characteristic of growth' (Piaget 191c. p.125). While he expressed some sympathy for Althusser and praised Godelier, Piaget was highly critical of Foucault for the arbitrariness of what he included in his concept of *episteme*, for failing to acknowledge different levels of analysis, and for rendering the sequence of *epistemes* incomprehensible.

Piaget's main interest was in the development of the most abstract forms of thinking, in showing how abstract logic and the most advanced developments in mathematics are ultimately grounded in the most basic forms of cognition developed very early in the young child's practical engagement with its environment. What fascinated Piaget was that as mathematics has become more abstract, in discovering the most fundamental forms of mathematical operations presupposed by the more concrete forms of mathematics which we learn first, what has been discovered are the most basic operations that are developed in sensori-motor coordinations of the young child. As he noted: 'It is remarkable that, psycho-genetically, topological structures antedate metric and projective structures, that psychogenesis inverts the historical development of geometry but matches the Bourbaki "genealogy" (Piaget 1971c, p.27). These more abstract forms of mathematics, he believed, would facilitate comprehension of the more complex aspects of structures.

Piaget also averred that as analytic tools evolve, it will become possible to describe mathematically the transitions from one structure to another (Piaget 1971c, p.127f.). This suggests that Piaget believed that as mathematics advanced, dialectics would be superseded, or that mathematics itself would incorporate dialectics. This would mean that it would be possible to mathematically model the development of mathematics, an idea that is not only highly implausible (the activity of formalization is not formalizable) but contradicts Piaget's whole project of explaining mathematics as a development of biological functioning. However, Piaget also noted the implications of Gödel's discovery, invalidating the received way of viewing theories 'as layers of a pyramid, each resting on the one below, the theory at ground level being the most secure because constituted by the simplest means, and the whole firmly poised on a self-sufficient base' (Piaget 1971c, p.34). The idea of *structure* as a system of transformations has to be linked to *construction* as continual formation, with knowledge being a spiral whose radius increases with each turn rather than as pyramid or building. Piaget also noted that the Bourbaki notion of structure was changing under the influence of Category Theory that involves a higher level of reflection and is more in accord with dialectical thinking (as will be explicated below).[4]

Despite his formalist ambition, Piaget embraced the work of Lucien Goldmann whose main interest was in the relationship between literature and society, identifying transindividual subjects and explaining their mental structures. Goldmann's work was an effort to integrate Marxist cultural theory as developed by Lukács with Piaget's theory of cognitive development, arguing that the mental structures produced in literature could be explained as the outcome of efforts to make sense of the situations of members of these transindividual subjects, while situations they had to deal with could be interpreted through the mental structures manifest in their literary creations. However, Piaget's suggestion that even these structures of consciousness would eventually be able to be comprehended mathematically, both as finished structures and in their formation and transformation was not accepted by Goldmann (Goldmann 1972, p.111). And it is evident that while Piaget was concerned with the social dimension of cognitive development, recognized the importance of affective relations and of children overcoming their early egocentric perspective, examined the development of ethics, and recognized that in different societies different levels of cognitive development are attained (Piaget 1995), he had an individualist bias and a bias towards cognition associated with mathematical reasoning – despite his sympathy for Goldmann's work.

Pierre Bourdieu as genetic structuralist and dialectician

In embracing genetic structuralism Bourdieu did not discuss Piaget's work and was critical of Goldmann. Boudieu's genetic structuralism was his own highly original effort to develop a new approach to understanding social dynamics, but it was building on their work. As noted, Bourdieu was concerned to explain the patterns that seemed to support Lévi-Strauss's structuralism, such as the patterns of binary oppositions in the interior of houses, the layout of buildings, and the layout of fields, as the effect of generalizing habitual ways of acting collectively from situation to situation. However, to explain these he developed a social version of Piaget's notion of cognitive structures, more dynamic than the cognitive structures of Goldmann's cultural theory and following Merleau-Ponty, emphasized the embodiment of experience and cognition. His aim was to avoid the realism of the structure engendered by objectivism while acknowledging the need for objectivism to avoid falling back into a subjectivism that could not account for the necessity of the social world by returning to practice as 'the site of the dialectic of the *opus operatum* and the *modus operandi*; of the objectified products and the incorporated products of historical practice…' (Bourdieu 1990, p.52).

Bourdieu's social theory deployed three basic concepts: '*habitus*', 'capital' and later, 'field'. He first introduced the concept of *habitus* in *Outline of a Theory of Practice*, characterizing it as a 'a system of lasting, transposable dispositions which, integrating past experiences, functions at every moment as a *matrix of perceptions, apperceptions, and actions* and makes possible the achievement of infinitely diversified tasks, thanks to analogical transfers of schemes permitting the solution of similarly shaped problems, and thanks to the unceasing corrections of the results obtained…' (Bourdieu 1977, p.82f.). While this definition captures its Kantian origins, the indebtedness of this notion to Piaget's notion of cognitive structures, and how this was modified to take into account and explain the continual reproduction and development of the relations between people, was more evident in later definitions of this concept. In *The Logic of Practice*, where Bourdieu also pointed out that his theory was aligned with Marx's *Theses on Feuerbach*, stepping down 'from the sovereign viewpoint from which objectivist idealism orders the world … without having to abandon it to the "active aspect" of apprehension of the world' (Bourdieu 1990, p.52), he offered his classic definition of *habitus* as:

> … systems of durable, transposable dispositions, structured structures, predisposed to function as structuring structures, that is, as principles which generate and organize practices and representations that can be objectively adapted to their outcomes without presupposing a conscious aiming at ends or an express mastery of the operations necessary in order to attain them. Objectively 'regulated' and 'regular' without being in any way the product of obedience to rules, they can be collectively orchestrated without being the product of the organizing action of a conductor.
>
> (Bourdieu 1990, p.53)

The second concept, 'capital', as conceived in this context is any form of power which enables actors to participate in society to gain further capital, thereby augmenting their position in society, for instance, social contacts (social capital), competence in deciphering cultural relations or cultural artefacts (cultural capital), and most importantly, the power gained, deriving from prestige and authority, to define reality (symbolic capital), including the significance of people, their acts and products.

When he returned to France and applied the concepts he had developed to interpret Kabyle society to French society, first of all in his study of education, Bourdieu embraced and developed his third core concept, the concept of 'field' as a theoretical object in Bachelard's sense, as an alternative to 'base' and 'superstructure', 'system' and Foucault's concept of 'discursive formation', in doing so, avoiding various forms of reductionism while transcending the apparently unbridgeable oppositions between the subjective and the objective, agency and structure. Although first used as a concept in social psychology by Kurt Lewin, Bourdieu's notion of field is really a generalization of Marx's analysis of bourgeois society or capitalism as an emergent phenomenon structured by economic categories, that once formed, reproduces and expands itself. Bourdieu accepted Marx's argument that what appear to be autonomous individuals acting according to their own interests are actually products of an emergent historically developing field of social relations constraining them to recognize each other and to compete with each other for socially recognized forms of power or 'capital', with the quest for capital now conceived in relation to fields rather than the nebulous 'society'. Bourdieu appreciated all three of the dialectical struggles identified by Hegel in his early works and which he had deployed in his study of world history, the dialectic of labour, the dialectic of recognition and the dialectic of representation. While appreciating the dialectic of labour and being centrally interested in the dialectic of representation, Bourdieu saw the primary motivating force, despite the language of 'capital', to be first and foremost the quest for recognition, that is 'symbolic capital', which also involves the power to define reality.[5] He pointed out that productive activities take place in a field of objective, historical formed relations between objective positions, with actors struggling against each other for various forms of 'capital', thereby reproducing this field while misrecognizing their relation to it and how their actions reproduce it. To enter and be a successful actor within the field it is necessary to have developed the right *habitus,* a transposable disposition to perceive, evaluate and act in certain ways, an appreciation of the value of the different forms of capital and a 'feel for the game'. *Habitus* is formed by fields and functions simultaneously to make people acceptable (or unacceptable) to other actors in the field, to enable them to cope with unforeseen and ever changing situations, and to act in a way that reproduces the field. Bourdieu argued that 'An institution, even an economy, is complete and fully viable only if it is durably objectified not only in things, that is, in the logic, transcending individual agents, of a particular field, but also in bodies, in durable dispositions to recognize and comply with the demands immanent in the field' (Bourdieu 1990, p.58).

This conceptual framework has proved enormously fruitful, since it is possible to allow for very complex relations between fields and to analyse their forms of autonomy and inter-dependence. When related to Piaget's work, the human form of cognition examined by Bourdieu can be situated in the broader context of the development of sentient life. With the development of humanity, it becomes possible to identify the emergent forms, including the development of philosophy and science as cultural fields. Cultural fields can be seen to consist of a diversity of sub-fields, including the field of literature, which in turn consists of fields of poetry, novel writing, drama etc. and all the conditions required for the reproduction of each of these (Bourdieu 1993). The cultural field as a whole and all its sub-fields can be understood in relation to political fields, economic fields, national fields and so on. In each case the autonomy of a field can be ascertained by whether there are specific forms of capital associated with it that people pursue in such a way as to maintain and augment the autonomy of the field. The notion of 'field' is scalable, so it is possible to identify global fields and then subfields within these, right down to very local fields such as families or groups of friends. It is possible to reinterpret what Foucault referred to as discursive formations as fields and thereby avoid the tendency towards reductionism implied by Foucault's concepts. It is also possible to interpret the development and interaction between fields in terms of Braudel's form of history involving different scales, temporalities and spatialities. Since Bourdieu developed his concepts while studying the Kabyle, they can be applied to all forms of societies, allowing Marx's achievements to be situated in a much more defensible general theoretical framework than was provided by Engels' historical materialism.

Also, these concepts could be and were applied to academia, to science, including social science, and to philosophy, making possible and calling for reflexivity, requiring of researchers that they understand their own motives to avoid biases (Bourdieu and Wacquant 1992). While Bourdieu discussed a dialectic of objectification and embodiment (Boudieu 1977, p.87ff.) and of 'objective structures and incorporated structures' (Bourdieu 1977, p.41), and defended an epistemological theory to guide sociology (Bourdieu, Chamboredon, and Passeron 1991), he did not characterize this quest for scientific knowledge in terms of dialectics. Given the confused state of the concept, this is hardly surprising. However, influenced by Bachelard, striving to overcome oppositions between subjective and objective, agency and structure, and synthesizing the partial insights of a wide range of theorists into a coherent conceptual framework, his approach was dialectical, producing a new conceptual synthesis that was further developed though assimilating and then accommodating to a very wide range of social phenomena. Furthermore, he provided a theoretical framework that dealt with and facilitated comprehension of the complex relationships that dialecticians traditionally have been concerned to do justice to, including the relationship between the knower and the known and between knowledge and social reality, and was able to offer a more subtle analysis of these relations, notably universities in his book *Homo Academicus* (1988), through his theoretical concepts. Bourdieu always appreciated that he was part of the social world that he was trying to understand, and that the knowledge he produced would have practical implications, changing people's understanding of themselves and how they acted and lived accordingly. Bourdieu's work was a major contribution to synthetic thought, providing a conceptual framework and applying it to transcend the oppositions within earlier social theory, anthropology and sociology. Most importantly, he provided the means to analyse the mediations that Sartre had recognized as important in society but, with his extreme voluntarism and anti-science bias, was unable to do justice to. In particular,

Bourdieu was concerned to reveal the conditions for achieving objective knowledge, conditions that require the scientific field to have autonomy so that those engaged in inquiry aspire for symbolic capital or recognition from other members of the field, with their work being judged by their competitors in the field, together with reflexivity about their conditions of enquiry. His last work, *Science of Science and Reflexivity* (2004), focused on these topics. When combined with Piaget's work as part of the genetic structuralist research program, Bourdieu's work provides the means to situation humans in the broader context of the evolution of sentient life that is consistent with the tradition of speculative naturalism inspired by Schelling.

Both Piaget and Bourdieu, after having become leading figures in their disciplines and beyond, throughout the world, were severely criticized after their deaths. This was more so with Piaget than Bourdieu. Specific criticisms of Piaget centred on the unevenness of cognitive development, with stages being nowhere near as neatly defined or as neatly sequential as he claimed. There were also problems with his claim that cognition developed first of all through action, since it was found that some people with severe cerebral palsy still developed intellectually. The most important criticism of his work is that it had an intellectual bias, and so even though he was interested in the development of morality and studied the way people in different societies developed differently, he was seen by many as not doing justice to emotional life and the complexity of interpersonal relations. These challenges to Piaget's thinking have been addressed by his followers, so there is now a flourishing school of neo-Piagetian psychology. Although these neo-Piagetians have not examined the work of Bourdieu, Bourdieu's work insofar as it has utilized and modified Piaget's central concepts of structuring structures could be utilized to overcome the individualist bias in Piaget's work.

The reaction to Bourdieu has not been so negative; however, even those aligned with Bourdieu came to the conclusion that his research failed to reveal the potential for ethical action. Having defined himself as a sociologist rather than as a philosopher, geographer or human ecologist, Bourdieu was free to ignore ways in which his work could be integrated with work in other disciplines to provide further justification for his conception of humans or to situate humanity in the context of the ecosystems within which they had emerged and evolved. He was not concerned to defend his conception of humans and society against reductionist forms of the natural sciences that are inconsistent with any notion of agency not determined by physical processes. That is, he was not concerned to challenge the dominant world-view which is still based on assumptions deriving from the seventeenth century scientific revolution. Nevertheless, his concepts imply a creative world in which there is real emergence and this is inconsistent with this reductionist cosmology. They are a challenge to it. Furthermore, his work on cultural fields and how they gain or lose autonomy is extremely important for revealing what are the conditions under which defective assumptions of our culture can be revealed and brought into question. Implicitly, he was upholding an ethics of integrity, revealing the importance to culture, society and humanity of those people who have augmented the autonomy of fields while their own work was unconsecrated, at least at the time (largely concurring with the values upheld by the Coen brothers' films). These are the people with a vested interest in upholding notions of truth, justice and workmanship. Conversely, he was critical of those people consecrated by existing cultural fields who served merely to legitimate existing inequalities in society, and highly critical of figures such as Derrida who advanced their careers by undermining the fields on which their symbolic power was dependent. Although Bourdieu appeared not to be interested in major transformations of people's *habitus* equivalent to Piaget's notion of accommodation, he was actually promoting such an accommodation by drawing attention to the interdependence and importance of autonomous fields for creating a less oppressive society. Not only should it be part of people's *habitus* to appreciate their dependence upon and work towards augmenting the fields in which they are pursuing symbolic capital, but their *habitus* should incorporate a conception of society as consisting of fields within fields, so revealing the broader conditions for maintaining the specific forms of capital of the fields within which they are participating. If all this appears complex, it should not be to academics because what Bourdieu's conceptual framework has revealed is the appalling lack of integrity and other virtues of academics over the last thirty years in allowing and often supporting the undermining of the autonomy of the academic field, along with other cultural fields, including science. This has had disastrous consequences not only for a great many academics, but for all those people adversely affected by neoliberalism and managerialism, society and humanity generally. Ultimately, their lack of the required virtues to defend their fields could seal the fate of the current regime of the global ecosystem.

The main criticism leveled against Bourdieu is that through his commitment to supplying objective knowledge which at the same time could function as critique, he still left those who recognized the forms of domination he identified with only limited resources to resist their domination. They could only learn to become better actors in their fields. As Luc Boltanski and Eve Chiapello, former colleagues of Bourdieu, complained:

> Pierre Bourdieu ... aims to unveil the 'mechanisms' through which a universal 'domination', presented as an iron law, is exercised, while at the same time seeking to advance the work of individual liberation, conceived as an emancipation from external powers and intervention. But if, in the final analysis, all relations are reducible to conflicts of interest and relations of force, and this is a 'law' immanent in the order of the 'social', what is the point of unmasking them in the indignant tones of critique, as opposed to registering them with the dispassion of the entomologist studying ant societies?
>
> (Boltanski and Chiapello 2007, p.x)

This criticism is related to another criticism. In addressing a major lacuna in social theory, the blindness to habituated tactical action which is not based on reflective thinking but which is at the core of all social life and the basis of all the structures of society, Bourdieu's work did not acknowledge or offer any means to comprehend more reflective strategic action. What else is required?

Narratology and dialectics

Piaget and Bourdieu each began their careers as students of philosophy, and broke away from philosophy because the philosophers they had to deal with were insufficiently appreciative of the importance of empirical research. Consequently, one became a psychologist, the other, a sociologist, although in both cases having an enormous range of interests that cut across most disciplinary boundaries. However, as self-consciously scientists, they differentiated themselves from academics in the humanities and both failed to appreciate important developments in the humanities that could have supplemented their work. Most importantly, they did not appreciate developments in narratology, or appreciate the importance of narratives to dialectics, and by virtue of this, to science itself. Here it is necessary to return to Piaget and examine earlier reactions to his work.

Lev Vygotsky was strongly influenced by Piaget and it is widely known that they differed in the significance they accorded to language in cognitive development. While the evidence is divided, Jerome Bruner, one of Piaget's early collaborators, aligned himself with Vygotsky in this regard and went on to argue that stories are just as important forms of cognition as mathematics and science (Bruner 1986, Ch.2). When this bias towards mathematics is understood, what also comes into focus is the odd place Piaget believed to be the pinnacle of cognitive development: formal operations. It is clear from Hans Furth's superb study of Piaget's work (1981), from Piaget's engagement with the work of others thereby producing a complex, coherent conceptual structure to characterize cognitive development, that Piaget himself was a brilliant dialectical thinker, and that if he simply had followed Plato, he would have had to have added a further stage in cognitive development beyond formal operations, the stage of dialectical thought. This is exactly what Klaus Riegel argued in 'Dialectical Operations: The Final Period of Cognitive Development' (Riegel 1973) and in other works (Riegel 1979). In doing so he argued for the importance of dialogue and narrative associated with the capacity retrace earlier forms of cognition (to appreciate the immediacy of sensori-motor intelligence, for instance) and thereby relate feeling, imagination and abstract thinking in this final stage of cognitive development. He did not mention this, but such a capacity is what is required to develop and deploy metaphors. Riegel's work has inspired other psychologists, and is now influencing research on organizations (Basseches 1984 and Lakse 2008).

Once dialectics as the final stage of cognitive development is acknowledged, it becomes possible to recover aspects of dialectical thinking that, because of a bias against the humanities, have been forgotten by proponents of dialectics. Firstly, dialectics implies dialogue, engaging with others in enquiry. Secondly, associated with dialogue, dialectics requires stories or narratives. While Plato in

The Republic defined dialectics formally as the stage beyond mathematics in which assumptions are treated as hypotheses, the whole book is a work of dialectics, and as such was written as a story. Nietzsche in *The Birth of Tragedy* characterized Plato's works as philosophical novels (Nietzsche 1956, XIV, p.88). Aristotle also gave a central place to presenting the history of philosophy in putting forward and defending his own ideas, particularly in *Metaphysics*. History was central to Hegel's dialectics in the *Phenomenology of Mind* and Schelling defended his work through a historical narrative in *On the History of Modern Philosophy*. The epistemological importance of these histories has been pointed out by Alasdair MacIntyre, in doing so, revealing how synoptic narratives are absolutely central to dialectics. At the same time, he showed the role of narratives in synopsis and synthetic thinking. Grappling with the relativistic conclusions that had been drawn from the work of philosophers of science such as Michael Polanyi, Thomas Kuhn and Paul Feyerabend who had exposed the gross deficiencies in the portrayal of science by logical positivists, Alasdair MacIntyre in 'Epistemological Crises, Dramatic Narrative and the Philosophy of Science' (1977) pointed out that the acceptance of radically new theories in science is dependent upon the capacity of their defenders to construct narratives from the perspectives provided by the new theories. Since major advances in knowledge transcend old assumptions and create new ways of arguing, changing the standards of relevance and proof, they cannot be evaluated in terms of existing criteria. The superiority of the new theories is only revealed by the comprehension these narratives facilitate of the achievements and limitations of the theories transcended, and of how the new theories overcome these limitations. In making this case, MacIntyre was pointing out that all research, and this is true of research in logic and mathematic as well as in science, requires narratives to define what has been achieved in the past, what are the rival research programs, what are the outstanding problems being addressed in the present, and what are the goals of inquiry. Destroy historical memory and you destroy all enquiry, although specialists in particular disciplines might not appreciate this immediately.

In grappling with the question, What are narratives? while advancing the tradition of hermeneutic phenomenology, Paul Ricoeur in conjunction with David Carr not only revealed the dialectical relationship between articulated narratives and life, but revealed the synthetic thinking of creative imagination in narratives. Ricoeur argued that narratives involve three forms of mimesis, the first being life which prefigures narratives, the second being configuration or emplotment in the production of narratives where diverse characters and events are integrated into the unity of a story, and the third being refiguration with the reception of stories. New narratives are emplotments consisting of 'configural acts' that 'grasp together' detailed actions which make up the story's incidents. Of these acts, Ricoeur wrote:

> I cannot overemphasize the kinship between this 'grasping together', proper to the configurational act, and what Kant has to say about the

operation of judging. It will be recalled that for Kant the transcendental meaning of judging consists not so much in joining a subject and a predicate as in placing an intuitive manifold under the rule of a concept. ... . Remaining in the Kantian vein, we ought not to hesitate in comparing the production of the configurational act to the work of the productive imagination. ... The productive imagination is not only rule-governed, it constitutes the generative matrix of rules. In Kant's first *Critique,* the categories of the understanding are first schematized by the productive imagination. The schematism has this power because the productive imagination fundamentally has a synthetic function. It connects understanding and intuition by engendering syntheses that are intellectual and intuitive at the same time. Emplotment, too, engenders mixed intelligibility between what has been called the point, theme, or thought of a story, and the intuitive presentation of circumstances, characters, episodes, and changes of fortune that make up the denouement. In this way, we may speak of a schematism of the narrative function.

(Ricoeur 1984, p.68)

Reception of new stories, whether historical or fictional, challenges people's horizons of expectations and enables them to refigure their ways of experiencing, their beliefs and the stories of their lives and thereby change the way they live, thereby incorporating such emplotments into social reality. These then prefigure later narrative production and reception, providing the inchoate narratives that provide the background assumptions and horizons of expectations that creative new emplotments can again challenge. While Ricoeur made no effort to relate his work on metaphor and narrative as central components of dialectical thinking as understood by Fichte, Schleiermacher and Schelling, it is nevertheless a major contribution to understanding this aspect of dialectical thought. As such, it complements the work of Piaget, and provides a way to think about broader projects of action than simply succeeding within existing fields.

Initially Ricoeur did not do full justice to inchoate narratives, or the influence of received narratives on how people live. For this he was criticized by David Carr who had already presented a very strong argument that complex actions and people's lives are lived as stories (Carr 1994, p.160ff.; Carr 1991). Ricoeur largely accepted Carr's argument that actions, especially where a number of people are involved, are lived stories requiring continual telling and retelling of the stories of the actions in which they are engaged. This is the case in building a house, fighting a war or creating a civilization. In Ricoeur's work on politics, *Ideology and Utopia* (1986), which is best interpreted through his theory of narratives, ideology functions as the sedimented component of traditions, preserving the identity of individuals or groups and facilitating their integration. These are the inchoate narratives that people are socialized into. Utopia, on the other hand, is a vision of a different and inspiring future that challenges current traditions. As the editor of this book, George Taylor explained in his introduction to this work:

The utopia puts in question what presently exists. ... We are forced to experience the contingency of the social order. The utopia is not only a dream, though, for it is a dream that wants to be realized. ... A society without utopia would be dead, because it would no longer have any project, and prospective goals.

(p.xxi)

It is, as Fred Polak characterized it, 'an image of the future' (Polak 1973). Such a dream requires new emplotments of the narratives that are being lived out, challenging these to reveal new possibilities for the future.

A further addition can be made to this framework by recognizing the distinction pointed out by Mikhail Bakhtin in *Problems of Dostoyevsky's Poetics* (Bakhtin 1984, p.62f.) between monologic and polyphonic, dialogic narratives. 'Polyphonic' or 'many voiced' language is language that incorporates into it appreciation of diverse voices, providing the conditions for a 'dialogic' relation in which different perspectives are brought into relation with each other. Polyphonic, dialogic narratives are characterized by a plurality of consciousnesses, each with its own world. They accord recognition to a diversity of voices and perspectives which can question each other and the narrative itself, and strive to reformulate the narratives they are living out. Dialogic narratives, which cultivate synoptic thinking in the highest degree, are the condition for synthetic thinking and are essential to dialectical thinking.

Synthesizing genetic structuralism and narratology to overcome Sartre's limitations

Conceived in this way it becomes possible to articulate Ricoeur's theory of narrative with Bourdieu's social theories in a way that augments the work of each theorist. There is nothing equivalent in Ricoeur's work to Bourdieu's concept of fields. However, Ricoeur also engaged with the work of the *Annales* school of historians, focusing on the work of Braudel, criticizing him for appearing to dismiss narratives in his concern to give a place to the long durée associated with geographical, economic and cultural structures (Ricoeur 1984, 101ff.). Ricoeur argued that the long durée still consists of events and requires narratives to describe them and to define the limits of any mathematical models used to analyse features of the long durée. While Ricoeur did not develop his views on this, he was clearly giving a place in narratives to events or processes of different durations which at the same time could give a place to aspects of social reality that could be modeled mathematically, and could give a place to geographical conditions of actions. While he never discussed Boudieu's notion of fields, embracing such complexity in narratives makes it easy to encompass and give a place to the autonomization of fields and their interactions. Furthermore, fields can be conceived of as consisting of inchoate narratives, and construing fields in this way is supported by Bourdieu's brief comments on the relationship between *habitus* and history. As Bourdieu put it in *The Logic of Practice*:

> The *habitus,* a product of history, produces individual and collective practices – more history – in accordance with the schemes generated by history. It ensures the active presence of past experiences, which, deposited in each organism in the form of schemes of perception, thought and action, tend to guarantee the 'correctness' of practices and their constancy over time, more reliably than all formal rules and explicit norms ... The *habitus* – embodied history, internalized as a second nature and so forgotten as history – is the active presence of the whole past of which it is the product. As such it is what gives practices their relative autonomy with respect to external determinations of the immediate present. ... The *habitus* is a spontaneity without consciousness or will, opposed as much to the mechanical necessity of things without history in mechanistic theories as it as to the reflexive freedom of subjects 'without inertia' in rationalist theories.
>
> (Bourdieu 1990, p.54/56)

With fields seen as embodying inchoate narratives as their history, the importance of the production and reception of stories should become immediately apparent. Bourdieu revealed the dialectic not only between *habitus* and fields but also and more broadly between objectifying forms of thinking that distance people from immediate engagement, and the logic involved in practical engagement as a subject. Narratives occupy an intermediate state between objectifying thought and engagement through which people can bring to consciousness and reflect on their engagement in the world in a less detached way than is usually associated with objective reflection.

With this integration of narratology and Bourdieusian social theory, it is then possible to revisit Sartre's work on dialectics and transcend its deficiencies. If Sartre's notion of dialectics had acknowledged the centrality of narratives in totalizations, detotalizations and retotalizations, he would have been able to deal with far greater complexity than he offered, both in comprehending the past and orienting people for action in the present and in working out what kind of future people should be striving to realize. Sartre still presupposed the Marxist categories of class where in the First World these were losing their relevance. Opposing oppression in the present requires far more than people in similar situations recognizing their common cause. It is necessary for people to recognize the oppression faced by others living very different lives and faced with very different problems, to identify the real causes of such oppression, to work out what kinds of futures are possible and to judge between these, and to find common interests despite this diversity in order to form effective social and political movements that can create a future better than the present. Through their understanding of history, they have to believe that they can create a better social order than that which presently exists. Furthermore, to be successful such movements cannot conceive their goal simply as seizing power from their oppressors. It requires the transformation of the organization of society to liberate people to fully realize themselves with the rights to assert themselves without fear of retribution, with the future society to be created being if anything more complex than present society. Sartre failed to appreciate the value of institutions that had defied or at least ameliorated the logic of the market and upheld fields through which the propensity of economic actors to commodify and instrumentalize everything had been resisted.

Associated with this, Sartre did not adequately deal with spatiality when, through the globalization of markets, transnational corporations were destroying what political control some nation-states had gained over the destructive and oppressive tendencies engendered by the quest for profit maximization, at least in their own territories. Concomitantly, he did not provide the means for understanding the production and organization of space through geological, ecological and human activities and processes through which some regions have been able to flourish and to exploit other regions, or to exclude or confine people from participation in their communities. Collective action against oppression is likely to be inspired by efforts to preserve existing institutions from destruction or corruption, for instance public institutions such as universities, rather than creating something completely new. To achieve relatively common understanding for such common action while avoiding the tendency for new power elites to impose their self-serving will on others against their common interests, polyphonic and dialogic narratives will be required that grant a place to diverse voices to participate in forming, questioning and reforming the narratives of their actions and institutions.

Given the complexity of the current world, it will be necessary to acknowledge the achievements and utilize the work of social theorists in such dialogical stories, recognizing the contribution that can and must be made by people who devote their lives to comprehending social reality. That is, it will be necessary to acknowledge the inadequacies in the dialectic in the form that Sartre conceived it that engendered dissatisfaction with his ideas. To recapitulate the story of the debate over dialectics between those aligned primarily with the humanities exemplified by the existentialist Hegelian Marxism of Sartre and those aligned primarily with structuralism and science, what we have seen is that the structuralist reaction to Sartre's dialectics produced a reaction in the form of genetic structuralism which gave a place to dialectics in the relationship between cognitive structures or *habituses*, fields and situations that individuals and groups have to grapple with, and between objectification and agency. While the limitations of this were then seen to require supplementing with work in narratology, narratives to be adequate have to incorporate the insights of the genetic structuralists.

As I have suggested, a further problem with Sartre's work is that he did not differentiate the dialectics of representation, recognition and labour found in Hegel's early work and therefore did not examine how these can, or can fail to be, coordinated, or understand the importance of the struggle for recognition and the significance of denial of recognition in motivating action. Bourdieu's notion of symbolic capital makes good this deficiency. It is also clear from Bourdieu's work that 'practico-inert fields' are not inert but have emergent dynamics that Sartre could not allow for, let alone explain. It is these dynamics that rival traditions of thought, developing ideas from science rather than the humanities, illuminated more successfully. Nor did Sartre provide the means to properly understand such semi-autonomous fields. This synthesis of Bourdieusian sociology with narratology provides a far more developed framework of concepts for analyzing the complexities of the social world, whether of traditional societies, the nation–state or globalized capitalism. Bourdieu's studies support Merleau-Ponty's misgivings about the direction of Sartre's philosophy, and in *Acts of Resistance: Against the Tyranny of the Market* (1998) and *Firing Back, Against the Tyranny of the Market 2* (2003), Bourdieu provided a powerful defense of pluralism and the need for autonomy of a multiplicity of cultural fields. However, the threat to this pluralism, as Bourdieu pointed out in these later works, with all the rhetorical force he could muster, now comes not from Sartrean ultra-Bolshevism but from neoliberalism. The problem now is how to mobilize people to preserve this pluralism against the quest by the global corporatocracy and their neoliberal allies to dissolve all institutions into the global market, including political institutions and public institutions such as universities and research organizations.[6] It is here that the dialectic associated with overcoming serialization, of forming into a self-conscious group or movement, and then through a series of totalizations, detotalizations and retotalizations, forming an effective collective will to transform society, appears to be what is required. For this to be even possible in the modern world, let alone achieving it without this leading to the dissolution of the partial autonomy of fields necessary to preserve liberty, it is also necessary to develop open, dialogic narratives, ranging from stories of individuals and small groups and cultural fields to grand narratives of civilizations, with everything in between, able to do justice to the complexity of the world and still orient people for action. This development of a more complex historical narrative should not be opposed to the human sciences as such, which are still required to understand geographical, social, economic and cultural formations and their dynamics. These need to be given a place in historical narratives, as the *Annales* school of historians attempted to do. It is necessary to construct the complex kind of narratives required to do justice to the thousand rivers of time and a multiplicity of spaces that Braudel asked historians to acknowledge.

The biggest problem of all with Sartre's philosophy is that, as with other 'Hegelian' Marxists, Sartre made no effort to reconcile his dialectics with his understanding of nature and the place of humanity within nature, including the cognitive development of non-human and human organisms, both historically and in each individual. Sartre had dismissed both 'the unfortunate theory of proletarian science' (Sartre 1976, p.802) and Darwinian evolutionary theory, virtually severing dialectics from engagement with the sciences and ignoring the major advances in Soviet science made possible in an intellectual environment conducive to non-reductionist thinking. Dialectics should be taken first and foremost as a characterization and the practice of enquiry and cognitive development, and one of the most important problems that must be faced is to comprehend how rationality of any kind can have emerged within nature and how dialectical rationality emerged, precariously, in human history, and then to understand the evolution of humanity in relation to the evolution and dynamics of nature.[7] Although Sartre recognized the importance of people achieving a comprehensive understanding of society and its history, he never considered the role of speculative philosophy in such totalizations and in the formation of a new social order. However, totalizations must be synthetic, and there is no reason why Sartre's concepts could not be further developed to characterize the longer term social dynamics that could give rise to new eras and even civilizations, and then to situate these within the dynamics of nature. To do so it is necessary to acknowledge the role that speculative philosophy must play in totalizations facilitating joint praxis on a massive scale, able to constitute the cultures of such eras and civilizations and redefine the place of humanity within nature.[8]

The limitations of Marxist dialectics

With this background, we can identify most of the achievements and limitations of Marxist contributions to dialectics, and the need to go beyond their limitations. For Marxists, dialectical inquiry is not constructing a deductive system from absolute foundations, nor is it a patchwork of empirical investigations collected together and systematically organized into a coherent logical structure for convenience, but open enquiry guided by the ultimate goal of achieving an integral, coherent comprehension of the whole as the background informing every enquiry into particulars, which has to include ourselves developing through our efforts to comprehend the world and ourselves as historical agents. As Lucian Goldmann wrote in *The Hidden God*:

> Both rationalism and empiricism are … opposed to dialectical thought, for this affirms that there are never any absolutely valid starting points, no problems which are finally and definitely solved, and that consequently thought never moves forward in a straight line, since each individual fact or idea assumes its significance only when it takes up its place in the whole, in the same way as the whole can be understood only by our increased knowledge of the partial and incomplete facts which constitute it. The advance of knowledge is thus to be considered as a perpetual movement to and fro, from the whole to the parts and from the parts back to the whole again, a movement in the course of which the whole and the parts throw light on each other.
>
> (Goldmann 1964, p.4f.)

And as Goldmann emphatically pointed out in 'The Dialectic Today' (1971, pp.108–122), this has to include the conditions of our existence – natural, social, cultural and our particular circumstances – that make this possible and could also be hindering our efforts. This implies awareness that in advancing towards such comprehension, people are participating in the formation and transformation of themselves, their culture, their society, and nature, which pre-existed human existence. This is universally accepted among dialecticians, although as we have seen, Hegelian Marxists sometimes ignore nature, treating it as a social category, or acknowledge it only insofar as it is transformable for human purposes.

Marxist dialecticians have also revealed some of the difficulties standing in the way of overcoming one-sided forms of knowledge and thought to gain such comprehensive understanding. Quite apart from the intrinsic difficulties standing in the way of advancing comprehension, Marxists have shown how people's thinking is bound to be constrained by the concepts embodied within and reproduced by social practices, institutions, traditions, instruments and other manufactured products, and broader social formations with their own inertia and emergent logics of development that constitute the context within which all enquiry and communication, including their own, takes place. Consequently, there is a propensity for developing and maintaining systematically distorted and misleading conceptions of reality, necessary falsehoods or necessary illusions reproduced as the condition for the functioning of existing institutions and social formations, contradicting other concepts and goals. Intellectual inquiry to advance requires ideology critique or a 'hermeneutics of suspicion', Marxist or Nietzschean. However, stopping at this, as postmodernists have tended to do, is self-defeating. Such suspicion can be used to justify complete relativism, usually interpreting all knowledge claims as manifestations of the quest for power, denying the possibility of overcoming at least to some extent prevailing beliefs and ways of thinking that are oppressive.

No Marxist dialectician, and certainly not Bertell Ollman who was quoted at the beginning of this chapter, is guilty of relativism. Marxists have successfully argued that the way to overcome such mystifications is through dialectics committed to overcoming one-sided ways of thinking. However, typifying Marxists, in presupposing the validity of his ontology Ollman himself is guilty of a form of one-sidedness. He assumes that 'the world really is an infinite number of mutually dependent processes that coalesce to form a structured whole or totality'. He then added that dialectics is 'the only sensible way to study a world composed of mutually dependent processes in constant evolution' (Ollman 2008, p.11). This is a good argument against any approach to comprehending the world that precludes recognizing that the world could consist of such mutually dependent processes in evolution, but provides no place for defending such an ontology or advancing beyond it. This one-sidedness has led to blind-spots, one of which is a lack of appreciation of the importance of new processes emerging, gaining and then maintaining some autonomy from the conditions of their emergence, and the conditions for their continued existence.

This one-sidedness underlies the complaint of David Harvey, one of the contributors to the Ollman and Smith anthology *Dialectics for the New Century* (2008). In 'The Dialectics of Spacetime' (pp.98–117), Harvey pointed to the tendency of Marxist dialecticians to ignore the importance of spatiality. This manifests a lack of appreciation of the partial autonomy implied by spatial separation created and maintained by natural processes and also by people, as in struggles for liberation and maintenance of territories by nations, or in built-up environments which separate and insulate areas from each other, and also in the more complex ways in which people can be liberated or dominated, as demonstrated by Foucault, and world-systems theorists and theorists of economic globalization such as Immanuel Wallerstein, Samir Amin and Giovanni Arrighi, among others, as well as Harvey (Harvey, 2000 and Arrighi, 2008). Recognizing partial autonomy of processes and the various kinds of spaces associated with them is important for understanding how people can be excluded, confined and exploited, but also the conditions for liberty, including the liberty for people to engage in critical and creative enquiry, bringing received beliefs and the social orders they legitimate into question and challenging those who hold these beliefs.

Boudieu's work illuminates this point. Bourdieu's genetic structuralism has much in common with Ollman's ontology, but it challenges it in one crucial respect. Bourdieu explicitly criticized Lucian Goldmann's approach to the study of literature based on Lukácsian dialectics, a conception of dialectics very similar to Ollman's, for failing to recognize the specific logic of cultural fields, and for failing to appreciate their autonomization. It is partially autonomous cultural fields supported by partially autonomous political fields, which in turn are based on partially autonomous economic fields (of a locality, a nation, a continent etc.) that are the condition for free enquiry and in relation to which cultural productions must be understood. That is, partially autonomous fields create social spaces, generally supported by transformations of the physical world that support such spaces, which provide the conditions for the pursuit of truth and justice. When cultural fields are reduced to instruments of politics (as occurred in the Soviet Union) or economics (as is now taking place throughout the world under the influence of neoliberalism) and their significance is defined entirely in terms of extrinsic criteria (means to control nature and people, or the means to make money, or both at once with neoliberalism), then the objective conditions for such enquiry no longer exist and the public sphere is impoverished or completely crippled, as Bourdieu (2004) has pointed out.

The main exception to the blindness to spatiality by a Western Marxist dialectician was Henri Lefebvre, who strongly influenced Harvey. Lefebvre was concerned with the kinds of spaces that are being produced and how these undermine or augment freedom, utilizing a complex and original notion of dialectics drawing on Hegel, Marx and Nietzsche (Lefebvre 1991; Schmid, 2008). However, while discussing socially produced spaces, even Lefebvre ignored the geological and ecological processes that have produced the spaces within which humanity evolved and continues to evolve, and the relationship between these 'naturally produced' spaces and the humanly produced spaces of built-up environments, economic activity and cultural life. What is required to acknowledge the emergence of socially produced spaces and specific fields in society is a more general theory of emergence whereby the emergence of humanity with its unique spatio-temporal characteristics and capacity to form autonomous fields can be made intelligible in the context of a dynamic, creative nature.

The idea of the social production of spaces (and associated times) and autonomization of fields, is incomprehensible from the perspective of a Newtonian conception of nature, and to be defended it is necessary to challenge the Newtonian framework of concepts and deeper assumptions about what counts as scientific knowledge. To do so is to follow Schelling's call for a speculative philosophy of nature to replace Newtonian physics and its reductionist assumptions in order to make the existence of humanity, in all its complexity, intelligible. From a Schellingian perspective, in which space and time are understood to be causally produced orders of potentialities for independence and interaction between differentiated and separated processes and their products in a creative world, the production of specifically human spaces in the context of geologically and ecologically produced spaces becomes intelligible, as does the emergence of cultural fields. Such a perspective also clarifies the significance and value of spatial separation and the consequence of failure to acknowledge its value. The 'conquest of space' in transport and communications celebrated by those who assume Newtonian categories has been disastrous for a vast numbers of ecosystems, species and people, beginning with invasion of the Americas and culminating with IBMs, with the global corporatocracy able to operate through their communication systems at a global level, factory fishing ships and digital surveillance now threatening everyone.

As we have seen, Engels did offer such a radically new conception of the world with his dialectics of nature that might have been developed to deal with space, but this was really a bowdlerized version of Schelling's philosophy of nature. Despite its limitations identified by Western Marxists, its development by orthodox Marxists in the Soviet Union and some Western Marxists was often creative (Graham 1971; Weiner 1988; Foster 2008). However, the positivistic way this conception of nature was formulated, and the combination of this with Stalin's efforts to control science to reduce it to an instrument of the economy, limited how far it could be developed in the Soviet Union. And it was an easy target for Western Marxists such as Lukács and Sartre. The failure of most Western Marxists who repudiated Engels' dialectics of nature to appreciate the significance of space and the autonomy of fields is part of a broader problem, to meet the challenge of accounting for the emergence of humanity and thereby comprehending the possibility that humanity might cease to exist, or alternatively, the need to envisage and create a radically new social order not based on the categories of current economics. As we have seen, Schelling argued in opposition to Kant that it is necessary to comprehend the formation of consciousness in nature, and through human history to comprehend and fully justify claims to knowledge in the present. This radicalization of Fichte's claim that it is possible to achieve synthetic knowledge of cognitive development in each individual was central to their development of dialectics. Despite the work of Piaget, Vygotsky, Riegel and the narratologists sympathetic to Marxism, most Western Marxists have failed to acknowledge the importance of cognitive development and the specific nature of dialectical thinking and the conditions for fostering its development, and maintaining it. There is little acknowledgement that while unreflective dialectics is central to every culture, very few cultures throughout history developed reflective dialectical thinking, and when they did so, it was achieved by only a relatively small number of people (although, as shown in Gare (1996, p.375f.), among the Fipa of Tanzania, its achievement appears to be almost universal), and it could disappear again. Few Marxists (with those influenced by Antonio Gramsci being a partial exception) acknowledge that the potential for thinking dialectically is a fragile achievement that needs to be cultivated in each individual as the condition for people to advance their comprehension and appreciation of the world and the situations they are in, to overcome oppressive formations and the categories on which they are based, and to defend not only what liberty has been achieved from oppressive formations, but to create new formations cultivating and maintaining new forms of liberty.

This brings us to the crux of the matter. From the perspective of dialectics as it was revived by Hegel, Schelling and Schleiermacher, developing better cognitive schemes or conceptual frameworks requires speculation. This aspect was downplayed by Hegel in his *Science of Logic*, the work that most influenced Marxists, and by treating dialectics as general laws of development, Engels not merely acknowledged the inseparability of epistemology and ontology but conflated them, in doing so, eliminating any place for speculative imagination. Dialectics that fails to give a place to speculative thinking by which more adequate perspectives and conceptual frameworks, including both theories of physical existence and concepts of humanity and society, could be created, proposed, elaborated and defended in response to the fragmentation of perspectives and contradictions and failures of concepts (prevailing or otherwise) revealed to be contradictory or otherwise deficient, excludes what should be one of the most important dimensions of dialectical thinking. As opposed to thinking that is purely analytical, dialectics can and should give a central place to constructive speculation involving creative imagination and synthesis along with analysis, providing new concepts for people to define themselves and their relationships to each other, to society, civilization and the rest of nature, in order to create the future.

Not all French Marxists were remiss in regard to speculation. As we have seen, Sartre and the genetic structuralists addressed some of the deficiencies of earlier Marxists. Sartre understood the importance of and appreciated some of the difficulties of achieving totalizations transcending and uniting particular perspectives and uniting oppressed people to create the future, but his concern to privilege agency led him to an inadequate appreciation of the importance of maintaining some degree of autonomy for members (whether individuals, communities, organizations or cultural fields) participating in these totalizations. Not unconnected to this, Sartre could not provide, or even allow for a form of totalization that could effectively unite and orient the whole of humanity to overcome the destructive dynamics of capitalism. Part of the problem with Sartre was a deficient understanding of the role of narrative, but more importantly, a dismissive attitude to contributions that could be made by science. He had no appreciation of the importance of speculative metaphysics, and most importantly, an almost complete lack of interest in nature and how it should be understood. Sartre did not confront the difficult problem that if the categories of economics are the forms of existence in a capitalist society, what categories could replace these to liberate people in a social and economic order that could be sustained and flourish without destroying the ecological conditions of its existence.

The work of the genetic structuralists and narratologists has provided the means to address some of these lacunae, but their work needs to be integrated and synthesized with Sartre's work and to further develop the philosophy of nature if it is to orient people for effective political action, and achieving this will require much more. Some French philosophers who contributed to the development of thought on dialectics did focus on the speculative philosophy of nature and on the development of the sciences. Piaget could be included here (although he was Swiss and tends not to be regarded as a philosopher), along with Gaston Bachelard and those he influenced. And Merleau-Ponty towards the end of his life was refocusing his whole philosophy by engaging with the philosophy of nature. But by this stage he had abandoned Marxism (Merleau-Ponty, 2003), and his work on the philosophy of nature was not developed by other French philosophers whom he influenced. French Marxists by and large, and this includes 'speculative materialists', have not seen the need for speculative thought to create the future, particularly, speculative thought about nature. Bachelard will be examined further in the next chapter.

Notes

1 This side of Marx's dialectics has been emphasized by Robert Albritton in *Dialectics and Deconstruction in Political Economy* (2001). Albritton builds on the work of Kozo Uno and Tom Sekine. See also the essays in *New Dialectics and Political Economy* (Albritton and Simoulidis 2003) and Albritton's *Economics Transformed: Discovering the Brilliance of Marx* (2007).

2 What potentialities are opened up by crises has been analysed from a Marxian perspective by James O'Connor in *The Meaning of Crisis* (1987). O'Connor reveals the complexity of crises in the present, which can be simultaneously economic, social, political and personal, and spatially differentiated.

3 This side of dialectics has been examined by Axel Honneth, *The Struggle for Recognition: The Moral Grammar of Social Conflict* (1996), and *Disrespect: The Normative Foundations of Critical Theory* (2007).

4 In fact, except for Charles Ehresmann and Andree Ehresmann, the Bourbaki group did not embrace Category Theory, even though their belief in mother structures could not be substantiated, as Leo Corry pointed out in *Modern Algebra and the Rise of Mathematical Structures* (2004), p.334.

5 Axel Honneth failed to recognize this in his critique of Bourdieu in 'The Fragmented World of Symbolic Forms: Reflections on Pierre Bourdieu's Sociology of Culture' (1995).

6 This agenda of the neoliberals has been well described by S.M. Amadae, *Rationalizing Capitalist Democracy* (2003), Dieter Plehwe, Bernard Walpen and Gisela Neunhöffer, eds. *Neoliberal Hegemony: A Global Critique* (2006), and Philip Mirowski (2009, 2011, 2013).

7 This was not faced up to by either Friedrich Engels who continued to treat dialectics as an ontology, nor by Györgi Lukács or Jean-Paul Sartre, who argued against a 'dialectic of nature' but then ignored nature. As Roy Bhaskar defined the problem in *Dialectic: the Pulse of Freedom*, 'in real emergence the processes are generally non-teleologically causal, only socio-spherically conceptual; and the higher level (in Hegel, absolute spirit or, to borrow Charles Taylor's felicitous expression, "cosmic Geist") does not posit, but is rather formed from, the lower cosmic level' (1993, p.50). From Bhaskar's naturalist perspective, social dynamics involve complex interactions between non-dialectical and dialectical natural, social and cultural processes, as Marx demonstrated in *Capital*. Marxists are still grappling with such issues (see Ollman and Smith 2008).

8 The study of the rise and fall of eras and civilizations reveals a much more brutal and complex history than Sartre allowed for, as should be evident from Peter Turchin's study, *War and Peace and War: The Rise and Fall of Empires* (2007). The study of the formation and rise of civilizations and eras also reveals a far greater role to culture, including speculative thought, as is evident in the work of Johann Arnason (2015, pp.146–176) building on the work of Elias and Eisenstadt.

4 The dialectics of speculative naturalism

To confront and overcome the inadequacies of current interpretative schemes, including those promulgated by the sciences and other privileged discourses (including ideas parading as Marxist) and those embodied in practices, institutions, built environments and technology, dialectical thinking that gives a place to all components of speculative thinking: analysis, synopsis and synthesis, that can reconceive humanity and its place in nature, is required. The most important interpretative schemes that need to be identified and confronted are those that are assumed by more consciously articulated interpretative schemes. It is these that are most difficult to question and replace because they are absorbed subconsciously in the process of being socialized into a culture and its practices. Embodied as *habituses* and accepted as *doxa*, it is extremely difficult for any individual to bring these assumptions to full consciousness. It is here that synopses that highlight the contradictions between different domains of life, experience and thought, and assumptions held at different times in history, are required. All forms of experience, whether the experience of the physical world, of being alive, aware or self-conscious, of being socially engaged or involved in empirical or theoretical research or artistic and religious contemplation, including the experiences of others and their utterances or writings, can be the basis for bringing into question and challenging prevailing interpretive schemes if they contradict experiences in any one of these. There are no absolute starting points or foundations for knowledge in this quest, either in reason or in experience, or in received claims to knowledge from the past (scientific or otherwise) and no conclusions that are beyond further questioning. Recognizing the role of speculation and synthetic thought while appreciating the unprethinkable Being that is always more than we can comprehend, exposes the fallibility of all claims to knowledge, whether comprehensive or narrowly focused, and the absurdity of foreclosing further questioning and speculation.

Dialectics achieves reflexivity through situating the present in broader contexts, real and imagined, enabling current assumptions and prejudices to be revealed and brought into question. The characterization of knowledge emerges with synoptic histories of competing claims to knowledge in which prevailing assumptions about what is knowledge have been or are challenged by alternatives. This also involves appreciating that current arguments, including arguments over what is knowledge, take place in the context of traditions of thought and inquiry. These are formed by a history of questioning, investigating, experimenting, extending experience, discussing and arguing, and are crystallized in canonical texts, institutions and in built-up environments that then channel thought and inquiry. To participate in traditions requires recognition of their past achievements and failures, what tradition or traditions are dominant in the present, and why they are dominant. It is for such reasons that synoptic histories of philosophy, traditions, institutions, formations and civilizations are central to the work of dialectical thinkers. Not only is such historical work part of the quest for comprehensive understanding of nature and humanity; it is only by providing synoptic histories that philosophers can reveal and bring into question the assumptions underlying rival ways of thinking and define and situate their own work in relation to evolving, often contradictory, traditions of research, and develop and then defend their own speculative ideas. Only through such histories can radically new conceptions of the world be elaborated and justified as superior to what had been achieved in the past, not as absolute claims to knowledge, but as programs for further research and as orientations for action to create the future.

Aleksandr Bogdanov (1873–1928), Ernst Bloch (1885–1977), Joseph Needham (1900–1995) and those influenced by them did not have the limitations of French Marxists, and their work highlights these limitations. Bogdanov embraced developments in thermodynamics and biology and set about constructing a highly original general theory of organizations, or 'tektology', a form of process philosophy that could replace the mechanistic view of nature, account for the emergence and development of humanity, explain social organization and the development and evolution of culture, while providing the concepts that would enable people to organize themselves. This is required to overcome the subordination of workers to managers which, according to Bogdanov, is the real source of oppression in the modern world rather than the bourgeoisie. Tektology also provides concepts to understand the development of cognition in culture, including in science and art. As such, it was a precursor to, probably influenced, and was superior to the systems theory of Ludwig von Bertalanffy (Gare 2000b). Bogdanov's ideas were developed by the *Proletkult* movement after the Bolshevik revolution with the aim of creating a new culture preserving the best of all past cultures in order to avoid transforming the Soviet Union into either a capitalist system controlled by a technocratic elite, the system that was developed under the New Economic Policy, or a form of 'war communism', the mobilization of society controlled by a bureaucracy, the path promoted by Trotsky and adopted by Stalin, which Bogdanov argued presciently, would lead to a new feudalism and stagnation. As I have argued, elsewhere, this is the path that was not taken, but should have been (Gare 1993c). Bogdanov was one of the first eco-Marxists, and his work is clearly relevant to the quest for an ecological civilization (Gare 1994).

Some aspects of Bogdanov's philosophy appear to have influenced Gramsci, but were not developed by him to the same extent. However, at the end of his life, after having observed the trajectory of the Soviet Union, Gramsci argued that to avoid becoming a mere mirror of what it was opposing, a communist society needed to create a new conception of the world (Ahearne 2012). Ernst Bloch, uninfluenced by Bogdanov, developed what John Ely characterizes as 'left-Aristotelianism' which:

> … emerges from the fringes of history in two key empty spaces generated by the ossification of Western Marxism. First, it emerges in the space left by an absent theory of 'nature', the 'objective' or 'substantive rationality' which could provide a practical alternative to the negative dialectic of 'subjective' or 'instrumental' rationality characterizing the central aporia of critical theory. Second, it offers a substantial theory in the second empty space, namely the absence in critical theory (and Marxism generally) of a theory of politics.
>
> (Ely 1996, p.137)

Bloch demanded a theoretically and empirically defensible interpretation of the cosmos drawing on Avicenna's and Averroes' re-interpretation of the Aristotelean *telos* as this had influenced the work of Giordano Bruno, and indirectly, Schelling. This interpretation emphasizes the inherent *nisus* or developmental tendency of matter. Recognizing this *nisus* provided Bloch with a reference point for developing a radical version of natural law theory of politics and law that incorporated a utopian vision of the future able to inspire hope (Hudson 1982). Joseph Needham was indirectly influenced by Bogdanov through contact with Soviet historians of science. While embracing a form of Marxism, Needham was also strongly influenced by the speculative philosophy of Whitehead, and he was centrally involved in efforts to develop theoretical biology. Subsequently he wrote major works on the history of Western science and then a massive study of science and civilization in China, developed from the perspective of and further developing his Whiteheadian Marxism. This work has played a significant role in the development of a global civilization.

Bogdanov, Bloch and Needham, each defending a form of process philosophy, give some idea of what direction Marxist dialecticians might have taken if they had given a place to all dimensions of dialectics. Apart from Marxists engaged in the history and philosophy of science and eco-Marxists, however, these thinkers have been almost completely ignored by the vast majority of those who claim to be Marxist dialecticians. And despite the work of James O'Connor who founded the journal *Capitalism, Nature, Socialism*, Western Marxists until recently did not pay much attention to the work of the eco-Marxists.[1] To properly appreciate and develop all dimensions and the full potential of this tradition of dialectical thought it is also necessary to examine and provide a synoptic history of non-Marxist defenders of dialectics, most importantly those who engaged with science and the philosophy of nature.

Extending dialectics into speculation: Collingwood, Peirce and Whitehead

Because 'dialectics' has been associated with Marxism, the term tends to be avoided by non-Marxists. However, other philosophers have also advanced dialectical thinking, most importantly in considering the role of speculation and synthetic thought. These are the speculative naturalists, who are all directly or indirectly influenced by Schelling, and all have been concerned to comprehend how nature could have engendered human consciousness and to question the assumptions of mainstream science in doing so. While Robin Collingwood (1889–1943), C.S. Peirce (1839–1914) and Alfred North Whitehead (1861–1947) are not usually considered as dialecticians, it is clear when their work is examined in the context of the development of dialectics, they have made major contributions to its development. Collingwood in an early work, *An Essay on Philosophical Method* (2005, pp.10–15), was explicitly engaged in debates over the nature of dialectics in Hegel's philosophy and presented his conception of philosophical method as a form of dialectics continuous with a tradition beginning with Socrates and Plato. His question and answer logic is clearly a clarification of what has always been centrally involved in dialectical thinking from Plato onwards. In *An Essay on Metaphysics,* Collingwood showed that it is only possible to properly understand and evaluate any action, product, statement or proposition by appreciating to what question the action, product or statement is an answer (Collingwood 2002, p.21ff.). He then showed how questions are based on a hierarchy of presuppositions, each of which can be called into question. He defended systematic philosophy, countering all objections to it that assume that systematic philosophy must be a claim to have the final truth. He pointed out that systematic philosophy does not require this, and it is scarcely ever the case that systematic philosophers make this claim (Collingwood 2005, pp.176–198, 327–355).

However, Collingwood argued that there are ultimate assumptions, identified as metaphysical presuppositions, such as 'every event has a cause', that cannot be brought into question. They are the presuppositions that define an era and are the condition for all questioning in that era and delimit what any systematic philosophy can achieve. So, while a question and answer logic can clarify what is involved in action, production and enquiry or research on specific topics, it can only reveal the presuppositions of the era, it cannot challenge, develop or replace these metaphysical presuppositions, even though it can be shown that they are different from the presuppositions of other eras. Those influenced by Collingwood have gained insight into the structures of cultures, their imperviousness to ideas that are inconsistent with prevailing assumptions, how these assumptions support each other in hierarchical order, and the difficulty of bringing such assumptions to consciousness and challenging them. Hintikka's work revealing the constricting effect of the assumption that logic and mathematics are a universal language and the influence this assumption has had in philosophy, illustrates the fruitfulness of a question and answer logic in exposing such assumptions.

Peirce was bolder than Collingwood. His philosophy is best seen as a reworking of Kant's philosophy along lines laid out by Schelling, at the same time drawing on more recent science and mathematics and a vast range of past philosophers. Aristotle and Duns Scotus were the most important of these. Peirce reduced Kant's twelve categories to three: Firstness, Secondness and Thirdness. These are the simplest categories and are applicable to *any* subject, whether merely possible or actually existing. First, there must be something. Second, there must be something other. Third, there must be mediation. Thirdness presupposes Secondness, and both presuppose Firstness. On this basis, Peirce argued that philosophy consists of three parts. Phenomenology is Firstness. The normative sciences consisting of aesthetics, ethics and logic, concerned with what is good and bad, is the realm of Secondness. Thirdness is metaphysics, which examines the most general features of real objects. Although arrived at independently, these categories clearly resonate with Hegelian dialectics, as is evident in *Pragmatism as a Principle and Method of Right Thinking* (1997, p.120). 'I consider Hegel's three stages as being, roughly speaking, the correct list of Universal Categories' he wrote (Peirce 1958, 5.43). However, Peirce defended a conception of cognitive development closer to that of Schelling's. As he put it, 'Hegelians overlook the facts of volitional action and reaction in the development of thought. I find myself in a world of forces which act upon me, and it is they and not the logical transformations of my thought which determine what I shall ultimately believe' he wrote in 'Comments on Royce's Philosophy' (Peirce 1958, 8.45 §2). This is essentially a Schellingian form of dialectics.

Peirce, following to some extent Kant, rejected the Parmenidean assumption that logically true things and the properties of real things coincide. The fact that aspects of the world can be understood through mathematically expressed laws should not be merely accepted but must be accounted for − as the result of evolution. He then speculated on how the world must be to account for the achievement of such knowledge. Peirce suggested that nature was initially 'absolutely undefined and unlimited possibility − boundless possibility' (Peirce 1958, 6.127) and 'a chaos of unpersonalized feeling' (Peirce 1992, 297.). Corresponding to Schelling's unprethinkable Being, this is presupposed by all thinking, practical and theoretical, unreflective and reflective. This is Firstness. Order emerged from this chaos of potentiality as chance generates determinate habits (becoming more limited in its freedom) (Peirce 1992, p.348f.). This is Secondness. As nature developed habits, thing-like entities came into existence behaving somewhat predictably, although never entirely so. These could then interact and come into conflict. This is the precondition for the emergence of signs by which these things could be related to each other and their behaviour then predicted. As such, signs are Thirdness. Peirce characterized the sign as 'anything which is so determined by something else, called its Object, and so determines an effect upon a person, which effect I call its Interpretant, that the latter is thereby mediately determined by the former'. He quickly corrected this definition, however, writing to Lady Welby, 'My insertion of "upon a person" is a sop to Cerberrus, because I despair of making my own broader conception understood' (Peirce 1998, p.478). For Peirce, signs and interpretation pervade nature. The universe, he wrote, 'is perfused with signs, if it is not composed exclusively of signs' (Peirce 1958, 5.448). Accordingly, he offered a more general definition: 'A Sign is anything which is related to a Second thing, its *Object*, in respect to a Quality, in such a way as to bring a Third thing, its *Interpretant,* into relation to the same Object' (Peirce 1958, p.92).

As such, the production and interpretation of signs, or 'semiosis', is triadic. It is because it is triadic that it lends itself to forming sequences and networks of semiosis, with interpretants in turn becoming signs, becoming increasingly complex. The study of semiosis consists of 'speculative grammar', the study of the modes of signifying in general, understood in relation to his evolutionary metaphysics, 'speculative critic' the science of 'the necessary conditions for attainment of truth' or 'the ways in which a sign can be related to an object independent of it', and 'speculative rhetoric', the science of the essential conditions under which a sign may determine an interpretant of itself, or bring about a physical result (Peirce 1998, p.297ff.). Deploying his three categories, Peirce analysed and classified the different kinds of signs, showing how they are related to each other and how the semiosis characteristic of humans alone, involved in art, science and philosophy, is made possible and is built upon simpler forms of semiosis (Thellefsen 2001). Logic was seen to be part of semiotics and examined as part of speculative critic, where utilizing his categories again, Peirce showed that induction and deduction do not exhaust reasoning; reasoning in all domains of inquiry requires also abduction (or hypothesis formation), which is really speculation; that is, as Karl-Otto Apel characterized it, a 'synthetic unified interpretation of the a manifold of sense data in a judgment of experience' (Apel 1995, p.40). In 'The Doctrine of Necessity Examined' Peirce referred to this as 'ampliative inference' (to emphasise its creative nature) (Peirce 1992. p.300). That is, Peirce ascribed a central role to creative imagination in inquiry, requiring an ability to produce hypotheses. An hypothesis, Peirce argued in 'The Nature of Mathematics', is 'a proposition imagined to be strictly true of an ideal state of things' (Peirce 1955, p.137). For instance, necessary conclusions are drawn by mathematicians through the use of diagrams which function as analogies to such hypotheses. As Peirce elucidated in 'On the Algebra of Logic':

> Mathematical deduction consists in constructing an icon or diagram the relations of whose parts shall present a complete analogy with those of the parts of the object of reasoning, or experimenting upon this image in the imagination, and of observing the result so as to discover unnoticed and hidden relations among the parts.
>
> (Peirce 1992, p.227)

While if an hypothesis turns out to be true of an actual state of affairs then conclusions drawn from it would be necessary, it can never be known with certainty (or apodictically) that the hypothesis is true of an actual state of affairs.

This characterization of semiosis as triadic contrasts with the dyadic thinking that has dominated and crimped the thinking of logical empiricists, including Quine and Co. (as well as Saussure). It not only gives a place to the synthetic judgments associated with hypothesis formation and to the subjects involved in such synthetic thinking, it acknowledges that all knowledge contained in an interpretant is mediated by previous claims to knowledge, that there is an intersubjective relation requiring interpretation of others and persuasion to achieve mutual agreement (thus giving a place to both hermeneutics and rhetoric), and that the object itself can be causally efficacious in forming and validating or invalidating an interpretant. There is no temptation to reduce the logic of science to the study of syntactical relations between signs and truth conditions, and there is no temptation to treat language as an all encompassing universal medium functioning as an iron curtain between us and reality.[2] All semiosis is understood in the context of the evolution of the cosmos, while the way the evolution of the cosmos is understood, granting a place to both chance and continuity, is required to make intelligible the possibility of semiosis. Speculative reasoning is not exhausted by mathematics and symbolic logic, however important these are, and requires the use of 'real vagues' (Peirce 1998, p.350f.), terms which are not and could not be precisely defined, and all conscious reasoning is founded on and can only be fully understood in relation to communities of enquirers practically engaged in the world. Finally, Peirce argued for 'synechism' as a regulative principle of logic or inquiry that there are no gaps in the intelligibility of the universe of being, that the universe exists as a whole of all its parts; that is, that everything in the universe is intelligible in relation to everything else and in relation to the universe as a whole.

While apparently not influenced by Collingwood or Peirce, Whitehead's work can be interpreted and then defended as combining their contributions. Understood in this way, Whitehead greatly clarified the goal of speculative philosophy and the nature of 'synthetic' thinking. Whitehead also is best interpreted as a post-Kantian philosopher in the Schellingian tradition, although this is not how he interpreted himself. He also developed an evolutionary cosmology and wrote in *Process and Reality* of his philosophy of organism that it 'aspires to construct a critique of pure feeling' such that 'Kant's "Transcendental Aesthetic" becomes a distorted fragment of what should have been his main topic' (Whitehead 1978, p.113). 'Feeling' for Whitehead is an aspect of what there is and of all thinking, and essential to account for synthesis in both being and thought. Like Collingwood, Whitehead was acutely aware that all thinking is historically situated and takes place within a context of unconscious presuppositions, and was concerned to show that the most important philosophical problems derived from these presuppositions. In fact, his arguments sometimes amount to simply revealing these presuppositions and then showing how they have fettered thought, and labeling them fallacies (for instance, 'the fallacy of simple location' and 'the fallacy of misplaced concreteness'). However, he also paid far more attention than Collingwood to what is involved in bringing these presuppositions into question and replacing them, including metaphysical presuppositions. Doing so involves developing radically new ideas and new language to express these, and it was this that he characterized as speculation (Gare 1999, pp.127–145; Siebers 2002).

However, not all presuppositions are problematic, and one of the goals of philosophy is to make explicit presuppositions that are the condition of any inquiry and need to be acknowledged as such to guide inquiry. For instance, Whitehead argued that the most important assumption of all inquiry, more important than logical consistency, is that the universe is coherent, and that therefore our comprehension of it is coherent. This corresponds to Peirce's synechism. The demand for coherence, Whitehead, argued, is 'the great preservative of rationalistic sanity' (Whitehead 1978, p.6). For Whitehead 'coherence':

> [...] means that the fundamental ideas, in terms of which the scheme is developed, presuppose each other so that in isolation they are meaningless. ... In other words, it is presupposed that no entity can be conceived in complete abstraction from the system of the universe, and that it is the business of speculative philosophy to exhibit this truth. This character is its coherence.
>
> (Whitehead 1978, p.3)

Speculative philosophy was described by Whitehead most succinctly in *Process and Reality*:

> Speculative Philosophy is the endeavour to frame a coherent, logical, necessary system of general ideas in terms of which every element of our experience can be interpreted. By this notion of 'interpretation' I mean that everything of which we are conscious, as enjoyed, perceived, willed, or thought, shall have the character of a particular instance of the general scheme. Thus the philosophical scheme should be coherent, logical, and in respect of interpretation, applicable and adequate. Here 'applicable' means that some items of experience are thus interpretable, and 'adequate' means that there are no items incapable of such interpretation.
>
> (Whitehead 1978, p.3)

Whitehead made it clear that speculation cannot be reduced to analytical thinking, and was highly critical of philosophy that gave no place to speculation. As he wrote in *Modes of Thought*:

> The fallacy of the perfect dictionary divides philosophy into two schools, namely, the 'Critical School', which repudiates speculative philosophy, and the 'Speculative School' which includes it. The critical school confines itself to verbal analysis within the limits of the dictionary. The speculative school appeals to direct insight, and endeavours to indicate the meanings by further appeal to situations which promote such specific insights. It then enlarges the dictionary.
>
> (Whitehead 1938, p.173)

He then proclaimed: 'Philosophy is the search for premises. It is not deduction. Such deductions as occur are for the purpose of testing the starting points by the evidence of the conclusions' (Whitehead 1938, p.105). Nor can premises be found though induction. Before correlations between observations can be of importance, it is first necessary to have schemes of ideas into which such observations can be fitted. These schemes precede systematic observation, and can be of the greatest significance even when they fail to achieve contact with observation. So rationality in its most basic form is neither deduction nor induction, but the search for principles or schemes of ideas. This involves developing new conceptual frameworks, or categories, an essentially post-Kantian, post-Hegelian project, as Zvie Bar-On has shown (1987).

How can this search be conducted? To begin with, Whitehead argued that there cannot be a method for this, since it is only through such schemes of ideas that methods are established. As he put it: 'The speculative Reason is in its essence untrammeled by method. Its function is to pierce into the general reasons beyond limited reasons, to understand all methods as coordinated in a nature of things only to be grasped by transcending all method' (Whitehead 1929, p.51). However, he qualified this, arguing that there is a method of sorts involved in reaching beyond set bounds, including all existing methods. It was this 'method' which was discovered by the Greeks, and why we now talk of speculative reason rather than inspiration. This cannot be understood as the application of a rigid formula. There cannot be a fixed, definite procedure of speculative reason such as that of deductive logic.

What then is speculative reason? And in particular, how does speculation operate in philosophy? Essentially, while as Broad argued, speculative philosophy requires analysis, synopses and synthesis, and while it is possible to engage in analysis and synopses without synthesis, speculative reason must involve synthetic thought as well. In Peirce's terminology, this is abduction, the development of a working hypotheses not merely to make predictions, but most importantly, and this was emphasized by Whitehead, to elucidate experience. Such working hypotheses are arrived at through the generalization of patterns experienced, recognized and studied in particular domains and then generalized, first to interpret one other domain, and then all domains of experience, a method that has been further developed by Felix Hong (2013). Only well developed areas of enquiry are likely to provide the requisite resources for such speculative generalization. Along with physics, physiology, psychology and sociology, Whitehead allowed that aesthetics, ethics and languages, conceived as storehouses of human experience, could be the source of speculative generalizations. This procedure is referred to by Whitehead as the method of 'descriptive generalization', meaning 'the utilization of specific notions, applying to a restricted group of facts, for the divination of the generic notions which apply to all facts' (Whitehead 1978, p.5, 10). Although Whitehead seldom uses the terms, a major component of this is elaborating analogies or metaphors. What is required to elaborate these metaphors is, as Whitehead put it, the 'free play of the imagination, controlled by the requirements of coherence and logic' (Whitehead 1978, p.5). Such imaginative thought is required to supply the differences which direct observation lacks. To ensure that such imaginative constructions have at least some application, 'this construction must have its origin in the generalization of particular factors discerned in particular topics of human interest' (Whitehead 1978, p.5).

What is aimed at is not a set of true sentences, but understanding. 'Truth is a generic quality with a variety of degrees and modes' he wrote in *Adventures of Ideas* (1933, p.241). Whitehead argued, that 'the logicians rigid alternative, "true and false", is … largely irrelevant for the pursuit of knowledge' (1978, p.11). Furthermore, all claims to understanding, including metaphysical claims, are fallible and therefore provisional. Metaphysical categories are 'tentative formulations of the ultimate generalities' (1978, p.8). And these formulations always will be tentative:

> Philosophers can never hope finally to formulate these metaphysical first principles. Weakness of insight and deficiencies of language stand in the way inexorably. Words and phrases must be stretched towards a generality foreign to their ordinary usage; and however such elements of language be stabilized as technicalities, they remain metaphors mutely appealing for an imaginative leap.
>
> (Whitehead 1978, p.5)

Whitehead called for the production of a diversity of metaphysical schemes. While 'we cannot produce that final adjustment of well-defined generalities which constitute a complete metaphysics… we can produce a variety of partial systems of limited generality' (Whitehead 1933, p.145). The resulting rival schemes, inconsistent with each other, but each with its own merits and its own failures, will then warn us of the limitations within which our intuitions are hedged.

Dialectical thinking in post-positivist philosophy of science

Whitehead has provided the best overall characterization and defense of speculative philosophy, and characterization of synthetic thought and dialectical reasoning associated with this, up to the present. However, work by historically oriented philosophers of science reacting against logical positivism and logical empiricism, often based on recovering the insights of Collingwood, Peirce and Whitehead, or more distantly, Schelling and Hegel, focused on and further illuminated specific aspects of dialectical thinking. While consistent with Whitehead's portrayal of speculative thinking, they were able to draw on more detailed studies of the history of thought and society and also on developments in psychology, particularly the Gestalt psychologists and Piaget's genetic epistemology. Even Karl Popper, whose original work differed only slightly from logical positivism (although he was also influenced by the Gestalt psychologist Karl Bühler, his dissertation advisor) and who was hostile to

Hegel's dialectical philosophy, as his philosophy evolved and he focused more on conjectures rather than refutations, came to similar conclusions as Whitehead and to appreciate the parallels between his own work and dialectics. In 'Back to the Presocratics' and 'What is Dialectic' published in *Conjectures and Refutations* (1969) he described how the pre-Socratic philosophers achieved their greatness by responding to perceived defects in the speculations of their predecessors, and then examined the insights of dialecticians in illuminating how later thinkers transcend while incorporating the insights of their predecessors. These developments should have been seen as a vindication of Collingwood, Peirce and Whitehead and of the tradition of dialectical thought deriving from Schelling and Hegel, against all forms of logical empiricism and naïve realism. Instead, the relation between these philosophers of science and the broader tradition of which they were part was ignored, along with their different conception of reasoning (Suppe 1997). Subsequently, logical empiricist or undialectical realist theories of science were revived. This state of philosophy of science was evident in the anthology edited by Boyd, Gasper and Trout, *The Philosophy of Science* (1991).

The revival, defence and development of dialectical thinking in the philosophy of science really began in France in the work of Gaston Bachelard (1884–1962). Bachelard began by rejecting both Cartesian and empiricist forms of foundationalism and explicitly defended a dialectical form of rationality. Science, he argued in *The Philosophy of No* (1969), achieves objectivity by continually questioning its own foundations, most importantly, the postulated objects being investigated, rejecting past positions through the process of correcting them, generating new concepts and ways of thinking which only make sense in opposition to what has been rejected. Consequently, the rationality of science has to be seen as essentially historical and developing through history, and while moving to greater objectivity through criticism of earlier beliefs, this could only be understood as a consequence of the activity and development of subjects. As Mary Tiles characterized Bachelard's orientation to the study of science:

> Bachelard is concerned with scientific thought not so much in the static form of deductively interconnected sets of statements constituting scientific theories, but with the dynamic process of correction, revision, rejection and creation of theories, with the dynamics of the experimental and theoretical practices of science. Again, his concern is not with scientific knowledge as expressed in theories, but with the knowledge and understanding of scientists which enables them to make scientific advances. The knowing subject is never absent from Bachelard's epistemology, and, perhaps most importantly, this subject is historically located.
>
> (Tiles 1984, p.9)

Bachelard argued that scientific theories always have tacit metaphysical foundations, but science develops by questioning these, producing epistemological ruptures or breaks with previous thinking. These ruptures begin with the questioning of common sense and common sense objects, developing new concepts and new theoretical objects and new experimental techniques to investigate these. In this development science has moved away from common sense objects and an ontology of things to an ontology of relations and processes. There were no rules for this development, but, as Tiles put it: 'critical reflection, leading to dialectical generalization, is a paradigmatically rational process, a process of discovery that yields 'justifications as well as innovations' (p.24). Such rational development is not merely a matter of developing more adequate conceptual structures but is an evolution in thought and ways of thinking.

One of Bachelard's major contributions to philosophy was his concept of the 'theoretical object'. In characterizing such objects he acknowledged the centrality of 'objective representations' and the difference between representations and their objects emphasized by Bolzano in his critique of Kant, while still granting a major place to imaginative construction that had been denied by Lotze, Frege and the mainstream tradition of analytic philosophy.

Beginning in the 1950s, Stephen Toulmin, Norwood Russell Hansen and other philosophers of science set out to demolish logical positivism in Britain and USA. They were influenced by the later work of Wittgenstein, but their historical orientation, and in Hansen's case in *Patterns of Discovery* (1958), by Gestalt psychology and Peirce's notion of abduction, aligned their ideas with the tradition of dialectical thinking. Michael Polanyi in *Personal Knowledge* (1958) and other works illuminated a different dimension of science. Clearly influenced by Merleau-Ponty and probably Heidegger and drawing on Gestalt psychology, he greatly advanced our understanding of synthetic thought, elucidating the role of theories, tacit assumptions and tacit knowledge in making sense of explicit claims to knowledge, and the difficult process by which experience is elucidated through theoretical ideas. Although he referred to 'personal knowledge', Polanyi was really showing that the goal of real science is, as Whitehead argued in *Modes of Thought* (1938), 'understanding', and he clarified what this involves. It involves 'indwelling' in theories so that experience is interpreted through these theories, so that we 'indwell' in what we are trying to understand. Whatever is focused upon, is always made sense of against the background that is 'dwelt within' by means of theories, which are also dwelt within. This includes cosmological theories. It is impossible to judge scientific theories without this tacit knowledge, and so it can only develop as a tradition in which advances are judged by other participants within the scientific tradition. It cannot be managed by bureaucracies without being wrecked. Probing these tacit assumptions, Polanyi also pointed out that scientists generally take for granted that experimenting generally involves setting up boundary conditions, which are then ignored. That is, to use Heidegger's terminology, they enframe the world to reveal it as a calculable coherence of forces, ignoring the enframing and the conditions for it. However, these define the domain of validity of theories, and are also important in nature where the boundary conditions are harnessed by higher levels of organization to serve new forms of activity, thereby forming a hierarchy of organizational levels. In this way, Polanyi largely inspired hierarchy theory, later developed in theoretical biology, particularly theoretical ecology.

Thomas Kuhn who was clearly influenced by Hansen and possibly Bachelard and Polanyi, was also influenced by James Conant, who in turn was influenced by Whitehead. He was also influenced by Gestalt psychology and the work of Piaget and his dialectic of assimilation of data and accommodation of the organism. Whether or not he was influenced by Collingwood, one of the important contributions of his famous work on paradigms was again to reveal how subconscious presuppositions can channel, facilitate and also severely constrain thinking over centuries, and how difficult it can be to overcome such presuppositions. He described in great detail in his most important works, *The Copernican Revolution* (1957) and *The Structure of Scientific Revolutions* (1962), the scientific revolution of the Sixteenth and Seventeenth Centuries where previously held deep assumptions were brought into question and replaced, and the radical change in concepts, ways of experiencing and thinking involved in this replacement. He also showed how new scientists are socialized into accepting unquestioningly these concepts and ways of experiencing, thinking and judging as a way of life, and how these then guide their research. His books confirmed Whitehead's claim that science as systematic enquiry is only possible after metaphysical first principles have been established, and that major advances in science cannot be characterized algorithmically through inductive and deductive logic. These philosophers of science inspired more work in the area that has clarified the problems and possibilities of challenging prevailing metaphysical assumptions.

Imré Lakatos in *Proofs and Refutations* (1986) developed a dialectical theory of the development of mathematical concepts, extending the falliblism of Hegel's epistemology to mathematics (p.139n1), and then elaborated a theory of science based on the notion of 'research programs' in an attempt to improve on Kuhn's account of science (Lakatos 1978). In doing so he pointed to the central place of 'hard cores' of these research programs, which are essentially metaphysical assumptions presupposed by and guiding all research (although Lakatos gave no indication of how these were developed in the first place). Programs consist of positive heuristics, indicating how the program is to be advanced, and negative heuristics, how to explain apparent evidence challenging this hard core. Lakatos' aim was to show that through a characterization of the difference between progressive and degenerating research programs, he could provide absolute, universal criteria for which research program to pursue.

Paul Feyerabend, whose understanding of scientific research largely concurred with Lakatos', argued convincingly that no such absolute criteria could be found, showing in *Against Method* (2010) that the history of science reveals the impossibility of specifying a universal, ahistorical method that would guarantee progress. While he claimed to be defending relativism and argued that in science 'anything goes', in fact he was really defending a more consistent dialectical view of science, pointing out the need for theories and research programs to proliferate to expose the failures of each other (a view that had already been argued by Whitehead), and for those committed to any research program to be prepared to respond to challenges to their ideas and to work to overcome objections to it. Only when these conditions are met can scientific research avoid stagnating. What distinguishes genuine science from fake science on Feyerabend's view is the commitment to honestly meeting objections and challenges to the basic ideas the scientist is developing. His guidance for science concurs with the view expressed by Whitehead in his Presidential Address the London Mathematical Association in 1914:

> The art of reasoning consists in getting hold of the subject at the right end, of seizing on the few general ideas that illuminate the whole, and of persistently organizing all subsidiary facts around them. Nobody can be a good reasoner unless by constant practice he has realised the importance of getting hold of the big ideas and hanging on to them like grim death.
>
> (Whitehead 1955)

Again, this corresponds to Alain Badiou's notion of 'fidelity to an event of truth'. Only through such commitment are insights developed and the limits of these general ideas revealed.

The role of metaphors in speculative thought was elucidated by Rom Harré (1970), David Bohm and David Peat (2000, 30ff.) and Mary Hesse (1966). Later, Hesse (1995) explicitly defended metaphors as a major component on dialectical thinking. Following Saunders Mac Lane's observation that all new developments in mathematics could be traced to different practices (counting, measuring, shaping, forming, proving, grouping etc.), George Lakoff (1987, Ch.20) and showed that mathematics can be interpreted as metaphorical elaborations of body schema. With Rafael E. Núñez, Lakoff developed this observation into a general theory of mathematics (Lakoff and Núñez 2000). Noting that through the deployment and development of metaphors more than can be grasped by inductive and deductive logic, Lakoff's colleague Mark Johnson pointed out that formal logic itself, including modal logic, are founded on metaphors (Johnson 1987, p.37ff.). As was noted in the previous chapter, combating the charge that acknowledging such major revolutions in thought affecting our experience, methods and even our ideas about what science is and what are its goals implies relativism, Alasdair MacIntyre in 'Epistemological Crises, Dramatic Narrative and the Philosophy of Science' showed the central role of synoptic narratives in legitimating radically new theories. He showed how new theories provide new perspectives for constructing histories of past ideas that clarify both the successes, failures and *aporias* of earlier theories, and thereby why these new theories, which overcome these failures and *aporias,* are superior. As he argued:

> Wherein lies the superiority of Galileo to his predecessors? The answer is that he, for the first time, enables the work of all his predecessors to be evaluated by a common set of standards. The contributions of Plato,

Aristotle, the scholars at Merton College, Oxford and Padua, the work of Copernicus himself at last all fall into place. Or to put matters in another and equivalent way: the history of late medieval science can finally be cast into a coherent narrative.... What the scientific genius, such as Galileo, achieves in his transitions, then, is not only a new way of understanding nature, but also and inseparably a new way of understanding the old sciences way of understanding... It is from the stand-point of the new science that the continuities of narrative history are reestablished.

(MacIntyre 1977, p.467)

In all cases, these post-positivist philosophers of science confirmed Schelling's and Whitehead's insights into speculative philosophy and further clarified the nature of and importance of synthetic thinking in the quest for knowledge. Having rejected the positivists' conception of rationality, they were charged with relativism, which led to a preoccupation in the philosophy of science with realism, ignoring the solution that Schelling had already provided to defend the role of synthetic thought and realism, overcoming the opposition between Idealism and realism. That these post-positivist philosophers of science were so often misunderstood and misinterpreted as relativists demonstrates the blindness to the tradition of speculative naturalism. Recent developments in the history and philosophy of science centred on the work of Michael Friedman, re-examining Kant and those he influenced, are again recovering the insights of this tradition of philosophy of science. In the long concluding essay to a major anthology devoted to this, Friedman discussed Schelling's contribution to the philosophy of science (Friedman 2010, pp.624–630).

Speculative naturalism versus the naturalism of analytic philosophers

Once the tradition of speculative naturalism is recognized and the nature and importance to it of dialectical thinking, it is possible to judge it in relation to the naturalism of the Quine inspired tradition of analytic philosophy. As noted, for the most part, American analytic philosophers simply ignore speculative naturalists, either not acknowledging their existence or, as with Peirce, misinterpreting their work, seeing them as philosophers attempting the impossible and therefore not to be taken seriously except for their contribution to philosophical analysis. Since they assume that careful analysis will produce indubitable arguments that can be added to the bucket of scientific knowledge, there has been very little engagement between these two traditions, despite the close relationship between Russell and Whitehead. There are two major exceptions, however, the work of Murray Code who has contrasted Peirce and Whitehead on the one hand with Russell and Quine on the other, and Nicholas Rescher who, strongly influenced by Peirce, has defended process metaphysics. Reviewing the work of Peirce, Whitehead, Russell and Quine, Code (1995) argues for the superiority of the former over the latter, and in a more recent work, has revealed the deficiencies in Philip Kitcher's naturalistic philosophy of mathematics. In response to Kitcher's work, Code, originally a mathematician, argues that an adequate naturalism requires the insights of Peirce and Whitehead with their much fuller account of experience and rationality, giving a place to vagueness, feeling, imagination and intuition, and most importantly, requires their speculative theories of nature that give a place to vagueness, feeling, imagination and intuition along with what can be comprehended through mathematics (Code 2005, pp.35–53).[3] Rescher, generally regarded as an analytic philosopher, in *Process Metaphysics* has simply defending process metaphysics as the most promising philosophy to 'articulate the set of concepts and ideational perspectives able to provide a thought-framework for understanding the world about us and our place within it' (Rescher 1996, p.1).

The problem is to understand why the work of Code and Rescher has been ignored by analytic philosophers. As we have seen, analytic philosophers have accepted the exclusion by Frege of the fundamental question that, as Aristotle had argued in *Metaphysics*, had always been the fundamental question of philosophy, more primordial than and presupposed by every other branch of philosophy: What is the nature of being?, a question which must include the first principles and primary factors of primary beings (Aristotle 1975, 1003b, pp.10–19). That is, they have ruled out asking what is self-explanatory being in terms of which all else could be interpreted and explained. Once philosophers have also accepted Frege's claim that logic provides a universal language and redefined philosophy through this, philosophy is confined to formalizing arguments and ignoring all purported arguments that cannot be formalized. More fundamentally, they have dismissed dialectical thinking whereby basic assumptions of traditions of thought could be challenged and replaced. Consequently, efforts such as Code's to reveal and defend the deeper concerns of Peirce and Whitehead and consequently, the reason for their defense of unformalizable aspects of reasoning associated with vagueness and imaginative generalization, can no longer be registered as intelligible arguments. This path has simply been blocked off in such a way that it has become illegitimate to even question this blockage. Quine and his disciples have been able to claim the title 'naturalism' for themselves and mainstream scientists, protected from any questioning of this by strictures accepted by other analytic philosophers on what can be considered valid philosophizing.

Hintikka's work, while challenging such narrowness and making excellent use of synopsis, does not challenge Quine's dogmatic form of naturalism because he does not follow the implications of his work and defend speculative philosophy. Excluding synthesis, philosophy not only rules out any questioning of the current metaphysical assumptions of mainstream reductionist science, but rules out replacing the strictures that rule this out. This has had a massive impact on philosophy departments since analytic philosophers have used their control over educational institutions to discredit philosophers who do not share their assumptions. In one case, McCumber reports, they recommended that the internationally renowned philosophy program at the New School of

Social Research in New York be disaccredited 'on the grounds that it was so far removed from the mainstream of American philosophy as to be overspecialized and sectarian' with Hannah Arendt deemed to be 'an unproductive drone because her works were not cited in important journals such as the *Journal of Philosophy* and *Philosophical Review*' (McCumber 2001, p.51). This intolerance and tunnel vision also has had implications for and affected mathematics and science, since it has influenced the standing of those attempting to question the assumptions of dominant research programs in order to advance radically new ideas, undermining their ability to gain academic appointments and research funding for their work. In this way, the assumptions of the entire culture of modernity have been locked in place, no matter how defective these might appear to the few who have questioned these assumptions.[4]

The weakness of naturalism as conceived by Quine and those he influenced relative to the naturalism of speculative naturalists is manifest in their assumption, which they offer no argument to defend, that mainstream science has found a method of acquiring and accumulating knowledge, and that speculative philosophy is irrelevant to this as well as to everything else. Not only have they devalued or attempted to invalidate the cognitive claims of wide areas of experience that could not be interpreted through current science, they have denied any place to philosophy in questioning the deep assumptions of existing science, or any place for developing alternative research programs. As a leading theoretical physicist, Carlo Rovelli complained, after noting that 'for thirty years we have failed. There hasn't been a major success in theoretical physics in the last few decades':

> The divorce between this strict dialogue between philosophers and sciences is very recent, in the second half of the 20th century. ... There is narrow-mindedness, if I may say so, in many of my colleagues who don't want to learn what's being said in the philosophy of science. There is also a narrow-mindedness in a lot of the areas of philosophy and the humanities, whose proponents don't want to learn about science, which is even more narrow-minded.
>
> (Rovelli 2014, p.215, 227, 228)

Essentially, by identifying naturalism with the view of reality and ambitions of mainstream science, these philosophers have simply embraced the basic assumptions about nature and how it is to be comprehended assumed by reductionist scientists against not only the humanities, and thereby greatly contributed to undermining the humanities – including philosophy, but against the most creative areas in the natural sciences. That is, they have ignored Whitehead's argument that:

> No science can be more secure than the unconscious metaphysics which tacitly it presupposes. The individual thing is necessarily a modification of its environment, and cannot be understood in disjunction. All reasoning,

apart from some metaphysical reference, is vicious. Thus the Certainties of Science are a delusion. They are hedged around with unexplored limitations. Our handling of scientific doctrines is controlled by the diffused metaphysical concepts of our epoch. Even so, we are continually led into errors of expectation. Also, whenever some new mode of observational experience is obtained the old doctrines crumble into a fog of inaccuracies.

(Whitehead 1933, p.154)

Consequently, they not only accepted, but defended the state of our culture where, as Whitehead complained: 'Philosophy has ceased to claim its proper generality, and natural science is content with the narrow round of its methods' (Whitehead, 1929, p.50).

While through their scientism these analytic philosophers have attempted to link their philosophy to the high status of science, and occasionally mathematics, effectively, this has been a form of slow intellectual suicide. It is also obscurantist, reinforcing the obscurantism of mainstream science by crippling the capacity of philosophy to bring this obscurantism into question. As Whitehead noted:

Obscurantism is the refusal to speculate freely on the limitations of traditional methods. It is more than that: it is the negation of the importance of such speculation, the insistence on incidental dangers. A few generations ago the clergy, or to speak more accurately, large sections of the clergy were standing examples of obscurantism. Today their place has been taken by scientists –

By merit raised to that bad eminence.

The obscurantists of any generation are in the main constituted by the greater part of the practitioners of the dominant methodology. Today scientific methods are dominant, and scientists are the obscurantists.

(Whitehead 1929, p.34f.)

Their apologetics for this obscurantism has rendered such analytic philosophers vulnerable to speculative naturalists and scientists aligned with them who have challenged the assumptions of mainstream science, challenges which have succeeded in advancing science.

To appreciate the impact of speculative naturalists and what is wrong with Quinean naturalism it is only necessary to read the work of historians of science. These historians have revealed the immense influence speculative naturalists have had on science and mathematics (Gare 2013b). To begin with, it is necessary to look at the origins of naturalism and what was its relationship to science. 'Naturalism' derives from the Latin *natura* which was coined by the Romans to translate the Greek word *physis*. It was derived from *natus*, 'born', which was the past participle of *nasci* 'to be born' or 'come into being', which is how the Roman philosophers understood the Greek term *physis*. *Physis* could refer to those beings which had their own nature, or collectively to all such beings. It in turn derived from the Greek φύ, 'to bring forth, produce, put forth; to beget, engender; to grow, wax, spring up or forth' (Leclerc 1972, p.102). Aristotle equated it to the immanent part of a growing thing, from which its growth first proceeds. The Ionians were naturalists because they believed that the cosmos was self-creating, growing out of itself, and were concerned to comprehend this self-creation. As Ivor Leclerc characterized their endeavour:

> [T]he Presocratics were endeavouring to find the *archē*, the principle, source, of all things, that is to say, that which is immanent in all and whereby things are what they are, that immanent something which ultimately accounts for 'the all' having the character which it does have.
>
> (Leclerc 1972, p.102)

Originally, this search was virtually equated with philosophy.

Anti-naturalist philosophers were those who offered explanations for the formation of the cosmos in terms of an agent or agents transcending the cosmos, acting as an external force or forces to create order.

Quine's philosophy is neither naturalistic nor anti-naturalistic in the sense of the early Greek philosophers. As we have seen, the quest to characterize the *archē* of beings to make everything intelligible involves posing a question that is ruled out by those, such as Quine, who have followed Frege's strictures on what questions can intelligibly be asked. Instead, Quine passively accepted that nature as characterized by physicists, along with behaviorist psychologists, is simply there to be described by sentences. Without being able to even ask the question What in the most fundamental sense is self-explanatory? (let alone proffer an answer to how the cosmos, including himself with his consciousness of the cosmos, could have been generated), Quine's promotion of naturalism was parasitic upon others who had asked this question. These were the philosophers who made science possible. Quine simply assumed the theoretical objects of mainstream physicists, ignoring their origins in the work of natural philosophers and ruling out the synthetic work involved in developing new, more adequate theoretical objects. Those analytic philosophers who have continued the tradition of Quine while rejecting Quine's strictures on what logical forms are acceptable, and thereby given a place to dispositions, or in some cases, a pre-eminent place to activities rather than objects, are still parasitic on the speculative philosophers who accorded a place to dispositions or activities in their efforts to characterize physical existence. Philosophy has been reduced by these philosophers to describing the world as it had been characterized by scientists developing the insights of earlier philosophers.

As historians of science have shown, it is impossible to understand the development of science either in the Ancient World or in modernity except in relation to the work of speculative philosophers. Leaving aside the Ancient Greeks, Romans, medieval and Renaissance thinkers, Burtt's *The Metaphysical Foundations of Modern Science* (1954) (first published in 1924) and Whitehead's

Science and the Modern World (1932) (first published 1925), research on the Seventeenth Century scientific revolution and the period leading up to this has revealed the extent to which the birth of modern science was essentially the product of speculative work of natural philosophers. These philosophers challenged the Aristotelian framework of concepts and developed radically new concepts in their efforts to make intelligible the physical phenomena they were investigating.[5] The concept of space, for instance, was an invention of the late Renaissance (of Bernardino Telesio and Giordano Bruno) which was taken up and redefined by Newton as a foundational concept of his new celestial mechanics, in place of the atomist notion of void and the Aristotelian notion of place. The concept of space provided a metaphor for developing a new concept of time that could be treated much like a dimension of space. This made possible the development of the new concept of inertia, to replace the concept of impetus. This in turn was associated with the development of a new concept of matter and thereby of bodies as inert, and the idea of laws of motion of these bodies as the basis of all valid explanation. All this provided the framework for developing a new way of describing acceleration mathematically, associated again with a series of radically innovations in mathematical thinking culminating in the development of the calculus. All this was required to explain the observations of the planet Mars and predict its subsequent movements (Gare 1996, Ch.5). Learning about this conceptual revolution is standard fare in early undergraduate courses in the history of science, and makes the dismissal of concepts by Quine and of conceptual frameworks and of the creative work involved in the development of new conceptual frameworks by Davidson appear bizarre.

Work focusing specifically on the natural philosophy of the time has revealed the differences between participants in the scientific revolution, and the extensive arguments over the philosophical assumptions about physical existence underpinning the development of experimental science. This has shown that it is not even possible to properly understand modern science except in relation to the conclusions reached on the basis of the speculative thinking of natural philosophers and the arguments generated between rival speculations about the best concepts to make nature comprehensible, and that these arguments have continuing relevance for current developments in science. Furthermore, it has become evident that modern science is far less coherent than it appears. While Newtonian physics won the day against followers of Descartes and Leibniz, scientists influenced by the latter thinkers continued as minor traditions and influenced the subsequent development of science. Earlier natural philosophers such as Bruno and Galileo were never entirely eclipsed, and Aristotelian thought has had a continuing influence in modern science. Newton himself had a more subtle conception of nature than his later followers since he did not believe that there could be action at a distance and regarded space as the sensorium of the deity and that through space the deity was continually active (McMullin 1978). This led James Clerk Maxwell to enlist Newton's philosophical reflections to support his field theories against Newtonians (Harman 1998, p.172). To understand Einstein's work it is necessary to appreciate the continuing influence on him of Newtonian science, but also of Galileo's arguments concerning relativity, the revival by him of a Leibnizian conception of relational space-time when he first formulated the special theory of relativity, which he abandoned for a more Cartesian conception of physical existence after Hermann Minkowski developed a geometrical representation of the theory. This assisted Einstein in developing his general theory, replacing Euclidean geometry with Riemannian geometry, on the basis of which he claimed that the experience of temporal becoming is an illusion. As G.J. Whitrow (1980) argued, Einstein's views were neither consistent nor necessarily the final word on these theories, however, and there are many proponents of the earlier Leibnizian interpretation of his work, or Schellingian interpretations, each defending the reality of temporal becoming, which seems to be required with the reintroduction of cosmic time.

Other theorists have re-examined Aristotle's philosophy of nature to reveal how it had been misrepresented by medieval Aristotelians, who were really neo-Platonists, and to highlight deficiencies in post-Newtonian science. They have then set about recovering some of these Aristotelian insights, most importantly, Aristotle's notion of causation and the place he accorded final causes.[6] These debates are not simply a matter of interpretation, and are central to theoretical disputes that are influencing directions in empirical research. Lee Smolin's challenge to mainstream physics in his book *Time Reborn: From the Crisis of Physics to the Future of the Universe* published in 2013 is an example of this. The works of the mathematician René Thom and the biomathematician Robert Rosen, influenced by Aristotle's arguments against Pythagorean thought, were directed at creating a mathematics of qualities that could give a place to final causes (Aubin 2004, Ch.3, Gare 2008a). These were conceived of by Thom as 'attractors'. In giving a place to final causes, these mathematicians are transcending the opposition between Aristotelian thought and Pythagorean Platonism by defending Aristotelian concepts through mathematics. With such historically oriented speculative thought among mathematicians and scientists, we now have the peculiar situation described by Joseph Esposito where: 'Since [Peirce's] time modern science has become increasingly creative, philosophical, and speculative, while philosophy, on the other hand, has lost its sense of quest and participation in the activity of science' (Esposito 1980, p.5).

Speculative naturalism and post-Newtonian science: the Schellingian tradition

It is against the background of this historical work on the scientific revolution that the significance of Schelling's work becomes fully apparent. Schelling challenged Newtonian physics because of its incapacity to account for life, let alone consciousness, radicalizing Kant's dynamism as put forward in *Metaphysical Foundations of Natural Science* and developed his conception of life as put forward in the *Critique of Judgment*. Here Kant defined organic bodies as bodies in which the parts 'combine into the unity of a whole because they are reciprocally cause and effect of their form' and 'the idea of the whole should conversely (reciprocally) determine the form and combination of all the parts' (Kant 1987, §65, p.252). An organism then is 'both an *organized* and a *self-organized* being' in which the parts produce each other both in their form and in their combination (Kant 1987, §65, p.253). Schelling generalized this to construe the entire universe as self-organizing processes (Heuser-Kessler 1992). In *First Outline of a System of the Philosophy of Nature* he argued for a speculative physics based on a conception of physical existence as activity or productivity, opposed forces and 'limiting', uniting the study of light, electricity and magnetism (Schelling, 2004). Nature then consists of 'productivity-products' or dynamical processes. On this basis, Schelling attempted to show how all the concepts of physics, including force, causation, space and time, could be made intelligible. Based on this new physics, chemicals and living organisms would be understood as products of nature formed by limiting of activity (productivity) through either passive (in the case of chemistry) or in the case of life, actively achieved, balances of opposing forces. Schelling argued that to actively maintain a balance of forces, organisms must define their environments as their worlds to which they then respond accordingly (Schelling 2004, p.106ff.). These ideas were used to justify an evolutionary cosmology.

Those influenced by Schelling, who included Hans Christian Oersted and Bernhardt Riemann, and in Britain a circle of scientists and mathematicians around Samuel Taylor Coleridge, including the mathematician William Hamilton and the scientist Michael Faraday, succeeded in this project. Although these physicists have had difficulty freeing themselves from Newtonian assumptions that have rendered real creativity unintelligible, it is the physics based on field theory (further developed by Maxwell, Einstein and others) and the notion of valency in chemistry that underpins much of post-Newtonian science, while the notion of actively maintained homeostasis is now central to biology (Esposito 1971, Ch.2). Schelling's notion of universal productivity also inspired the postulation of the first law of thermodynamics, and Schelling anticipated systems theory, cybernetics, complexity theory and hierarchy theory (Heuser-Kessler 1992; Gare 2011a). Defending and extending Kant's constructivist philosophy of mathematics, Schelling developed ideas on mathematics that influenced Hermann Grassmann (Otte 2011). Echoing Schelling, Grassmann argued that philosophy and mathematics are different and complementary, writing:

> The contrast between the general and the particular ... produces the division of the formal sciences into dialectics and mathematics. The first is a philosophical science, since it seeks the unity in all thought, while mathematics has the opposite orientation in that it regards each individual thought as a particular.
>
> (Grassmann 1995, p.24)

As Grassmann's biographer Hans-Joachim Petsche wrote, 'Hermann Grassmann assumed that thinking is the activity of uniting, opposing and equating, or conjoining and separating: a dialectical process' (Petsche 2009, p.235). He was not only the father of multidimensional space and vector and tensor algebra central to modern physics, but anticipated the development of Category Theory, one of the most active fields in current mathematics. As William Lawvere, a major figure in the development of Category Theory, wrote:

> In several key connections in the foundations of geometrical algebra Grassmann makes significant use of the dialectical philosophy of 150 years ago. ... Grassmann in his philosophical introduction describes the two-fold division of formal sciences, that is, the science of thinking, into dialectics and mathematics. He briefly describes dialectics as seeking the unity in all things, and he describes mathematics as the art and practice of taking each thought in its particularity and pursuing it to the end. There is a need for an instrument which will guide students to follow in a unified way both of these activities, passing from the general to the particular and from the particular to the general. ... I believe that the theory of mathematical categories ... can serve as such an instrument. ... Looking more closely into Grassmann, Stephen Schanuel and I found numerous ways in which it could be justified to say that Grassmann was a pre-cursor of category theory.
>
> (Lawvere 1996, p.255)

Schelling's speculative naturalism inspired the tradition of process metaphysic that has been central to more recent advances in science (Gare 2011a). The work of Peirce, Bergson, Bogdanov and Whitehead can be seen as expressions of a renaissance of this tradition, a renaissance that was marginalized under the influence of analytic philosophy but had an enduring influence on science and is now being revived at present in what could be a new renaissance. Also, as already noted, Bogdanov's tektology almost certainly influenced von Bertalanffy, and through him, systems theory. Logic and set theory beloved by analytic philosophers is proving increasingly irrelevant to understanding advances in contemporary mathematics, and mathematicians attempting to provide a synthetic theory of mathematics adequate to this task have turned back to Peirce's philosophy to provide this, and aligned themselves with Category Theory (Zalamea 2012, Ch.3, 5; Moore 2010). However, it has been the works of Bergson, Whitehead and Peirce which have been the main points of reference for those defending this Schellingian tradition of natural philosophy with Whitehead and Bergson coming into prominence in the late 1960s through to the 1980s, largely through the work of C.H. Waddington in Britain and John Cobb Jr. and David Ray Griffin in USA (Waddington 2010; Cobb Jr., and Griffin, 1976; Griffin 1986), while inspired by Thomas Sebeok, Jesper Hoffmeyer, and Kalevi Kull, Peirce's natural philosophy, integrated with the ideas of Jacob von Uexküll, has been vigorously promoted by biosemioticians in more recent decades (Perron et al. 2000, Hoffmeyer 1993, Kull 2009).

Bergson's philosophy has been shown to have promise for interpreting and integrating relativity theory and quantum theory (Čapek 1971). Whitehead's ideas have also been a major influence on physics, chemistry, post-reductionist biology and neuroscience (Eastman and Keaton 2004; Henning and Scarfe 2013). David Bohm, an original natural philosopher in his own right as well as a theoretical physicist, developed a version of process metaphysics in order to overcome the incoherencies and deficiencies of quantum mechanics (Bohm 1980; Bohm and Peat 2000). Henry Stapp's interpretation of quantum mechanics, which is then used to develop a concept of mind and consciousness, draws on Whitehead's analysis of actual occasions as prehensions of prior acts in a novel but unified way (Stapp 2006, Ch.13). Recently, the quantum physicist Brian Josephson has invoked Peirce's work on semiotics to interpret quantum theory, and thereby contribute to overcoming reductionism in biology (Josephson 2013). Bergson and Whitehead were a major influence on Ilya Prigogine's work on far from equilibrium thermodynamic systems which has been central to the development of complexity theory and post-reductionist biology (Prigogine 1980). The claim by Ilya Prigogine and Isabelle Stengers that the study of dissipative structures through non-linear thermodynamics heralded a new alliance between science and the humanities (Prigogine and Stengers 1984), should be treated as a proclamation of the triumph of Schellingian speculative naturalism over Newtonian science.

Similar ideas have been defended recently by Roberto Mangabeira Unger and Lee Smolin in *The Singular Universe and the Reality of Time,* acknowledging Bergson as a precursor. They call for a reinvention of natural philosophy focusing on nature, that is, not science, but the world itself. Dialectically related to science, and 'unlike much of the now established philosophy of science', the intentions of natural philosophy 'may be revisionist, not merely analytic or interpretive' (Unger and Smolin 2015, p.76). Their radical revision, echoing Schelling, Peirce, Bergson and Whitehead, is to take time as creative causal process as fundamental to being. This involves inverting the relationship in cosmology between mathematics, through which we explain structures and their transformations, and history in which we grasp temporal becoming. As Unger put it:

> We are accustomed by the dominant tradition of physics, established as the supreme model of successful science, to regard historical explanation as ancillary to structural explanation [through mathematics]. On the view that we here defend, this hierarchy must be reversed: structure results from history. Historical explanation is, thus, more fundamental than structural explanation. Cosmology affirms the ambition to be the most comprehensive natural science when it understands itself as a historical science first, and as a structural [mathematical] science only second.
>
> (Unger and Smolin 2015, p.42)

Whitehead was a major influence on the mathematico-physico-chemical morphologists led by Joseph Needham and C.H. Waddington. Needham integrated ideas from Engels and Whitehead to develop the notion of hierarchical order in theoretical biology. Waddington's core concept of 'chreod' as 'self-stabilizing time-path' central to epigenesis, modeled mathematically by René Thom as the basis of catastrophe theory, was inspired by Whitehead's concept of concrescence and D'Arcy Thompson's notion of form (Waddington 2010, pp.72–81). Waddington's ideas have been further developed by Brian Goodwin (among others) who examined the temporal organization of cells and morphogenesis (Goodwin 1963; Goodwin 1976; Goodwin 1994). The study of symbiosis in ecosystems was also stimulated by Whitehead who observed that Darwin had treated the environment that determines survival of organisms as fixed, whereas it is modified by organisms, and it is through augmenting rather than undermining their environmental conditions of existence that organisms survive.[7] Whitehead's philosophy has also been drawn upon by Nicholas Georgesçu-Roegen, Herman Daly and John Cobb Jr. to critique mainstream economics and lay the foundations for ecological economics (Gare 2008b).

Schelling's notion of organisms having worlds did not have any direct influence on subsequent thinkers, but the biosemioticians such as Kalevi Kull and Jesper Hoffmeyer, influenced by Jacob von Uexküll and C.S. Peirce, have rediscovered this insight and are making rapid progress in their research on this basis (Barbieri 2008; Favareau 2010; Emmeche and Kull 2011; Schilhab, Stjernfelt and Deacon 2012). For such thinkers, life is the action of signs and humans are the symbolic species. Developing these ideas, they have embraced the transdiscilinary work of Gregory Bateson who himself was influenced by Peirce and Whitehead (Hoffmeyer 2008, p.5). Building on biosemiotics and integrating it with Bateson's work on cybernetics and his definition of information as a difference that makes a difference, along with Heinz von Foerster's work on second order cybernetics, Søren Brier has elaborated a unifying non-mechanistic conceptual framework of cyber-semiotics, bridging the gap between the natural and human sciences (2010). This work has been augmented by the rediscovery by Howard Pattee and Robert Rosen, and following them, Timothy Allen, Stanley Salthe and Alicia Juarrero, of Schelling's insight that emergence involves new limits on activity, or as Pattee and Rosen referred to these, constraints. Pattee, originally a theoretical physicist before moving into theoretical biology, was concerned to explain the emergence of hierarchical orders of control and symbols. He developed Michael Polanyi's conception of hierarchy based on the observation that deterministic laws presuppose and operate within boundary conditions, and higher level orders exploit the boundary conditions produced by lower level orders (Polanyi 1958; Polanyi 1969). Pattee developed this by using Heinrich Hertz's development of Helmholtz's theory of perception in terms of signs into a theory of images and symbols and his work on different forms of constraint in physics, including non-holonomic constraints where behavior is the result of configuration (Ferrari and Stamatescu 2002). Pattee focused on control in organisms and the symbols required for this. He showed that constraints can be facilitative or enabling, creating new forms of existence with new possibilities. As he wrote in *Hierarchy Theory: The Challenge of Complex Systems*:

> The constraints of the genetic code on ordinary chemistry make possible the diversity of living forms. At the next level, the additional constraints of genetic suppressors make possible the integrated development of functional organs and multi-cellular individuals. At the highest levels of control we know that legal constraints are necessary to establish a free society, and constraints of spelling and syntax are prerequisites for free expression of thought.
>
> (Pattee 1973, p.73f.)

These ideas were further developed and Pattee's classic papers are now available in *Laws, Language and Life* (Pattee and Rączascek-Leonardi 2012).

Stan Salthe, in major works of synthesis, integrated Prigogine's non-linear thermodynamics, Pattee's hierarchy theory, Peircian semiotics, dialectical materialism and endophysics as developed by David Finkelstein, Otto Rössler and George Kampis (Salthe 1985; Salthe 1993: Salthe 2005; 2012; Vijver, Salthe and Delpos 1998). Endophysics, again echoing Schelling, acknowledges that scientists are participating in the world they are observing and striving to comprehend, and since this is ultimately inescapable, knowledge of systems from the inside has to be seen as more basic than 'external' knowledge of systems (Kampis and Weibel 1998; Rössler 1998). Part of the problem with the view of emergence through constraints is that it assumes that fractionated components exist self-sufficiently and are somehow constrained to form part of the emergent system. This is associated with a tendency to see emergent entities as supervening over smaller entities, ignoring the environment in which these entities were able to exist in the first place, and then the new environment created by the emergent system. Salthe corrected this view, pointing out that emergence, in both evolution and development, is associated with interpolation between processes of smaller and larger scales and faster and slower rate processes, modifying both the longer and the shorter scale processes. Granting a place to scalar hierarchies was then used to characterize and explain final causes. As Salthe observed: 'constraints from the higher level not only help to select the lower level-trajectory but also pull it into its future at the same time. Top-down causality is a form of final causality' (Salthe 1993, p.270).

Combining Peirce's semiotics with Jacob von Üexkull's biology to explain how all organisms, including plants, define their environments as meaningful surrounding worlds (*Umwelten*) and then the sequence of more complex worlds (perception worlds, action worlds and inner-worlds) leading up to and including humans' with-worlds (*Mitwelten*) and self-worlds (*Eigenwelten*), biosemioticians have effectively overcome Cartesian dualism and shown what is involved in the development of human culture and reflective consciousness very much in accordance with the insights of Schelling (Gare 2002a; Gare 2009). Influenced by Salthe, Alicia Juarrero in *Dynamics in Action: Intentional Behavior as a Complex System* (2002) has made highly original contributions to complexity theory and hierarchy theory in making intelligible on naturalistic foundations intentional behavior and consciousness.

In developing their ideas on cognition, Francisço Varela and Evan Thomson, influenced by Merleau-Ponty, followed a similar intellectual path, a path that is now embraced by philosophers and cognitive scientists who are attempting to 'naturalize' phenomenology (Varela, Thompson and Rosch 1993; Thompson 2007; Gallagher and Schmicking 2010; Simeonov, Gare and Rosen 2015). These philosopher-scientists have noted developments in the natural sciences that manifest the influence of speculative philosophers, and shown why it is necessary to free science and philosophy from the entrenched assumptions of reductionist science and align science with the humanities. Frederik Stjernfelt in *Diagrammatology: An Investigation on the Borderlines of Phenomenology, Ontology, and Semiotic* (2007) has taken this further by integrating Peircian semiotics and phenomenology. At the same time, this has allowed the insights of the humanities to contribute to science. Through such work, the affinities and complementary nature of the work of all those philosophers who have taken the reality of mind seriously and attempted to reform science on the basis of a conception of physical existence consistent with this reality, have been revealed, as has been pointed out in Kauffman and Gare, 'Beyond Descartes and Newton: Recovering life and humanity' (2015).

Another speculative naturalist, Rom Harré, initially inspired by the dynamism of Roger Boscovich (1711–1787), a natural philosopher who had attempted to overcome the opposition between Newton's and Leibniz's philosophies, has critiqued mainstream psychology and contributed to the development of a rigorous humanistic psychology, and his onetime student, Roy Bhaskar developed a dialectical critical realism that has contributed significantly to the defence and development of transdisciplinary post-reductionist social science, including economics. Bhaskar has deployed this perspective to the problem of dealing with climate change (Bhaskar 2010) and his work on this has been taken further by Jenneth Parker (2014). Bohm's natural philosophy developed as part of his effort to overcome problems in quantum mechanics has subsequently influenced work in biology and neuroscience (Bohm and Peat 2004). Mae-Wan Ho (2008), Karl Pibram (1991), Paavo Pylkkänen (2007)– have each drawn on and developed Bohm's ideas to advance biology and neuroscience. Speculative naturalism is now flourishing among the most original scientists struggling to overcome the deficiencies of mainstream physics (S. Rosen 2008) and comprehend the complexity of life (Simeonov, Smith and Ehresmann 2012). This is inspiring new development in holistic biomathematics, or as Plamen Simeonov has characterized this in a major anthology and special editions of the journal *Progress in Biophysics & Molecular Biology* on this, 'integral biomathics' (Simeonov, Matsuno, and Root-Bernstein, 2013; Simeonov, Gare, and Rosen 2015). The apparently analytic approach of proponents of natural philosophy associated with the philosophy of science referred to in the introduction, such as Mark Bickhard, Cliff Hooker and Alicia Juarrero, are contributing to philosophy by aligning themselves with such revolutionary scientists, contributing to advancing this new conceptual revolution. For instance, Bickhard (2004) defends emergence based on rigorous analytic arguments, but his work depends on the synthetic work of process metaphysicians, as he acknowledges.[8] Confronted with arguments by Jaegwon Kim against the reality of emergence, he had to reveal Kim's implicit metaphysical assumptions and point out that without these, which process metaphysicians had already rejected, his arguments carried no weight.

In short, by refusing to subordinate philosophy to science or to be overawed by past achievements of science, being prepared to question the foundations and assumptions of mainstream science and to elaborate radically new ways of thinking about nature, speculative naturalists, unlike analytic philosophers, have had and continue to have a profound and creative influence on science. While analytic philosophers are apologists for 'normal' science, speculative naturalists have been and are essential to 'revolutionary' science. Not only have analytic philosophers failed to contribute to science, their promotion of scientism and their fawning attitude towards scientists and mathematicians has failed to impress their idols. Gian-Carlo Rota, a mathematician and physicist in post-WWII USA, friend of John von Neumann and Stanislav Ulam and a professor of applied mathematics and philosophy at MIT, wrote in 'The Pernicious Influence of Mathematics Upon Philosophy':

> The fake philosophical terminology of mathematical logic has misled philosophers into believing that mathematical logic deals with the truth in the philosophical sense. But this is a mistake. ... The snobbish symbol-dropping found nowadays in philosophical papers raises eyebrows among mathematicians, like someone paying his grocery bill with Monopoly money.
>
> (Rota 1996, p.93)

The most influential US mathematician of the Twentieth Century, Saunders Mac Lane was also unimpressed with these philosophers, noting that 'current publications in the philosophy of mathematics, from Putnam to Quine to Wang, show little new insight and no new input from mathematics' (Mac Lane 1981, p.463).

To fill this gap, leading scientists and mathematicians are extending their work into philosophy and taking up and contributing to the tradition of speculative naturalism, filling the vacuum created by academic philosophers who are abrogating their responsibilities. Joseph Needham, Michael Polanyi, Ludwig von Bertalanffy, David Bohm, Ilya Prigogine and Robert Rosen towards the end of the Twentieth Century and Murray Code, Howard Pattee, Stan Salthe, Joseph Earley, Kalevi Kull, Jesper Hoffmeyer, Stuart Kauffman, Robert Ulanowicz, Mae-Wan Ho, George Lakoff and Donald Mikulecky in the present are obvious examples of this, but this is nothing new. Peirce and Whitehead were originally mathematicians and scientists before becoming philosophers.

Speculative naturalism versus speculative materialism/realism: Alain Badiou or Robert Rosen

Not all efforts to revive speculative thought have come from speculative naturalists or speculative idealists, however. In recent years another intellectual movement has developed within philosophy to revive speculation. Its proponents have characterized themselves as speculative materialists (or speculative realists). While there are great differences between them, what unifies them is opposition to 'correlationism', that is, the doctrine that, as Quentin Meillassoux put it, 'consists in disqualifying the claim that it is possible to consider the realms of subjectivity and objectivity independently of one another', a doctrine originating in Kant. In opposition to correlationism, these philosophers are reviving the distinction between the sensible that 'only exists as a subject's relation to the world' and 'mathematizable properties of the object' that 'are exempt from the constraint of such a relation' and 'are effectively in the object in the way in which I conceive them…' (Meillassoux 2012, p.3, 5). Speculative materialism has gained some traction, and it is in contrast to this that the distinctive significance and implications of new developments in speculative naturalism can be understood.

By far the most important of the speculative materialists (leaving aside Slavoj Žižek, who despite his support for speculative materialists, could never be taken to be aligned with pre-Kantian thought) is the French philosopher Alain Badiou who is now also commonly seen as one of the world's foremost defenders of Marxism. According to Badiou, philosophy invents itself by violating itself, by transforming its terms – its concepts, questions and problems, and it can succeed only if it remains exposed to itself and its own violence. That is, philosophy should be attuned to its origins if it hopes to continue being philosophical. He has taken a stand against what he argues are the three main schools of philosophy: hermeneutics, the analytic orientation and postmodernism, each of which has concluded that the metaphysics of truth has become impossible, that language is the crucial site of thought, and that consequently the question of meaning replaces the question of truth (Badiou 2005b, p.31ff.). His own position, which could be called 'Platonic Marxism', derives from structuralism, although it contains existentialist themes that could have come straight from the early work of Sartre. He began his philosophical career as a follower of Althusser and Jacques Lacan, but has defended his position from a mathematical perspective. He has also embraced elements of Bachelard's philosophy of science and mathematics. His work involves simultaneously privileging the status of mathematics to the centre of philosophy while showing that through mathematics it is possible to theorise novel events such as, but not only, the epistemological ruptures or breaks as characterized by Bachelard.

On the basis of set theory, Badiou argued that situations are inconsistent multiplicities and must be presented as inconsistent. All multiples, he argued in Section II (Hegel) and Section III of *Logics of Worlds: Being and Event II* (2009), must themselves consist of multiples without there being a total multiple. There is no 'whole' as this was defended most rigorously by Hegel. In every situation there is also the being of the 'nothing' which cannot be presented, but is involved in constituting a situation (the Sartrean element in Badiou's thinking, although it could be taken as going back to Anaximander's concept of the *apeiron,* the unlimited). It is because situations are multiple that there can be novel events where a possibility is embraced as a truth. For Badiou 'a truth is that by which "we", of the human species, are committed to a trans-specific procedure, a procedure which opens us to the possibility of being Immortals. A truth is thus undoubtedly an experience of the inhuman' (Badiou 2009, p.71). It is inhuman because it involves the construction of an infinite set. A truth procedure is the process by which a truth is developed in a situation in which there is a decision to recognize within a situation an event. An example of this was the rebellion by Spartacus where the affirmative thoughts of slaves countered the power of the state which had no place for such affirmation, just as in the present an event of truth would be to take a stand against the circuits of Capital that demand the destruction of public services (Badiou 2009, p.69). Emerging from this, Badiou argued for fidelity to events of truth. This concurs with Whitehead's injunction to seize on big ideas that illuminate the whole and then to hang on to them like grim death, but this injunction is extended into ethics and politics. In his most widely read and most accessible work, *Ethics: An Essay on the Understanding of Evil* (2001, p.41) Badiou defended an heroic ethics of fidelity to such events of truth, a post-Cartesian decision and commitment to these events against forces trying to suppress them, but without totalizing the recasting of ontology occasioned by such events. As the translator of Badiou's *Ethics,* Peter Hallward, summed up Badiou's project in his Introduction to this work:

> Badiou's philosophy seems to expose and make sense of the potential for radical innovation (revolution, invention, transfiguration …) in every situation. Simplifying things considerably, we might say that he divides the sphere of human action into two overlapping but sharply differentiated sub-spheres: (a) the 'ordinary' realm of established interests and differences, of approved *knowledges* that serve to name, recognize and *place* consolidated identities; and (b) an 'exceptional' realm of singular innovations or *truths,* which persist only through the militant proclamation of those rare individuals who constitute themselves as *subjects* of a truth, as the 'militants' of their cause.
>
> (Hallward 2001, p.viii)

Not all commitment is connected to truth, however. Evil is also an event in a situation, but as with the Nazis, it is an event that is not universally addressed and therefore is incapable of any truth.

Badiou characterizes his work as a philosophy of mathematics in the grand style in opposition to philosophy of mathematics in the little style. The little style is associated 'philosophy of mathematics' which treats it as an object for philosophical scrutiny. In doing so, it 'strives to dissolve the ontological sovereignty of mathematics, its aristocratic self-sufficiency, its unrivalled mastery, by confining its dramatic, almost baffling existence to a stale compartment of academic specialization'. By contrast, 'The grand style is entirely different. It stipulates that mathematics provides a direct illumination of philosophy, rather than the opposite, and that this illumination is carried out through a forced or even violent intervention at the core of these issues' (Badiou 2004a, p.3, 7). Most importantly, Badiou has defended the centrality of mathematics to philosophy, claiming that although mathematicians do not know this, mathematics is ontology. He reformulated the classic concepts of ontology – being, relations and qualities – in mathematical terms. Examples of practitioners the grand style are Descartes, Spinoza, Kant, Hegel and Lautrèamont. Badiou also identified himself with a tradition of 'mathematizing idealism' which included Brunschvicg, Cavaillès, Lautman, Desant, Althusser and Lacan, in opposition to another tradition running through Bergson, Canguilhem, Foucault, Simondon and Deleuze which he characterized as 'vitalist mysticism' (Badiou 2009, p.7). Effectively, as Sakari Hänninen (2015, p.217f.) argued, Badiou has aligned himself with Parmenides against Heraclitus, focusing on Being while excluding Becoming. This reflects an alignment not only with mathematics, but also with physics against biology, which he associated with 'democratic materialism'. Elsewhere, he wrote that 'Biology, for the time being, is thus nothing but a collection of findings [*trouvailles*] anarchically correlated to a powerful apparatus of experimentation' (Badiou 2004b, 223). The rejection of 'vitalist mysticism' and denigration of biology goes along with a critical attitude to the very idea of nature. 'Nature Does not Exist', he argued in *Being and Event*, because 'a new theorem of ontology declares that such a set is not compatible with the axioms of the multiple, and could not be admitted as existent within the frame of onto-logy. Nature has no sayable being' (Badiou 2005a, p.140).

This philosophy is opposed to speculative naturalism on a number of grounds, beginning with its questioning of the very idea of nature. More fundamentally, it is assumed in this questioning that for nature to exist it would have to be a denumerable set, denying Schelling's claim that there is an unprethinkable Being preceding all thought, that as such, could never be fully grasped as an object of thought. Badiou's philosophy goes along with assuming an ontology of 'definite and distinct objects of our intuition or of our thought', as Cantor described what could be collected into a set, an assumption criticized as by Castoriadis (who quoted this passage) in 'The Logic of Magmas and the Question of Autonomy' (Castoriadis 1997a, p.290) as part of the 'ensemblistic-identitary' logic that must be assumed if ontology is defined through mathematics. This then renders human freedom almost unintelligible. In arguing this, Badiou is defending a form of Platonism, and belongs to that tradition of philosophy criticized by Hintikka which claims to be providing a *Lingua Universalis*, a universal language such that it is impossible to acknowledge anything not characterizable through it. Speculative naturalism, more Aristotelian than Platonist in its conception of mathematics, is aligned with what Badiou categorizes derogatorily as 'life mysticism', and biology is privileged rather than denigrated. Speculative naturalism as post-Kantian does not reject correlationism, but radicalizes it by situating the knowing, self-conscious subject not only within society but within and as part of nature, reconceiving nature to make this intelligible. From the perspective of speculative naturalism, speculative materialism as exemplified by Badiou is a return to pre-Kantian approaches to philosophy of Archimedean Platonists such as Galileo, while speculative naturalism elevates the role accorded to the subject and synthesis and maintains (as James Bradley put it in 'Philosophy and Trinity'): 'self-synthesis to be a real and universal feature of things, with the corollary that all things stand in a communicative relation to one another by way of their antecedent conditions and subsequent relations' (Bradley 2012, p.159). Humanity is seen as an emergent phenomenon with unique characteristics and unique abilities to develop art, literature, philosophy, mathematics and science, but even in developing these, as always participating in the creative becoming of nature which, as Schelling argued, must be conceived as the evolving process that we as sentient, self-conscious humans have evolved from and within.

However, speculative naturalism and speculative materialism are not entirely antithetical. Proponents of speculative naturalism are committed to upholding the quest for truth, and while mathematics is not given the exalted status accorded to it by Badiou, in being committed to developing an ontology adequate to all dimensions of experience, speculative naturalists regard advances in mathematics as being at least as important for philosophy as does Badiou. It is taken for granted that philosophy must recognize the demonstrated comprehensibility of much of the world through mathematics along with conscious beings who can develop and deploy mathematics to this end. Schelling, Peirce and Whitehead can also be seen as developing philosophies of mathematics in the grand style, with Whitehead having broken with the little style of philosophizing with which he had previously been engaged. Schelling inspired many of the great advances in mathematics, and both Peirce and Whitehead made major contributions to mathematics. What is significant about the mathematical ideas developed within this tradition is that in their opposition to Cartesian dualism they were inspired by the quest to do justice to the reality of life. In doing so, they have differed fundamentally from Badiou in rejecting the possibility of identifying mathematics with ontology, or assuming that mathematics ever could be developed as a universal language to define every aspect of being. For Whitehead, to believe that this is even possible is to commit the fallacy of misplaced concreteness. Just as Hintikka differed from Quine in rejecting the possibility of developing logic as a universal language, the speculative naturalists differ from Badiou by being aligned with a tradition of mathematical thought which rejects even the aspiration to develop mathematics as a universal system capable of defining all aspects of being.[9] Consequently, these philosophers tend to be interested in different developments in mathematics, most importantly, the extension theory of Hermann Grassmann whose work in mathematics was indirectly inspired by Schelling, as Michael Otte (2011) argued and as we have already noted. And as William Lawvere (1996) has pointed out, Grassmann's work, which was designed to be a general foundation for all mathematics, anticipated the development of Category Theory that is currently challenging set theory as the foundation for all mathematics.

The figure that most clearly highlights the difference between speculative naturalism and speculative materialism is Robert Rosen, both a major theoretical biologist and mathematician who made a number of forays into philosophy.[10] Rosen pointed out in a *Festschrift* for the theoretical physicist David Bohm that: 'In every confrontation between universal physics and special biology, it is physics which has always had to give ground' (Rosen 1987, p.315). Rosen's work was distinguished by a determination to develop mathematical models adequate to life as it appears to us, rather than imposing a research program coming from the physical sciences onto biology. He contributed to the development of and utilized Category Theory to examine the assumptions of Aristotelian and Newtonian science and the relationship between Newton's assumptions and the mathematics deployed by him and his successors. He revealed thereby how science had locked itself into a path that denied the objective reality of function, and more fundamentally, of final causes, and thereby excluded the fundamental question 'What is Life?' Rosen showed how reductionists avoid this question by constructing a small surrogate universe of various fractionated components of organisms that can be explained by methods that have sometimes worked in other areas of science, and then taking these isolated fractions as the surrogate for the whole living system. They then identify science with the methods used to investigate these fractions. One of the most central problems, Rosen argued, is that Newton had eliminated any role for constraints associated with configurations. Life involves 'non-holonomic' constraints that cannot be expressed as a global relation among configuration variables. Configuration determines what happens, not initial and boundary conditions. As noted, this notion of non-holonomic constraints, echoing Schelling's notion of 'limiting', was also developed by Howard Pattee and further developed by Stan Salthe and others and is now central to the development of bio-semiotics inspired by Peirce.

Recognizing a place for final causes, Rosen set out to model anticipatory systems, systems which do not simply respond to their environments but anticipate and respond to what will happen in the future. Modeling anticipatory systems involves modeling systems that produce their own components (in accordance with how Kant and Schelling understood living organisms) based on models of themselves (as von Neumann argued). Such systems, Rosen showed, can be represented through synthetic models in which functional components are the direct product of the system. Genuine complex systems require multiple formal descriptions which are not derivable from each other, to capture all their properties. That is, for such systems there must be multiple models of which none is the largest model from which all the others can be derived. Furthermore, it is impossible to fully model the context or ambience of such a system. The example Rosen produced to illustrate this was his metabolism, repair, reproduction models (the M-R- systems). These models consist of three algebraic maps, one of which represents the efficient cause of metabolism in a cell, another, the efficient cause of repair (that repairs damage to the metabolic processes), and the third represents replication which repairs damage to the repair process. Each of these maps has one of the other two as a member of its co-domain, and is itself a member of the co-domain of the remaining map. The maps thus form a loop of mutual containment.

In developing these ideas Rosen was rethinking the nature of mathematics and its relation to the world. He argued 'that mathematics took a disastrous wrong turn some time in the sixth century B.C' (Rosen 2000, p.63), identifying effectiveness with computability. He argued that mathematics should be understood as a way of modeling, and used Category Theory to characterize this. Category Theory, unlike set theory, is essentially holistic, focusing on patterns and providing the means to model one domain of mathematic by another. This enables us to understand what is involved in modeling what is in the world. In doing so, it highlights the way in which modeling always involves simplification of that which is modeled. Modeling is really only a special instance of analogical thinking, ubiquitous in everyday life where the study of one system is used to learn something about another that is judged to be congruent with it. As Peirce argued, mathematical modeling is essentially diagrammatic reasoning, in which mathematical 'diagrams' are studied to learn about what is modeled (Gare 2016, Ch.3). Modeling, Rosen argued, 'is the art of bringing entailment structures into congruence'. He continued. 'It is indeed an art, just as surely as poetry, music, and painting, are. Indeed, the essence of art is that, at root, it rests on the unentailed, on the intuitive leap' (Rosen 1991, p.152).

In the first chapter of *Life Itself: A Comprehensive Inquiry into the Nature, Origin, and Fabrication of Life,* 'Praeludium', Rosen grappled with the 'problem' of the two cultures – 'science and art and science and humanism', and the division between 'hard' and 'soft' sciences (Rosen 1991, p.1ff.). He argued that what Gödel's Theorem showed was that the model of arithmetic by logic and set theory could not capture the richness of arithmetic. Arithmetic is 'soft' relative to logic and set theory, but richer. Similarly, whatever is modeled by arithmetic will be richer than the model of it. Consequently, as Judith Rosen, his daughter, writing in the preface to the second edition of one of his major works, *Anticipatory Systems: Philosophical, Mathematical and Methodological Foundations* to warn the reader not to be intimidated by the mathematical notation, recounted what her father had told her: 'the mathematics represent *additional illustration of ideas already described in the prose*' (Rosen 2012, p.iv). Rosen characterized mathematical modeling as only one example of analogical thinking, whereby what is being investigated, in this case, living systems, is comprehended through the study of something else, in this case, mathematical models. It is not a matter of two cultures, but gradations of rigour and richness. This concurs with the conclusions reached by the complexity theorist and theoretical biologist Stuart Kauffman in his essay 'Emergence and Story:

Beyond Newton, Einstein and Bohr?' arguing the impossibility of continuing with the Newtonian assumptions that were still presupposed by Einstein and Bohr, namely that to explain anything we must first pre-state the configuration space, that is, the set of all possible solutions:

> If we cannot have all the categories that may be of relevance finitely prestated ahead of time, how else should we talk about the emergence of the biosphere or in our history – a piece of the biosphere – of new relevant categories, new functionalities, new ways of making a living? These are the doings of autonomous agents. Stories not only are relevant, they are how we tell ourselves what happened and its significance – its semantic import.[11]
> (Kauffman 2000, p.134f.)

Mathematics has to be complemented by the humanities, and in particular, by stories, and it is only through stories that it is possible to understand the intuitive leaps involved in mathematical modeling.

Rosen's work frees science from assumptions that put science and the humanities in opposition to each other, reinstating final causes through mathematics while also acknowledging the importance of non-mathematical models. Rosen's work has also freed mathematicians from Newtonian assumptions to explore the possibilities opened up by Category Theory. He has been a source of inspiration for an increasing number of mathematicians and theorists, beginning with his students. A.H. Louie, the most prominent of his students, subsequently published *More Than Life Itself: A Synthetic Continuation in Relational Biology* (2009), and *The Reflection of Life: Functional Entailment and Imminence in Relational Biology* (2013). Rosen also paved the way for further development of Category Theory to develop a process relational view of reality. Andrée Ehresmann and Jean-Paul Vanbremeersch in *Memory Evolutive Systems* began by noting that while it is necessary for humans to distinguish objects and their relations, we should not allow ourselves to be dominated by the very limited notion of objects as physical objects located in space; these should include 'a musical tone, an odour or an internal feeling. The word *phenomenon* (used by Kant, 1790) or *event* (in the terminology of Whitehead, 1925) would perhaps be more appropriate' (Ehresmann and Vanbremeersch 2007, p.21). An 'object' can be a body, property, event, process, conception, perception or sensation, and it is also necessary to take into account more or less temporary relations between such objects. As Ehresmann and Vanbremeersch put it: 'Long ago, the Taoists imagined the universe as dynamic web of relations, whose events constitute the nodes; each action of a living creature modifies its relations with its environment, and the consequences gradually propagate to the whole of the universe'. In their models they 'make use of fundamental constructions, to give an internal analysis of the structure of the dynamics of the system' (p.33). Work inspired by Rosen and Ehresmann has been continued through the energetic efforts of Plamen Simeonov, who has brought together major theoreticians from science, mathematics and philosophy to develop holistic biomathematics or 'biomathics', published as *Integral Biomathics: Tracing the Road to Reality* (Simeonov, Smith and Ehresmann 2012), and then two focused editions of the journal *Progress in Biophysics & Molecular Biology* (2013 and 2015). Work on integral biomathics continues.

Rosen highlighted the central place models have in all living systems, including societies where models are central to defining themselves and their place in the world. Once this is understood and it is appreciated that with life, including all human organizations, modeling is ubiquitous, Rosen's work on modeling should be seen as relevant to societies and the functioning of democracies. What is required is an interrogation of the models that societies have of themselves and their relationship to their ambience or environments. In contrast to Badiou who expressed contempt for discussion aiming at consensus, Rosen endorsed the views of Robert M. Hutchins who had invited him to be a Visiting Fellow at the Center for the Study of Democratic Institutions in Santa Barbara, California. As Rosen wrote of this center:

> The Center's spirit and modus operandi revolved around the concept of the Dialog. The Dialog was indispensible in Hutchin's thought, because he believed it to be the instrument through which an intellectual community is created. He felt that 'the reason why an intellectual community is necessary is that it offers the only hope of grasping the whole'. 'The whole', for him, was nothing less than discovering the means and ends of human society: 'The real question to which we seek answers are, what should I do, what should we do, why should we do these things? What are the purposes of human life and of organized society?' The operative word here is 'ought', without a conception of 'ought' there could be no guide to politics, which, as he often said, quoting Aristotle, 'is architectonic', That is to say, he felt that politics, in the broadest sense, is ultimately the most important thing in the world.
>
> (Rosen 2012, p.1)

It is not only the sciences that are dominated by assumptions deriving from Newtonian scientific models (and these assumptions have not been replaced by relativity theory, quantum theory or mainstream complexity theory); these assumptions dominate economics, as a consequence of which societies have acted on and continue to act on fundamentally defective models of themselves. It is through reformulating their models that societies form and transform themselves, and Judith Rosen in her preface to *Anticipatory Systems* pointed out that this is now essential if we are to work out how to choose 'the most optimal pathways towards a healthy and sustainable future' (J. Rosen 2012, p.xiv).

Judging between Badiou and Rosen should ultimately be based on the coherence and fruitfulness of their ideas. Despite Badiou's celebration of mathematics, his work has been severely criticized by mathematicians such as Antti Veilahti (2015) and David Nirenberg (2011) on details, and for the limited range of mathematics that he has embraced (with Badiou later responding to the second critic). Despite some engagement with Category Theory and references to topos theory in *Logics of Worlds*, Badiou chose a framework that does not represent a genuine departure from set theory. His topos-theoretic formalism meant to give some place to becoming turns out to be confined only to a limited, set theoretically bounded branch of this. And in *The Concept of Model* (2007) Badiou simply dismissed questions of how to judge the efficacy of mathematical models in science. Rosen, on the other hand, has extended Category Theory, and used it to clarify the relationship between mathematics and science. The main criticism of Rosen is that his work is only a beginning in developing the potential of Category Theory, and needs to be taken much further, which would be even further from Badiou's fixation on set theory. Rosen's work, centrally concerned to recognize the reality of life itself, provides much better practical guidance than Badiou has provided for criticizing and mobilizing against the quest by neoliberals to force every society and every individual to define themselves and their relationships to each other, to their communities and to nature, through the categories of neo-classical economics formulated on Newtonian assumptions, and then to subordinate themselves to the twisted logic of the global market. It is an ideology that does not acknowledge the reality of life.

Efforts to address this problem, inspired by Rosen's work, are underway. James Coffman and Donald Mikulecky's study *Global Insanity: How Homo sapiens Lost Touch with Reality while Transforming the World,* for instance, begins: 'The thesis of this essay is that Western science has misconceived life. As a consequence, civilized humanity, by way of its scientifically informed industrial economy cum existential nihilism cum retreat into fantasy, is destroying the biosphere – and hence itself' (Coffman and Mikulecky 2012, p.1). In a later essay, they summarized their argument:

> [T]he Western world model and consumer economy works as a complex system to thwart, neutralize, or co-opt for its own ends any effort to bring about the kind of radical change that is needed to avert global ecological catastrophe and societal collapse. This resistance to change stems from the need, inherent in the Western model, to continually grow the consumer economy. The media's continued portrayal of consumptive economic growth as a good thing, the widely held belief that the Economy is paramount, and current political and technological trends all manifest the system's active resistance to change. From the perspective of the mature economic system, any work that does not serve to grow the Economy is counterproductive, and viewed as unnecessary, a luxury, or subversive.
>
> (Coffman and Mikulecky 2015, p.1)

Through Rosen's work, the nature of the problem and what is required to overcome it have been recognized and brought into sharp focus.

Notes

1 Eco-Marxists were led in USA by James O'Connor following the establishment of the journal *Capitalism, Nature, Socialism*, and his successor as editor of this, Joel Kovel. See O 'Connor, *Natural Causes: Essays in Ecological Marxism* (1998), the essays in *The Greening of Marxism* edited by Ted Benton (1996), Kovel (2007) and Enrique Leff's book, *Green Production: Toward an Environmental Rationality* (1995). André Gorz and Jean-Paul Deléage in France, Ivan Frolov in the former Soviet Union and in Russia and Pan Yue in China are other leading eco-Marxists. Other US eco-Marxists are Stephen Bunker, John Bellamy Foster and Brett Clark. Alf Hornborg in Sweden is building on the work of Bunker.

2 Hintikka expressed profound appreciation of Peirce for this, and showed how it accounted for the failure to appreciate his contributions to logic by mainstream philosophers. See 'The Place of C.S. Peirce in the History of Logical Theory' (Hintikka 1996).

3 The importance of these has been the focus of much of Code's work, for instance, in his paper 'On the Poverty of Scientism, or: The Ineluctable Roughness of Rationality' (1997, pp.102–122), and more broadly in his book *Process, Reality, and the Power of Symbols: Thinking with A.N.Whitehead* (2007).

4 It could be argued that work in natural philosophy that incorporates modal logic and gives a place to dispositions, as defended by Brian Ellis and Alexander Bird, does replace Quine's conception of nature; but these philosophers are merely re-describing the speculative work of Rom Harré in the language of modal logic. Harré is an important speculative naturalist, although less ambitious in his speculations than Schelling, Peirce or Whitehead. Bhaskar, another important naturalist referred to earlier, originally was a student of Harré.

5 Burtt and Whitehead were followed by E.J. Dijksterhuis, Alexadre Koyré, John Herman Randall Jr., Thomas Kuhn, Arthur Koestler, I Bernard Cohen among many others. See also the work of Stephen Gaukroger, including *The Emergence of a Scientific Culture: Science and the Shaping of Modernity 1210–1685* (2009) and *The Collapse of Mechanism and the Rise of Sensibility: Science and the Shaping of Modernity, 1680–1760* (2012).

6 The most important work on this, that has not received the attention it deserves, is Ivor Leclerc's *The Nature of Physical Existence* (1972), and *The Philosophy of Nature* (1986). The relevance of this research to current science was demonstrated in a Festschrift for Leclerc edited by Bogaard and Treash, *Metaphysics as Foundation: Essays in Honor of Ivor Leclerc* (1993).

7 The importance of symbiosis had already been recognized in Russia by Boris Mikhaylovic Kozo-Polyansky and Peter Kropotkin, among others. The importance of Russian science in this regard has been shown by Giulia Rispoli (2014).

8 This is the case also with the papers collected and edited by Andersen et al., *Downward Causation* (2000), and by Johanna Seibt, *Process Theories: Crossdisciplinary Studies in Dynamic Categories* (2003). Both these include this paper by Bickhard, and the former a paper by Kim.

9 That such a division among mathematicians exists, paralleling the division between logicians, has been pointed out by Johannes Lenhard and Michael Otte in 'Two Types of Mathematization', *Philosophical Perspectives on Mathematics* (2010).

10 On the significance of his work for both biology and for philosophy see Arran Gare, 'Overcoming the Newtonian paradigm: the unfinished project of theoretical biology from a Schellingian perspective' (2013b).

11 This argument has been further developed in Stuart Kauffman and Arran Gare in 'Beyond Descartes and Newton: Recovering life and humanity' (2015). Kauffman's interrogation of the assumptions of science complements the work of Robert Rosen, and before Rosen, Schelling, Peirce, Whitehead and Bergson.

5 Reviving the radical enlightenment through speculative naturalism

What I have tried to show so far is that the core problem of the culture of modernity is that in its quest for total rational mastery over the world it privileges the discourse of techno-science over all other discourses. Consequently, the main forms of our natural and human sciences are committed to explaining away not only consciousness, but life itself, as nothing but physical and chemical processes, supporting a debased view of humanity and life that legitimates greed as the driving force of the economy and of the evolution of nature, imposing thereby a fundamentally flawed model of reality on humanity. Philosophers, as physicians of culture, should be challenging and working to overcome this defective civilization, but philosophy is dominated by schools of thought that have blocked such work, locking in place this defective model of reality. While acting on the basis of this model, now incorporated into peoples' *habituses*, is creating, as Mike Davis put it in the title of his book, *A Planet of Slums* (2007), and is destroying the global ecosystem, there is no place for acknowledging the possibility of human subjects able to create a different future and no place for valuing life as such. Implicitly, mainstream reductionist scientists, with the support of their apologists amond analytic philosophers, are committed to reducing everything, including humans, into predictable instruments of the global economic machine, or to eliminating them, and they believe that they have been and will continue to be successful at this. And if this machine destroys the ecological conditions for humanity, not only can nothing can be done about it, but there is no reason for doing anything about it, unless this affects one personally. Modernity has never been dominated by this model of reality so completely. This reductionist world-view is incorporated and reproduced in our dominant institutions, and supported and maintained by the new globalized managerial ruling class, the corporatocracy, in alliance with a technocratic elite.

William I. Robinson in *A Theory of Global Capitalism: Production, Class, and State in a Transnational World* (2004) argues convincingly that what we are seeing at present is the takeover of the institutions of nation states and their transformation into institutions serving global exploitation by transnational corporations. In the process, they have plundered public assets, creating what James Galbraith has characterized as *The Predator State* (2009). This has been associated with the growth of what Leslie Sklair characterized as *The Transnational Capitalist Class* (2001), or as John Perkins referred to them, the 'corporatocracy' (Perkins 2006, p.31). This is a class without loyalty to any nation, although different fractions of it are dependent upon the governments of different countries to project their power. The members of this global corporatocracy generally have no more compassion for ordinary people than ordinary people have for the cattle from which they make hamburgers, although there are obvious exceptions to this. Members of this class have furthered their ends by supporting a global web of neoliberal think-tanks while deploying the mind control industries of public relations and advertising to ensure that people, including politicians, behave as they want them to (Beder 2006a).

While neoliberals claim to be on the side of freedom, it is clear that their agenda all along has been to subvert democracy. This was revealed by S.M. Amadae in *Rationalizing Capitalist Democracy* (2003) and the contributors to Philip Mirowski and Dieter Plehwe's anthology, *The Road from Mont Pèlerin: The Making of the Neoliberal Thought Collective* (2009). As we have seen, they embraced Walter Lippmann's claims made in the 1920s that the world is too complex for democracy and ruling elites should aim to manufacture consent, rejecting John Dewey's claim that education could enable people to function properly as citizens of democracies. The essays in this latter book point to the complexity and diversity in neoliberalism, showing that not all neoliberals have been opposed to the welfare state or aligned with the corporatocracy. However, there is a common focus on using markets in place of political processes to define human relationships, and while the concern might be to oppose bureaucracy, it also rules out democracy. That this is the case has been recognized by Al Gore, a former US vice president and contender for presidency in his book *The Assault on Reason* (2007). Through their interventions in politics, society and culture, the new global ruling class have undermined the capacity of people to anticipate the future and respond to it creatively except at the crudest level of anticipating how to make more money and increase consumption, supporting Margaret Thatcher's claim that 'there is no alternative'. Any institution not aligned with this culture is now being transformed or eliminated, as Sharon Beder (2007) among others have documented. Mass media is dominated by a small number of media moguls, while schools, universities and research organizations are being transformed into business corporations, snuffing out almost all enquiry that does not support increased profitability, advance weapons technology, or provide means for social control. As Marx predicted, commodification has intensified, both extensively and intensively. From commodifying labour-power, the economy now commodifies life itself. As Mauritzo Lazzarato succinctly characterized the current world-order:

> We are ... faced with a form of capitalist accumulation that is no longer only based on the exploitation of labour in the industrial sense, but also on that of knowledge, life, health, leisure, culture etc. What organizations

produce and sell not only includes material or immaterial goods, but also forms of communication, standards of socialization, perception, education, housing, transportation etc. The explosion of services is directly linked to this evolution; and this does not only involve industrial services but also the mechanisms that organize and control ways of life. The globalization that we are currently living is not only extensive (delocalization, global market) but also intensive; it involves cognitive, cultural, affective and communicative resources (the life of individuals) as much as territories, genetic heritage (plants, animals and humans), the resources necessary to the survival of the species and the planet (water, air, etc.).

(Lazzarato 2004, p.205)

Science itself, transformed into the knowledge industry, has been almost completely commodified, and as such, reproduces and extends this false model of reality. All these developments have undermined the quest for truth (or redefined truth as that which improves the profitability of corporations) and all but eradicated responsibility for the future. The scientism supported by the corporatocracy then legitimates efforts to replace democratic institutions by markets and bureaucracies run by technocrats, transforming public institutions into quasi-business organizations.

The triumph of techno-science over the humanities and its consequences

Do we still need the humanities? Do we need to cultivate people with *humanitas* willing to take responsibility for their communities and for creating the future? Could we not eliminate the quest for understanding and accept the redefinition of science as nothing but techno-science, allowing only forms of science to be funded that treat nature and people as of significance only insofar as they can be transformed to serve the quest by companies to maximize profitability and governments to maximize GNP? 'Subjectivities' of a kind will still be formed by the mind control industries, supplemented by psychiatrists, psychologists, sociologists and criminologists dealing with intransigent cases. The market as a self-regulating mechanism being imposed throughout the world to define all human relationships provides all the feedback needed to generate economic progress. Science, integrated and identified with technological research, no longer requires people inspired by the quest for truth; science graduates can be controlled like all other employees by human resource managers trained to extract the maximum output of profitable products for minimal inputs. The contradiction between a form of science that makes the very existence of science and scientists unintelligible can be ignored because scientists can now be treated as instruments for producing profitable technology, not heroic figures striving for true understanding of nature. Such is the thinking of neoliberals and their patrons. This is the age of 'Megabuck Science' predicted by Norbert Wiener.

What has been the effect of transforming education and research institutions into quasi-business organizations and defining their ends by market criteria? While there have been some technological advances, the picture that is emerging is of the degeneration of culture, the fragmentation of enquiry, the multiplication of disciplines and subdisciplines (approximately 4000 of these) ignoring each other, and a noise explosion hiding stagnation in intellectual life. Theodore Dalrymple, the psychiatrist working with poor people and prisoners in Britain referred to in Chapter One, in *Our Culture, What's Left of It: The Mandarins and the Masses* characterized the disintegration of contemporary culture as a manifestly pathological deterioration of fundamental values. This, he argues, has been brought about by an unholy alliance of neoliberals, who believe that consumer choice is the answer to all social questions, and purportedly radical intellectuals who promote rights without duties (Dalrymple 2005, p.14). The rise of postmodern art, and deconstructionist dismissal of any critical evaluation of this, is an expression of this decay of values. While the humanities are being eliminated, science is also suffering. As Bruce Charlton (also referred to in Chapter One) argued, we now have the mass production of defective scientific papers that are clogging the channels of communication. There do appear to be advances in cosmology, theoretical biology and cognitive science, some of which challenge reductionist science. However, while it is often held to be a golden age of cosmology, this is associated with new observations rather than deeper understanding. As Lee Smolin pointed out recently, theoretically, cosmology has been a disaster (Smolin 2014), reinforcing the conclusions he drew in *The Trouble with Physics* (2007) and Peter Woit drew in *Not Even Wrong* (2007). There have been no significant advances in chemistry to match the advances of mid-twentieth century, despite vast numbers of publications.

As we have seen, there appears to have been more creative work in theoretical biology and cognitive science. The recent much celebrated publication in 2013 of Terrence Deacon's *Incomplete Nature: How Mind Emerged from Matter*, following his earlier book, The Symbolic Species: The Co-evolution of Language and the Brain published in 1997, illustrates advances in science that are no longer in thrall of reductionism, and there are a number of works in which semiotics, complexity theory, hierarchy theory, non-linear thermodynamics and evolutionary theory have been synthesized. The work of the biosemioticians such as Kalevi Kull, Jesper Hoffmeyer, Marcello Barbieri and the work on complexity of Stuart Kauffman (1993), Howard Pattee and Stan Salthe, not to mention Herman Haken's work on synergetics (1984) and all the work of the Santa Fe Institute on complex adaptive systems, suggest great creative intellectual ferment. Much of this goes unrecognized by mainstream scientists, however. The synthesis produced by Stan Salthe, *Development and Evolution: Complexity and Change in Evolution* published in 1993, which first integrated hierarchy theory, Peircian biosemiotics, non-linear thermodynamics and dialectical materialism and is in many ways superior to Deacon's work, has been ignored by mainstream biologists. This is also true of the work of the earlier theoretical biology movement associated with C.H. Waddington and Joseph Needham and carried on by Brian Goodwin, Mae-Wan Ho and Gerry Webster, among others. For instance, Ho's book, *The Rainbow and the Worm* (2008), a major work of synthesis guided by Bergson and Whitehead, integrating thermodynamics and complexity theory while arguing for a central role of quantum fields and quantum coherence in biological organization, is ignored by most biologists, although her claims for the importance of quantum coherence are now supported by the recent work on quantum criticality. Examining what is going on, it becomes evident that except in a few strongholds, those challenging mainstream science and the reduction of science to techno-science have been marginalized, working in a few, often insecure niches, almost all of them being older academics. Cognitive science is heavily funded not because this holds prospects of deepening our understanding of life and humanity, but because it could facilitate better control of people, or better still, their replacement by new forms of information technology, or information technology that can kill people more efficiently. Academics succeed by embracing this role and those that do are hostile to those challenging their reductionist assumptions. Whatever cannot be made sense of by such reductionist science is ignored by mainstream academics, as shown in the science writer Michael Brooks' study, *13 Things that Don't Make Sense: The Most Baffling Scientific Mysteries of Our Time* (2008). This is the natural sciences.

The human sciences are worse because what is produced is positively and immediately destructive. This is clearly the case with mainstream economics. This has been supported and has flourished because it provides ideological support for the neoliberal agenda of 'disembedding markets' from communities and forcing communities to abandon democracy and subordinate themselves to the imperatives of a global market, to use the terminology of Karl Polanyi (1957) and Takis Fotopoulous (1997). This is why it displaced Keynesian economics, not because neo-classical economists won intellectual debates. In fact it has been argued that the revival of neo-classical economics by John Nash, Gerard Debrau and Kenneth Arrow and their epigone in the 1950s was hollow from the beginning, and yet in USA managed to displace not only the economics of the New Dealers such as John Kenneth Galbraith, but also the efforts of John von Neumann to develop mathematical modeling adequate the the complexity and historical development of actual economic systems. As Varoufakis, Halevi and Theocarakis wrote in *Modern Political Economics: Making sense of the post-2008 world* (2011, p.257), 'the joint defeat of the New Dealers and the *Scientists,* at the hands of the new neoclassicism, deprived post-war economics of all useful knowledge that had been learned the hard way during the hideous 1930s and 1940s' (p.257). Where Keynesianism survived, as in the work of Paul Samuelson, it was in a bowdlerized form, interpreted through neo-classical economics. Later, the Cambridge political economists led by Joan Robinson won the intellectual debates against the neo-classical economists, as even Samuelson acknowledged, to no effect. An explanation for what happened had already been provided before all this happened. John Maynard Keynes' colleague Michal

Kalecki in 'Political Aspects of Full Employment' (1943) had predicted that despite having worked out how to manage the economy so that there would be permanent full employment with continuous economic growth, that the business class would rebel against this order, accepting a less healthy economy as a means to keep workers in a subordinate position.

It is not difficult to criticize 'mainstream' economics, the economics expounded in textbooks because, as Edward Nell wrote (quoting Geoffrey Harcourt), it is really 'billabong' economics, a stagnant pond (Nell 1996, p.17). It is not a moving target, and criticisms from decades ago are just as relevant today as when they were made – and ignored. For instance, the Nobel Laureate Wassily Leontief wrote in 1982 of academic publications in economics: 'Page after page of professional economic journals are filled with mathematical formulas leading the reader from sets of more or less plausible but entirely arbitrary assumptions to precisely stated but irrelevant theoretical conclusions' (Leontief 1982, p.104). This situation had not changed when that statement was quoted by Geoffrey Hodgson in *Evolution and Institutions* (1999), and it has not changed to the present. Such criticisms have had little impact on economics where mainstream economists have powerful patrons. Hodgson points out how few places there now are for dissident economists to get academic appointments or to have their voices heard. He refers to Japan as the main exception, with USA because of its enormous diversity offering a few niches for dissidents. What mainstream economists have done, with the support of their patrons, is impose fundamentally defective models of societies on themselves and their major policy makers that are blinding them to the cultural, social and ecological destruction they are wreaking.

The revival of neo-classical economics, along with social Darwinism, has been accompanied by the almost complete dominance of positivistic forms of human science focused on how to efficiently control people, and 'scientific management' or 'Taylorism', building on the work of Frederick Winslow Taylor. Taylorism dominates the management faculties that have flourished under neoliberalism. Scientific management involves concentrating knowledge and decision-making powers with managers and simplifying work and disempowering subordinates so that they become little more than trained gorillas (to use Gramsci's apt characterization of the consequences of Taylorism). Its triumph, characterized by George Ritzer (1993) as 'McDonaldization', is manifest in the renaming of 'personnel' departments in organizations, including universities, as 'human resources' departments, and efforts to impose quantitative criteria to define and judge employee performance while distinguishing themselves by their capacity to cut labour costs.

Public institutions that stand outside markets are essential for preventing markets corrupting themselves and for achieving and maintaining democracy. However, as we have seen, the aim of neoliberals has been to eliminate such independence and the social responsibility that public institutions traditionally have been concerned to foster. In place of democracy and the institutions required to sustain it, we have a new 'technocracy' aligned with the global corporatocracy taking over public institutions. This was characterized by Bourdieu as a 'new state nobility', 'a small group of academically educated elites [which] feels entitled to rearrange society top to bottom because of its superior knowledge and its economist approach'. As Bourdieu put it in *Acts of Resistance: Against the Tyranny of the Market*:

> This state-nobility, preaching the retreat of the state and the undivided rule of market and consumer – this commercial substitute of the citizen – has monopolized the state. It has transformed public into private property and made the public matter of the republic its own private concern. What matters today is reclaiming of democracy and its victory over technocracy.
> (Bourdieu 1998, p.25f)

Bourdieu wrote of this 'ideology of competence' or 'racism of intelligence': 'In fact, the power of neoliberal hegemony is based on a new form of social Darwinism: In the words of Harvard, "the best and the most remarkable" win the race' (p.42).

Unconstrained markets, legitimated by mainstream economics, concentrate wealth and thereby power in regions, countries and corporations as well as in individuals, until they cripple the economy, corrupt politics and destroy communities, exhaust reserves, destroy resources, and wreck ecosystems, especially when the economy comes to be dominated by the finance sector.[1] It is not possible to lead ecologically sustainable lives while decisions are made on the basis of monetary calculations in a society dominated by corporations and Taylorist managerialism in which spaces where people have in the past gained some autonomy have been destroyed. As Alf Hornborg pointed out in 'Money and the Semiotics of Ecosystem Dissolution' (1999), money is a code with only one sign, or a language with only one phoneme. It cannot possibly provide the feedback required to deal properly with complex situations, and in fact is guiding humanity to ecological destruction. Taylorist managerialism also works with grossly deficient signs that lead to one blunder after another, and to the crushing of any creativity. As Beder (2006b) among others have shown, it will be impossible to address ecological problems by tweaking markets to take into account externalities and rely on technological fixes in a neoliberal managerialist framework.

Stephen Bunker's study of the exploitation of Amazonia illustrated the effect of supposedly free markets in the past. They have transferred most of the usable energy in living and fossilized plants to a small part or the world, generating ecologically costly over-exploitation of natural resources in the periphery of the world economy and socially costly hypercoherence in the global system. And as he pointed out in *Underdeveloping the Amazon* (1986):

> Hypercoherence ultimately leads to ecological and social collapse as increasingly stratified systems undermine their own resource base. ... The exchange relations which bind this system together depend on locally

dominant groups to reorganize local modes of production and extraction in response to world demand, but the ultimate collapse will be global, not local. The continued impoverishment of peripheral regions finally damages the entire system.

(p.253)

Instead of being addressed, this tendency has been exacerbated under the global neoliberal regime. As the theoretical biologist Mae-Wan Ho and the theoretical ecologist Robert Ulanowicz pointed out in 'Sustainable systems as organisms?' (2005):

> The economic globalization promoted by the rich countries in the World Trade Organization is aimed at removing all barriers to trade, finance and procurement, which is tantamount to destroying the system's intricate space-time structure. This inevitably results in the over-exploitation of the poor, especially in third world countries, that will impoverish the whole economic system. But that is not all. As the global economic system is embedded in the global ecosystem, over-exploitation in the global economy will drive people to use natural resources at unsustainable rates, so that the global ecosystem increasingly fails to renew itself. This leads to diminished input into the economic system so that even more natural resources will have to be harvested, resulting in a vicious cycle that will ultimately destroy both the global economy and the earth's ecosystem.
>
> (p.47)

Giovanni Arrighi and Beverly J. Silver in *Chaos and Governance in the Modern World System* (1999, p.288f.) argue that these policies are the consequence of the government of USA attempting to cement its slipping pre-eminence into exploitative domination, a strategy which is undermining its power and is bound to fail while generating system-wide chaos. After the collapse of the Argentine economy and the global financial crisis of 2007 brought about by the policies promoted by neo-classical economists, thereby verifying theoretical criticisms of neo-classical economics, these economists continued to dominate government economic policies. This was despite the alternatives offered by the theoretically more defensible traditions of Keynesian economics, political economy and institutionalist economics.[2] These traditions have had almost no impact on mainstream economics or government policies, however.

What this shows is that with the success of the market displacing the quest for truth and comprehension as the criterion for determining research funding, a process well described by Mirowski in *Science-Mart: Privatising American Science* (2011), ideas that augment the power of the powerful dominate no matter how irrational and no matter what the consequences. Of course, the quest for truth has not been entirely eliminated, as leaked documents about the dire future we face from the Pentagon or from transnational companies such as Exxon-Mobil reveal. Exxon-Mobil knew about global warming in 1981, but set about lobbying to prevent this being found out or acted upon. Documents ascertaining the truth are produced by the ruling elites for themselves, and have to be leaked for the public for them to find out what they conclude (Taylor, 2014). The founder of Wikileaks has been vilified for making such documents accessible to the public. However, it is becoming increasingly difficult for anyone outside transnational corporations to develop alternative ideas, or if they are developed, to disseminate them or have them taken seriously. Psychology and sociology illustrate this. Habermas' claim in 'Ideologies and Societies in the Post-War World' (1986, p.52) that 'the social sciences can only be preserved from declining into a sterile positivism by functioning within the framework of a philosophy-based theory of society' has been borne out. Despite the work of a brilliant minority of theoreticians, developing a tradition that can be seen to go back to Herder, Fichte, Hegel and Schelling, much of what now purports to be scientific research in these subjects, aimed at providing knowledge to bureaucracies and business organizations to augment their quest to control people, consists of handing out questionnaires and using statistical packages to reveal correlations in the results, then offering ad hoc theories to explain whatever correlations are found. This does not bear an even superficial resemblance to real science, and it is this which most students of sociology will be taught at universities.[3]

All this does not mean that the broader culture is characterized by a general acceptance of scientific materialism. In the vacuum that has been created by the nihilism of this world-view, many people live in a state of confusion, concluding as ruling elites and their priests, the economists, want them to conclude, that intellectual life apart from that devoted to control is merely a form of entertainment, and that the only end in life that has any value is consuming and having the means to consume more. In affluent countries, this view is pervasive, and it is responsible for the depoliticization of the population, which in turn is responsible for the undermining of the welfare state, growing inequalities, the elimination of job security, and growing personal debt, so that the outcome of consumerism is growing indebtedness, insecurity and anxiety. As Zygmunt Bauman put, people are *Living on Borrowed Time* (2010). Consequently, people are turning to religious fundamentalism and paranoid nationalism, with increasing tendencies to violence. Such irrationalism and violence are likely to increase in the future.

The neoliberal agenda has largely crippled institutions of learning and research, stunted intellectual inquiry, created a nihilistic culture and locked humanity into a trajectory that will lead to increasing concentrations of wealth and income and financial and commercial collapse, followed by political, social and cultural collapse.[4] More significantly, it has locked humanity into a trajectory of ecological collapse. It is now abundantly clear that unconstrained markets dominated by the corporatocracy and promoting techno-science and the distraction of the masses through entertainment, do not provide the feedback necessary to generate appropriate responses to ecological destruction; they have accelerated ecologically destructive economic activity. As the ecological economist, Kozo Mayumi pointed out in *The Origins of Ecological Economics* (2001, p.125), in the global economy created by the dogma of free trade, economic enterprises that are ecologically sustainable are not economically viable, while those economic enterprises that are economically viable are ecologically unsustainable.

The radical enlightenment and the struggle for democracy

For philosophers such as Castoriadis who have examined the birth of democracy in Ancient Greece, it should come as no surprise that the value accorded the quest for truth is disappearing. The creation of Greek politics and philosophy emerged together with democracy. Here we find people explicitly deliberating about the laws and changing those laws, and that led to questions such as What is it for a law to be right or wrong? That is, What is justice? Here also we find people for the first time explicitly questioning the instituted collective representation of the world and proposing alternatives. They quickly moved from questions about whether some representations of the world are true to the question What is truth? (Castoriadis 1997, pp.267–289). The most important power in any society is the power to define reality. Tyrants and oligarchs operate by imposing a definition of reality on the people they dominate. They have no place for people questing after truth (except in very limited domains), or justice, or who have integrity; they only want instrumental knowledge. As genuine democracy disappears, so does the value accorded to the quest for truth, justice, integrity and high standards of workmanship. Reviving the quest for truth and the conditions for pursuing it are inseparable from the struggle for autonomy and liberty. Liberty means not being enslaved, and avoiding this requires participation in the governance of one's communities where these communities themselves are not enslaved. Overcoming the enslavement of countries, communities, economic organizations and individuals to the managers of transnational corporations and their political allies, surmounting managerialism and the imposition of the laws of the market on humanity and the reduction of workers to trained gorillas, requires not a command economy with central planning, as orthodox Marxists are still prone to believe, but the revival of democratic politics and self-management and the values and virtues required for these.

There is a crisis in political philosophy at present, however, at least for those who are not content to see democracy hollowed out and destroyed. Effectively, the drive for democracy, which gathered momentum from the end of the Nineteenth Century until the 1960s, was halted and reversed from the 1970s onwards. What we have seen, largely as a consequence of the triumph of analytic philosophy, is the revival of the tradition of ethics and political philosophy that began with Thomas Hobbes (1588–1679) and developed through John Locke (1632–1704), Adam Smith (1723–1790), Jeremy Bentham (1748–1832) and Herbert Spencer (1820–1903). What Hobbes was promoting was, as C.B. Macpherson characterized it in *The Political Theory of Possessive*

Individualism: Hobbes to Locke (1964) was 'possessive individualism', and depoliticization of the population. Locke reformulated Hobbes' notion of rights to life based on a social contract to claim that the prime goal of the social and political contracts on which society is founded is to preserve people's property, that is, what people have mixed their labour with. Although Bentham, the main proponent of utilitarianism, was hostile to the idea of rights deriving from Locke, utilitarianism also derived from Locke's equation of good with what is pleasurable and bad with what is painful. The conception of rights based on contract and utilitarianism complement each other in modern societies. As Alasdair MacIntyre pointed out in *After Virtue* (2007) they are 'a matching pair of incommensurable fictions' (p.91). This becomes intelligible when Locke and Bentham are recognized as epigone of Hobbes. These are the ideas that were incorporated into classical economic theory, with *homo-economicus,* efficiently calculating sociopaths, portrayed as the ideal rational human being. Social Darwinism, using classical economic theory as a metaphor for nature, was a further articulation of Hobbes' mechanistic view of humans and provided the overarching framework delimiting the extent to which rights and utility would be taken seriously. Philosophers who ignore this history and promote negative liberty as freedom from any constraint, along with the notion of the 'unencumbered self' in which what counts as a person with supposedly a capacity to choose is sharply separated from the values they choose, who then promote rights to choose over any notion of the good and focus on procedure over ends, as Michael Sandel suggested in 'The Procedural Republic and the Unencumbered Self' (2005), are really supporting Hobbes' project of eliminating liberty and enslaving people.

To develop genuine democracy (in the sense of government of the people, by the people, for the people), requires a rejection of this whole Hobbesian tradition of thought, and the re-establishment of democratic control over the economy. This makes new demands on ethical and political philosophy. The problem is how to subordinate markets to democratic institutions of communities, reducing markets to instruments to augment these communities, and create and maintain the social spaces required for this, in a globalized world. This will involve limiting the extent of commodification, eliminating Taylorist managerialism, and eliminating the conditions in which out-of-control feedback loops concentrate power and subvert such democratic organization. Localizing production where-ever possible is one solution to this, but even achieving this is problematic. To meet these challenges it will be necessary to recover and rethink political philosophy and ethics. As Castoriadis pointed out in 'The Greek *Polis* and the Creation of Democracy' (1997a, pp. 267–289), politics, which originated with the Ancient Greeks, is the domain in which communities and their members question and take responsibility for their beliefs and institutions and struggle to govern themselves, control their destinies and augment the conditions of their existence. It is here that people struggled for autonomy. Politics has always been associated with ethics because autonomous communities can only function properly when people have the required virtues. Political and ethical philosophy are, and always have been, central to the humanities, as Hans Baron has pointed out in his study *The Crisis of the Early Italian Renaissance* (1966). They are required to provide the concepts to orient people to find and appreciate the highest values, choose what to aim at in life, how to organize themselves, how to live and how to act, what kinds of people they should be striving to become, what and how they should produce and how they should distribute what they produce.

Political and ethical philosophers should have been grappling with these problems, putting into perspective the greater complexity of the world, and some have been doing this. However, the subdisciplines of political philosophy and ethics, like most other disciplines, have been differentiated from each other, from the rest of philosophy and from other disciplines in the humanities and the sciences, from art, literature and often history, while dividing even these sub-disciplines, especially ethics, into a multiplicity of sub-sub-disciplines and special topics.[5] There has been strong opposition to this, but in most philosophy departments, opposition has been marginalized, and most people have turned to economists and psychologists for guidance on politics and ethics. With a few exceptions, philosophers of ethics and politics who were aligned with democracy have lost the plot, and to recover this, requires above all a return to history. It is here that the most important work on ethics and political philosophy has been and is being undertaken.

Such historical work is required just to recover very simple but extremely important ideas, such as Aristotle's postulation that the *arche* or first principle of ethics and politics, without which people will simply talk past each other, is agreeing that the basic problem is to work out what is the ultimate good (or goods) that people should aim at, basing this on the most defensible conception of humans and their place in the cosmos, and then working out how the polis (or state) can be organized to facilitate people living a good life. The tradition of natural law jurisprudence is based on this *arche*. Even more fundamentally, politics for the Greeks was based on the belief, first defended by Heraclitus, that people are responsible for their actions. Subsequently, Greek democracy was predicated on this assumption, and participants in political life were held responsible for the outcome of decisions of the ecclesia they had influenced long after the decisions had been made. It was also assumed that rulers should govern for the common good. Good constitutions, whether rule be by the many, by an elite or by one, were characterized by Aristotle as those where rulers ruled for the common good; the others being regarded as defective constitutional forms. What is required is a dialectical reconstruction of the development of political philosophy from this starting point, utilizing synopsis, analysis and synthesis to identify and recover the major advances in its history, and to integrate these to provide solid foundations for developing a philosophy adequate to present circumstances. It will be necessary to incorporate the insights of Pericles, Plato, Aristotle, Polybius, Cicero, Aquinas, the Renaissance civic humanists along with more recent work in ethics and political philosophy.

In reconstructing a dialectical history of political philosophy, the Renaissance has a particular significance. It was centred on the quest by 'civic humanists' to defend their liberty as liberty had been understood by the defenders of the Roman republic. In *Hobbes and Republican Liberty,* Quentin Skinner characterized the core ideas of republican theory, quoting from the *Digest of Justinian:*

> ... the *libertas* enjoyed by free-men consists in their being 'in their own power' as opposed to being 'under the power of someone else'... and hence in subjection to his *arbitrarium* or arbitrary will. The nerve of the republican theory is thus that freedom within civil associations is subverted by the mere presence of arbitrary power, the effect of which is to reduce members of such associations from the status of free-men to that of slaves.
>
> (Skinner 2008, p.x)

Building on the work of the Ancient Greeks and Romans, one of their greatest contributions to political philosophy was to recognize the importance of diverse centres of power, going beyond Polybius' defence of a mixed constitution as it existed in the Roman republic, with power divided between the consuls, the senate and the people's tribunals, to argue for a separation between the legislative and the executive branches of government. Later, Bolingbroke and Montesquieu argued for the independence of the judiciary, and then Kant and Wilhelm von Humboldt argued for some autonomy for universities and Hegel for the civil service. The other great achievement of the Renaissance republicans was the development of the humanities as a form of education to develop *humanitas.*

It soon becomes evident when studying civic humanism and its reception that political philosophy promoting liberty has always been a struggle against powerful opponents. For Renaissance thinkers struggling to preserve what liberty they had gained from the German kings and the Papacy it was necessary to recover what had been lost through the success of such opponents. A 'rebirth' or 'renaissance' of the culture of Republican Rome and democratic Greece was required. Later, their civic republicanism was defended and radicalized by Nature Enthusiasts such as Giordano Bruno and Tommaso Campanella. The Nature Enthusiasts revived pre-Socratic philosophies of nature to provide a cosmology justifying their radical political ideas.

The work of Mersenne, Gassendi, Descartes and Hobbes, developing a mechanistic view of nature and humans and promoting possessive individualism, was the most concerted effort to subvert this quest for liberty ever made. Marin Mersenne, a lifelong friend of Descartes, in 1624 characterized Bruno as 'one of the wickedest men whom the earth has ever supported ... who seems to have invented a new manner of philosophizing only in order to make underhand attacks on the Christian religion' (Mersenne 1974, p.317). Gassendi and Descartes, inspired by Mersenne, not only opposed the influence of Bruno and Nature Enthusiasm generally but strove to provide an alternative to this cosmology. This was the new 'mechanical philosophy'. Descartes and Hobbes also rejected civic humanism, and Hobbes undertook to replace it, along with Aristotelian political philosophy, with a complete social, political and ethical philosophy based on mechanistic materialism. Hobbes was the crucial figure, having set out not merely to argue against the civic humanism of the Renaissance republicans with their commitment to liberty and self-governance, but to transform language by articulating a mechanistic view of nature and humans in accordance with Galilean science so that the liberty they aspired to would become unintelligible (Skinner 1998; Skinner 2002; Skinner 2008). As Stephen Toulmin has shown in *Cosmopolis: The Hidden Agenda of Modernity*, the hidden agenda of these mechanistic philosophies, which Toulmin characterized as the 'counter-Renaissance', was not only to dominate nature, but to create a social order in which people would be completely controlled (Toulmin 1994, p.24). Toulmin's research has been supported Xavier Martin's study of the assumptions about humans and the goals of the French revolutionaries (2001). Hobbes provided the social and political philosophy to serve this end. Reformulated by Locke and Newton and further developed in France, Scotland and Britain, this movement was largely successful. This is what Jonathan Israel in *The Radical Enlightenment: Philosophy and the Making of Modernity 1650–1750* (2002) characterized as the 'Moderate Enlightenment', committed to possessive individualism and defending tolerance as a weak alternative to democracy.

Renaissance ideas were not buried without a struggle. There had been a reaction against the atomism, utilitarianism and nihilistic implications of this Moderate Enlightenment and a concerted effort to defend liberty and democracy, reviving Renaissance civic humanism and Nature Enthusiasm. Those involved were really striving for another renaissance, recovering and reformulating the ideas of the Ancient Greeks and Romans as well as the Renaissance of the Fifteenth Century. This is the tradition characterized by Margaret Jacob in *The Radical Enlightenment: Pantheists, Freemasons and Republicans*, as the 'Radical Enlightenment', a term that was taken up and further developed by Israel (2002). In Gare (2008c) I equated the Radical Enlightenment with the 'genuine' Enlightenment and the Moderate Enlightenment with the 'fake' Enlightenment. While driven underground in the early Eighteenth Century, it was this Radical Enlightenment that emerged in the explosion of ideas in late Eighteenth and early Nineteenth Century Germany, inspired by Jean-Jacques Rousseau's and Kant's defence of freedom. This was a new Renaissance which not only continued the trajectory of Renaissance thought in the quest for liberty, but reworked the concept of freedom and redefined the nature of humanity, rethinking traditional political and ethical philosophy in the context of the much more complex social order of the modern world. Natural philosophy was revived to neutralize or oppose the mechanistic world-view.

The revival within philosophy of the Hobbesian tradition and the neutralization of the German Renaissance can only be fully understood by tracing the influence of Bolzano, Frege, Russell, the logical positivists and Quine. They also have attempted to promote a language so impoverished that the struggle for liberty and democracy are made unintelligible. Most analytic philosophers have either defended complete nihilism, openly as with the logical positivist A.J. Ayer, or implicitly as with Quine, or defended contractarian notions of rights or utilitarianism. By recognizing the fundamentally opposed traditions of Enlightenment thinking, we can now recognize neoliberalism not only as a revival of the Moderate Enlightenment, but the significance of this. It is not only subverting democracy, but is a renewed attack on the Renaissance idea of liberty and the value accorded to nature by the Nature Enthusiasts and the Romantic philosophers who had revived their exalted view of life. Most of those purportedly opposed to neoliberalism appear to have forgotten this tradition. Effectively they have 'lost the plot' of the Radical Enlightenment. We need to recover the plot.

To recover the plot it is necessary to look more closely at German philosophy to reveal the significance of Kant's second Copernican revolution defending the reality of freedom of the will, and the divergent developments of Kant's philosophy. While the Radical Enlightenment had a significant if subordinate influence in the Dutch Republic, Britain and France and in the American and French revolutions, it was in Germany that it flowered intellectually. Kant (1724–1804), Hegel (1870–1831) and Schelling (1775–1854), and particularly Hegel's *Philosophy of History* and *Philosophy of Right,* strongly influenced by Kant's students Johann Herder (1744–1803) and J.G. Fichte (1762–1814) and focused on the evolution of the advance of freedom, are the crucial reference points for understanding this tradition. By virtue of Hegel's own historical and integrative work and thereby his contribution to social, political and ethical thought, the Radical Enlightenment in Germany can be identified with the neo-Hegelian tradition of social philosophy, although it should not be identified with Hegel's philosophy. The naturalization of this tradition of thought can only be fully understood in relation to Schelling's philosophy and its influence.

After it had been subordinated in Germany, the Radical Enlightenment was revived and further advanced towards the end of the Nineteenth Century and the early decades of the Twentieth Century by British, American and Italian Idealists, Hegelian Marxists, American pragmatists, process metaphysicians and a good proportion of the phenomenologists. The social liberalism (or liberal socialism) of the Idealists, embraced by pragmatists, process philosophers and humanistic Marxists, was committed to liberty and freeing people from all forms of enslavement, removing obstacles to people's self-realization and cultivating individual responsibility and the virtues required to uphold liberty. For the British Idealists, this required people to have some private property to foster individual responsibility – providing others were not excluded from having private property. Private properly was seen by them as a means, not an end, and expropriating of excessive wealth can not only be justified by this philosophy, but is required by it. The market itself was seen as a public institution requiring an ethical framework that was not egoistic. This revival of German thought could be regarded as another renaissance of the Radical Enlightenment, and the development of analytic philosophy as an intellectual subversion of this

Renaissance. Stalinism and Naziism, each of which was strongly influenced by Taylor's scientific management theory associated with the development of a new managerial class, identified as such by James Burnham in *The Managerial Revolution* (1945), were also assaults on the Radical Enlightenment, assaults which failed. Neoliberalism has been succeeding where they failed.

We need a new Renaissance. This has been undertaken by historically oriented political philosophers. As we have seen, Castoriadis has revived interest in the emergence of democracy and the quest for autonomy in Ancient Greece. Quentin Skinner, J.G.A. Pocock, Philip Pettit and Michael Sandel have defended and developed the central ideas of the Renaissance civic republican tradition, while neo-Hegelian communitarianism has been ably defended by Charles Taylor in North America, David Miller in Britain, by Paul Ricoeur in France and by Axel Honneth in Germany.[6] The civic republican tradition, focusing on what is required to defend liberty and avoid slavery complements and strengthens neo-Hegelian thought in opposing neoliberalism, while neo-Aristotelian philosophy brings into focus what politics and ethics are all about. There is now also a growing appreciation of how important was the ethics and political philosophy of the Nineteenth Century neo-Hegelians (or neo-Fichteans), T.H. Green and the British and American Idealists (including Josiah Royce), for combating the ideas now being revived by the neoliberals, since the neoliberals are reviving precisely the doctrines these philosophers fought against. Their philosophy provides a framework for integrating recent advances in neo-Hegelian and republican political philosophy.[7] This complements efforts to integrate the civic republicanism of the civic humanists, the communitarianism of Hegelian and neo-Hegelian political philosophy and neo-Aristotelian political and ethical philosophy.[8]

Speculative naturalism, philosophical anthropology and the humanities

However, it is also necessary to show that the cosmology and conception of humans developed by Hobbes and his epigone to oppose democracy are false. As work on theoretical biology by Rosen, Pattee, Salthe and others suggests, however, to evaluate the alternative on the basis of its logical coherence and superior contributions to science and mathematics alone would be to miss its full significance. Speculative naturalism justifies not only the cognitive claims but also the values and significance of the humanities, including philosophy and the arts. It situates humans as conscious, reflective social beings participating in the creative becoming of humanity and nature, which now can be seen to include philosophers striving for a comprehensive understanding of the world and themselves and their possibilities, and justifies holding them responsible for the future. Post-Newtonian science inspired and guided by speculative naturalism now justifies this conception of humans as capable to some extent of creating themselves.

The triumph of reductionist science involved treating life and mind as epiphenomena of physico-chemical entities, relations and processes, and more fundamentally, denying the efficacy of final causes. This denial has been built into the assumptions of mainstream science from Francis Bacon and Newton onwards. This rendered the notion of humanity that could be cultivated and liberty as something to be fought for, along with the quest for truth and justice, meaningless illusions. In place of this, we have had Hobbes' conception of humans as mechanisms moved by appetites and aversions, in which all thinking is adding and subtracting, and knowledge is equated with knowing how to control the world to satisfy these appetites and avoid aversions. Augmenting Hobbes' philosophy is Social Darwinism portraying life as a struggle for survival between competing mechanisms, evaluating everything in terms of their instrumental value in this struggle for survival. In Richard Dawkins' formulation of this, the struggle is ultimately between different genes or strings of DNA, and organisms are their survival machines. Filled out with metaphors from information technology, this is now identified as the scientific view of humans, carrying all the authority accorded to science. Political theorists who have attempted to make the study of politics more scientific are also for the most part distant disciples of Hobbes. With this conception of humans, the validity claims and thereby the significance of the arts and the humanities, and the possibility of creating a less oppressive, ecologically sustainable global civilization, are denied. The capitulation of philosophy to scientism by Quine and his disciples involved crippling opposition to such views. This has been central to marginalizing the Radical Enlightenment.

Reviving the Radical Enlightenment is not just a matter of believing what we would like to believe, or avoiding the disastrous consequences of a reductionist conception of the world, or even a matter of defending democracy against an increasingly parasitic global managerial class. The strategy within the humanities of simply ignoring developments in science and upholding a more exalted view of humanity, sometimes aligned with various forms of Idealism, has clearly failed. It is first of all a matter of defending the quest for truth and the conditions for advancing and upholding it as a condition for challenging the reductionist conception of the world and the nihilism that follows from it, then showing that this Hobbesian view of humans is false and should be replaced. This highlights the importance of the central claim of speculative naturalism from Schelling to present day speculative naturalists: just to account for the possibility of science, let alone to do justice to the cognitive claims of the humanities as a condition for defending democracy, nature must be conceived in such a way that it is intelligible that humans, who have evolved within it as feeling, imaginative, conscious and potentially creative social subjects able to pursue truth, justice and beauty, reflect upon and transform their culture and themselves, and thereby their relationship to the rest of nature, could have evolved from and within it. This is a condition for accounting for the possibility of science. A conception of nature that denies this possibility is self-contradictory and therefore, must be false. Reductionist science along with the reductionist forms of explanation privileged by it, denying the reality of or causal efficacy of consciousness, and thereby the possibility of science, is incoherent, and in the name of truth, must be replaced.

Conversely, as Broad pointed out, the goal of speculative philosophy is to take into account the whole range of human experience – scientific, social, ethical, aesthetic and religious, and to develop a coherent conception of reality that does justice to all of these. In contrast to the naturalism of analytic philosophers, speculative naturalism not only affirms the ambitions of philosophy in the grand manner against any tendency to dissolve philosophy into apologetics for mainstream science; it has provided the basis for overcoming the deficiencies of mainstream science, and along with it, the Hobbesian conception of humans. Schelling's work exemplified this quest. As Devin Zane Shaw (2010) has shown, with some initial success (which he then failed to build upon), he attempted to forge a new synthesis of natural philosophy, art and history that would overcome the dualisms and gulfs within Kant's philosophy, and this has been the aim of speculative naturalism ever since. Consequently, this tradition has embraced Schelling's proclamation in *The Grounding of Positive Philosophy*, based on his notion of dialectics, that '[t]he true understanding of the world is provided by precisely the right metaphysics' (Schelling 2007, p.107), where metaphysics is speculative philosophy. That is, metaphysics or speculative philosophy is the basis of a coherent understanding of the world, including other people and ourselves, and for solidarity between people, and metaphysics guides all enquiry and all action. For this reason, as Karl Jaspers put it, 'Philosophy must enter into life. That applies not only to the individual but also to the condition of the time, to history and to humanity. The power of philosophy must penetrate everything, because one cannot live without it' (Jaspers 1993, p.144). These sentiments inspired and continue to inspire the modern tradition of speculative naturalism, which includes the modern traditions of eco-Marxism, process metaphysics, Peircian semiotics and naturalized phenomenology. By acknowledging and giving a place to real teleology and real creativity in nature and society, these inter-related traditions justify the assumption of the humanities that humans are genuinely creative, and that the arts and the disciplines of the humanities, particularly stories or narratives, are required along with the sciences to participate with the rest of nature in creating the future.

Speculative naturalism demands above all that the efficacy of final causes be recognized. What we see all around us are living beings actively involved in determining the future through anticipating and responding to anticipated possibilities. This cannot be explained through mere variation and selection. Idealism gives a place to free consciousness, but then cannot adequately explain nature and evolution. What is required is a form of science that can make intelligible the emergence of conscious beings not determined by the activities of their components, and this is science based on the process-relational thinking developed by speculative naturalists. As Schelling showed, this is the conception of the world that makes the possibility of life, consciousness and science intelligible. This insight has had to be rediscovered over and over again, with the most recent rediscovery having been made by Smolin in *Time Reborn: From the Crisis in Physics to the Future of the Universe*

(2013) and Unger and Smolin in *The Singular Universe and the Reality of Time* (2015). As shown in the previous chapter, evolutionary theory requires hierarchy theory as foreshadowed by Schelling and then revived and developed by Rosen, Pattee and Salthe in which emergence, involving new forms of downward causation through new constraints characterized by different process rates, is recognized. On this basis, Pattee provided a physical account of control, which, he argued, requires of systems that they generate models of themselves, and showed how physical processes could generate such symbols or signs. Salthe, a major figure in the further development of hierarchy theory, interpreted and defended Peircian semiotics through hierarchy theory, at the same time showing how emergence involves interpolation of new levels of constraint between shorter and longer scales and faster and slower rate processes. As noted in the previous chapter, he was able to explain the emergence of final causes through these concepts. In his study of anticipatory systems, Rosen showed that such final causes can be understood through mathematical models of systems that have models of themselves and their environments or ambiance. Life itself becomes intelligible as such, and science need no longer be committed to explaining it away as nothing but complexes of chemicals. Such models can be characterized through Peircian semiotics, and life and its evolution defined through the development of more and more complex forms of semiosis. While there are clearly differences between the genetic structuralism of Piaget and Peircian biosemiotics, work on the concept of causation could allow these traditions of thought, both strongly influenced by Kant, to be integrated. Theoretical biology now supports philosophical biology focused on characterizing the nature of life.

This alliance of theoretical biology and philosophical biology in turn support and are supported by the conception of humans and humanity developed in philosophical anthropology. Philosophical anthropology, along with philosophical biology, gained prominence in the early decades of the Twentieth Century through the work of Max Scheler, Helmuth Plessner, Arnold Gehlen and others (Fischer 2009). These philosophers were attempting to naturalize phenomenology, attempting to characterize the distinctive features of life and then of humans manifest in experience, rejecting both Husserl's Idealism as well as mechanistic models of life and humanity that simply ignored dimensions of experience inconsistent with reductionist science. However, philosophical anthropology had been developed more than a century earlier to oppose the Hobbesian tradition of thought, first by A.G. Baumgarten, and then by Kant, who argued in his lectures published as *Introduction to Logic* that the question 'What is Man? is the fundament question of philosophy and the key to answering the questions, 'What can I know? How should I act? and What can I hope for?' (Kant 1971, p.17). Through philosophical anthropology we should comprehend what is unique to humans, what humans have been, what they could be and what they should aspire to be. It engages dialectically with the sciences (critiquing, guiding and learning from particular scientific research) while simultaneously being central to the humanities, including political and ethical philosophy. John Zammito (2002) argues that Kant's student, Herder, carried on Kant's earlier work and made philosophical anthropology central to his own philosophy, developing a conception of humans as cultural beings, a conception that was then further developed by Schelling, Hegel and Marx and virtually all anti-reductionist, humanistic forms of the human sciences.

Kant had argued that the condition of the possibility of science, which at the same time provided the basis for upholding the reality of freedom as the foundation for ethics, is the self-identical 'I' which persists through all our changing experiences. This had been accepted by Kant's followers, but Fichte in his *Foundations of Natural Right* (2000, p.29) had shown that such an 'I' could only develop and sustain itself as such through limiting itself through recognizing and respecting others as free agents who in turn reciprocate this recognition, recognizing its own freedom. Following Fichte, Hegel rejected Kant's notion of the preformed ego, the 'I' represented as a pure unity relating to itself, and portrayed the ego as the result of the development, from immediate sensitivity to self-awareness, then to self-consciousness gained through achieving reciprocity of recognition in interpersonal relationships, and finally to universality through participation in ethical and cultural life, which he characterized as Spirit. Hegel characterized this formative process as part of three interdependent dialectical patterns: symbolic representation which operates through the medium of language; the labour process which operates through the medium of the tool; and interaction on the basis of reciprocity of recognition which operates through the medium of moral relations. While Habermas (1974) who first drew attention to these three interwoven dialectical processes he claimed that Hegel abandoned this trichotomy, Robert Williams (1997) showed that Hegel incorporated this dialectic into his later philosophy with its trichotomy of Subjective, Objective and Absolute Spirit.

Schelling's work can be seen as an earlier and similar attempt to naturalize the insights gained by Idealists. By situating these dialectical patterns (most importantly, the dialectic of recognition) in the context of the rest of nature, Schelling gave a place to the freedom of individuals to reject or embrace ethico-cultural life and also to transform it. That is, through his speculative naturalism, Schelling had already developed a philosophical anthropology by naturalizing the insights of the Idealists, notably Fichte. With the revival of philosophical anthropology in the Twentieth Century associated with the development of phenomenology, philosophers rediscovered the work of those influenced by Schelling, including the young Marx, Kierkegaard, Dostoyevsky and Nietzsche, and integrated their insights with those of the philosophical anthropologists inspired by phenomenology. While most of these were in Germany, Maurice Merleau-Ponty was also exemplary figure in this regard. Similar ideas were developed in the Soviet Union by Mikhail Bakhtin and the circle of thinkers influenced by him (Todorov 1984, Ch.7). On this basis Bakhtin developed his theory of dialogism which was further developed by the Moscow-Tartu school of semiotics. Philosophical anthropology, closely related to the tradition of hermeneutics, also has been central to German philosophy and has been strongly defended by Axel Honneth and Hans Joas (1988). This development has been associated with a new appreciation of the philosophical importance of the American philosophers, of William James by Sami Pihlström (1998) and George Herbert Mead by Hans Joas (1997), while these philosophers are ignored by most Anglophone philosophers.

The insights of these philosophical anthropologists can be further developed through Peircian semiotics, Piaget's genetic structuralism, non-linear thermodynamics and hierarchy theory, as I have shown (largely following Stan Salthe (1993)) in 'Philosophical Anthropology, Ethics and Political Philosophy in an Age of Impending Catastrophe' (Gare 2009). From this perspective, new levels of semiosis can be understood as the interpolation of new levels of constraint on the transformation of exergy into entropy so that humans not only constrain their activities in response to their surrounding worlds, but constrain their activities in recognition of others and of their shared world, and in relation to their own representations of themselves as participants in such shared worlds. It is by virtue of these more complex forms of semiosis associated with culture that humans have the capacity to form institutions and develop technologies, and then to understand not only their present situations but to anticipate the distant future. Furthermore, they have the capacity to question their models of themselves embodied in their interpretative schemes and the institutions based on and reproducing these schemes, and to modify these or even create entirely new schemes of interpretation, institutions and technologies. Humans are thereby able to see themselves as part of the future they will have participated in creating, and thereby to take responsibility for their future. Making intelligible a view of ourselves as anticipatory systems not only supports, but requires the humanities as the set of disciplines focusing on understanding and evaluating the present, developing new ideas and forms of thinking and deciding what futures we should be striving to create, and mobilizing people to create such futures. As such, the humanities should give a central place to the philosophy of nature, which should include philosophical biology and philosophical anthropology.

Conceived in this way, humans must be seen to have the capacity to act back on the conditions of their emergence, and this implies the possibility of altering the trajectories of their natural and social communities. If the conditions are maintained for pursuing and disseminating the truth, it can be demonstrated we are not condemned to destroying the conditions of our existence. It is the commitment to truth and the conditions for pursuing it that could provide the ultimate foundation and unity for an environmental movement able to successfully challenge neoliberalism, or rather, managerialist market fundamentalism, and create a new, global civilization. The most illuminating way to comprehend the significance of this view is to consider the work of a recent defender of the humanities, the Russian philosopher Mikhail Epstein, referred to earlier.

Epstein in *The Transformative Humanities* offers not only a defense and guidance for reviving the humanities, but more importantly, a crucial clarification of what the humanities are and what role they should play. Succinctly:

The crucial distinction between the humanities and the sciences is that in the humanities the subject and the object of study coincide; in the humanities, humans are studied by humans and for humans. Therefore, to study the human being also means to create humanness itself; every act of the description of the human is, by the same token, an event of one's self construction. In a wholly practical sense, the humanities create the human, as human beings are transformed by the study of literature, art, languages, history and philosophy: the humanities humanize.

(Epstein 2012, p.7)

Humans create themselves by creating 'new images, signs and concepts of themselves ... humans do not so much discover something in the world of objects as build their very subjectivity by way of self-description and self-projection' (Epstein 2012, p.8). Following Rosen, we can also add: new models of nature and of ourselves within it. It is by virtue of this self-reflexivity that the humanities are more fundamental than the sciences. Alluding to the way meta-mathematics and the theory of computation founder on problems of self-reference, Epstein notes that 'the natural sciences are most interested in what makes the humanities "less scientific", their subject-object reversibility, for example, their semantic fuzziness, and even the metaphoric nature of their language. The natural sciences cannot strive for the pinnacle of self-organized and self-reflective knowledge without the humanities' critical contribution' (Epstein 2012, p.8f.) It is by virtue of this critical contribution that the humanities are not merely a supplement to science, but must lead it. As Epstein noted, 'the humanities used to determine, and give meaning to historic eras. The era of Enlightenment was inaugurated by philosophy and literature..., the era of Romanticism came into being thanks to the creative efforts of literary critics, linguists, poets and writers.... It has traditionally been the role of the humanities to lead humankind' (Epstein 2012, p.12). It is on this basis that Epstein quoted with approval Whitehead's proclamation in *Modes of Thought* that 'the task of a University is the creation of the future, so far as rational thought, and civilized modes of appreciation, affect the issue' (Whitehead 1938, p.171).

Clarifying this further, Epstein pointed out that the natural sciences are concerned with nature, and the practical extension of science is technology through which we transform nature. The human sciences study society, and their practical extension is politics through which society is transformed. The humanities focus on culture, and the practical extension of this is the transformation of culture. But we are not separate from culture, and to transform culture is to transform ourselves. In the humanities, the subject and the object of inquiry coincide. It is through the transformation of culture that we create ourselves as human. The humanities create new subjectivities, and such subjectivities are required if people are to take responsibility for the future and govern themselves accordingly. The natural sciences and the capacity to transform nature and the human sciences and the political power bequeathed by the social sciences to transform society are each part of culture, while culture is an essential constituent of society and has evolved from and within nature. While culture is a product of nature and develops through society, the natural scientist and the social scientist are themselves formations and products of culture. The whole project of understanding nature in order to transform it was launched by Francis Bacon, and it was the philosopher William Whewell in the Nineteenth Century who coined the term 'scientist'. The concept and role of the scientist were created by the humanities, and it is through the humanities that this project and the role of scientists can be defended, questioned, criticized and modified. The study of nature and society by the natural and social sciences are not only projects to comprehend these to facilitate their transformation; they are part of a humanities inspired project to define and form our relationship to nature and society to create the future.

Naturalizing neo-Hegelian social philosophy: the radical spirit

The Radical Enlightenment, committed to a process-relational metaphysics supported by post-reductionist natural philosophy and science, situates people in the context of humanity's self-creation within nature through history, moving towards a new civilization where the destructive conflicts between tribes, civilizations and nations will have been overcome. Advancing the Radical Enlightenment at present involves unifying the whole of humanity in a commitment to advancing the health of the global ecosystem and its subordinate communities. The argument here is that this goal should be understood as the quest for a global ecological civilization. While the notion of civilization has not been central to political philosophy, it is in fact a notion that encompasses within it all the ideals of the Radical Enlightenment. The term derives from the Latin *civitas,* the social body of the *cives,* or citizens, united by law that binds them together, giving them responsibilities on the one hand and rights of citizenship on the other. The law has a life of its own, creating a *res publica* or 'public entity' (synonymous with *civitas*). As the Roman Empire expanded the term was used for those kingdoms that were allowed some measure of self-governance. So, to be civilized means to be able to govern oneself, having been educated to do so, and thereby having acquired the virtues of *humanitas,* or humanity.

As noted, the pivotal figures in the German Renaissance were Kant, Herder, Fichte, Schelling and Hegel, with Hegel providing the fullest development of social and political philosophy. However, Hegel was an Idealist, arguing that the ground-plan of nature and human history pre-existed their creation, and that Nature was posited by Spirit as its Other in opposition to which it could develop itself. He offered a grand narrative of progress defined as the advance of freedom and consciousness, along with the technological conditions for achieving this, but his Idealist metaphysics is no longer credible, and its implausibility has weakened the influence of Hegel's social philosophy and those influenced by it. Rather than putting Hegel on his feet, as Marx claimed to have done, it is necessary in order to revive this tradition to turn Hegel's philosophy inside out, with humanity seen as emergent within nature and individuals as emergent from and within communities and cultures, which themselves are generative of and susceptible to the emergence of self-reproducing economic, social and cultural formations with their own, partially autonomous dynamics.

Following Hegel's philosophical anthropology developed in his early works, the advance of this capacity for self-governance and the associated freedom, the development of the State through history can be characterized as the advance of the interwoven dialectical patterns of recognition, representation and labour driving the quest for justice, truth and empowerment. This can be conceived as the development of 'Spirit', as Hegel portrayed it. It is also necessary to recognize the three aspects of Spirit identified by Hegel in his later work: Subjective, Objective and Absolute Spirit, corresponding to the concepts of 'personality' 'society' and 'culture' deployed by the Russian/American sociologist Pitirim Sorokin (1947) and those he influenced. However, to defend these ideas against positivist reductionism they need to be understood through Schelling's philosophy and speculative naturalism rather than Hegel's Idealism. As with the dialectics of representation, recognition and labour, Subjective, Objective and Absolute Spirit are components of each other without being reducible to each other. 'Spirit' here should always be understood as inspiration that is generated by and keeps alive historically developing communities such that it is appropriate for people to think of themselves as 'we', united in their struggle to advance civilization, as David Carr argued in *Time, Narrative, and History* (1991, p.138ff.). Naturalizing both the notion of Spirit and the Absolute, it should be noted that 'the Absolute' (i.e, the 'unconditioned') from a Schellingian perspective is the self-organizing universe in process of becoming, becoming conscious of itself, while Spirit is the impetus for the self-creation of humans as communities participating in this self-organizing universe. Following Joel Kovel (1991), 'Spirit' should always be understood in relation to 'inspiration', associated with engagement in the dialectics of representation, recognition and labour with others in pursuit of truth, justice, and empowerment. Inspiration comes from appreciating that one is part of a meaningful whole of which one is at least potentially a significant participant. 'Spirit' should not be reified as a transcendent entity using individuals as instruments, any more than the 'Absolute' should be understood as a transcendent being.

Objective and Absolute Spirit

Objective Spirit, in Hegel's philosophy, is the realm of institutions. As the philosophical anthropologist, Arnold Gehlen, argued, with their unformed nature and cognitive potential, humans can and must institutionalize their practices (Honneth and Joas 1988, p.48f.). Reacting to both the failures of the French revolution and the rise of Britain as the dominant world power based on atomic individualism and utilitarianism, Hegel was concerned to identify the diverse institutions that had evolved to make up the modern State, understood in the broader sense, which for Hegel included a people or nation, their territory and their institutions of government through which they are recognized as free, and could participate in maintaining their freedom. It is necessary to appreciate that this Hegelian notion of the State accords with the Greek notion of polis and the Renaissance notion of the State. 'State', as Quentin Skinner (2002, p.13) pointed out, is an abbreviation of '*stati liberi*', a differentiated self-governing community being in a state of freedom, as opposed to being subject to the arbitrary will of rulers on whom they are dependent. Objective Spirit includes the family, the economic institutions of civil society, including corporations (trade unions and professional bodies) through which workers could protect their livelihoods and gain recognition for their significance, and the institutions of the State understood in a narrower sense as the strictly political state or government, unifying the principles of the family and civil society and according people and these institutions due recognition through the laws that it promulgates and enforces and through the public institutions which it finances and sustains. The State in this sense includes legal and regulatory bodies and enforcement agencies, health, education and research institutions, social security systems, public works systems that build and maintain water and power supplies and transport and communications infrastructure, financial institutions required for the functioning of markets and diplomatic and defence organizations, along with the legislative and executive institutions of local, provincial and national governments. These make and oversee the enforcement of laws and regulations, levy taxes, determine and monitor public expenditure, and set up, monitor and reform other institutions, including economic enterprises, to ensure they serve the State (in the broader sense), while gaining recognition from, negotiating agreements with or declaring war on other States.

Along with the mobilization and coordination of activities required to sustain and augment life, these institutions crystallize recognition of people's freedom and significance, so to define one's situation through received concepts that structure these institutions and define roles and actions and relations between them, to do one's duty as a participant in these institutions, is to realize this recognition. Freedom here is understood as the freedom to live as one should, upholding and augmenting freedom. Acting dutifully requires some measure of 'inspiration', that is, to be moved by the spirit of these institutions. As F.H. Bradley argued in 'My Station and its Duties' in *Ethical Studies* (1962, Essay 5), people must develop the appropriate virtues to fill conceptually defined roles in these institutions, which should include understanding and appreciating their function in the broader society or societies. This is particularly important for maintaining the civil service and legal and political institutions and the Humboldtian form of the university, but in fact almost all institutions in society, including those associated with the family and the economy, require the cultivation of such specific virtues.

Schelling in *System of Transcendental Idealism* (1997, p.198) added to this tradition by calling for an international political organization and legal institutions to recognize and defend the autonomy of nations (essentially, what became the United Nations). Similar ideas were developed by the Hegelian philosopher, Friedrich Carové. Carové, originally a student of Hegel, argued against Hegel's celebration of the particular State, arguing that (as Edward Toews interpreted him), 'only mankind as a totality, as an inwardly differentiated, universal community, could constitute the Kingdom of God in this earth' (Toews 1985, p.139). In the modern world it should be apparent that such institutionalized recognition of freedom requires multiple levels of political organization, with major regions organized to protect more localized communities, governments and economies from subjugation and exploitation, and the United Nations or its equivalent required to uphold this structure. The world should be constituted as communities of communities, the autonomy of which should be protected, so long as these communities are augmenting rather than destroying the conditions for other such communities. The ultimate end of these communities of communities should be the creation of an ecological sustainable civilization.

Participating in Objective Spirit requires participation in the realm of 'Absolute Spirit'. Through Absolute Spirit, awareness and consciousness associated with the dialectic of representation (or orientation) are developed. This is the dialectic in which people struggle to orient themselves and make sense of their lives and their social and natural worlds and become fully conscious of themselves and their significance as the products of evolution and history. Unless participants in institutions are able to appreciate the broader historical and cosmological contexts of the institutions of Objective Spirit, these inevitably degenerate or become malignant. When institutions are corrupted by uninspired careerists, the communities of which they are part become decadent; that is, they decay. Institutions become malignant when they become entirely self-serving, expanding in a way that damages, oppresses, enslaves or destroys the communities of which they are part. In the contemporary world, universities are central to the dialectic of representation and should function as centers for preserving, criticizing, developing and passing on the culture (or Spirit) of nations and civilizations from generation to generation. True universities thereby play an essential role in achieving, maintaining and advancing the dialectic of recognition and the struggle for freedom. The media should also be recognized as such a set of institutions, institutions that, as Sandra Borden described in *Journalism as Practice: MacIntyre, Virtue Ethics and the Press* (2010), have been severely corrupted by media moguls.

Hegel subdivided Absolute Spirit into art, religion and philosophy. Although Hegel did not conceive Absolute Spirit in this way, it is through art, religion and philosophy that imagination is fostered, the historical and cosmological significance and proper ends of life, humanity, communities, these institutions and individual lives are revealed, understood, appreciated and questioned, and pathologies identified and successes celebrated. It is through participating in Absolute Spirit that people respond creatively to conflicts of obligations and other deficiencies in their cultures and societies, whether these have revealed themselves in crises or not. While it might be thought that Absolute Spirit is most removed from nature, and to some extent this is true of Hegel's understanding of Absolute Spirit, it is through Absolute Spirit that the full significance of being part of nature can and should be comprehended. Schelling, a source of inspiration for the development of thermodynamics, field theory, systems theory, complexity theory and hierarchy theory, had shown how final causes could be reintroduced into science, and the emergence of humanity concerned to achieve higher forms of consciousness made intelligible.

Hegel privileged philosophy over art and religion. Philosophy for Hegel included science, mathematics, history and political economy. To participate in the life of philosophy requires first and foremost that people take responsibility for their own and others' beliefs and ways of understanding the world, and a commitment to improving these, participating in the ongoing dialogue that is central to a healthy cultural life. This involves people respecting each other's points of view while questing for deeper and broader understanding, acknowledging the limitations, fallibility and possible falsity of their own and other's views. It also involves at least tacit appreciation of the social and historical context of each dialogue, acknowledging genres and traditions utilized or drawn upon and the cultural fields that provide the conditions for these, while being open to questioning of these and of themselves, and to innovation. All this requires an appreciation of history and the historicity of existence, which was central to Hegel's thinking but which he did not discuss in relation to Absolute Spirit. These are the virtues required for dialectical thinking. Through the work of Bourdieu, we can also appreciate the importance of developing a *habitus* that acknowledges and augments the autonomy of cultural fields, including the academic field, and resists tendencies to undermine this autonomy (as is occurring at present), or which trivialize the field's significance, for instance, by consecrating only cultural productions that are irrelevant to everything else as when art is promoted as art for art's sake, or philosophy is reduced to academic parlour games. The importance of cultivating the virtues for participating in the realm of Absolute Spirit becomes even greater when people with different cultural and civilizational backgrounds engage in dialogue.

For Hegel, art includes music, all the plastic arts – painting, sculpture and architecture, and literature, which he saw as mere steps on the way to philosophy. The arts were held to be more significant by Friedrich Schiller and Schelling before him, and after him, by Peirce, John Dewey, Scheler, Heidegger and most recently Mark Johnson. Schiller's *On the Aesthetic Education of Man* (1982) defended the objectivity of beauty and characterized human development from a first phase of unselfconscious, to a second phase of reflective lucidity, to a third phase, achieved through art, combining the virtues of both to achieve a new kind of spontaneity in which people with cultivated taste are not constrained by a rigid Kantian moralism but are self-constraining through spontaneous inclination, consummating 'the will of the whole through the nature of the individual' (p.215). Art is the organ of philosophy through which anyone can gain an appreciation of and be inspired by the Absolute (the unconditioned) of which we are part and in which we are participants, Schelling argued in *The Philosophy of Art* (1989). The art object unites the sensible with the intelligible, and artistic activity realizes the ideas of philosophy in the world.[9] In his later work, Schelling argued in opposition to Hegel that human reason cannot explain human existence. The insights of art are also required, and so art cannot be treated as merely a stage on the way to philosophical consciousness of the Absolute.

Peirce concurred with Schiller and Schelling, as Vincent Potter has shown in *Charles S. Peirce: On Norms & Ideals* (1997). He claimed that just as logic presupposes ethics, and can be regarded as a branch of ethics, ethics presupposes aesthetics which determines what is admirable. Participation in Absolute Spirit is education of one's feelings and emotions through art (including crafts, architecture and literature). Peirce's ideas were taken up and further developed by William James and John Dewey. Mark Johnson (2007), drawing on Dewey, argues that the arts are the culmination of efforts by humanity to find meaning. Suzanne Langer, influenced by Whitehead and Ernst Cassirer, placed art at the centre of her philosophical anthropology developed as the culmination of her work in *Mind: An Essay on Human Feeling* (1970–1984). She argued that works of art symbolize feeling, which is a form of knowledge. Martin Heidegger (1971) and Theodor Adorno (1984) revived claims for primacy of art over science in Germany. In Britain, Wendy Wheeler in *The Whole Creature* (2006) has defended the humanistic Marxism of the literary theorist Raymond Williams by interpreting it through complexity theory, Michael Polanyi's philosophy of science and Peircian biosemiotics, again defending the central place for art in life. What all such work suggests, is that without properly educated feelings and the insights gained from this, augmented through practical activities, people are blind to meaning and so will be unlikely to undertake the hard work of engaging in philosophy or to make the effort to live wisely in accordance with philosophy. It is on such grounds that Paul Schafer argued in *Revolution or Renaissance: Making the Transition form an Economic Age to a Cultural Age* (2008) that the goal of life now should be greater wisdom rather than owning more consumer goods.

What is involved in the realization of philosophy in the world through art as Schelling characterized it is illuminated by the architectural theorist, Christopher Alexander. Attempting to overcome the disastrous influence of mechanistic thinking in architecture and town planning, Alexander showed how the creation of beautiful buildings requires the cultivation of a feel for the whole, which also transforms the person. As he put it *The Nature of Order: An Essay on the Art of Building and the Nature of the Universe: Book Four*:

> Gradually, as the greater and greater experience of true feeling occurs in a person, as true feeling therefore grows more and more clear within you, you are learning something about *yourself*. ... so, what happens is that you, in this state, experience more and more truly the feeling of being free. ...

You experience art, grass, leaves, and sky as connectedness towards the I, that you are part of the great I along with the grass and the sky.

(Alexander 2004, p.267)

As I have argued, Alexander's work is an advance over Heidegger's philosophy in developing an ecological ethos for humanity (Gare 2003/2004). Interpreted through Peircian biosemiotics, building as Alexander conceived it is a form of morphogenesis, should be seen as participation in the vegetative semiosis of nature (Gare 2007/2008).

Religion will also be central to the creation of an ecological civilization. Observing economic imperatives, Schelling anticipated the unification of humanity in one civilization. This would lead to the development of a world consciousness requiring the development of a 'philosophical religion' transcending the parochialism of the specific religions of particular civilizations, while incorporating the truths of each (Schelling 2007, p.83). Similar arguments were made by Friedrich Carové, who 'conceived the breakthrough to a universal human community, primarily, or at least in the last instance, as a transformation of consciousness, as a product of cultural education' (Toews 1985, p.139). Speculative naturalism clarifies and advances this quest, continuing the efforts to replace reductionist materialism, understanding complexity, defending the efficacy of final causes, recognizing the problems of creating a global civilization and providing the basis for this philosophical religion. The education of feeling combined with a deeper understanding of nature achieved through such philosophy should be central to the development of such a religion,understanding 'religion' in its original sense as 'reconnection'. This religion could be either a form of pantheism or panentheism or a non-theistic religion; for instance, a development of Daoism. Clearly, this is what Peirce, Max Scheler, Bergson, Collingwood, Whitehead and Heidegger, often influenced by Asian religions, were striving to provide.

Subjective Spirit

Subjective Spirit can only be understood in relation to Objective Spirit and Absolute Spirit, but it is not reducible to them. Cognition develops in each individual through stages and to become a fully developed political and ethical subject requires the capacity for dialectical thinking. Dialectical thinking involves not only the capacity to engage in dialogue, question existing institutions and assumptions and develop radically new ways of thinking, but also the imaginative capacity to relate abstract thinking to feeling and emotion, to relate science to art and to utilize metaphors and to construct and reconstruct compelling narratives. It is the capacity to utilize analysis, synopsis and synthesis. This is what is required to fully participate in the dialectical advance of a pre-existing Objective and Absolute Spirit. Dialectical thinking involves openness to others and a willingness to have one's horizons of expectations challenged, and willingness to rethink one's understanding of the world and oneself accordingly. This is not the end of the matter, particularly for those influenced by Schelling, directly or indirectly, from Kierkegaard, Nietzsche, Mikhail Bakhtin and Heidegger to the existentialists. There are also issues associated with how individuals deal with their particular situations and relationships, make choices and commit themselves to causes in what are often unique situations and contexts. At issue here is what is involved in taking responsibility for one's life, becoming reflexive, cultivating one's abilities and developing and maintaining such virtues as integrity, authenticity, sagacity, courage, a feel for the whole and loyalty in one's particular circumstances. These should be understood in relation to the roles individuals take on and the practices they participate in. The commitments they make are associated with these roles, but they are not reducible to them.

One of the best worked out versions of ethical philosophy to come from this neo-Hegelian tradition, highlighting the institutions and community context within which people are situated and what is involved in participating in institutions, while acknowledging the importance of the subject and individual freedom, was developed by Josiah Royce (1855–1916), the American neo-Hegelian philosopher. Privileging the virtue of loyalty, his ethico-political ideas were grounded in an analysis of the conditions necessary for an individual life to become meaningful. Kelley Parker summarized Royce's conclusions:

> To lead a morally significant life, one's actions must express a self-consciously asserted will. They must contribute toward realizing a plan of life, a plan that is itself unified by some freely chosen aim. Such an aim and its corresponding plan of life could not easily be created by an individual out of the chaos of conflicting personal desires and impulses that we all encounter. Rather, such aims and plans are found already largely formed in social experience: we come to consciousness in a world that proffers countless well-defined causes and programs for their accomplishment. These programs extend through time and require the contributions of many individuals for their advancement. When one judges a cause to be worthwhile and fully embraces such a program, several momentous things happen. The individual's will is focused and defined in terms of the shared cause. The individual becomes allied with a community of others who are also committed to the same cause. Finally, a morally significant commitment to the cause and to the community develops. This commitment is what Royce calls 'loyalty'. The moral life may be understood in terms of the multiple loyalties that a person exhibits.
>
> (Parker 2004, p.6)

For Royce, community precedes the individual. Responding to Nietzsche, Royce argued that my life means nothing unless I am a member of a community. It is through membership of communities and playing roles in its institutions that it becomes possible to harmonize desires and integrate them into a self. Community and the formation of a collective will do not involve the dissolution of individualism, however, but are the conditions for becoming an individual. A community is constituted by people accepting as part of their own individual lives the same past events and the same expectations: they must be a community of memory and a community of expectation and hope.

Not any loyalty makes actions morally valid. Royce recognized that some of the most hideous acts in history have followed from loyalty to causes. To be morally valid the cause to which loyalty is given must be consistent with loyalty generally. Loyalty also requires that individuals scrutinize the aims and actions of the communities of which they are part to reform their 'disloyal' aspects. This should involve questioning these institutions, the concepts that define them and their functions, taking responsibility for them. To this degree, Royce's philosophy accords with Castoriadis' defence of autonomy. For Royce, the highest moral achievements involve individuals' loyalty to ideals that promote the formation and expansion of communities of loyalty. As Royce put it, 'A cause is good, not only for me, but for mankind, in so far as it is essentially a *loyalty to loyalty,* that is, an aid and a furtherance of loyalty in my fellows. It is an evil cause in so far as, despite the loyalty that it arouses in me, it is destructive of loyalty in the world of my fellows' (Royce 1995, p.56). It is not difficult to see from this that embracing the cause of endlessly increasing power or wealth, whether of individuals or nations, is an evil. For people to gain meaning in their lives by being loyal to causes, they must first be free to make such commitments and then free to be loyal. To be loyal to loyalty, causes must be pursued in a way which upholds the conditions of others to make such commitments.

On this principle, other people, whether colleagues loyal to the same cause, or people pursuing other causes, must never be treated as mere instruments to be used or exploited for profit. Taylorist managerialism, whereby knowledge and decision-making are concentrated in the hands of managers, and workers are treated as instruments of organizations evaluated according to how much they contribute to their profitability, should be seen as not only soul destroying, but inimical to life, corrupting of the virtues required to augment Objective Spirit. People should be recognized as free subjects and the causes which they have committed themselves to and by which they have given meaning to their lives must also be recognized if Objective Spirit is to be maintained and advanced. Considering the global ecological crisis, all specific causes and the institutions that embody them should accord with and be judged in terms of the ultimate cause of creating a global ecological civilization. While this requires international institutions such as the United Nations to achieve this, this ultimate cause should be continually reworked to take into account and adjust to local and more specific causes.

Commitment to causes and conscientiousness in social roles is not merely a matter of making decisions. It requires the habituation of virtues required by these roles, along with a proper appreciation of the significance of these causes, and the courage to question and take a stand against existing authorities and structures of power and to defend the practices required to advance these causes. It requires an appreciation of the cultural, social and economic fields within which people are participating and commitment to maintaining the autonomy of these fields. To do so, each individual should organize their lives into the unity of a biography, and relate the narrative of their own lives to the narratives of the causes they are committed to, to institutions, communities, cultural fields, civilization and more broadly, ecosystems within which they are participating. People should understand their lives as unfinished stories, relating these to the narratives of other individuals, organizations and communities at every level, situating themselves in relation to all of these, interrogating, supporting or challenging and participating in reformulating the narratives by which each person, organization and community is currently defined. They should cultivate as practices the virtues required to uphold the ideals and goals of these stories. This is the essence of authentic self-realization. To properly understand what all this involves it is not only necessary to understand Subjective Spirit in the context of Objective and Absolute Spirit and emergent cultural, social and economic formations, it is also necessary to understand Spirit as part of and participation in nature, as eco-poiesis.

Notes

1 Controlling the finance sector has always been a central concern of institutionalists, particularly Thorstein Veblen. The problems of out of control financial institutions and how to bring them back under control have been the focus of work by Hyman P. Minsky (2008) and Massimo Amato and Luca Fantacci (2012).

2 A number of superb works have been written on this, including Philip Mirowski, *Never Let a Serious Crisis go to Waste* (2013) and John Quiggin, *Zombie Economics: How Dead Ideas Still Walk Amongst Us: A Chilling Tale by John Quiggin* (2010). For a synthetic work developing out of the political economy movement that developed at Cambridge University led by Joan Robinson, see Edward J. Nell, *The General Theory of Transformational Growth: Keynes After Sraffa* (1998). For an institutionalist approach, See also Geoffrey M. Hodgson, *From Pleasure Machines to Moral Communities: An Evolutionary Economics Without Homo Economicus* (2013). For an alternative set of policies based on the tradition of historical, institutionalist economics, see Erik S. Reinert ed., *Globalization, Economic Development and Inequality: An Alternative Perspective* (2004).

3 On the state of sociology, see Carlos Frade, 'The Sociological Imagination and Its Promise Fifty Years Later: Is There a Future for the Social Sciences as a *Free* Form of Enquiry?' (2009) This confirms the diagnosis of sociology made in the appendix to Anton C. Zijderveld, *On Clichés: The Supersedure of Meaning by Function in Modernity* (1979). Zijderveld pointed out that sociology had almost completely broken with the great sociologists of the past to undertake empirical research. Frade confirms this and shows how it has eliminated critical perspectives.

4 The destruction of education is documented in Richard Arum and Josipa Roksa, *Academically Adrift: Limited Learning on College Campuses* (2011). The debasement of the sciences has been analysed by Carl Boggs in *Intellectuals and the Crisis of Modernity* (2003). On where this is leading, see Dmitry Orlov, *The Five Stages of Collapse: Survivor's Toolkit* (2013) The black humour with which this book is written should not blind readers to the profundity of Orlov's observations. Much the same conclusions are reached in the anthology *The Politics of Empire: Globalisation in Crisis* edited by Alan Freeman and Boris Kagarlitsky (2004), published before the global financial crisis. Evidence for growing and unsustainable wealth concentration has been provided by Ann Pettifor, *The Coming First World Debt Crisis* (2006)

and more recently, Thomas Piketty, *Capital in the Twenty-First Century* (2014). Stephen Hymer had predicted that this, along with the destruction of the welfare state – and effectively the nation-state as a self-governing community, would be the inevitable outcome of the growth of multinational corporations in the late 1960s. See his posthumously published essays in Stephen Herbert Hymer, *The Multinational Corporation* (1979).

5 This is evident in Anglophone political philosophy. Anthologies such as *Contemporary Debates in Political Philosophy* edited by Thomas Christiano and John Christman (2009), *A Companion to Contemporary Political Philosophy, two volumes* edited by Robert E. Goodin, Philip Pettit and Thomas Pogge (2007), and *Debates in Contemporary Political Philosophy: An Anthology* edited by Derek Matavers and Jon Pike (2005) illustrate this. European political philosophy does not offer much more, as is evident in Oliver Marchart's, *Post-Foundational Political Thought* (2007).

6 An excellent synoptic work examining the history of democratic thought in all its varieties is David Held's, *Models of Democracy* (2006). Charles Taylor's work is well known. Also of importance are works by Axel Honneth *The Pathologies of Individual Freedom: Hegel's Social Theory* (2010) and Philip Pettit, *On the People's Terms: A Republican Theory and Model of Democracy* (2012). David Miller has defended communitarianism in *Citizenship and National Identity* (2000) and *Justice for Earthlings* (2013).

7 See for instance, Avital Simhony and David Weinstein's anthology *The New Liberalism: Reconciling Liberty and Community* (2001). Since this book was published there has been a flood of books on Green and the British Idealists. One of the more recent is W.J. Mander, *British Idealism: A History* (2011) and the two volume work by Colin Tyler, *The Liberal Socialism of Thomas Hill Green, Part 1: The Metaphysics of Self-realisation and Freedom* (2010) and *Part II, Civil Society, Capitalism and the State* (2012). See also the anthology edited by ed. Maria Dimova-Cookson and W.J. Mander, *T.H. Green: Ethics, Metaphysics, and Political Philosophy* (2006) and David Boucher and Andrew Vincent, *British Idealism and Political Theory* (2000).

8 An exemplary work attempting to confront the present by drawing on the history of political philosophy are the essays in Quentin Skinner and Bo Stråth's anthology *States and Citizens: History, Theory, Prospects* (2003). Key essays associated with these efforts can be found in *The Liberty Reader*, edited by David Miller (2006). Neo-Hegelianism has been developed by a range of authors, beginning with Hegel's contemporaries, liberals such as Eduard Gans who were disowned by Hegel and for a long time were overshadowed by Young Hegelians, Marx and Marxists. These were brought to light by Edward Toews *Hegelianism: the Path Toward Dialectical Humanism, 1805–1841* (1985).

9 The whole development of aesthetics in German philosophy, which is the reference point for all work in aesthetics, is described by Andrew Bowie, *From Romanticism to Critical Theory* 1997) and *Aesthetics and Subjectivity: From Kant to Nietzsche* (2013) and Kai Hammermeister, *The German Aesthetic Tradition* (2002).

6 From the radical enlightenment to ecological civilization

Creating the future

Making science consistent with the reality of humans and their potential for understanding, responsibility and creativity not only is an advance of science; it is a transformation of culture and therefore a development of the humanities. Since culture is a component of society, this is also a transformation of society, and since culture as a complex of different forms of semiosis is a component of the semiosphere, it is also a transformation of nature, altering how we act and live within society and nature and what and how we produce. It involves transforming the concepts or categories through which we define our relationships to each other, to society and to nature, and to ourselves; that is, to use Marx's apt terminology, our 'forms of existence'. This is what is required to create an ecologically sustainable civilization; that is, an ecological civilization.

The discipline that focuses all this and upholds or provides the concepts needed to replace the concepts that are the forms of existence in the present order, is ecology. Ecology, the study of 'households' in biotic communities, where emergence, hierarchical order, semiosis, symbiosis, and anticipatory systems are central, is pre-eminently an anti-reductionist science exemplifying, and further developing process-relational thinking. As Donald Worster (1994) and Douglas Weiner (1988) showed in their classic histories of the science of ecology in the West and in Russia respectively, it was a discipline engendered by, influenced by and is reciprocally influencing the tradition of speculative naturalism. A leading theoretical ecologist, Robert Ulanowicz, points out that ecology brings into focus what are now coming to be seen as the core problems that have to be addressed to advance science in all fields. All sciences are having to acknowledge the reality of organized complexity and its emergence, and ecology is the field in which these can most easily be studied. As he put it in his book *Ecology, The Ascendent Perspective*:

> Ecology occupies the propitious middle ground. ... Indeed ecology may well provide a *preferred* theatre in which to search for principles that might offer very broad implications for science in general. If we loosen the grip of our prejudice in favour of mechanism as the general principle, we see in this thought the first inkling that ecology, the sick discipline, could in fact become the key to a radical leap in scientific thought. A new perspective

on how things happen in the ecological world might conceivably break the conceptual logjams that currently hinder progress in understanding evolutionary phenomena, development biology, the rest of the life sciences, and, conceivably, even physics.

(Ulanowicz 1997, p.6)

Ulanowicz argues for a 'process ecology' which should serve as the foundation for 'an ecological metaphysic' (Ulanowicz 2009, Ch.6). In accordance with the tradition of speculative naturalism, the ultimate existents of the universe would have to be seen as creative processes, or durational self-constraining patterns of activity, and configurations of such processes at multiple scales in dynamic interaction, rather than objects or things, which are taken to have only a derivative status. This is also the view of ecology defended by hierarchy theorists such as Tim Allen and Stan Salthe (Allen and Starr 1982; O'Neill et al. 1986; Salthe 1993). The focus of science is on processes and chance events, rather than law, since as Ulanowicz put it: 'laws emerged out of inchoate processes eventually to become static, degenerate forms of the latter' (2009, p.164). Ecology has become the focal point for recovering and developing the tradition of speculative naturalism that began with Herder, Goethe and Schelling. While the focus on complexity is strongly associated the advance of thermodynamics, ecology also serves to bring into focus the relationship between quantum dynamics, energetic processes and structures. Acknowledging energy transformations, hierarchical order and a proper place for final causes in living processes facilitates an appreciation of how physical and chemical structures have been harnessed and developed by dissipative structures and have facilitated more complex forms of life. It is now also coming to be seen how life is made possible by the peculiar aspects of reality revealed by quantum mechanics, and how quantum processes have also been harnessed with the evolution of life. A study of the interaction between vibrations and molecular noise in bacterial phytosynthetic complexes has revealed that quantum transport of energy is not only utilized but is optimal around the temperatures at which plants photosynthesise. What this indicates, as Jim Al-Khalili and Johnjoe McFadden pointed out in *Life on the Edge: The Coming of Age of Quantum Biology* (2014), is that 'three billion years of natural selection have fine-tuned the quantum-level evolutionary engineering of exciton [i.e. free electrons] transport to optimize the most important biochemical reaction in the biosphere' (p.303). Such research has stimulated further work on how biomolecules are able to sustain such quantum coherence at normal temperatures. This has revealed the centrality of quantum coherence to biological organization, including cognition and consciousness, and thereby its role in the evolution of ecosystems, supporting the conjectures of Mae-Wan Ho that only by taking into account quantum coherence (and electro-magnetic fields) can biological phenomena be explained. Such work is not only utilizing ideas from quantum mechanics, but is facilitating further development of this field of research.

Ecology so conceived provides a site for the study of semiosis (the production and interpretation of signs) and its evolution into more complex forms associated with new levels of constraint. As Jacob von Uexküll argued, each organism has an *Umwelt* or surrounding world that has meaning for it, which it senses or perceives, grows or acts in response to. (Uexküll 1926, Ch.5). Surrounding worlds can include other organisms and can engender inner-worlds. The development, response to and interaction between such surrounding worlds can be understood and analysed through Peircian semiotics and hierarchy theory and is central to symbiosis and co-evolution. Organisms, from prokaryotic cells to humans themselves are now regarded as highly integrated ecosystems 'in which the thermodynamic patterns seen in ecological ascendancy achieve high boundedness, stability, and predictability' (Depew and Weber 1996, p.474). They are characterized by a diversity of increasingly complex forms of semiosis (including vegetative, animal and symbolic), while semiosis is essential to the global ecosystem, generating a global semiosphere. (Hoffmeyer 1993; Emmeche and Kull 2011). As Kalevi Kull (2010) argued, ecosystems are made of semiotic bonds.

Ecology, eco-semiotics and human ecology

In 'Vegetative, Animal, and Cultural Semiosis: The semiotic threshold zones' (2009) Kull also argued that humans, defined by more complex forms of semiosis, should be understood in the context of these ecosystems. Their surrounding worlds are augmented through the development of *Mitwelten* or with-worlds, and then *Eigenwelten*, or self-worlds, which emerge when individuals reflect on their lives and situations. The dialectical patterns of representation, recognition and labour identified by Hegel can be understood in the context of ecosystems as semiotic developments. Associated with their worlds, humans form technologies, institutions and cultural fields, or forms of Spirit, that provide the conditions for the further development of these dialectical patterns (Gare 2002a). Conceiving humans in this way, recognizing their increased capacity for creativity, also involves recognizing their capacity for destruction, and focuses attention on the conditions for the emergence and continued survival of civilization and humanity.

To privilege ecology over the physical sciences and then to define humans through human ecology is to redefine our place in the world, practically as well as theoretically. It is to embrace a life affirming metaphor explicitly affirming our own potential for creativity in place of life denying mechanistic metaphors, and thereby to replace the dominant models of nature and our place within it by virtue of which we are currently destroying the global ecosystem. As Roy Rappaport observed in developing an ecosystem approach to anthropology:

> In a world in which the lawful and the meaningful, the discovered and the constructed, are inseparable the concept of ecosystem *is not simply a theoretical framework* within which the world can be analyzed. It is itself an element of the world, one that is crucial in maintaining that world's integrity in the face of mounting insults to it. To put this a little differently,

the concept of the ecosystem is not simply descriptive ... It is also 'performative'; the ecosystem concept and actions informed by it are *part of the world's means for maintaining, if not indeed constructing, ecosystems.*

(Rapaport 1990, p.68f.)

This has come to be appreciated by a number of philosophers, including Lorraine Code in *Ecological Thinking* (2006) and Sean Esbjörn-Hargens and Michael E. Zimmerman in their book *Integral Ecology* (2009). It is what is required to purge and replace our current symbols, as Murray Code, amplifying the ideas of Coleridge, Nietzsche, Peirce and Whitehead, called for (Code 2007).

Ecosystems can be healthy or unhealthy (or, more broadly, can have or lack integrity). This claim has been contested, particularly by Mark Sagoff, but it has been defended, notably by Ernest Partridge and Robert E. Ulanowicz among others (Costanza, Norton, and Haskell 1992; Pimentel, Westra, and Noss 2000). Health is characterized by mutual augmenting of the whole community and the component communities of each other, facilitating their continued successful functioning, their resilience in response to perturbations, new situations and stress, and for ongoing development and creativity to maximize developmental options, and can be measured as such (Ulanowicz 2000, p.99). Characteristically, health is associated with the generation of forms consisting of mutually augmenting centers at multiple scales. The breakdown of health can have many causes, but it is characterized by loss of coordination, excessive differentiation and specialization undermining the possibility for communication, corruption or breakdown of semiosis, loss of balance between centres, breakdown in constraints associated with different scales and process rates, resulting in destruction of the conditions for creative responses to new situations. Salthe has examined the tendency to 'senescence' in systems, characterized by 'too much information crammed into a system with limited channels and decaying energy flow' (Salthe 1993, p.265). These causes can be generated outside the ecosystem, but can also be endogenous, often involving semiotic debilities. Endogenous debilities are frequently associated with the breakdown of constraints on component communities as occurs for instance in cancer, where cell reproduction produces tumours which, if they do not destroy vital organs, corrupt semiosis and absorb all nutrients and starve the rest of the organism. 'Death' is the final breakdown of such coordination and thereby the destruction of the homes conducive to the flourishing of component systems. We should think of all ecological communities, ranging from single cells to multi-celled organisms to local ecosystems and the global ecosystem, as being alive.

Through speculative naturalism we can now see that ecosystems, including the global ecosystem, do have a *telos*. As Salthe (2010) agued, it is to maximize the rate at which the energy gradient produced by the Sun's energy is degraded. However, with life, this should be seen as the long term *telos*, achieved by augmenting the conditions for life through creating and maintaining energy gradients and controlling how and when these are degraded into entropy and how entropy is dissipated. It is in this way that the Earth has become far more efficient at transforming energy and dissipating entropy than a life-less planet such as Venus. It has achieved this by providing the conditions for the flourishing of those forms of life that contribute to this augmentation, and eliminating those which foul their own nests. Life, which originated as a means, has itself become the end, and the *telos* of life is augmenting the conditions for the flourishing of life. This *telos* allows for experimentation, so that each life form has the freedom to explore possibilities and new synergies and to develop its own unique potentialities, and in the long run will survive or be eliminated according to whether or not the potentialities developed augment the flourishing of the synergetic relations and ecosystems of which they are part.

Humans as ecosystems themselves and participants in ecosystems can be augmenting or undermining the health of each of these. The challenge for humans is to create socio-economic formations that constrain human activities so they do not destroy the conditions for humanity's continued existence, or destroy the maintained energy gradients necessary for the continued flourishing of ecosystems (such as buried carbon or the ecological processes that are burying it) but augment these conditions, including the conditions for the life of the global ecosystem (Gare 2000a). More fundamentally, it is necessary to institutionalize this way of understanding nature, institutionalizing recognition of the value of life, including non-human life forms and ecosystems, so that only those practices are allowed to flourish that augment ecosystems. Central to achieving this is deepening understanding of nature and the place of humanity, with all its complexity, within the global ecosystem, and constraining its activities accordingly. It will be necessary to understand the thermodynamic, semiotic and ecological impacts of various physical, biological, social and cultural transformations of nature. It will also be necessary to understand which cultural forms, institutional structures and forms of economic organization constrain people to be ecologically destructive and which could enable people to augment the resilience of their ecosystems, and then to inspire them to do so and overcome those that are destructive. This is essentially what is shown by Richard Newbold Adams in *The Eighth Day: Social Evolution as the Self-Organization of Energy* (1988), Stephen Bunker in *Underdeveloping the Amazon* (1988) and Alf Hornborg in *Global Ecology and Unequal Exchange* (2011). In 'The Semiotics of Global Warming: Combating Semiotic Corruption' (2007), I examined the creative and destructive forms of semiosis from this perspective. At present, the power elites, the global corporatocracy and those who serve them, are effectively a cancerous tumour in the global ecosystem. As David Korten wrote in *The Post-Corporate World*:

> Cancer occurs when genetic damage causes a cell to forget that it is part of a large body, the healthy function of which is essential to its own survival. The cell begins to seek its own growth without regard to the consequences for the whole, and ultimately destroys the body that feeds it. As I learned more about the course of cancer's development within the body, I came

to realize that the reference to capitalism as a cancer is less a metaphor than a clinical diagnosis of a pathology to which market economies are prone in the absence of adequate citizen and government oversight.

(Korten 2000, p.15)

This is the situation that must be overcome.

The most important problem that has to be overcome if an ecological civilization is to be achieved is the hypercoherence of the ruling elites of the core zones of the world economy, channeling exponentially increasing amounts of energy and nutrients of the global ecosystem and global economy into its further growth, empowering themselves at the expense not only of humanity, but the ecological conditions for humanity's flourishing. As noted, these ruling elites can now be recognized as a component of a cancerous tumour within the current global ecosystem, an ecosystem peculiarly suited to human life. A remission will require slowing the flows of energy and nutrients to this tumour. The perspective of human ecology demands a radical reduction in the economic interactions between different regions of the world to undermine regional exploitation, combined with a revaluation of labour and nature, overcoming class divisions, particularly in the peripheral and semi-peripheral regions of the world economy and respect for ecosystems. If humanity suffers from the feedback loops generated by the interaction between the regulative and productive sectors of society, then it is also necessary to constrain these interactions to eliminate such feedback loops. That is, it is necessary to develop organizations in which the differentiations between organizers and the organized are minimized. As the theoretical biologists Mae-Wan Ho and Robert Ulanowicz argued:

> We can deal with sustainable economic systems by embedding the global economic system in the global ecosystem. ... The global economic system will have an intricate structure encompassing many national economies. Ideally, the intricate structure of the global economy should look like the many nested subcycles that make up the organisms' life cycle. ... And each national economy, in turn, would have its own intricate structure that is self-similar to the global. If the entire global system is to be sustainable, there has to be a proper balance between the local and the global, the same kind of reciprocal, symmetrical coupled relationship that one finds in organisms ... Furthermore, the global economy is coupled to the global ecosystem, which too, has to have its own balance ... so that both can survive.

(Ho, and Ulanowicz 2005, p.43)

Simon Levin (1999) has proposed principles for governance in accordance with these ideas: maintain heterogeneity, sustain modularity, preserve redundancy, tighten feedback loops, minimize entropy production, produce nothing that cannot be recycled and recycle everything, build trust, and do unto others as you would have them do unto you. Such principles, requiring multi-level governance, are being adhered to in efforts to govern and manage ecosystems at local levels, at least where the political environment allows for such multi-level governance (Armitage, Berkes, and Doubleday 2007; Waltner-Toews, Kay, and Lister 2008). However, these do not consider how to provide the niches where people applying such principles can survive and flourish.

The politics of eco-poiesis

While there has been much activity in political philosophy, some of it attempting to grapple with the problems of a globalized economy and the threat of ecological destruction, it is clear from the failure to combat neoliberalism that the task facing political philosophy has barely begun to be addressed. There has been an explosion of work striving to come to grips with globalization and its implications. However, there are few books relating political philosophy directly to the problem of achieving ecological sustainability. These include Prugh, Costanza and Daly Jr.'s short book, *The Local Politics of Global Sustainability* (2000), and Robyn Eckersley's *The Green State: Rethinking Democracy and Sovereignty* (2004). However, not even these integrate political philosophy with ecology.

This brings into focus the importance of speculative naturalism and ecological thought in overcoming the inadequacy of current institutions, ways of thinking and models of reality if we are to confront and overcome the massive environmental problems created by modern Western civilization. This leads us back to the humanities as such and the place of manifestos. It is in this context that a political and ethical philosophy of eco-poiesis (home-making) should be understood. As I have already suggested, the most promising path to achieve this is by synthesizing the neo-Hegelian political philosophy interpreted on naturalistic foundations, with the older Aristotelian tradition committed to organizing the polis to provide the conditions for realizing people's highest ends, and the republican tradition of political thought committed to liberty and self-governance in opposition to slavery. Hegelian philosophical history should then be reworked to portray the development of politics as the advance of the Radical Spirit. This involves upholding Hegel's anthropology characterizing the development of humanity through the three interdependent dialectical patterns of representation, recognition and labour interpreted as developments of semiosis understood through hierarchy theory, together with the three interdependent dimensions of Spirit: Objective, Absolute and Subjective, along with the social forms and fields that emerge from these dialectics to take on a life of their own. These formations range from friendships, to bureaucracies, discursive formations, cultural fields and socio-economic formations to the globalized market economy dominated by transnational corporations. From a neo-Hegelian perspective, to uphold freedom the market should be bounded by family relations, 'corporations' or professional bodies or unions, the public sphere and emergent cultural fields, and then the institutions of government, including legal and educational institutions as well as legislative and executive bodies of government. The extension of market principles into these institutions and cultural fields should be identified as corruption. It is necessary to work out how this structure can function in a globalized world involving multiple levels of federation. The challenge now is to use the concepts of ecological theory to rethink such political philosophy to apply to a multi-leveled federalism of human communities of communities from the local to the global level, acknowledging broad regions, nations, provinces and localities, where human communities are understood as participating in the complex of biotic communities of communities ranging up to the global ecosystem, or Gaia.

Conceiving humans as participants in (i.e. internally related to) evolving ecosystems and historically developing communities structured according to such neo-Hegelian principles, a political philosophy (together with ethics) of eco-poiesis is the definitive challenge to the reductionist naturalism of the Hobbesian/Lockean/Social Darwinist agenda of surrendering politics and ethics to the laws of the market and the Darwinian struggle for domination. To be adequate to this challenge, political and ethical philosophy should orient people to live and organize politically in a globalized world with all its inter-related global, regional, national and local problems, involving legal, economic, social and political processes conceived as part of nature, as operating within ecosystems also operating at multiple spatial and temporal scales. More than integrating and building on the insights of the political philosophers or European civilization is required for this. To create an ecological civilization, it will be necessary to overcome the parochialism of each civilization and incorporate the major insights from all civilizations while conceiving the development of humanity in the context of the ecosystems of which humans are part. For instance, as I argued in 'Daoic Philosophy and Process Metaphysics: Overcoming the Nihilism of Western Civilization' (Gare 2014b), it is necessary for those whose heritage is European civilization to appreciate the insights of the Daoic philosophies of China, as Joseph Needham and Heidegger have clearly done in the past.[1] Then it is necessary to critically reinterpret all such philosophies from the process-relational perspective of ecology.[2]

From this perspective, the goal of politics should be defined as eco-poiesis – making and augmenting homes or households of 'people', whether the 'people' are individuals, local communities, nations or humanity as a whole, to provide the conditions for them to freely explore their possibilities and fulfil their potential to further augment life. This can be seen to resonate with the Swedish social democratic politics of *folkshemspolitik* – society conceived as the people's home without any unwanted stepchildren. The philosophy underpinning this has been examined by Winton Higgins and Geoff Dow in *Politics Against Pessimism: social democratic possibilities since Ernst Wigforss* (2013). *Folkshemspolitik* in turn resonates with George Lakoff's promotion of the 'caring family' model for society to replace the 'patriarchal family' model promoted by neo-conservatives (Lakoff 1996)., but this should be developed to include the whole of humanity federated into a multiplicity of communities of communities. Societies should be judged according to what kinds of 'homes' they provide, where homes are the places where various capabilities can or cannot be expressed. And as Amartya Sen (1999) argued, the conditions to express capabilities are the basis of 'substantive freedoms', the 'freedoms he or she enjoys to lead the kind of life he or she has reason to value' (p.87). This is essentially the task being taken up by political ecology, an intellectual movement that began with the work of Harold Innis (1894–1952) (Keil et al. 1998), although the foundations for it had been provided by Patrick Geddes (1854–1932). It emphasizes that human communities are ecological communities with a metabolism, and that all human activity is simultaneously cultural, social, biological and physical. A major advance of this movement was Richard Newbold Adam's reconceptualization of social power as an energetic phenomenon in *Energy and Structure: A Theory of Social Power* (1975), with power seen as control over the triggers which release transformations of exergy into entropy, and the most important power being over the environments of others. Work on the politics of urban metabolism such as Heynen, Kaika and Swyngedouw's 'Urban Political Ecology' (Heynen, Kaika and Swyngedouw 2006, pp.1–20), exemplifies this ecological approach. As an intellectual movement, political ecology now has some momentum, but a great deal of work is required to elaborate such ideas so they can replace those which now dominate.

Rethinking political philosophy as part of political ecology involves reconceptualizing the relationship between social, political and economic life, institutions and ecological processes, including the relationship of different geographic and socially produced spaces and regions to each other. With the dissolution or subversion of non-economic institutions by neoliberals, people are losing job security and are thereby being enslaved, albeit, in the developed countries, becoming house slaves rather than field slaves. The goal should be to orient people to create new forms of life and associated institutions, and to organize spaces to achieve social cohesion and liberate themselves and their communities from such enslavements to the global and local forces driving ecological destruction. People need the spaces to develop their full potential to lead ecologically sustainable lives. A good overview of what is required is provided by Howard T. Odum and Elisabeth C. Odum in *A Prosperous Way Down: Principles and Policies* (2008). Such changes require spaces that simultaneously insulate people from broader environments while enabling them to interact with these environments. Central to achieving this is the form they give to their built-up environments. Comparative studies of cities undertaken in Timothy Beatley's anthology *Green Cities of Europe: Global Lessons on Green Urbanism* (2012) illustrate this. It is not simply a matter of efficiency. European cities are becoming a major force for ecological sustainability because they have been built to foster community and thereby empower people, while US cities, with a few exceptions, are built to isolate people, fostering consumerism and competition for money.

A number of measures can be taken to bring the market under control to prevent it undermining such spaces. Local currencies and trade barriers can be used to insulate markets from each other and from the global market. The process of commodification can be rolled back to revive communities and their institutions. There should be public ownership of financial institutions, natural resources and natural monopolies along with schools, universities and prisons. It should be made illegal for companies to take over other companies, as used to be the case in West Germany. And as André Gorz, a humanist eco-Marxist argued in *Paths to Paradise* (1985), the aim of politics should be to provide the conditions where people can fulfill themselves in their work. The tendency of markets to generate egoism and calculative reasoning has suggested to many that they should be eliminated entirely, but eliminating markets does not eliminate calculative reasoning, as the Soviet Union demonstrated, and markets properly controlled can not only free people from oppressive communities and bureaucracies and foster a sense of individual responsibility, but can foster solidarity in communities, as economic anthropologists such as Stephen Gudeman and David Graeber have shown (Gudeman 2008; Graeber 2011). The best way to utilize markets while avoiding their tendency to corrupt institutions is through forms of market socialism in which cooperatives are privileged, while educating the population to ensure that they understand that the Hobbesian tradition of thought now dominating economics and psychology that portrays societies as collections of calculating individualists, is pernicious and false.[3]

The importance of egalitarianism is difficult to underestimate. Richard Wilkinson and Kate Picket in *The Spirit Level: Why More Equal Societies Almost Always do Better* (2009) showed the correlation between inequalities in society and a range of social ills, while Peter Turchin in *War and Peace and War* (2007) showed that egalitarianism is a condition for achieving the solidarity among large numbers of people required for them to coordinate their activities. Great inequalities can be regarded as a sickness of societies, making them less resilient and prone to further diseases, such as semiotic corruption, despondency and mental illness, particularly among those engaged in productive work who tend to be despised by the 'predators' or 'macroparasites' who make their fortunes through wealth extraction (Galbraith 2009). 'Predators', identified as such by Veblen, are really macroparasites. 'Macroparasitism' is a term introduced by William H. McNeill in *The Human Condition: An Ecological and Historical View* (1980) to complement his study of 'microparasitism' – infectious diseases. At present, macroparasites, particularly those associated with transnational corporations and international finance, are the more threatening disease. Income distribution policies can be implemented to determine returns to factors of production in place of manipulated markets, identifying and eliminating wherever possible macroparasitism. Semiotic corruption by the public relations arms of private corporations, along with donations to politicians and political parties, can and should be made illegal. Even with market socialism, progressive taxation and death duties will be necessary to redistribute income and wealth to create and maintain egalitarian societies and to finance public institutions and provide incomes for those engaged in tasks and projects serving the common good, particularly over the long term, since these tasks and projects will never be adequately supported by markets. Other sources of public revenue can come from publically owned natural resources and assets generated by past public investments. 'Privatizing' or selling off such public assets, particularly when this is to foreign investors, should be treated as a treasonable offence, for which politicians should be held responsible long after they have left their political offices. Advocating such 'privatization' should be identified with sedition.

Hours of work should be reduced so that people can fulfil their functions as citizens, and people should be required to and be paid for fulfilling their obligations as citizens, which should include acquiring and maintaining the education necessary for citizenship. Citizenship also requires an economic safety net of social security to prevent people being forced into positions where they can be arbitrarily harmed by the decisions of others on whom they are dependent; that is, enslaved. To recover maintain genuine democracy it will be also necessary to make corporate governance more democratic, putting in place structures to empower stake-holders (workers, people living in the vicinity of corporate activity etc.) to ensure that their interests prevail over shareholders, to increase transparency in the activities of transnational corporations and to enforce income distribution policies (Sturm 1998). These are the structures imposed on West Germany and Austria after the Second World War and proved to be highly successful. In implementing these measures it will be necessary to foster the institutional and environmental conditions for developing and maintaining the autonomy of cultural fields and the public sphere from economically and politically defined ends. Those in control of the media should be obliged to maintain the autonomy of the journalistic field defined by its commitment to revealing the truth. Educational and research institutions can be restored as public institutions with their goals defined as core cultural institutions supporting, preserving, developing and passing on from generation to generation the culture of nations and civilizations, not in terms of profitability.

Generally, all these measures involve expanding the number and size of the institutions of States, where States are understood as the complex of institutions through which communities govern themselves. To avoid the tendency to bureaucratization, civil servants need to be professionalized, with job security and autonomy to carry out their work, and open, required to publish their policy recommendations – as was traditionally the case in the Swedish civil service. Civil servants, as with the population in general, should have the freedom to speak out in public without fear of retribution, and public criticism of the civil service and its members should not only be allowed, but facilitated. Most of these measures have been tried and tested in different places, most notably Sweden (Fulton 1968). All this requires increasing demands on individuals to sustain public institutions without corruption, a challenge which had been fully recognized by Geoffrey Vickers when he wrote *Making Institutions Work* (1973). Strongly influenced by Michael Polanyi on the importance of tacit knowledge, Vickers had published a series of works on public policy formation in the context of complex institutions. More relevant than ever, these are now largely forgotten.

Such changes will also place new demands on legal systems at multiple levels of governance, requiring major changes in how these are conceived and function. From the Ancient Greeks onwards, law applicable to all has been understood as the basis of political community and central to the recognition of the significance, freedom and capacity for responsibility of individuals, holding individuals accountable for their actions. This is built into the notion of 'autonomy', legislating one's own laws. Legislation should be recognized as one of most important means by which people govern themselves, and law so conceived should be understood as facilitative constraints protecting rights but also fostering virtues and providing the conditions for people (both individuals and communities) to maintain their liberty and realize themselves by augmenting life. Central to this development is the development of responsibility and accountability and the means to hold people accountable. With an ecological civilization it will be necessary to extend accountability from individuals in isolation to individuals as participants in communities and to communities as such at multiple levels, for their actions or failure to act not only in the immediate past in relation to contemporary problems, but over generations to take into account the origins of contemporary problems and problems that can be anticipated for the future. Thus, people of European descent should be held responsible for the plight of people in the present descended from people Europeans subjugated in the past, for ecological damage caused by these European conquerors manifest in the present and for anticipated damage that will be brought about in the future if people do not act now and change the way they live.

All this requires a rethinking of what laws are. Roberto Unger exposed the parlous state of jurisprudence in his 'The Critical Legal Studies Movement' published in the *Harvard Law Review* (Unger 1983), In place of legal positivism deriving from Hobbes, who argued that justice is defined by enacted law, a synthesis of Aristotelian, republican and neo-Hegelian legal theory through speculative naturalism can reinstate the notion of justice as proper recognition as the core of legal systems, through which positive laws can be judged. This synthesis involves advancing the 'process natural law' theories of Ernst Bloch and Mark Modak-Truran to overcome the current crisis in jurisprudence and law, particularly in Anglophone countries. Ernst Bloch's major work on law is *Natural Law and Human Dignity* (1986), defended natural law through a radicalized Aristotelianism and Schellingian philosophy. The full significance of Bloch's work is spelt out by John Ely (1986). In 'Prolegomena to a Process Theory of Natural Law', Mark Modak-Truran (2008) revived a version of natural law theory through Whitehead's version of process philosophy. In 'Law, Process Philosophy and Ecological Civilization' (Gare 2011b) I sketched a synthesis of process natural law and neo-Hegelian legal theory. This involved conceiving the development of natural law, not just positive law, as a development of the dialectic of recognition.

The core of natural law theory is St Augustine's injunction that 'An unjust law is no law at all', and that the function of law is to foster the common good and the virtues required for this. On this basis it can be argued that property laws which enable massive concentrations of wealth that lead to the subversion of public institutions, the plundering of public assets, the crippling of economies, the corruption of governments and massive ecological destruction are not laws at all and should not be recognized as such, either by individuals or governments. The same can be said of purported international laws through which governments are able to sign away the liberty of the nations they purport to represent, such as those associated with the World Trade Organization and international trade agreements.[4] The challenge now is how to hold people, both as individuals and as members of communities, responsible and accountable for the effects of their actions which are often far ranging, spatially and temporally, and are the joint effects of a great many people. This should not be allowed to absolve people from responsibility. In general, laws should be easy to understand and presuppose a virtuous population capable of judging what is just. 'Fuzzy law' which is general and requires of participants that they understand the spirit of the law, should be used rather than 'black letter' law in which legislators try to prescribe in detail the circumstances for applying the law, which then generates a host of lawyers attempting to work out how to get around the law. And as an unjust law is no law at all, the absence of positive law should not be allowed to excuse people from ignoring just laws that should have been enacted. Politicians should also be held accountable for their decisions and actions. The precedent of the Nuremberg trials should be upheld. This concurs with Ancient Greek principles of governance where, as Prugh, Costanza, and Daly Jr. (2000, p.131) pointed out, people could be fined, disenfranchised, or even put to death for persuading the ecclesia to act in ways they should not have.

However, there can be no simple recipe to deal with all problems, and cultivation of virtues including creative thinking guided by more adequate natural and social philosophy is and will be increasingly required. To foster such creative thinking and creating people with the character able to create an ecological civilization it will be necessary to uphold, in opposition to consumerism, the superior ideal of civilized life in which people can and do govern themselves as citizens and as workers. Civilization implies people constraining themselves through their habitualized commitment to truth, justice and workmanship, their appreciation of life and beauty, and the need to harmonize these, and to embrace the challenge posed by their communities' problems to develop their full potential to contribute to the common good and to adventure on new paths into the future.

As noted, the most promising vision of the future to achieve this is of humanity organized into a hierarchy of egalitarian communities characterized by organized decentralization, fostering a high level of civilization at all levels of these communities. As Herman Daly and John Cobb Jr. argued in *For the Common Good* (1994, Ch.9), the world should be organized as 'communities of communities' (which they opposed to 'cosmopolitanism'), building on the principles underpinning the United Nations of upholding and protecting the quest by communities to govern themselves insofar as this is consistent with others doing likewise. In doing so, they supported Dudley Seers' defence in *The Political Economy of Nationalim* (1983) of extended nationalism encompassing major regions, such as Latin America or Europe. In terms of the concepts of eco-poiesis, broader communities should provide the homes for more local communities, constraining the way they develop, preventing conflict and exploitation, while enabling and inspiring them to develop their full potential to augment the life of their own and broader communities, while empowering these local communities to constrain the broader communities to ensure they work for the common good of more local communities. Economies also should be organized in this way, protecting local economies (which could be a continent, such as South America, or region within a nation) through control of trade and capital flows from destructive exploitation and competition while at the same time fostering the conditions for the kinds of interaction that can generate new synergies. The importance to evolution of limiting competition to facilitate experimentation has been argued by Robert Reid in *Biological Emergences: Evolution by Natural Experiment* (2007). Reid shows that it is not natural selection that produces evolutionary development but the autonomous exploration of new possibilities resulting in new emergences or natural experiments that can be hindered by too much competition. Peter Corning in *Holistic Darwinism: Synergy, Cybernetics, and the Bioeconomics of Evolution* (2005) has argued tht it is synergies that are the most important principle in evolution. The implications for human societies should be obvious – traditional social Darwinism based on traditional Darwinian theory has provided a grotesquely misleading guide to its followers, whether Spencer, Hitler or Milton Friedman. As Richard Norgaard argued in his call for a 'coevolutionary revisioning of the future', rather than a global economy in which everyone is in competition with everyone else, the economy of the future should be envisaged as a 'coevolving patchwork quilt' (Norgaard 1994, p.165). This will require a multi-level federalism with some global governance, governance of major regions such as Western Europe and South America, of nations, of regions within nations and then of local communities, in which power is decentralized to local levels, with economies localized as much as possible to facilitate and create the conditions for strong democracies. Switzerland, which inspired Benjamin Barber's book, *Strong Democracy: Participatory Politics for a New Age* (1984), provides a partial model of what can and should be done. In this way economic activity should be made to serve the public by being subordinated to public institutions, cultural fields and democratic processes, while freeing people from enslavement and economic exploitation.

Organized decentralization should foster diversity rather than homogeneity. Valuing diversity without relativism can be achieved through a commitment to 'dialogism' and 'transculturalism'. Communities should have the courage to be open to each other while recognizing the uniqueness and value and possible limitations of their own cultures, at the same time respecting and striving to understand and learn from each other. In this way they should develop critical perspectives on their own culture, freeing themselves from sterile parochialism. They should at the same time expect reciprocal recognition and be prepared to criticize what they find defective in other cultures, and to demand of people of other cultures that they also take into account their own insufficiency. As Mikhail Epstein argued in *After the Future*, 'the fundamental principle of transcultural thinking and existence' is the '[l]iberation from culture through culture itself', generating a 'transcultural world which lies not apart from, but within all existing cultures' (Epstein 1995, p.298f.). This is the condition for creativity in the quest for truth, justice and liberty, for as the Russian philosopher Vladimir Bibler observed, 'Culture can live and develop, as culture, only on the borders of cultures' (Epstein 1995, p.291).

Dialogism and transculturalism require narratives. An exemplary narrative illustrating transculturalism is Joseph Needham's monumental study *Science and Civilization in China*. However, more than historical narratives are required. Formulating policies will require the development of dialogic narratives that simultaneously project visions of the future while taking into account the very different histories of diverse people and communities of communities in defining the present, cultivating a capacity for scenario visualizations with a diversity of temporal and spatial scales. Taking into account this diversity of time and space scales is particularly important and a major challenge. It involves recognizing slow rate processes that people have been blinded to through seeing everything from the perspective of market exchange value. Some idea of what this involves is provided by the papers in *Political Ecology across Spaces, Scales, and Social Groups* edited by Paulson and Gezon (2005) and *Adaptive Co-Management: Collaboration, Learning, and Multi-Level Governance* edited by Armitage, Berkes and Doubleday (2007). A different perspective is provided by the contributions to *Sustainability or Collapse? An Integrated History and Future of People on Earth* edited by Costanza, Graumlich and Steffen (2005). While there is important work underway contributing to these developments, human ecology incorporating the notion of eco-poiesis can provide the coordinating framework for carrying through this new synthesis.

With all this in mind, it is necessary to reconceive policy formation and enactment of policies. The recent tendency has been for those not satisfied with letting market operations decide the direction societies take to promote increasingly more complex forms of cost-benefit or risk-benefit analysis. They almost always involve efforts to make values commensurable by using exchange value as a reference point, and ascribing a monetary value to costs and benefits not properly factored into the decisions of economic actors, dealing with these by working out what people would be willing to pay to bring about or prevent various outcomes. This ignores the qualitative distinctions between different kinds of values, such as values associated with the health or otherwise of life-forms, or values of justice, values associated with healthy living and values associated with defining social status or entertainment. It also places decision-making in a new class of policy scientists. It is also associated with a very limited acknowledgement of the capacity of humans to anticipate the future and the importance of this for making sense of their lives. The alternative that avoids this is 'retrospective-path analysis' as developed by Clifford Hooker (1982). As I wrote of this approach in an earlier work, *Nihilism Inc.*:

> Retrospective path analysis consists in firstly the selection of macro-economic goals by considering a variety of end-points forty to fifty years in the future, and then secondly examining various paths to the desired future state. However there is no reason why this cannot be extended to considering goals for the whole of civilization several centuries into the future, and considering a variety of sub-goals for achieving these. This procedure departs from the normal approach in calculating a course of action retrospectively from some future date, specifying those key transitions in social structure and functioning generally which, taken in proper sequence, will lead from the present to the desired future social condition. Such an approach focuses attention on the conditions necessary for achieving the desired future states, on the tendencies inimical to the realization of such ends, and on the crucial societal decisions at the branchpoints of different possible paths of development.
>
> (Gare 1996, p.404f.)

Retrospective path analysis can be augmented by more recent work on scenario visualization, such as Robert Arp's *Scenario Visualization: An Evolutionary Account of Creative Problem Solving* (2008). This is commensurate with Hintikka's epistemic and interrogative logics concerned with discovering and choosing between scenarios. This way of thinking is very much in accord with how people normally define their goals and how they strive to realize them. It amounts to construing engagement in the world as a narrative form to be lived out, with a complex structure of sub-projects as sub-narratives and can augment such works as Emory Roe's *Narrative Policy Analysis* (1994) that have developed a narrative approach to policy analysis. Retrospective path analysis should provide people with unfinished complexes of stories within which they should be able to situate themselves as creative agents able to question and participate in modifying these stories as they are being lived out. Taking this potential into account, such stories should include such interventions and arguments over how these stories should be reformulated as part of the story, recognizing diversities of perspectives as not only inevitable but valuable, along with the institutions required to all allow such diversity to be developed and for diverse people to assert themselves and express these different perspectives. That is, retrospective path analysis should generate narratives that are dialogic rather than monologic, avoiding thereby the tendency to reduce other people who are to be involved in striving to realize ends into instruments. The struggle for consensus should lead to fundamental questioning of what kind of beings we are, what is our place in the cosmos and what are our potentialities. As I wrote in *Nihilism Inc.*: 'Such a decision procedure would contribute to transforming people's attitudes from a mechanistic world-orientation to a process world-orientation, from seeing themselves as beings standing outside the world trying to control it to experiencing themselves as processes of becoming actively participating as cultural beings in the becoming of the world' (Gare 1996, p.405).

The ethics of eco-poiesis

What then is an ethics of eco-poiesis? And how can it orient people to create an ecological civilization? Speculative naturalism will challenge the fundamental assumption of current public policy that a thing is right when it tends to increase the profitability of transnational corporations, and is wrong when it tends otherwise, and replace it with Aldo Leopold's dictum that: 'A thing is right when it tends to preserve the integrity, stability, and beauty of the biotic community. It is wrong when it tends otherwise' (Leopold 1949, p.224f.). In quoting this line from Leopold it is important not to under-estimate the profundity of his thinking. Leopold was interpreting ethics through ecology. On this basis he argued:

> The extension of ethics, so far studied only by philosophers, is actually a process in ecological evolution. Its sequences may be described in ecological as well as in philosophical terms. An ethic, ecologically, is a limitation on freedom of action in the struggle for existence. An ethic, philosophically, is a differentiation of social from anti-social conduct. These are two definitions of one thing. The thing has its origin in the tendency of interdependent individuals or groups to evolve modes of co-operation. The ecologist calls these symbioses. Politics and economics are advanced symbioses in which the original free-for-all competition has been replaced, in part, by co-operative mechanisms with an ethical content.... All ethics so far evolved rest upon a single premise: that the individual is a member of a community of interdependent parts. ... The land ethic simply enlarges the boundaries of the community to include soils, waters, plants, and animals, or collectively: the land.
>
> (Leopold 1949, p.202ff.)

We can now extend this to include the oceans and the atmosphere.

There is far more required of ethics than this, however. Ethics is not just a matter of limiting freedom. It involves motivating and inspiring people to develop constraints that are facilitative or enabling and, by making democratic institutions viable, open up new realms of freedom for myself and others. A more fundamental rethinking of the very nature of ethics is called for. As C.S. Peirce pointed out: 'We are too apt to define ethics to ourselves as the science of right and wrong. That cannot be correct, for the reason that right and wrong are ethical conceptions which it is the business of that science to develop and to justify'. He continued: 'The fundamental problem of ethics is not, therefore, What is right, but, What am I prepared deliberately to accept as the statement of what I want to do, what am I to aim at, what am I after? To what is the force of my will to be directed? …Life can have but one end. It is Ethics which defines that end' (Peirce 1958, 2.198). As such, ethics presupposes aesthetics through which we study what is admirable in and of itself. Such a view of ethics is more in accordance with the Chinese conception of philosophy as finding and walking on the right path or *Dao,* free of the assumption that this involves sacrificing one's personal interests for the good of others or the collective good. Or following Aristotle, we can take the right path to be a fulfilling and fulfilled life, achieved through augmenting the life of one's community or communities. What are required are constraints that provide people with the freedom to augment life.

In searching for the right path, it is necessary to understand the potential humans have to augment as well as damage their ecosystems. For instance, humans have enriched soil in various parts of the world by burying charcoal, producing *terra preta* soil, thereby augmenting the metabolism of the ecosystems of which they are part. The carbon augments the ecology of the soil by providing niches where micro-organisms can flourish that make available to plants the water and minerals from rain and other precipitation. This is also a way of removing greenhouse gases from the atmosphere. More recently, soil has been enriched by using trace elements. The western honey bee, humans and flowering plants have co-evolved over several thousand years, and beekeepers have facilitated the flourishing of both bees and the plants they pollinate, augmenting the health of ecosystems. The built environments of humans are also ecosystems serving both themselves and other organisms. These can be designed, as they tend to be when people's thinking is dominated by mechanistic metaphors, as nothing but machines for living to achieve efficiency in regenerating labour-power and moving goods and people, reducing people to cogs in the economic machine who occasionally need entertaining to keep them functioning properly. Alternatively, as the architectural theorist Christopher Alexander has argued, building our environments can be understood as contributing to morphogenesis in nature, a major aspect of life and should be judged according to whether it contributes to augmenting life – biological, social and cultural. As he put it in 'Sustainability and Rebirth of a Living World':

> The important thing about morphogenesis, in all its biological forms, is that highly complex, ordered structure is created in such a way that it is in balance with its environment. It is not too much to say that the enormous and extensive co-adaptive harmony of organisms in Nature is altogether due to morphogenesis.
>
> (Alexander 2007/2008, p.12)

Such morphogenesis is important not only for the health or otherwise of ecosystems but also for the life of human communities. It is in relation to the art of building, that the relationship between aesthetics and ethics is most clearly manifested. Built environments can and should be designed to augment community life, enabling people to live in a way that augments their own life, the life of others, the life of the community and the life of their co-evolved species and ecological communities (Heynen, Kaika and Swyngedouw 2006; Bueren et al. 2012). They should be more alive. Such environments should foster the subjectivities with the appropriate emotional commitment able to create an ecological civilization. Alexander showed that it is what is seen as alive and conducive to life that is seen as beautiful by the vast majority of people, justifying the central place accorded to beauty by Leopold, along with most of the great philosophers from Plato to Whitehead. It is what Peirce referred to as 'admirable'. It appears that just as we have evolved to be able to judge (not infallibly) which food is good to eat by smelling and tasting it, we have evolved to be able to judge what is alive and conducive to life and thereby what is of intrinsic significance, including the conditions for creativity and the development of new synergies that further augment life, through our appreciation of beauty, and what is inimical to life by what we perceive as ugly. Actions, characters, people, organizations or organizational structures, buildings or cities as well as biological forms can be beautiful or ugly. The emotions evoked by aversion to ugliness and attraction to beauty are required to achieve the commitment to long-term goals necessary to achieve anything worthwhile.

Ethical philosophy should provide the means for people to understand all this. It should provide more adequate concepts through which they can challenge existing 'categories of existence' and redefine their place in the world, in history and society, redefine their relations to each other, to institutions and to natural processes, and to redefine their particular situations. In this way it should orient people to live in their specific circumstances, to define what to aim at in life, what kinds of people they should be striving to become, and how these ends in turn relate to the ends of their communities, ranging from their villages, suburbs, towns, cities, countries and civilizations to the whole of humanity, and to their local and the global ecosystems.

The work of Alasdair MacIntyre, based on his study of the whole history of ethical philosophy in the West and in China, provides a good starting point for advancing such ethical philosophy. In *After Virtue* MacIntyre pointed out the central place of stories in defining right action. 'I can only answer the question 'What am I to do? If I can answer the prior question "Of what story or stories do I find myself a part?"' he wrote (MacIntyre 2007, p.216). If this is the case, then central to ethical philosophy must be the interrogation of these stories, questioning the assumptions on which they are based. This could lead to attempts to replace these assumptions and then to refigure the story that one is participating in. MacIntyre did not defend such radical questioning and refiguring of stories, but this is what he did. His own engagement with ethical philosophy can itself be understood as situating himself in the story of its development, in turn understood in terms of the broader story to civilization, in doing so, bringing into question the assumptions underlying modern ethical philosophy. Although he himself saw the problem with modern ethics the Protestant reaction against tradition, what he really revealed was the failure of the modernist project of developing ethics on Hobbesian assumptions. This tradition of ethics focused on finding universally acceptable reasons for constraining the egoism of individuals conceived in abstraction from any community membership and tradition of thought. MacIntyre showed there is no basis for choosing between utilitarianism and contractarian notions of rights, the most influential ethical philosophies that emerged with modernity, and even if there were, neither of these provide the basis for achieving rational consensus on what actions or political and economic arrangements are right. Nor did Kantian ethics provide a decision procedure. Kierkegaard and Nietzsche were right; modernism led to nihilism. As MacIntyre observed:

> It is precisely because there is in our society no established way of deciding between [moral] claims that moral argument appears to be necessarily interminable. From our rival conclusions we can argue back to our original premises, but when we do arrive at our premises argument ceases and the invocation of one premise against another becomes a matter of pure assertion and counter-assertion.
>
> (MacIntyre 2007, p.8)

MacIntyre argued from this conclusion that it is necessary to return to the tradition of Aristotelian and Thomist conceptions of ethics focused on working out what virtues should be cultivated to produce good character. Again, this accords with Peirce's argument that the core of ethics is about what is admirable, or conversely, what is not admirable but despicable. The virtues and good character are what are admirable; vices and vicious character are what are despicable. MacIntyre argued that characterizing virtues is possible only in the context of developing traditions of practices. As he put it: 'A virtue is an acquired human quality the possession or exercise of which tends to enable us to achieve those goods which are internal to practices and the lack of which effectively prevents us from achieving any such goods' (MacIntyre 2007, p.109). He then set about clarifying the relationship between virtues and forms of life and the relationship between these, arguing that what is most important in any society is to maintain the conditions for developing self-knowledge and learning more about what is the good for humans. He concluded:

> The virtues ... are to be understood as those dispositions which will not only sustain practices and enable us to achieve the goods internal to practices, but which will also sustain us in the relevant kind of quest for the good, by enabling us to overcome the harms, dangers, temptations and distractions which we encounter, and which will furnish us with increasing self-knowledge and increasing knowledge of the good. The catalogue of the virtues will therefore include the virtues required to sustain the kind of households and the kind of political communities in which men and women can seek for the good together and the virtues necessary for philosophical enquiry about the character of the good.
>
> (MacIntyre 2007, p.220)

What is noteworthy about this view is that it is an effort to revive classical ethical philosophy without the broader philosophies developed by Aristotle and Aquinas that had situated and supported their work on ethics. This brings us to the major gap in MacIntyre's virtue ethics, the failure to relate his ideas on ethics to nature as a whole. Even while acknowledging the importance of assuming a human *telos* and seeing humans as dependent rational animals, MacIntyre made no effort to challenge the heritage of the Seventeenth Century metaphysical revolution that had excluded final causes, and consciousness, from nature. MacIntyre also abstracted ethics from politics (although he criticized the separation of ethical philosophy from political philosophy) and at this stage he had attempted to do without a conception of what humans are and what is their place in the cosmos and their *telos* in terms of which the character of the good could be ascertained. Later, in *Dependent Rational Animals: Why Human Beings Need the Virtues* (1999), MacIntyre did develop a form of philosophical anthropology in which he ascribed to humans a *telos* of sorts, but this was only a beginning. While his work was a major advance over modernist ethics, as he demonstrated through the reconfigured story of the development of ethical philosophy he was able to provide from this perspective, it still was not adequate. It needs to be framed by not just the history of civilization but by natural philosophy which situates humanity in the cosmos.

To complete MacIntyre's recovery of virtue ethics there are several other issues that have to be addressed. Firstly, there are lacunae due to inadequate consideration of the relationship between all the different practices that make up a community, and the relationship between different communities. Partly, this is a consequence of the limited number of philosophers recognized by MacIntyre as being in the tradition of virtue ethics and, as a consequence, that he drew upon. This is manifest when comparing MacIntyre's *After Virtue* with Charles Taylor's *Sources of the Self* (1989) in which a far greater diversity of ideas is acknowledged. MacIntyre did not consider the insights of the Roman and Renaissance republicans, most importantly, Cicero, and then the Renaissance civic humanists who reflected on the decadence of the Roman republic that undermined it and the liberty of its citizens, a process that was repeating itself in Renaissance Florence. The Romans and the Renaissance civic humanists focused on the virtues required to avoid decadence and enslavement and to defend and maintain liberty, ends essential to upholding the virtues and forms of life defended by MacIntyre. Nor did MacIntyre consider the work of more recent philosophers who, even if they did not focus on virtues, did acknowledge their importance, such as the neo-Hegelians and British and American Idealists such as T.H. Green, F.H. Bradley and Josiah Royce. These philosophers have focused on the problems raised for virtue ethics by the far greater complexity of modern societies, with people required to specialize, so that along with new general virtues such as loyalty and conscientiousness, it is also necessary to give a place to virtues specific to an individual's station or role in society. It is necessary to recognize the importance of work, and to effectively oppose Taylorism, to uphold the virtues associated with workmanship and professionalism.

Recognition of the importance of these virtues was implicitly in the early works of Marx, but were more explicitly recognized and defended by John Ruskin and William Morris (1999), whose ideas were valued by the early labour movement in Britain. However, these thinkers were eclipsed by the utilitarian thinking and the rise of the social imaginary of pseudo-rational mastery of those who came to dominate labour politics. Christopher Alexander's challenge to current building practices along with recognition of the superiority of the Japanese approaches to management, as described in Tanner and Athos's book *The Art of Japanese Management* (1986), where it is held that work should be spiritually fulfilling, provides a starting point for reviving and further developing this alternative tradition of thought. However, it is also necessary to evaluate such work, institutions and the causes they are committed to in relation to each other, and to choose which causes to commit to. Ultimately, it is necessary to be committed to the creation and maintenance of a global ecological civilization, as suggested in the last chapter when considering Josiah Royce's neo-Hegelian ethical philosophy. We can clarify what is involved in aligning causes with each other through the notion of eco-poiesis. It is not simply a matter of aligning ends and respecting other causes, but of respecting, augmenting and even providing the conditions, that is, the 'homes', where causes augmenting life and the institutions formed to further them can flourish and provide the conditions for the flourishing of others.

While there are a number of general and specific virtues required to participate in institutions and to advance such causes, these are not enough to maintain people's liberty to pursue these causes. One of the most important virtues, or complex of virtues, as Peter Turchin recently has argued, is the capacity to achieve and maintain collective solidarity so that large numbers of people can cooperate in complex ways to defend themselves and their causes and impose their will on others. As Turchin argued in *War and Peace and War: The Rise and Fall of Empires* (2007, p.91), this is what the fourteenth century Islamic social theorist, Ibn Khaldun, referred to as *asabiya*. Clearly, this is something that the global corporatocracy and their neoliberal allies have succeeded in gaining, while the labour movement, civil servants and academics in most countries have lost this solidarity. The Green movement does not yet have the virtues required for it to prevail over its opponents. What is required above all to achieve *asabiya* is the cultivation of the virtue of loyalty to one's communities and its members. Sustaining this virtue generally requires avoidance of luxury and gross inequalities between people, and a central place for education as *paideia,* promoting a strong commitment to justice for the members of one's communities and loyalty to their ideals and the just causes to which they are committed. The more enlightened proponents of markets as the basis for organizing social relations are skeptical about achieving this solidarity for any length of time, and they defend markets as a way of organizing relations between people, partly on these grounds. For those wishing to subordinate markets to communities through democratic structures and civil services responsible to the public, it is a major challenge to maintain the virtues required to create and sustain these institutions without their being corrupted. Virtue ethics needs to be reformulated and defended from this broader perspective to meet this challenge.

Ultimately, the problem is to define and develop the virtues required to create and make function institutions of an ecological civilization augmenting the life of ecosystems and communities, including the institutions which foster these virtues, and to control or destroy those inimical to life. It is also necessary to work out, as Elinor Ostrom in *Governing for the Commons: the Evolution of Institutions for Collective Action* (1990) and Arild Vatn in *Institutions and the Environment* (2005) have striven to work out, which institutions are conducive to effectively dealing with environmental issues, including fostering the kinds of people with the virtues required for this. Markets and bureaucracies are institutions that, if they are uncontrolled by democratic processes, can corrode such virtues. As Korten (2000) argued, without being constrained by other institutions that demand this of economic organizations, economic organizations are prone to becoming cancerous tumours. Markets and bureaucracies should always be organized to foster mutual recognition for people who work and for the life of the communities of which they are part. To maintain institutions that can constrain the seductions of markets, it is also necessary to foster the virtues required for upholding liberty of individuals and communities. Above all, it is necessary to develop the virtues needed to provide and sustain the conditions for people to reflect on life and enquire into the character of the good through which current practices and institutions can be judged; that is, to foster and sustain a vigorous cultural life uncorrupted by commercial interests or bureaucratic control.

Human ecology, the human sciences and technology

As noted, political and ethical action requires adequate models of reality. Understanding the predicament people are now in and escaping it, both as members of communities and as individuals, requires the human sciences as well as the natural sciences to develop such models, but these need to be reconceived in accordance with the alliance of post-reductionist science and the humanities effected through speculative naturalism. They need to incorporate and be guided by the conception of humans developed through philosophical anthropology, understood through ecology and human ecology. On this basis, they should be explicitly evaluative. As Mikhail Epstein argued, the practical outcome of the human sciences is the transformation of society through politics. Creating models is not merely an interpretative endeavour; humans participate in creating themselves and their relations to each other and to rest of nature through the models they promulgate. The human sciences should always be seen as developments of political philosophy and ethics. This means rejecting completely positivist conceptions of the human sciences.

The humanities preceded the development of the human sciences, which were often developed to oppose the humanities. This was followed by a counter-reaction to develop forms of human science supporting and aligned with the humanities. This dialectic clarifies what is at stake, the significance of the broader opposition between science and the humanities and of the speculative naturalist quest to overcome this opposition in favour of the humanities. As we have seen, the humanities were developed in Renaissance Italy at a time when the liberty of its republics was under threat. This was a revival of the kind of education deemed necessary by Cicero, under the influence of the Greek idea of *paideia*, to produce citizens with '*humanitas*' and other virtues required to uphold and defend the liberty of the Roman republic. As noted, the rise of the mechanistic world-view was part of the 'counter-Renaissance', a movement of thought in France and Britain opposed to republicanism and its ideas of liberty as self-governance of the civic humanists. As Hobbes, a major figure in this counter-Renaissance, sought to characterize humans in a way that would render the civic humanist notion of liberty unintelligible, Giambattista Vico (1668–1744) defended a new science upholding the humanities. This defence was continued by Herder, a defender of democracy and the first person to develop the concept of culture in its modern sense, using the word in the plural. It is now possible to develop the ideas of Vico and Herder through the development of human ecology.

The fundamental issue dividing mainstream human sciences from the humanities and humanistic human sciences is whether people are to be studied in order to control them, or whether they are be studied to reveal the conditions for the full development of their potential for liberty and democracy. This opposition runs through all the human sciences. Erik Reinert (2007) has recovered the work of Renaissance economics where the focus was on the conditions for fostering the development of people and their arts. By contrast, Adam Smith's economics entrenched the possessive individualism of Hobbes and Locke as a way of distracting people from politics. The historical school, influenced by Herder, kept alive the Renaissance tradition, while institutionalist economics as developed by Friedrich List and Thorstein Veblen, kept alive and developed the historical school. Karl Polanyi (1957) also played a major role in reviving this tradition. It was List's recommendations put forward in *National System of Political Economy* (2006), based on the idea of the national economy, which accounted for the rise of wealthy countries, not Adam Smith's promotion of free-trade, which as Eric Reinert (2007) has argued, has kept poor countries poor. Psychology, sociology and geography are all divided by this opposition between 'scientistic' and humanistic approaches, which is manifest also in the opposition between orthodox Marxism (the form of Marxism that led Marx to write that all he knew was that he was not a Marxist) and humanist Marxism, and even between the institutionalists and the 'new institutionalists' who have attempted to rethink institutionalist economics by assuming calculating individuals and then attempting to explain the development of institutions on this basis, falsifying the evidence to do so (Gudeman 2008, p.115ff.). In the opposition between these, the anti-humanists have always promoted themselves as 'scientific', attacking, undermining and debunking the 'comforting illusions' and 'unscientific' approaches of the humanists and the values they have sought to uphold.

Speculative naturalism and the scientific work that it has inspired changes all this. Reconceiving the nature of life and humanity while at the same time advancing the physical sciences, it is the humanistic human sciences such as humanistic psychology and institutionalist economics, along with the humanities generally, that can now find support in the natural sciences. This is most evident in the work on non-linear thermodynamics, complexity theory, hierarchy theory, the theory of anticipatory systems and bio- and eco-semiotics. At the same time, however, speculative naturalism requires a radical rethinking of these humanistic approaches. The humanism of these now needs to be upheld while simultaneously seeing humans as part of and as participating within the creative advance of nature, associated with transformations of energy and matter constrained by various forms of semiosis that constitute ecosystems. As Bogdanov, the human ecologist Leslie White, and following them, Juan Martinez-Alier (1987), Richard Newbold Adams (1975, 1988), Stephen Bunker (1988), Kozo Mayumi (2001) and Alf Hornborg (2001) have argued, humans exist in the process of transforming usable energy into entropy. They are a particularly complex kind of dissipative structure, to use the language of Prigogine. The unique forms of semiosis which defines humans as characterized by philosophical anthropologists, such as heightened reflexivity, ability to anticipate the distant future and to choose which possibilities to realize, the ability to organize their activities as lived stories and to reflect on and reconfigure these stories, the ability to develop new forms of technology as well as to more abstract forms of semiosis associated with philosophy, science, mathematics and logic, are based on, emerged out of, and are dependent upon more primitive forms of bio- and eco-semiosis that emerge in these transforming processes. It is these higher forms of semiosis that have engendered the dialectics of labour, recognition and representation, each being a component of the others while not reducible to them, which, working through various social formations these dialectics have engendered, have unfolded through human history. The discipline that examines humans in the context of nature so conceived is human ecology, the history of which has been told by Kormondy and Brown (1988).

If, as Epstein argued, the practical extension of the humanities is the transformation of culture, and the practical extension of the social sciences is the transformation of society through politics, then the humanistic human sciences supported and reformulated through speculative naturalism will combine these transformations. The goal of social transformation, the way that such transformation is conceived and how it is implemented will be fundamentally different than that of mainstream 'scientific' social science. It will not be driven by the quest to make people governable, which as Foucault showed, has been their main role in the past, but to be self-governing by inspiring them to embrace the perspectives provided by such social sciences. That is, the humanistic social sciences should aim to transform culture to create the natural and social forms, the built-up environments and institutions that will augment people's liberty and humanity and augment the natural and social conditions for life. Based in human ecology, deploying such social science will be a politics of 'eco-poiesis'; that is, of 'home-making' or 'household-making', replacing the categories through which people currently define themselves and their relationships to others and the world and reforming society on this basis, a task begun in my 'Toward an Ecological Civilization: The Science, Ethics, and Politics of Eco-Poiesis' (Gare 2010). The development of retrospective path analysis based on the assumption that policies should be developed in the form of stories, and positional analysis as developed by Peter Söderbaum in *Ecological Economics* (2000, Ch.5, 6), which analyses and takes into account the diversity of actors involved in any situation, can be deployed to achieve this. This is the direction institutionalist ecological economics is taking, and it needs to be developed to replace orthodox neo-classical economics as the basis for policy formation.

Much of the failure to advance this project can be attributed to the influence of logical positivism which has been used by Milton Friedman and others to defend and promote neo-classical economics emphasizing idealized mathematical models of the economy to justify imposing markets to replace democratic processes. The influence of logical positivism has been exposed as pernicious by Martin Hollis and Edward Nell. Reviewing Quine's 'conceptual pragmatism' and its influence on economics, they concluded 'We hope we have now paid out enough rope and that the pragmatist has duly hanged himself. Choice which includes choice of its own guidelines is the negation of science and of all systematic thought' (Hollis and Nell 1975, p.169). Philosophers of science, most importantly Philip Mirowski in *More Heat than Light* (1989) have exposed the superficial resemblance of economics to nineteenth century physics to be for the most part a sham based on a misunderstanding of the appropriate conditions for deploying its mathematical models. Some economists have shown how the quest to understand the economy entirely in mathematical or engineering terms must lead to logical inconsistencies (Varoufakis 2011). Other economists, influenced by Whitehead such as Nicholas Georgesçu-Roegen in *The Entropy Law and the Economic Process* (1971) and his student Herman Daly Jr. in *Steady-State Economics* (1977) have criticized economists for their pre-occupation with abstract mathematical models Georgesçu-Roegen criticised what he called 'arithmomania' and the dominance of 'arithmomorphic concepts and models' and called for the use of 'dialectical concepts' which are not sharply defined and overlap with their opposites (Georgesçu-Roegen 1971, p.44ff.), while Daly and Cobb criticised the fallacy of misplaced concreteness. Exponents of complexity theory such as Brian Arthur (1994), Paul Ormerod (1998), and Kozo Mayumi (2001); that is, those economists who understand the role mathematics can and should play in science, have shown that economic systems generally do not have a tendency to move to equilibrium as assumed by neoclassical economists but are characterized by path dependence, multiple equilibria, 'increasing returns' and 'catastrophes', all operating at multiple scales which are partially insulated from each other, but also interacting in complex ways. Complexity theory undermines the basis for claiming that free markets are efficient means for allocating resources, and that this should be the main focus of economic theory. Arthur's work on positive feedback loops and increasing returns focusses attention on the role of technological innovations and creativity in economies (as Stuart Kauffman (2008) pointed out (p.157) but can also be used to confirm Sismondi's observation of 1819 that markets concentrate wealth and income in the hands of employers to such an extent that they create periodic depressions of under-consumption. It can be used to show that unconstrained markets concentrate wealth and economic activity in companies and in regions, leaving other regions impoverished and economically crippled. Even greater complexity is recognized by political economists and institutionalist economists who include political actors and institutions in their analyses of economic processes. Appreciating this reveals that income distribution has always been largely determined by political factors, as members of the political economy movement argued (Nell 1984), and who prevails in political struggles is dependent on institutions. Consequently, the most important political struggles are really over what institutions are put in place or maintained and who is to be empowered by them.

While the humanism of political and institutionalist economics can be defended through speculative naturalism, there is also an expectation that such economics be developed as ecological economics, which in turn should be understood in the context of human ecology (Gare 2008b).[5] Ecological economics has generated alternative indicators for judging economic performance, but for the most part still assume the goal of economic activity is sustainable production of commodities to be judged by technocrats (Lawn 2006). Apart from emphasizing more fully the physical and biological aspects of human existence, human ecology also emphasizes the uniquely human aspects of humanity. As Roy Allen pointed out in *Human Ecology Economics*:

> The human ecology approach to economics ... is similar to the relatively recent in field of 'ecological economics' .... The emphasis on *human* ecology combined with economics brings the '*humanities*' as well as the physical science-based field of ecology to the study of economics, and the framework is thus broader than ecological economics. For example ... ideologies and 'ways of being' (as defined through fields such as philosophy, psychology, sociology, religious studies, literature etc.) are important structural components of the economic system, and they are not given sufficient attention within the fields of ecology, economics, or ecological economics.
> (Allen 2005, p.4)

As Arild Vatn (2005, Ch.2), an institutionalist ecological economist aligned with human ecology noted, institutionalist economists reject the assumption that humans are simply mechanisms reacting to price signals. This is supported by complexity theory. Following Robert Rosen, humans as communities and as individuals can now be conceived of as anticipatory systems. Following

Robert Rosen, humans as communities and as individuals can now be conceived of as anticipatory systems. They act on the basis of models of the world and themselves, and can modify these models. They are formed by and with the capacity to form institutions, to define their lives, their communities and institutions through stories, accord mutual recognition, gain fulfillment in their work, and choose careers and live as citizens serving the common good and to engage in power struggles. To successfully uphold the common good, it is necessary as Elinor Ostrom (1990) showed, to have institutions that empower democratically organized communities to participate in developing and reforming institutions. Multiple levels of institutions are required to supply and modify institutions to which people can then make credible commitments, which can be mutually monitored to ensure compliance with their purported goals, and which can then constrain markets to serve these communities. This has been the focus of her work. Through these institutions, markets should be reduced to instruments for decentralizing decision-making, while basing returns to factors of production on principles of justice, rather than as they presently are – instruments of domination disguised as market imperatives. This requires institutions to insulate markets from each other, opposing the dogma of free trade that has been so devastating for genuine democracy. It should be noted that David Ricardo's classic defense of free trade in *On the Principles of Political Economy and Taxation,* the first edition of which was published in 1819, was explicitly predicated on capital not being mobile between nations. With this in mind, it is necessary to heed the conclusions of John Maynard Keynes (1933) reflecting on the conditions for controlling economies for the common good, avoiding the race between countries to hold down wages and costs of business to improve competitive advantage and the resultant catastrophes of depression, authoritarian governments and war. As he wrote:

> I sympathize, therefore, with those who would minimize, rather than with those who would maximize, economic entanglement among nations. Ideas, knowledge, science, hospitality, travel – these are the things which should of their nature be international. But let goods be homespun whenever it is reasonably and conveniently possible, and, above all, let finance be primarily national.

> (p.756)

Apart from tariffs, one of the most important means for achieving this will be the introduction of a Currency Transaction Tax as proposed by James Tobin, the Tobin tax (Patomäki 2015, p.184ff.). This would not only check the parasitism and destabilizing effects of currency speculators, thereby strengthening democratic control by nations of their economies; it could finance the United Nations. This can be taken further than confining commerce to nations. The 'Bristol Pound' and other local currencies in Britain designed to achieve some degree of economic autonomy for cities, illustrates what is possible at a more local level. At an even more local level again, there are the

LETS (Local Exchange Trading System) schemes, which I have argued could form the power base for struggles to recapture the institutions of the State from transnational corporations (Gare 2000c). Hornborg (2013, Ch.8) argues that to gain the full benefits for such local currencies it is necessary to divide their functions, with one currency serving as a means of payment and as a medium of exchange, serving local reproduction of community protected from global competition, but not yielding interest nor being able to be accumulated, and a different currency serving capital goods and flows of capital. These currencies should not be exchangeable. Usury should be abolished to avoid the growth of indebtedness, which as David Graeber revealed in *Debt: The First 5000 Years* (2011), is the essence of slavery. As Thomas Greco pointed out in *The End of Money and the Future of Civilization* (2010, p.68), this does not mean that people should not be able to profit from lending, but their returns should be based on taking a share of the added income of the lendee. This should be associated with reconceiving the role of money in the economy and the transformation of financial institutions accordingly, as Greco has called for. Similar arguments have been made by Amato and Fantacci in *The End of Finance* (2012, Part III). Money should not be allowed to be seen as an unlimited repository of credit and power. Then to limit predatory behavior among corporations, it should be made illegal for companies to take over or merge with other companies, as used to be the case in Germany until recently. All this is in the service of re-embedding markets within communities, to use the terminology of Karl Polanyi (1957).

By subordinating markets to genuine democracy committed to augmenting the common good, recognizing that not all values are commensurable, we will have the conditions to determine that resources not be destroyed and reserves be utilized sustainably, and that finance, insurance and real estate and the extractive component of economies not be permitted to metastasize and dominate markets and politics. Further, private interests should not be permitted to control the media or financial institutions, communities should never be enslaved to markets, either local, and more importantly, global, and individuals must be able to gain the incomes, wealth and economic security required to live well, meet their obligations as citizens and develop their full potential to augment the life of their communities. That is, the productive sectors of economies will prevail over extractive sectors. These are the condition for people to form new symbiotic relations and innovate technologically, which, as Renaissance economists realized from the example of Venice, are the basis of real advances in wealth. Institutionalist economics originating in this Renaissance tradition of thought, developed by Veblen and his disciples, and backed by speculative naturalism, implies the possibility of achieving such institutional arrangements (Reinert and Viano, 2012). Economic anthropologists have also thrown light on what is required, showing at the same time that the 'new institutionalists', having embraced a Hobbesian conception of humans have abandoned what made institutionalist economics superior (Gudeman 2008, p.158). Apart from recognizing the essentially social nature of humans and the primordial role of the dialectic of recognition, it is also necessary to appreciate the dialectic of representation and the role of rhetoric (and more generally, dialogue) in achieving, maintaining and developing common understanding (Gudeman 2009).

Humanistic approaches in political science, sociology and geography, usually associated with hermeneutics, symbolic interactionism, phenomenology, humanistic Marxism and genetic structuralism, also find support in such science, but they also need to be developed as part of human ecology. Political ecology and human ecology, are now the sites along with ecological economics of some of the most advanced thinking on nature and society.[6] However, there is much more that could be done to creatively reconceptualize the various human sciences in terms of these disciplines. For instance, human ecology should provide support for landscape geography, revitalizing by integrating physical and human geography, at the same time highlighting the energetic nature of all living processes, emergent constraints associated with various forms of semiosis, and the importance of space and its production and organization. It should take into account while reinterpreting all the physical, biological, economic, social, cultural and psychological processes and structures that constitute human ecosystems. This should then provide support for and advance the work of the *Annales* school of historians such as Fernand Braudel who have attempted to integrate history and geography and allowed for multiple temporalities and spatialities associated with different formations.

Bourdieu's notion of fields, along with such further developments of the field concept in social theory by Fligstein and McAdam, *A Theory of Fields* (2012), can be interpreted within this framework as emergent ecosystems. As such, they can be seen to be constituted through the highly developed forms of practical and reflexive semiosis characteristic of humans that have engendered the dialectics of representation, recognition and labour, constraining and then being reproduced by these dialectics. The emergence and development of these fields create the niches where individuals can pursue their ends with some autonomy, in doing so reproducing these fields or 'systems of homes', with all the complexity of the relationships between fields interpreted in terms of the relationships within and between ecosystems. That is, Boudieu's sociology, along with the subtle analysis of emergent fields and their forms of power, can be interpreted through, integrated with, and then developed as human ecology, thereby vastly enriching human ecology. Along with privileging human ecology and recognizing the energetic basis of life, human semiosis associated with culture should be understood as participating in the semiosphere of the global ecosystem, and should be developed accordingly. Understood in relation to political philosophy and ethics, it implies an imperative to maintain the autonomy and health of fields, whether economic, political or cultural, and a condemnation of those who prosper by undermining the fields on which they are dependent.

Finally, if the practical outcome of the sciences is technology, human ecology will also lead to a different way of understanding what is technology, and work. That is, Jürgen Habermas' dismissal of Herbert Marcuse's critique of modern science and technology in *Toward a Rational Society* where he claimed that 'there is no more "humane" substitute' (Habermas 1971, p.88) can itself be dismissed. 'Technology' and 'labour-power' will be de-reified. 'Technology', as with 'labor power', is reified when it is defined in abstraction from the social relations of which it is part. As the human ecologist Alf Hornborg observed:

> [T]echnologies require and reproduce specific forms of social organization ... Machines are not 'productive' – they do not 'produce', other than from a socially restricted perspective. To visualize the machine as a productive force *in itself* is to submit to a misleading distinction between technology and economy, the material and the social. Industrial machines *are* social phenomena.
>
> (Hornborg 2001, p.107)

It is the reification of technology and machines that has blinded people to oppressive relations that are imposed by introducing inappropriate technology. Supposedly increasing efficiency in the above senses, very often it simply alters who undertakes labour and whose resources are exploited. In this process, both nature and people are reduced to predictable material and instruments (or as Heidegger put it in *The Question Concerning Technology* (1970, p.20) to 'standing reserves'). It was this that Marcuse, who synthesized Heidegger's ideas with Marxism, was objecting to. Marcuse's synthesis that has been examined in depth and defended by Andrew Feenberg in *Heidegger and Marcuse: The Catastrophe and Redemption of History* (2005).

A demystified technology will have as its goal augmenting the conditions, that is, the homes, systems of home or ecosystems, for the flourishing of life, taking into account that as active agents formed by culture and utilizing manufactured instruments, people are autonomous participants within ecosystems. Their primary concern as agents 'managing' these ecosystems must always be to maintain or augment the health of these ecosystems, including themselves as participants within these, rather than to maximize yield. This is the approach called for by T.F.H. Allen, Joseph A. Tainter and Thomas W. Hoekstra in *Supply-Side Sustainability* (2002) and Peter Andrews in *Back from the Brink* (2006). To this end it is necessary to embrace the principles enunciated by McDonough and Braungart in *Cradle to Cradle* (2002) according to which production must be designed so all outputs augment the conditions for mor life, enriching our ecosystems.

Rather than treating people as instruments (or 'labour-power') to serve as cogs in the production of commodities, people will be recognized as workers whose powers should be extended by 'machines', that is, produced means of production and communication, in their productive work of wealth creation, transforming nature in the process of living and of augmenting the life of their communities. Transforming nature should be regarded as vegetative semiosis. The flourishing of life, both human and non-human, involves creativity and the development of new synergies, including new technologies, that further augment the conditions for life, including the conditions of such creativity. As Stuart Kauffman has argued, it is impossible to predict such creativity because each new development opens new possibilities that could not have been anticipated beforehand (Kauffman 2008, Ch.11). These conditions for such flourishing of life must include people's built-up and social environments and the local and the global ecosystems of which they are a part, augmenting at the same time their liberty to augment life and its conditions.

The dialogic grand narrative of ecological civilization

As Epstein argued, a work in the humanities that explicitly sets out to transform culture is a manifesto, and as such, can create new eras. This manifesto for speculative naturalism and ecological civilization is a quest to revive philosophy, and more generally, the humanities, forging a new direction for them and for humanity. It is a call to carry through and further advance the project begun by Herder, Goethe and Schelling to replace the Cartesian/Newtonian conception of the world, including the conception of physical existence, of life and of humans, and thereby of the place of humanity in nature, opening up new possibilities for what humanity and nature can become, and to rethink ethics and political philosophy accordingly. It is a manifesto to replace the grand narratives of progress understood as the pseudo-rational technological mastery of nature by Cartesian/Hobbesian subjects, driven by greed and the Darwinian competitive struggle for survival that has produced the unholy alliance of the global corporatocracy, corrupt politicians and narrowly educated technocrats who are crippling democracy, taking over and transforming public institutions into business enterprises and plundering public assets while through the mind control industries, promoting decadence among the general population to render them politically inert.[7] It is to overcome what Sheldon Wolin in *Democracy Inc.: Managed Democracy and the Spectre of Inverted Totalitarianism* (2008), aptly identified as a regime of 'inverted totalitarianism' on a trajectory to global ecological catastrophe. It is a manifesto for liberty and democracy, offering a new dialogic grand narrative based on understanding humanity through human ecology as a participant in the creative advance of nature, of the global ecosystem, and of the semiosphere.

This development of a dialogic grand narrative aiming to create an ecological civilization can be seen as the coming of age of the Radical Enlightenment. It can be characterized as a retotalization after the detotalization of the old grand narratives of emancipation, but a far more complex retotalization than Sartre envisaged, incorporating the interests of the whole of humanity (with its three dialectical patterns driven by the quest for recognition, orientation and empowerment) and most other life forms in all their diversity, in the struggle for the survival of civilization and the current regime of the global ecosystem. It is a retotalization based on a comprehensive understanding of the world through speculative naturalism and process metaphysics, orienting people to participate in this retotalization through a new grand narrative committed to averting ecocide. I have described what is involved in this in 'Narratives and the Ethics and Politics of Environmentalism: The Transformative Power of Stories (2001).[8] Progress will then be defined in terms of eco-poiesis as augmenting life and the conditions for it, including human life and all the co-evolved life forms with which humans are participating in the global ecosystem. As noted, this will not be a monologic narrative with one dominating perspective reducing everyone and everything to instruments for realizing the goals defined through this perspective, as is the case with the prevailing grand narrative and its former rivals. A dialogic grand narrative is required, allowing for the diverse voices of participants, situated in diverse and complexly related communities, organizations and economic, social and cultural fields with diverse histories, to question and participate in revising, reformulating and developing the narratives they are living out, from the local to the global level, preserving the autonomy of their communities, institutions and fields as the condition for such participation. This complex of narratives must itself be understood as a component of the global semiosphere and formulated as such. To be participating in forming and reforming these narratives is participating in the development of the semiosphere.[9]

The quest for such a grand narrative that can mobilize people to create a better future requires a religious dimension, and this justifies James Lovelock's naming the global ecosystem 'Gaia' and the efforts by process philosophers to re-enchant science.[10] It is this realm of 'Absolute Spirit' that should inspire people by fostering their imaginations and developing a 'feel for the whole', to use Christopher Alexander's perspicuous terminology. One of the most important virtues required for this is advancing understanding of nature, thereby enabling people to more fully 'indwell' in nature, to use Michael Polanyi's term, appreciating the reality and dynamics of the life of individuals, ecosystems and Gaia viscerally. Indwelling is required for achieving that 'feel for the whole' that has to be cultivated by town planners, architects and builders in order to produce beautiful built-up environments and to appreciate their work as participating in the morphogenesis of nature. This, Alexander argued, is crucially important for changing our relationship to the land. As he put it:

> ... we shall all gradually come to feel a concrete and realistic obligation to make sure that every action taken, by anyone, in any place, always, heals the land. A widespread ethical change begins to appear. Healing the land is understood by more and more people: Throughout society, slowly each person comes to recognize his or her fundamental obligation to make sure that in every act of every kind, each person does what he or she can do to heal the land and to regenerate, shape, form, decorate, and improve the living Earth of which it is part.
>
> (Alexander 2002, p.548)

Such a feel for the whole, achieved through indwelling, is required by everyone if they are to augment life, particularly when involved in participating in their society's governance and developing policies, as well as when engaged in work. This is the ultimate virtue is required to support all the other virtues.

Virtues have to be understood in relation to the stories people are living out, with the broadest story being the grand narrative defining the goals of civilization and humanity. With the aid of speculative naturalism, the new dialogic grand narrative should emerge from the quest by individuals, communities and civilizations to formulate their own narratives and relate these to each other's narratives and to the narrative of the whole of humanity, of terrestrial life and of the cosmos, and this should come to be understood as part of the process through which life, with its associated semiosphere, is becoming more conscious of itself and its significance in all its diversity. This narrative should accord proper recognition to all forms of life, including the life of ecosystems and of Gaia, of life forms that are augmenting Gaia and those that are undermining it. It should not be a free-floating body of thought but developed in the contexts of practices in which people are making a living, defending their liberty, striving to govern themselves, engaged in inquiry and transforming their cultures as members of what Alasdair MacIntyre described as 'practice-based forms of local participatory community' (2006, p.157). Along with speculative naturalism and the explicitly articulated grand narrative formulated in terms of it, this is what is required to revitalize the public sphere that Jürgen Habermas recognized as central to democracy, but could not provide a sufficient basis for supporting, nor even comprehending the conditions where it could function.[11]

To elaborate this narrative, it will be necessary to create images of the future through which individuals and communities and individuals can define themselves and their goals and be inspired to act. This will involve deploying 'vague' terms such as 'life', 'civilization', 'liberty', 'justice' and 'eco-poiesis', terms which can function as life-affirming symbols to replace the mind-numbing, life-denying and paralyzing symbols deriving from machine metaphors which currently dominate the civilization of modernity. These are 'real vagues' as Peirce characterized them because they are necessarily incomplete. Their meaning can only be defined more precisely through the efforts of diverse people in the present and future to understand the world and to define themselves and their aspirations through them, and then to struggle to realize these aspirations, in so doing, embodying them in their practices and built-up environments. The ultimate concept that must be developed is the new social imaginary of a global ecological civilization, and it is in relation to this that all other aspects of culture should be understood and evaluated, and acted upon. As Ernst Bloch proclaimed in his book *The Spirit of Utopia*:

I am. We are.

That is enough. Now we have to begin. Life has been put in our hands.
(Bloch 2000, p.1)

Notes

1 Much work has been undertaken to integrate Western and Chinese traditions of thought, the most important being the work of Joseph Needham. Recent work on this has been published in Guo Yi, Sasa Josifovic and Auman Lätzer-Lasar eds. *Metaphysical Foundations of Knowledge and Ethics in Chinese and European Philosophy* (2013). Conversely it is necessary for the Chinese to appreciate the achievements of the West other than science and technology. Arran Gare, 'Law, Process Philosophy and Ecological Civilization' (2011), originally presented at a conference in China, illustrates such work.

2 This is being undertaken by the Canada based Global Ecological Integrity Project led by Laura Westra. For such work see *Reconciling Human Existence with Ecological Integrity,* edited by Laura Westra, Klaus Bosselmann and Richard Westra (2008). See in particular 'Part V – Future Policy Paths for Ecological Integrity'.

3 The classic defence of market socialism was provided by Alex Nove in *The Economics of Feasible Socialism* (1983). These ideas were further developed by David Miller in *Market, State and Community: Theoretical Foundations of Market Socialism* (1990). Debates on market socialism were aired in *Why Market Socialism?* edited by Frank Roosevelt and David Belkin (1994). How far the markets can be controlled even with market socialism is a matter of dispute. Joel Kovel argued against markets altogether in *The Enemy of Nature: The End of Capitalism or the End of the World?* (2007), as did Robin Hahnel in *Economic Justice and Democracy: From Competition to Cooperation* (2005). Takis Fotopoulos in *Towards an Inclusive Democracy* (1997) argues that the market can be replaced and has shown how its mechanisms can be simulated without its destructive effects.

4 Efforts to develop appropriate international law are being made, illustrated by Laura Westra, Klaus Bosselmann and Colin Soskolne's *Globalisation and Ecological Integrity in Science and International Law* (2011, Part III).

5 The most important works in the emerging tradition of ecological economics are Herman Daly and John Cobb, Jr., *For the Common Good*, 2nd ed., (1994), Richard B. Norgaard, *Development Betrayed: The end of progress and a coevolutionary revisioning of the future*, (1994) Peter Söderbaum, *Ecological Economics*, (2000) and *Understanding Sustainability Economics* (2008), Philip Lawn, *Frontier Issues in Ecological Economics* (2007), and M. Rothschild, *Bionomics: Economy as Ecosystem* (1990), Mario Giampietro *Multi-Scale Integrated Analysis of Agroecosystems* (2005), Mario Giampietro, Kozo Mayumi and Alevgül H. Sorman's anthology *The Metabolic Pattern of Societies: Where Economists Fall Short* (2012) and from a Marxist perspective, Albritton, Jessop and Westra, *Political Economy and Global Capitalism,* (2010). Roy Allen has produced an anthology devoted to rethinking economics as part of human ecology, *Human Ecology Economics: A new framework for global sustainability* (2008). The institutions and policies required for ecological sustainability have been examined by Arild Vatn in *Institutions and the Environment*, (2005), Robert Costanza et al. eds. in *Institutions, Ecosystems, and Sustainability* (2001) and in the work of Elinor Ostrom and her colleagues, including her own book Ostrom, *Governing the Commons* (1990) and the anthology Ostrom et al. *The Drama of the Commons* (2002). Efforts to develop alternatives to neoliberalism and economic globalization are John Cavanagh and Jerry Mander's, *Alternatives to Economic Globalization* (2002), produced by the International Forum on Globalization, the anthology *Confronting Global Neoliberalism: Third World Resistanc and Development Strategies* edited by Richard Westra (2010), and David Korten's *The Post-Corporate World* (2000). In *The Corporation: The Pathological Pursuit of Profit and Power* (2004, Ch.6) Joel Bakan has suggested a number of measures to bring corporations under control.

6 Examples of such work are Coffman and Mikulecky, *Global Insanity*, (2012), Hornborg, Clark, and Hermele, eds. *Ecology and Power* (2012), Hornborg, *Global Ecology and Unequal Exchange: Fetishism in a zero-sum world*, Oxford: Routledge, (2011), Hornborg and Crumley, eds., *The World System and the Earth System* (2007), Westra, Bosselmann and Westra *Reconciling Human Existence with Ecological Integrity*, (2008), Waltner-Toews, Kay

and Lister, eds. *The Ecosystem Approach: Complexity, Uncertainty, and Managing for Sustainability,* (2008), Gunderson and Holling, eds. *Panarchy: Understanding Transformations in Human and Natural Systems,* (2002) and Peter Bunyard, ed., *Gaia in Action: Science of a Living Earth,* (1996). In *The Ecosystem Approach* see in particular Silvio Funtowicz and Jerry Ravetz, 'Beyond Complex Systems: Emergent Complexity and Social Solidarity', Ch.17.

7 The depoliticization of young people has been noted in China and Europe as well as USA. See Wang Hui, *The End of the Revolution: China and the Limits of Modernity* (2011) and Ingerid Straume and J.F. Humphrey in *Depoliticization: The Political Imaginary of Global Capitalism* (2011).

8 Carl Boggs was clearly thinking along these lines from a Gramscian perspective in *Ecology and Revolution: Global Crisis and the Political Challenge* (2012). This work highlights the difficulty of achieving such a reorientation without far more theoretical and philosophical work.

9 The bridge between eco-semiotics and human culture is under construction, with a major impetus having been provided by Thomas A. Sebeok's 'Semiotics as a Bridge Between the Humanities and the Sciences', in *Semiotics as a Bridge Between the Humanities and the Sciences* (2000) pp.76–100, and Wendy Wheeler's *The Whole Creature: Complexity, Biosemiotics and eh Evolution of Culture* (2006). See also, Arran Gare, *The Semiotics of Global Warming* (2007).

10 See for instance David Ray Griffin ed., *The Re-Enchantment of Science* (1988). Peirce, Whitehead, Heidegger and James Lovelock can all be seen as contributing to the development of such a philosophical religion.

11 Habermas described this in *The Structural Transformation of the Public Sphere* (1992). It should now be clear that his subsequent efforts to justify and revive this failed, and for two reasons. Firstly, as Pierre Bourdieu argued in *Language and Symbolic Power* (1991, Ch.3), Habermas did not understand the conditions under which utterances would carry authority, that is, the power relations required to sustain a public sphere, and secondly, he had undermined the philosophical assumptions which would provide people with the framework shown by Aristotle to be required for intelligible political disputation to take place. His students, Axel Honneth and Hans Joas in turning to and developing philosophical anthropology are far superior in this regard. See *Social Action and Human Nature,* (1988).

Conclusion

Ecological civilization and 'Life, Liberty and the Pursuit of Happiness'

The quest for an ecological civilization can give new meaning to and revive the quest for Life, Liberty and the Pursuit of Happiness, the ultimate ends promulgated by the United States Declaration of Independence. Each of these words is problematic.[1] The word 'happiness' has come to understood through Benthamite utilitarianism as a subjective state of mind of 'feeling good' or pleasure, but its original meaning was 'favored by fortune', and through its association with the Aristotelian notion of *eudaimonia* it can also have a more profound meaning. The most accurate translation of *eudaimonia* is 'a fulfilling and fulfilled life'.[2] An important feature of this as conceived by Aristotle that the whole duration of a life is what had to be judged, so the end was not a point in time in the future. As with melodies in a symphony, no part could be considered as a mere instrument serving some extrinsic end in the future. Almost the whole of Aristotle's *Nicomachean Ethics* was concerned with working out what is a fulfilling and fulfilled life, and he argued cogently that pleasure is a byproduct of having chosen the right ends; pursued as an end in itself it is elusive, an observation now robustly confirmed. Subsequently philosophers in Hellenistic Greece, in Rome, in medieval Europe and in Renaissance Italy, continued their investigations into this question building on Aristotle's insights. It was Hobbes attempting to counter all this who, on the basis of his conception of humans as complex machines moved by appetites and aversions, paved the way for Bentham's crude utilitarianism and made individual pleasure appear to be the highest end to be pursued. As we saw in Chapter Five, the neo-Hegelian tradition, building on Rousseau, Kant, Herder and Fichte as well as Hegel, defended a different conception of humans as essentially cultural beings in which fulfillment is conceived as self-realization through participating in the dialectics of labour, recognition and representation in the context of the institutions of society. For some neo-Hegelians (as for Schelling), it is also necessary to consider the global community and relations between nations, with institutions constraining States to respect each other and work for the common good of humanity. For Schelling and the tradition of natural philosophy he inspired, self-realization should involve working for the common good of life.

The most underestimated dialectic in the modern world is the dialectic of recognition associated, as Axel Honneth (1996, pp.92–130) argued, with love (which includes friendship), rights, and solidarity (through which each individual's unique contribution to the community is acknowledged). It is through this dialectic that people gain and accord significant identities and a sense of their own and each other's significance. It is the condition for the development of institutions, and once people's most basic needs are met, the most important motivating force for human endeavour. However, without 'representation' or the means to orient themselves in the world and identify what ends are most worth striving for, the dialectic of recognition could not function. Quite apart from this, advancing comprehension, understanding and wisdom through the dialectics of representation is itself a grossly underestimated motivating force. No-one can be regarded as living a fulfilled life unless they have achieved economic security and been able to realize their creative potential through their work, gained recognition from others who they themselves recognize as significant, and developed a world-orientation through which they can understand and make sense of the world and themselves and the significance and meaning of life, including their own lives. When recognition of the value of human endeavor is genuinely forthcoming and is based on a comprehensive understanding of the world, even the most arduous and dangerous work can be fulfilling. As Nietzsche put it in *Twilight of the Idols:* 'If we possess the *why* of life, we can put up with almost any *how*. Man does not strive after happiness. Only the Englishman does that' (Nietzsche 1990, p.33).

As we have seen, those analytic philosophers who promote scientism undermine all this by locking in place a Hobbesian/Darwinian conception of nature and of humans that reduces all life to the struggle to satisfy appetites and to be more efficient than others in doing so, a struggle which is simply the manifestation of deterministic physical and chemical laws. Tacitly, this justifies dominating others and reducing everything and everyone to instruments or resources to be efficiently exploited. Speculative naturalism, embracing the dialectic of representation as a development within the global semiosphere not only acknowledges the reality of final ends and upholds the Aristotelian/neo-Hegelian vision of the good life, but situates this in the much broader context of terrestrial life and its evolution, upholding a perspective from which the basis for being recognized as of intrinsic significance through the dialectic of recognition can be justified. From this perspective, the pursuit of happiness entails realizing oneself, embracing challenges worthy of one's abilities and gaining meaning in life through the dialectics of labour, recognition and representation, living in a way that augments the life of one's communities (Gare 2009). This does not mean ignoring self-interest, but recognizing that there is more to life than this. As Bar-Hillel (1:14) observed two thousand years ago, 'If I am not for myself, who will be for me? But if I am only for myself, who am I? If not now, when?'

The pursuit of happiness so conceived presupposes liberty in its original sense; that is, as the Romans understood it, as not being in a position where one can be arbitrarily harmed by the decisions or acts of those on whom one is dependent; that is, not being enslaved. Liberty also involves autonomy as this emerged in Ancient Greece with all institutions and beliefs being put into question and, as

Cornelius Castoriadis noted, people recognize themselves as the creators of their institutions and their beliefs. This means taking responsibility for these institutions and beliefs and self-limiting accordingly. Liberty is more fundamental than happiness, and people will sacrifice their lives to defend their liberty and the liberty of their communities. Liberty is different from and incompatible with the current dominant goal of modernity of maximizing economic growth through the pseudo-rational quest for the total mastery of nature. Liberty implies the right to assert oneself without fear of retribution, and this in turn is what is required for a vibrant public sphere, which in turn is required for genuine democracy in which people really govern themselves. As such, liberty requires a social order in which people (individuals, societies or nations) are not indebted to others and are recognized as free, responsible agents. It was always understood that while this required space to make one's own choices, it cannot be equated with freedom from any constraint to do whatever one feels like. This is the form of freedom aspired to be tyrants and slaves, and it is incompatible with the virtues required of members of a community to maintain their liberty. It inevitably leads to their enslavement. All this was understood by Hobbes who redefined liberty to mean freedom from any constraint to justify rule by a tyrant and the acceptance by the general population of their enslavement (although these are not the words he used) having only the right to life, and set about changing language to make it impossible to even think about liberty as previously it had been understood.

Rousseau, Kant, Herder, Fichte, Hegel, Schelling and those influenced by them developed a more robust notion of freedom that could counter this Hobbesian nightmare, leading to the notion of freedom as something positive, the freedom to live with integrity and to engage in worthwhile activities with others and to be properly recognized for this. In the modern world, this requires economic security and a livelihood (as Fichte argued in *Foundations of Natural Rights* (Fichte 2000, §19D, p.202ff.) where people's freedom is respected and they can work autonomously, where they have the conditions to realize their full potential to advance causes worthy of this potential and be properly recognized for what they are, what they have endured, what they have achieved, what they are doing and what they aspire to achieve. As the British Idealist T.H. Green (1836–1882) argued, freedom is gained by participating in democratic communities united in the quest for a common good; most importantly, the quest to develop people's potential to participate in community life. 'When we speak of freedom' he wrote, 'we mean a positive power or capacity of doing or enjoying something worth doing or enjoying, and that, too, something that we do or enjoy in common with others'. Green continued:

> When we measure the progress of a society by its growth in freedom, we measure it by the increasing development and exercise *on the whole* of those powers of contributing to social good with which we believe the members of the society to be endowed; in short, by the greater power on the part of the citizens as a body to make the most and best of themselves.
>
> (Green 1986, p.199)

The highest good, never fully realized, is human perfection pursued through institutions. As Green proclaimed in his main work, *Prolegomena to Ethics*:

> There are arts and institutions and rules of life, in which the human spirit has so far incompletely realized its idea of a possible Best; and the individual in whom the idea is at work will derive from it a general injunction to further these arts, to maintain and, so far as he can, improve these institutions.
>
> (Green 2003, p.431)

The State's mission is to nurture the potential of its citizens to live the best possible life by enabling them to participate in these projects.

However, this self-realization through participation in social projects should not be conceived of as something separate from nature. This is why the work of Christopher Alexander on architecture and building as morphogenesis is so important. Alexander pointed out that freedom or liberty implies that we can participate in an unfolding of the creative process of generating form guided by feeling for the whole:

> Why is freedom associated with the morphogenetic character of social processes? Because it is the shape-creating, organization-generating, aspect of process which ultimately allows people to do what they want, what they desire, what they need, and what is deeply adapted to life as it is lived and to experience as it is felt. The *humanity* of the environment comes about only when the processes are morphogenetic, are whole seeking, are placed in a context that gradually allows people to work towards a living whole in which each person plays a part.
>
> (Alexander 2002, p.509)

This can be generalized from building to all forms of work, however apparently remote these might appear to be from the actual construction of built-up environments.

What is most important for achieving liberty, as the Greeks, the Roman defenders of the republic, the Renaissance civic humanists, the early Romantics and later, the neo-Hegelians and process philosophers appreciated, is an education that enables people to understand all this and to understand what is happening in the world so they can participate in sustaining the institutions and the governance of their communities and morphogenesis within nature. The Roman republicans, inspired by the Greek notion of *paideia*, developed the *artes liberalis* (what is now known as the 'liberal arts', although it included science), as a general education for free people (an *enkyklios paideia*), as opposed to a specialist education deemed suitable only for slaves (Gare 2012). That is, people need an education that provides a comprehensive world-orientation or wisdom to enable them to understand and contextualize each particular situation and issue they are likely to confront in their lives.

The scientism of Quinean analytic philosophers, continuing Hobbes' project, has subverted the influence of the Radical Enlightenment and made the doublespeak of neoliberals, purportedly defending freedom when they mean by this freedom of the corporatocracy to massively concentrate wealth and income, plunder public assets, subvert democracy and enslave people, difficult to counter. It has led to a situation where even the British who, as Quentin Skinner observed in 'States and the freedom of citizens':

> for so long prided themselves on the enjoyment of their liberties ... now find themselves living more and more under asymmetrical relations of power and powerlessness [where] free markets, with the concomitant collapse of trade union movements, has left successive governments subject to blackmail by multinational corporations while leaving the work-force increasingly dependent on the arbitrary power of employers.
>
> (Skinner 2003, p.25)

This is true of almost every nation at present, including USA and other Anglophone countries.

Again, speculative naturalism, whereby emergence is characterized as new enabling constraints that define the very being of any emergent process, provides the basis for a coherent world-orientation through which the traditional notions of autonomy of the Greeks and of liberty of the Romans and the Renaissance civic humanists can be integrated with the neo-Hegelian notion of positive freedom and defended. From this perspective, the most important liberty is having the conditions to live in a way that augments the ecological conditions of existence, and the worst form of slavery is having the conditions of life organized so that the only way to prosper in life is to participate in undermining these conditions. This parallels the slavery that existed in Auschwitz where as Hermann Langbein observed of 'Jewish VIPs' in *People in Auschwitz* (2004, pp.169–190), the way to survive the longest was to become a kapo, which some Jewish prisoners did, and in some cases became more brutal towards other prisoners than the Gestapo. According to process natural law, no purported law or contract that enslaves people, whether individuals or nations, can be regarded as genuine law, and should not be regarded as binding. This includes the purported laws that protect the property rights of transnational corporations and financial institutions that have used their influence over politicians to plunder public property, or sign trade or financial agreements that lead to massive national debts, as occurred with Argentina and Greece.

Liberty presupposes life, the most fundamental end of all and the condition for liberty and happiness. It is life which gives meaning to liberty and happiness. Adopting the perspective of speculative naturalism, 'life' should now be extended to the life of the 'ecological' communities, both human and non-human, within which people are participating, which they are internally related to as well as being the conditions for their existence. It is this intimate relation that makes it senseless to attempt to measure quantitatively the services of these communities. It is the experience of life that lays claim on one and underpins all other values. 'Life' should also include the vitality generated by participating in healthy communities in beautiful environments; the kind of vitality that inspires people to develop their potential to augment the life and vitality of these communities and the conditions for life. Unless people can live in a way that augments the life of their communities and have the economic security to have and raise families, they do not have liberty, and their lives cannot be fulfilling.

Members of a community who act in a way that threatens its liberty are guilty of treason; those who threaten the life of the communities and ecosystems of which they are part are guilty of far worse. These are the necrophiliacs described by Erich Fromm in 'Malignant Aggression: Necrophilia' in *The Anatomy of Human Destructiveness* (1973, pp.411–481), the 'morbid aggressors' who through history have celebrated death. Although primarily interested in explaining Naziism, Fromm found support for this diagnosis of morbid aggression in the work of Lewis Mumford. In *The Myth of the Machine* Mumford observed that the 'protoscientific ideology' of Ancient Egypt in quest of 'constant increase of order, power, predictability, and above all control' generated 'a corresponding regimentation and degradation of once-autonomous human activities: "mass culture" and "mass control" made their first appearance'. Fromm continued:

> With mordant symbolism, the ultimate products of the megamachine in Egypt were colossal tombs, inhabited by mummified corpses; while later in Assyria, as repeatedly in every other expanding empire, the chief testimony to its technical efficiency was a waste of destroyed villages and cities, and poisoned soils: the prototype of similar 'civilized' atrocities today.
>
> (Fromm 1973, p.342)

Just as it is only possible to pursue true happiness insofar as it does not compromise liberty, and should augment liberty, it is only possible to pursue genuine happiness and strive for liberty insofar as these do not compromise life, and the pursuit of these should augment life. Conversely, it is only through being inspired by their appreciation of life that people will have the will to fight for their liberty and be truly happy, achieving fulfillment in life.

Revitalizing old and creating new concepts able to orient and inspire people will only be possible when the paralyzing assumptions of the seventeenth century metaphysical revolution, the 'ontology of death' as Paul Tillich called it, now locked in place by scientism, have been replaced by the speculative naturalists. Upholding the conception of humanity that recognizes their potential for achieving liberty, it is a call for people to embrace responsibility for their culture and its transformation as the basis for all other forms of liberty – political, economic and social, most importantly, the liberty to live in a way that augments life and the ecological conditions for it. Reformulating culture through speculative naturalism will create new subjectivities, subjectivities committed to addressing and overcoming the threats to democracy, civilization, humanity and terrestrial life from ecological destruction, and in doing so, creating a new civilization; an ecological civilization.

Notes

1 The assumption that these terms should be understood through the philosophy of John Locke was strongly challenged by J.G.A. Pocock in the *Machiavellian Moment: Florentine Political Thought and the Atlantic Republican Tradition* (1975). Pocock revealed the influence of Renaissance civic humanism on the foundation of the US republic and the significance of this. Thomas Jefferson was particularly influenced by the civic humanist Swiss political philosopher Jean-Jacques Burlamaqui. Civic humanism is commensurable with Josiah Royce's and John Dewey's neo-Hegelian influenced political philosophies. This interpretation of history would suggest that the neoliberals and neoconservatives who now dominate US politics have betrayed the founding principles of the United States.

2 See Aristotle, *Nicomachean Ethics*. For Aristotle, eudaimonia (which means literally 'having a good indwelling spirit') is distinguished from pleasure, and pertains both the life as it is lived and to people's whole lives. 'Fulfilling and fulfilled lives' captures both these dimensions. 'Flourishing' is a bad translation. Nobody takes 'flourishing' as their final end in life. 'Living an inspired life' would also be a good translation.

Bibliography

Abram, David. 1996. 'Merleau-Ponty and the Voice of the Earth'. *In:* D. Macauley ed. *Minding Nature: The Philosophers of Ecology.* New York: The Guilford Press, 82–101.

Adams, Richard Newbold. 1975. *Energy and Structure: A Theory of Social Power.* Austin: University of Texas Press.

Adams, Richard Newbold. 1988. *The Eighth Day: Social Evolution as the Self-Organization of Energy.* Austin: University of Texas Press.

Adams, Suzi. 2011. *Castoriadis's Ontology: Being and Creation.* New York: Fordham University Press.

Adorno, Theodor. 1984. *Aesthetic Theory* [1970]. Trans. Lenhardt, London: Routledge and Kegan Paul.

Ahearn, Gerard 2012. 'Towards an Ecological Civilization: A Gramscian Strategy for a New Political Subject', *Cosmos and History: The Journal of Natural and Social Philosophy,* 9(1): 317–326.

Al-Khalili, Jim and Johnjoe McFadden. 2014. *Life on the Edge: The Coming of Age of Quantum Biology.* London: Bantam Press.

Albritton, Robert. 2001. *Dialectics and Deconstruction in Political Economy.* Houndmills: Palgrave.

Albritton, Robert and John Simoulidis, eds. 2003. *New Dialectics and Political Economy.* Houndmills: Palgrave.

Albritton, Robert. 2007. *Economics Transformed: Discovering the Brilliance of Marx.* London: Pluto.

Albritton, Robert, Bob Jessop, and Richard Westra. 2010. *Political Economy and Global Capitalism: The 21st Century, Present and Future.* London: Anthem Press.

Alexander, Christopher. 2002. *The Nature of Order: The Process of Creating Life: Book Two.* Berkeley: The Center for Environmental Structure.

Alexander, Christopher. 2004. *The Nature of Order: An Essay on the Art of Building and the Nature of the Universe: Book Four.* Berkeley: The Center for Environmental Structure.

Alexander, Christopher. 2007/2008. 'Sustainability and Morphogenesis: The Rebirth of a Living World', *The Structurist.* 47/48: 12–19.

Allen, Roy E. 2008. *Human Ecology Economics: A new framework for global sustainability.* Abingdon: Routledge.

Allen, T.F.H. and Thomas B. Starr. 1982. *Hierarchy: Perspectives for Ecological Complexity.* Chicago: University of Chicago Press.

Allen, T.F.H. and Thomas W. Hoekstra. 1992. *Toward a Unified Ecology.* New York: Columbia University Press.

Allen, T.F.H., A. Tainter, and Thomas W. Hoekstra. 2002. *Supply-Side Sustainability.* New York: Columbia University Press.

Althusser, Louis. 1977. *For Marx.* [1965]. Trans. Ben Brewster, London: Verso.

Althusser, Louis and Etienne Balibar. 1977. *Reading Capital,* 2nd ed. [1968]. Trans. Ben Brewster, London: N.L.B.

Althusser, Louis. 1983. *Essays on Ideology.* London: Verso.

Amadae, S.M. 2003. *Rationalizing Capitalist Democracy.* Chicago: University of Chicago Press.

Amato, Massimo and Luca Fantacci. 2012. *The End of Finance.* Cambridge: Polity.

Andersen, Peer Bøgh, et al. eds. 2000, *Downward Causation: Minds, Bodies and Matter.* Langelandsgade: Aarhus University Press.

Andrews, Peter. 2006. *Back from the Brink.* Sydney: ABC Books.

Apel, Karl-Otto. 1995. *From Pragmatism to Pragmaticism.* Trans. John Michael Krois, New Jersey: Humanities Press.

Aristotle, 1962. *Nicomachean Ethics.* Trans. Martin Ostwald, Indianapolis: Bobbs-Merrill.

Aristotle, 1975. *Metaphysics.* Trans. Richard Hope, Michigan: Ann Arbor.

Armitage, Derek, Fikret Berkes, and Nancy Doubleday, eds. 2007. *Adaptive Co-Management: Collaboration, Learning and Multi-Level Governance.* Vancouver: UBC Press.

Arnason, Joseph P. 2015. 'Elias and Eisenstadt: The Multiple Meanings of Civilization'. *Social Imaginaries.* 1(2) Autumn: 146–176.

Arp, Robert. 2008. *Scenario Visualization: An Evolutionary Account of Creative Problem Solving.* Cambridge, MA: MIT Press.

Arrighi, Giovanni and Beverly J. Silver. 1999. *Chaos and Governance in the Modern World System.* Minneapolis: Minnesota University Press.

Arrighi, Giovanni. 2008. *Adam Smith in Beijing: Lineages of the Twenty-First Century.* London: Verso.

Arthur, W. Brian. 1994. *Increasing Returns and Path Dependence in the Economy.* Ann Arbor: Michigan University Press.

Arum, Richard and Josipa Roksa. 2011. *Academically Adrift: Limited Learning on College Campuses,* Chicago: University of Chicago Press.

Aubin, David. 2004. 'Forms of explanation in the catastrophe theory of René Thom: topology, morphogenesis, and structuralism', *In:* M. Norton Wise, ed. *Growing Explanations: Historical Perspectives on Recent Science.* Durham: Duke University Press, 95–132.

Bachelard, Gaston. 1969. *The Philosophy of No: A Philosophy of the New Scientific Mind,* [1940]. Trans. G.C. Waterston, New York: Viking Press.

Badiou, Alain. 2001. *Ethics: An Essay on the Understanding of Evil.* Trans. Peter Hallward, London: Verso.

Badiou, Alain. 2004a. *Theoretical Writings.* Trans. Ray Brassier and Aberto Toscano, London: Continuum.

Badiou, Alain. 2004b. *Think Again: Alain Badiou and the Future of Philosophy.* London: Continuum.

Badiou, Alain. 2005a. *Being and Event.* Trans. Oliver Feltham, London: Continuum, 2005.

Badiou, Alain. 2005b. *Infinite Thought: Truth and the Return of Philosophy.* Trans. Oliver Feltham and Justin Clemens, London: Continuum.

Badiou, Alain. 2007. *The Concept of Model.* Melbourne: re. press.

Badiou, Alain. 2009. *Logics of Worlds: Being and Event II.* Trans. Alberto Toscano, London: Continuum.

Bakan, Joel. 2004. *The Corporation: The Pathological Pursuit of Profit and Power.* New York: Free Press.

Bakhtin, Mikhail. 1984. *Problems of Dostoyevsky's Poetics.* Trans. Caryl Emerson, Minneapolis: Minnesota University Press.

Barber, Benjamin R. 1984. *Strong Democracy: Participatory Politics for a New Age.* Berkeley: University of California Press.

Barbieri, Marcello, ed. 2008. *Introduction to Biosemiotics: The New Biological Synthesis.* Dordrecht: Springer.

Baron, Hans. 1966. *Crisis of the Early Italian Renaissance: Civic Humanism and Republican Liberty in an Age of Classicism and Tyranny.* Princeton: Princeton University Press.

Bar-Hillel. *Ethics of the Fathers,* 1: 14. http://www.chabad.org/library/article_cdo/aid/2165/jewish/Chapter-One.htm [Accessed 17 January 2016].

Bar-On, Zvie. 1987. *The Categories and the Principle of Coherence: Whitehead's Theory of Categories in Historical Perspective.* Dordrecht: Martinus Nijhoff.

Barwise, Jon and John Perry. 1987. *Goodbye, Descartes: The End of Logic and the Search for a New Cosmology of the Mind.* Chichester: Wiley.

Basseches, Michael. 1984. *Dialectical Thinking and Adult Development.* Norwood: Ablex.

Bauman, Zygmunt. 2010. *Living on Borrowed Time.* Cambridge: Polity.

Beach, Edward A. 1990. 'The Later Schelling's Conception of Dialectical Method in Contradistinction to Hegel's'. *The Owl of Minerva,* 22(1): 35–54.

Beach, Edward Allen. 1994. *The Potencies of God(s): Schelling's Philosophy of Mythology.* New York: SUNY Press.

Beatley, Timothy, ed. 2012. *Green Cities of Europe: Global Lessons on Green Urbanism.* Washington: Island Press.

Beck, Ulrich. 1992. 'From Industrial Society to Risk Society'. *In* Mike Featherstone ed. *Cultural Theory and Cultural Change.* London: Sage.

Beck, Ulrich. 1996. 'Risk Society and the Provident State'. *In* ed. Scott Lash, Bronislaw Szerszynski and Brian Wynne eds. *Risk, Environment & Modernity.* London: Sage.

Beck, Ulrich. 2000. *What is Globalization?* Trans. Patrick Camiller, Cambridge: Polity Press.

Beder, Sharon. 2006a. *Suiting Themselves: How Corporations Drive the Global Agenda.* London: Earthscan.

Beder, Sharon. 2006b. *Environmental Principles and Policies.* London: Earthscan.

Beder, Sharon. 2007. *Free Market Missionaries: The Corporate Manipulation of Community Values.* London: Earthscan.

Beiser, Frederick C. 2002. *German Idealism: The Struggle Against Subjectivism, 1781–1801.* Cambridge: Cambridge University Press.

Beiser, Frederick. 2005. *Hegel.* New York: Routledge.

Beiser, Frederick. 2008. *Schiller as Philosopher: A Re-Examination.* Oxford: Clarendon.

Benardete, José A. 1989. *Metaphysics: The Logical Approach.* Oxford: Oxford University Press.

Benessia, Alice, et al. 2012 'Hybridizing sustainability: Towards a New Praxis for the Present Predicament', *Sustainability Science.* 7 (Supplement 1): 75–89.

Benton, Ted. 1996. *The Greening of Marxism.* New York: Guilford.

Berto, Francesco and Matteo Plebani. 2015. *Ontology and Metaontology: A Contemporary Guide.* London: Bloomsbury.

Bhaskar, Roy. 1993. *Dialectic: The Pulse of Freedom.* London: Verso.

Bhaskar, Roy. 2010. 'Contexts of interdisciplinarity: Interdisciplinarity and climate change'. *In* Roy Bhaskar et al. *Interdisciplinarity and Climate Change: Transforming Knowledge and Practice for our Global Future.* Abingdon: Routledge, 1–24.

Bickhard, Mark H. 2004. 'Process and Emergence: Normative Function and Representation'. *Axiomathes* 14: 121–155.

Bird, Alexander. 2010. *Nature's Metaphysics: Laws and Properties.* Oxford: Oxford University Press.

Bloch, Ernst. 1986. *Natural Law and Human Dignity.* Trans. Dennis J. Schmidt, Cambridge: MIT Press.

Bloch, Ernst. 2000. *The Spirit of Utopia,* [1964]. Trans. Anthony A. Nassar, Stanford: Stanford University Press.

Bogaard, Paul A. and Gordon Treash. eds. 1993. *Metaphysics as Foundation: Essays in Honor of Ivor Leclerc*. New York: SUNY Press.

Boggs, Carl. 1993. *Intellectuals and the Crisis of Modernity*. New York: SUNY Press.

Boggs, Carl. 2000. *The End of Politics: Corporate Power and the Decline f the Public Sphere*. New York: Guilford Press.

Boggs, Carl. 2012. *Ecology and Revolution: Global Crisis and the Political Challenge*. Palgrave: Macmillan.

Bohm, David. 1980. *Wholeness and Implicate Order*. London: Routledge and Kegan Paul.

Bohm, David and David F. Peat. 2000. *Science, Order, and Creativity*, 2nd ed. Toronto: Bantam Books.

Boltanski, Luc and Eve Chiapello. 2007. *The New Spirit of Capitalism*. Trans. Gregory Elliot, London: Verso.

Borden, Sandra L. 2010. *Journalism as Practice: MacIntyre, Virtue Ethics and the Press*. New York: Routledge.

Boucher, David and Andrew Vincent. 2000. *British Idealism and Political Theory*. Edinburgh: Edinburgh University Press.

Bourdieu, Pierre. 1977. *Outline of a Theory of Practice*, [1972]. Trans. Richard Nice, Cambridge: Cambridge University Press.

Bourdieu, Pierre. 1988. *Homo Academicus*. Trans. Peter Collier, Cambridge: Polity Press.

Bourdieu, Pierre. 1990. *The Logic of Practice*. Trans. Richard Nice, Cambridge: Polity Press.

Bourdieu, Pierre. 1991. *Language and Symbolic Power*. Trans. Gino Raymond and Matthew Adamson, Cambridge: Polity Press.

Bourdieu, Pierre. 1993. *The Field of Cultural Production: Essays on Art and Literature*. Randal Johnson ed. Cambridge: Polity Press.

Bourdieu, Pierre. 1998. *Acts of Resistance: Against the Tyranny of the Market*. Trans. Richard Nice, New York: New Press.

Bourdieu, Pierre. 2003. *Firing Back, Against the Tyranny of the Market 2*. Trans. Richard Nice, London: Verso.

Bourdieu, Pierre. 2004. *Science of Science and Reflexivity*. Trans. Richard Nice, Chicago: University of Chicago Press.

Bourdieu, Pierre, Jean-Claude Chamoredon, and Jean-Claude Passeron. 1991. *The Craft of Sociology: Epistemological Preliminaries*. Trans. Richard Nice, Berlin: Walter de Gruyter.

Bourdieu, Pierre and Loïc J.D Wacquant. 1992. *An Invitation to Reflexive Sociology*. Chicago: University of Chicago Press.

Bowie, Andrew. 1997. *From Romanticism to Critical Theory*. London: Routledge.

Bowie, Andrew. 2013. *Aesthetics and Subjectivity: From Kant to Nietzsche*, 2nd ed., Manchester: Manchester University Press.

Bowie, Andrew 2005. 'The Philosophical Significance of Schleiermacher's Hermeneutics'. *In* Jacqueline Mariña, ed. *The Cambridge Companion to Schleiermacher*. Cambridge: Cambridge University Press, 73–90.

Boyd, Richard, Philip Gasper, and J.D. Trout. 1991. *The Philosophy of Science*. Cambridge: MIT Press.

Bradley, F.H. 1962. *Ethical Studies,* 2nd ed. [1927]. Oxford: Oxford University Press.

Bradley, James. 2004. 'Speculative and Analytical Philosophy, Theories of Existence, and the Generalization of the Mathematical Function'. *In:* William Sweet. *Approaches to Metaphysics*. Dordrecht: Kluwer, 209–226.

Bradley, James. 2012. 'Philosophy and Trinity'. *Symposium,* 16(1) Spring: 155–178.

Braudel, Fernand. 1980. *On History*. Trans. Sarah Matthews. Chicago: University of Chicago Press.

Braver, Lee. 2007. *A Thing of This World: A History of Continental Anti-Realism*. Evanston: Northwestern University Press.

Breazeale, Daniel. 2010. 'Doing Philosophy: Fichte vs. Kant on Transcendental Method', in *Fichte, German Idealism, and Early Romanticism*. Rodopi: New York.

Brier, Søren. 2010. *Cyber-semiotics: Why Information is Not Enough*. Toronto: University of Toronto Press.

Broad, C.D. 1924. 'Critical and Speculative Philosophy', *In:* J. H. Muirhead ed. *Contemporary British Philosophy: Personal Statements* (First Series), London: G. Allen and Unwin: 77–100.

Broad, Professor C.D. 1947. 'Some Methods of Speculative Philosophy', *Aristotelian Society Supplement* 21: 1–32.

Brooks, Michael. 2008. *13 Things that Don't Make Sense: The Most Baffling Scientific Mysteries of Our Time*. New York: Doubleday.

Bruner, Jerome. 1986. *Actual Minds, Possible Worlds*. Cambridge: Harvard University Press.

Bryant, Levi, Nick Srnicek, and Graham Harman, eds. 2011. *The Speculative Turn: Continental Materialism and Realism*. Melbourne: re. press, 1–18.

Bueren, Ellen van et al. eds. 2012. *Sustainable Urban Environments: An Ecosystem Approach*. Dordrecht: Springer.

Bunge, Mario. 2001. *Philosophy in Crisis: The Need for Reconstruction*. Amherst: Prometheus Books.

Bunker, Stephen G. 1988. *Underdeveloping the Amazon: Extraction, Unequal Exchange, and the Failure of the Modern State*. Chicago: University of Chicago Press.

Bunyard, Peter. 1996. *Gaia in Action: Science of a Living Earth*. Edinburgh: Floris Books.

Burnham, James. 1945. *The Managerial Revolution*. Harmondsworth: Penguin.

Burtt, Edwin Arthur. 1954. *The Metaphysical Foundations of Modern Science*. New York: Anchor Books.

Čapek, Milič. 1971. *Bergson and Modern Physics*. Dordrecht: Reidel.

Caro, Mario De and David MacArthur, eds. 2004. *Naturalism in Question*. Cambridge, MA: Harvard University Press.

Caro, Mario De and David MacArthur, eds. 2010. *Naturalism and Normativity*. New York: Columbia University Press.

Carr, David. 1991. *Time, Narrative, and History*. Bloomington: Indiana University Press.

Carr, David, Charles Taylor, and Paul Ricoeur. 1994. 'Discussion: Ricoeur on narrative'. *In* David Wood ed. *On Paul Ricoeur: Narrative and Interpretation*, London: Routledge.

Castoriadis, Cornelius. 1987. *The Imaginary Institution of Society*. Trans. Kathleen Blamey, Cambridge: Polity Press.

Castoriadis, Cornelius. 1997a. *The Castoriadis Reader*, David Ames Curtis ed. Oxford: Blackwell.

Castoriadis, Cornelius. 1997b. *World in Fragments*. Trans. David Ames Curtis, Stanford: Stanford University Press.

Cavanagh, John and Jerry Mander. 2002. *Alternatives to Economic Globalization: A Better World is Possible: A Report of the International Forum on Globalization*. San Francisco: Berrett-Koehler.

Caygill, Howard. 1995. *A Kant Dictionary*. Oxford: Blackwell.

Charlton, Bruce G. 2012. *Not Even Trying: The Corruption of Real Science*. Buckingham: University of Buckingham Press.

Christiano, Thomas and John Christman. 2009. *Contemporary Debates in Political Philosophy*. Oxford: Wiley Blackwell.

Cobb Jr, John B. and David Ray Griffin. 1976. *Mind in Nature: Essays on the Interface of Science and Philosophy*. Washington: University Press of America.

Code, Lorraine. 2006. *Ecological Thinking: The Politics of Epistemic Location.* Oxford: Oxford University Press.

Code, Murray. 1995. *Myths of Reason: Vagueness, Rationality and the Lure of Logic.* New Jersey: Humanities Press.

Code, Murray. 1997. 'On the Poverty of Scientism, or: The Ineluctable Roughness of Rationality'. *Metaphilosophy,* 28(1/2): 102–122.

Code, Murray. 2005. 'Mathematical Naturalism and the Powers of Symbolisms'. *Cosmos and History,* 1 (1), 2005: 35–53.

Code, Murray. 2007. *Process, Reality, and the Power of Symbols: Thinking with A.N. Whitehead.* Houndmills: Palgrave.

Coffman, James A. and Donald C Mikulecky. 2012. *Global Insanity: How Homo Sapiens Lost Touch with Reality while Transforming the World.* Litchfield Park: Emergent Publications.

Coffman, James A. and Donald C Mikulecky. 2015. 'Global Insanity *Redux'. Cosmos and History,* 11(1): 1–14.

Coffa, J. Alberto. 1991. *The Semantic Tradition from Kant to Carnap: To the Vienna Station.* Cambridge: Cambridge University Press.

Collingwood, Robin. 1939. *An Autobiography.* Oxford: Clarendon Press.

Collingwood, R.G. 1945. *The Idea of Nature.* London: Oxford University Press.

Collingwood, R.G. 2002. *An Essay on Metaphysics,* [1940], revised ed. Oxford: Clarendon.

Collingwood, R.G. 2005. *An Essay on Philosophical Method.* New Edition, James Connerly and Guiseppina D'Oro eds. Oxford: The Clarendon Press.

Corning, Peter A. 2005. *Holistic Darwinism: Synergy, Cybernetics, and the Bioeconomics of Evolution.* Chicago: University of Chicago Press.

Corry, Leo. 2004. *Modern Algebra and the Rise of Mathematical Structures,* 2nd edn., Basel: Birkhäuser.

Costanza, Robert, Bryan G. Norton, and , Benjamin D. Haskell. eds 1992. *Ecosystem Health: New Goals for Environmental Management.* Washington D.C.: Island Press.

Costanza, Robert, et.al. eds. 2001. *Institutions, Ecosystems, and Sustainability.* Boca Raton, CRC Press.

Costanza, Robert, Graumlich, Lisa J. and Steffen, Will. 2005. *Sustainability or Collapse? An Integrated History and Future of People on Earth.* Cambridge, MA.: MIT Press.

Cottingham, John. 2012. Quoted by Murray Code, 'Vital Concerns and Vital Illusions'. *Cosmos and History,* 8(1): 18–46, 25.

Dalrymple, Theodore. 2005. *Our Culture, What's Left of It: The Mandarins and the Masses.* Chicago: Ivan R. Dee.

Daly, Herman E. 1977. *Steady-State Economics.* San Francisco: Freeman and Co.

Daly, Herman E. and John B Cobb Jr. 1994. *For the Common Good: Redirecting the Economy toward Community, the Environment, and a Sustainable Future,* 2nd ed. Boston: Beacon Press.

Davis, Mike. 2007. *Planet of Slums.* London: Verso.

Davidson, Donald and Jaakko Hintikka, eds. *Words and Objections: Essays on the Work of W.V. Quine,* rev. ed., Dordrecht: Reidel, 1975.

Davidson, Donald. 1984. *Inquiries into Truth & Interpretation.* Oxford: Clarendon Press.

Deacon, Terrence W. 1997. *The Symbolic Species: The Co-Evolution of Language and the Brain.* New York: Norton.

Deacon, Terrence. 2013. *Incomplete Nature: How Mind Emerged from Matter.* New York: Norton.

Demetriou, Andreas, Michael Shayer, and Anastasi Efklides. 1992. *Neo-Piagetian Theories of Cognitive Development.* London: Routledge.

Dennett, Daniel. 1991. *Consciousness Explained.* Boston: Little Brown.

Dennett, Daniel. 1994. *Darwin's Dangerous Idea.* New York: Simon and Schuster.

Depew, David J. and Bruce H. Weber. *Darwinism Evolving: Systems Dynamics and the Genealogy of Natural Selection.* Cambridge, MA: MIT Press.

Dimova-Cookson, Maria and W.J. Mander, eds. 2006. *T.H. Green: Ethics, Metaphysics, and Political Philosophy.* Oxford: Clarendon Press.

Domsky, Mary and Michael Dickson, eds. 2010. *Discourse on a New Method: Reinvigorating the Marriage of History and Philosophy of Science.* Chicago: Open Court.

Dummett, Michael. 1981. *Frege: Philosophy of Language,* 2nd ed. Cambridge, MA: Harvard University Press.

Eastman, Timothy E. and Hank Keeton, eds. 2004. *Physics and Whitehead: Quantum, Process, and Experience.* New York: State University of N.Y. Press.

Eckersley, Robyn. 2004. *The Green State: Rethinking Democracy and Sovereignty.* Cambridge, MA: MIT Press.

Ehresmann, Andrée C. and Jean-Paul Vanbremeersch. 2007. *Memory Evolutive Systems: Hierarchy, Emergence, Cognition.* Amsterdam: Elsevier.

Ellis, Brian. 2002. *The Philosophy of Nature: A Guide to the New Essentialism.* Chesham: Acumen.

Ely, John. 1996. 'Ernst Bloch, Natural Rights, and the Greens'. *In:* David Macauley ed., *Minding Nature: The Philosophers of Ecology.* New York: Guilford, 134–166.

Emmeche, Claus and Kalevi Kull, eds. 2011. *Towards a Semiotic Biology: Life is the Action of Signs.* London: Imperial College Press.

Engels, Friedrich. 1962. 'Feuerbach and the End of Classical German Philosophy' and 'Socialism: Utopian and Scientific' *In*: Karl Marx and Friedrich Engels, *Selected Works, Volume II.* Moscow: Foreign Languages Publishing House.

Engels, Friedrich. 1975. *Anti-Dühring.* Moscow: Progress Publishers.

Epstein, Mikhail N. 1995. *After the Future.* Trans. Anesa Miller-Pogacar, Amherst: The University of Massachusetts Press.

Epstein, Mikhail. 2012. *Transformative Humanities: A Manifesto.* New York: Bloomsbury.

Esbjörn-Hargens, Sean and Michael E. Zimmerman. 2009. *Integral Ecology: Uniting Multiple Perspectives on the Natural World.* Boston: Integral.

Esposito, Joseph L. 1977. *Schelling's Idealism and Philosophy of Nature.* Lewisburg: Bucknell University Press.

Esposito, Joseph l. 1980. *Evolutionary Metaphysics: The Development of Peirce's Theory of Categories.* Athens: Ohio University Press.

Estes, Yolanda. 2010. 'Intellectual Intuition: Reconsidering Continuity in Kant, Fichte, and Schelling'. *In:* Daniel Breazeale and Tom Rockmore eds. *Fichte, German Idealism, and Early Romanticism.* Amsterdam: Rodopi, 164–177.

Favareau, Don, ed. 2010. *Essential Readings in Biosemiotics: Anthology and Commentary.* Dordrecht: Springer.

Feenberg, Andrew. 2005. *Heidegger and Marcuse: The Catastrophe and Redemption of History.* London: Routledge.

Ferrari, M. and I.O. Stamatescu. 2002. *Symbol and Physical Knowledge.* Berlin: Springer-Verlag.

Feyerabend, Paul. 2010. *Against Method.* London: Verso.

Feynman, Richard P. 1986. *Surely You're Joking, Mr.Feynman.* London: Unwin.

Fichte, J.G. 1982. *The Science of Knowledge.* Trans. Peter Heath and John Lachs. Cambridge: Cambridge University Press.

Fichte, J.G. 2000. *Foundations of Natural Right* [1796–97]. Frederick Neuhouser, ed. Trans. Michael Baur, Cambridge: Cambridge University Press.

Finocchiaro, Maurice A. 2002. *Gramsci and the History of Dialectical Thought.* Cambridge: Cambridge University Press.

Fischer, Joachim. 2009. 'Exploring the Core Identity of Philosophical Anthropology through the Works of Max Scheler, Helmuth Plessner, and Arnold Gehlen'. *Iris*, I, April: 153–170.

Fligstein, Neil and Doug McAdam. 2012. *A Theory of Fields*. Oxford: Oxford University Press.

Føllesdal, Dagfinn. 1996. 'Analytic Philosophy: What is it and Why Should one Engage in It?'. *Ratio*. 9(3): 193–208.

Foster, John Bellamy. 2008. 'The Dialectics of Nature and Marxist Ecology'. *In:* Bertell Ollman and Tony Smith, eds. *Dialectics for the New Century*. London: Palgrave, 2008, 50–82.

Fotopoulos, Takis. 1997. *Towards an Inclusive Democracy*. London: Cassell.

Foucault, Michel. 1980. 'Truth and Power'. *In:* Michel Foucault. *Power/Knowledge*. Trans. Colin Gordon et. al. Brighton: Harvester Press.

Frade. Carlos. 2009. '*The Sociological Imagination* and Its Promise Fifty Years Later: Is There a Future for the Social Sciences as a *Free* Form of Enquiry?' *Cosmos and History*, 5(2): 9–39.

Frank, Thomas. 2000. *One Market Under God: Extreme Capitalism, Market Populism, and the End of Economic Democracy*. New York: Anchor.

Freeman, Alan and Boris Kagarlitsky. 2004. *The Politics of Empire: Globalisation in Crisis*. London: Pluto Press.

Frege, Gottlob. 1950. *The Foundations of Arithmetic*. Trans. J.L. Austin. Oxford: Blackwell.

Freundlieb, Dieter. 2003. *Dieter Henrich and Contemporary Philosophy: The Return to Subjectivity*. Farnham: Ashgate.

Friedman, Jonathan. 2005. 'Plus Ça Change, On Not Learning from History', *In:* Jonathan Friedman and Christopher Chas-Dunn, eds. *Hegemonic Declines: Past and Present*. Boulder: Paradigm Publishers.

Friedman, Michael. 2000. *The Parting of the Ways: Carnap, Cassirer, and Heidegger*, Peru; Illinois: Open Court.

Friedman, Michael. 2010. 'Synthetic History Reconsidered', *In:* Domsky, Mary and Michael Dickson, eds. *Discourse on a New Method: Reinvigorating the Marriage of History and Philosophy of Science*. Chicago: Open Court.

Fromm, Erich. 1973. *The Anatomy of Human Destructiveness*. New York: Holt, Rinehart and Winston.

Fulton, Lord. 1968. 'Appendix C – Sweden', *In:* Chairman: Lord Fulton, *The Civil Service, Vol. 1, Report of the Committee 1966–68*. London: Her Majesty's Stationary Office, 138–140.

Funtowicz, Silvio and Jerry Ravetz. 2008. 'Beyond Complex Systems: Emergent Complexity and Social Solidarity'. *In:* David Waltner-Toews, James J. Kay and Nina-Marie E Lister, eds. *The Ecosystem Approach: Complexity, Uncertainty, and Managing for Sustainability*. New York: Columbia University Press, 309–322.

Furth, Hans G. 1981. *Piaget & Knowledge: Theoretical Foundations*, 2nd ed. Chicago: University of Chicago Press.

Gabriel, Gottfried. 2002. 'Frege, Lotze, and the Continental Roots of Early Analytic Philosophy'. *In:* Erich H. Reck ed. *From Frege to Wittgenstein*. Oxford: Oxford University Press, 39–51.

Gadamer, Hans-Geog. 1976. *Hegel's Dialectic: Five Hermeneutical Studies*. Trans. P. Christopher Smith, New Haven: Yale University Press.

Gadamer, Hans Georg. 2004. *Truth and Method*, 2nd ed. Trans. revised by Joel Weinsheimer and Donald G. Marshall, London: Continuum.

Galbraith, James K. 2009. *The Predator State*. New York: Free Press.

Gallagher, Shaun and Daniel Schmicking, eds. 2010. *Handbook of Phenomenology and Cognitive Science*. Dordrecht: Springer.

Gare, Arran. 1993a. *Beyond European Civilization: Marxism, Process Philosophy and the Environment*. Bungendore: Eco-Logical Press and Cambridge: Whitehorse Press.

Gare, Arran. 1993b. *Nihilism Incorporated: European Civilization and Environmental Destruction*. Bungendore: Eco-Logical Press and Cambridge: Whitehorse Press.

Gare, Arran. 1993c. 'Soviet Environmentalism: The Path Not Taken'. *Capitalism, Nature, Socialism*, 4 (3), Sept: 69–88.

Gare, Arran. 1994. 'Aleksandr Bogdanov: Proletkult and Conservation'. *Capitalism, Nature, Socialism*, 5 (2) June: 65–94.

Gare, Arran E. 1995. *Postmodernism and the Environmental Crisis*. London: Routledge.

Gare, Arran. 1996. *Nihilism Inc.: Environmental Destruction and the Metaphysics of Sustainability*. Sydney: Eco-Logical Press.

Gare, Arran. 1999. 'Speculative Metaphysics and the Future of Philosophy: The Contemporary Relevance of Whitehead's Defense of Speculative Metaphysics'. *Australasian Journal of Philosophy*, 77 (2) June: 127–145.

Gare, Arran E. 2000a. 'Is it Possible to Create an Ecologically Sustainable World Order: The Implications of Hierarchy Theory for Human Ecology'. *International Journal of Sustainable Development and World Ecology*, 7(4) Dec: 277–290.

Gare, Arran. 2000b. 'Aleksandr Bogdanov's History, Sociology and Philosophy of Science', *Studies in the History and Philosophy of Science*, 31(2): 231–248.

Gare, Arran. 2000c. 'Creating and Ecological Socialist Future', *Capitalism, Nature, Socialism*, 11(2): 23–40.

Gare, Arran. 2001. 'Narratives and the Ethics and Politics of Environmentalism: The Transformative Power of Stories', *Theory & Science*, 2 (1) Spring, (no page numbers). Available at: http://theoryandscience.icaap.org/content/vol002.001/04gare.html [Accessed 18 January 2016].

Gare, Arran. 2002a. 'Process Philosophy and the Emergent Theory of Mind: Whitehead, Lloyd Morgan and Schelling', *Concrescence: The Australasian Journal for Process Thought: An Online Journal*, 3: 1–12.

Gare, Arran. 2002b. 'Human Ecology and Public Policy: Overcoming the Hegemony of Economics', *Democracy and Nature*, 8(1): 131–141.

Gare, Arran. 2003/2004. 'Architecture and the Global Ecological Crisis: From Heidegger to Christopher Alexander'. *The Structurist*, No. 43/44 – Special issue: 'Toward an Ecological Ethos in Art and Architecture': 30–37.

Gare, Arran. 2007. 'The Semiotics of Global Warming: Combating Semiotic Corruption'. *Theory & Science*: 1–33, http://theoryandscience.icaap.org/content/vol9.2/Gare.html

Gare, Arran. 2007/2008. 'The Arts and the Radical Enlightenment: Gaining Liberty to Save the Planet'. *The Structurist*, No. 47/48: 20–27.

Gare, Arran. 2008a. 'Approaches to the Question 'What is Life?': Reconciling Theoretical Biology with Philosophical Biology'. *Cosmos and History*, 4(1–2): 53–77.

Gare, Arran. 2008b. 'Ecological Economics and Human Ecology', *In:* ed. Michel Weber and Will Desmond. *Handbook of Whiteheadian Process Thought, Volume 1*. Frankfurt: Ontos Verlag: 161–176.

Gare, Arran. 2008c. 'Reviving the Radical Enlightenment: Process Philosophy and the Struggle for Democracy', *In:* Franz Riffert and Hans-Joachim Sander, eds. *Researching with Whitehead: System and Adventure*. Freiberg/München: Verlag Karl Alber, 25–58.

Gare, Arran. 2009. 'Philosophical Anthropology, Ethics and Political Philosophy in an Age of Impending Catastrophe', *Cosmos and History*, 5 (2): 264–286.

Gare, Arran. 2010. 'Toward an Ecological Civilization: The Science, Ethics, and Politics of Eco-Poiesis', *Process Studies*, 39(1): 5–38.

Gare, Arran. 2011a. 'From Kant to Schelling to Process Metaphysics: On the Way to Ecological Civilization', *Cosmos and History*, 7(2): 26–69.

Gare, Arran. 2011b. 'Law, Process Philosophy and Ecological Civilization', *Chromatikon VII* sous la direction de Michel Weber et de Ronny Desmet, Louvain-la-Neuve: Les Éditions Chromatika, 133–160.

Gare, Arran. 2012a. 'China and the Struggle for Ecological Civilization', *Capitalism, Nature, Socialism,* 23(4) Dec: 10–26.

Gare, Arran. 2012b. 'The Liberal Arts, the Radical Enlightenment and the War Against Democracy'. *In:* Luciano Boschiero, *On the Purpose of a University Education.* North Melbourne: Australian Scholarly Publishing, 67–102.

Gare, Arran. 2013a. 'From Kant to Schelling: The Subject, the Object, and Life'. *In:* Gertrudis Van de Vijver and Boris Demarest eds. *Objectivity after Kant.* Hildescheim: Georg Olms Verlag, 129–140.

Gare, Arran. 2013b. 'Overcoming the Newtonian Paradigm: The Unfinished Project of Theoretical Biology from a Schellingian Perspective'. *Progress in Biophysics & Molecular Biology.* 113(1) Sept: 5–24.

Gare, Arran. 2014a. 'Colliding with Reality: Liquid Modernity and the Environment'. *In:* Jim Norwine, ed. *A World After Climate Change and Culture-Shift.* Dordrecht: Springer, 363–392.

Gare, Arran. 2014b. 'Daoic Philosophy and Process Metaphysics: Overcoming the Nihilism of Western Civilization'. *In:* Guo Yi, Sasa Josifovic and Asuman Lätzer-Lasar eds. *Metaphysical Foundations of Knowledge and Ethics in Chinese and European Philosophy.* Fink Wilhelm Gmbh + Co, 111–136.

Gare, Arran. 2016. 'Creating a New Mathematics'. *In:* Ronny Desmet, ed. *Intuition in Mathematics and Physics: A Whiteheadian Approach.* Anoka: Process Century Press, Ch.7.

Gaukroger, Stephen. 2009. *The Emergence of a Scientific Culture: Science and the Shaping of Modernity 1210–1685.* Oxford: Oxford University Press.

Gaukroger, Stephen. 2012. *The Collapse of Mechanism and the Rise of Sensibility: Science and the Shaping of Modernity. 1680–1760.* Oxford: Oxford University Press.

Georgesçu-Roegen, Nicholas. 1971. *The Entropy Law and the Economic Process.* Cambridge: Cambridge University Press.

Giampietro, Mario. 2005. *Multi-Scale Integrated Analysis.* Boca Raton: CRC Press.

Giampietro, Mario, Kozo Mayumi, and Alevgül H. Sorman, eds. 2012. *The Metabolic Pattern of Societies: Where Economists Fall Short.* Abingdon and New York: Routledge.

Glock, Hans.-Johann. 2008. *What Is Analytic Philosophy?* Cambridge University Press.

Godelier, Maurice. 1967. 'System, Structure and Contradiction in *Capital'*, *In:* Ralph Miliband and John Saville, eds. *The Socialist Register, 1967.* London: Merlin Press, 91–119.

Godelier, Maurice. 1986. *The Mental and the Material.* Trans. Martin Thom, London: Verso.

Goldmann, Lucien. 1964. *The Hidden God: A Study of Tragic Vision.* Trans. Philip Thody, London: Routledge and Kegan Paul.

Goldmann, Lucian. 1972. 'Structure: Human Reality and Methodological Concept'. *In:* Richard Macksey and Eugenio Donato, eds. *The Structuralist Controversy.* Baltimore: John Hopkins University, 98–124.

Goldmann, Lucian. 1976. 'The Dialectic Today'. *In:* Lucian Goldmann, *Cultural Creation in Modern Society.* Trans. Bart Grahl, Saint Louis: Telos, 108–122.

Goodin, Robert E., Philip Pettit, and Thomas Pogge, eds. 2007. *A Companion to Contemporary Political Philosophy.* 2 volumes, 2nd ed. Malden, MA, Oxford and Carlton: Blackwell.

Goodwin, B.C. 1963. *The Temporal Organization in Cells.* London: Academic Press.

Goodwin, B.C. 1976. *Analytic Physiology of Cells and Developing Organisms.* London: Academic Press.

Goodwin, Brian. 1994. *How the Leopard Changed its Spots.* London: Weidenfeld and Nicoslon.

Gore, Al. 2007. *The Assault on Reason.* New York: Penguin.

Gorz, André. 1985. *Paths to Paradise: On the Liberation from Work*. Trans. Malcolm Imrie, London: Pluto Press.

Graeber, David. 2011. *Debt: The First 5,000 Years*. Brooklyn: Melville House.

Graham, Loren R. 1971. *Science & Philosophy in the Soviet Union*. London: Allen Lane.

Grassmann, Hermann. 1995. *A New Branch of Mathematics: the Ausdehnungslehere of 1844, and Other Works*. Trans. Lloyd C. Kannenberg, Chicago: Open Court.

Greco, Jr. Thomas H. 2010. *The End of Money and the Future of Civilization*, Edinburgh: Floris Books.

Green, T.H. 1986. *Lectures on the Principles of Political Obligation and Other Writings*. Paul Harris and John Morrow, ed. Cambridge, Cambridge University Press.

Green, T.H. 2003. *Prolegomena to Ethics*. ed. David O. Brink, Oxford: Clarendon.

Griffin, David R. ed. 1986. *Physics and the Ultimate Significance of Time*. New York: SUNY Press.

Griffin, David Ray ed., 1988. *The Re-Enchantment of Science*. Albany: SUNY Press.

Gudeman, Stephen. 2008. *Economy's Tension: The Dialectics of Community and Market*. New York: Berghahn Books.

Gudeman, Stephen, ed. 2009. *Economic Persuasions*. New York: Berghahn Books.

Gunderson, Lance H. and C.S. Holling, eds. 2002. *Panarchy: Understanding Transformations in Human and Natural Systems*. Washington: Island Press.

Habermas, Jürgen. 1971. *Toward a Rational Society*. Trans. Jeremy J. Shapiro, London: Heinemann.

Habermas, Jürgen 1974. 'Labor and Interaction: Remarks on Hegel's Jena *Philosophy of Mind*'. In: Jürgen Habermas. *Theory and Practice*. Trans. John Viertel, London: Heinemann, 142–169.

Habermas, Jürgen. 1986. 'Ideologies and Societies in the Post-War World', In: Peter Dews, *Habermas: Autonomy & Solidarity: Interviews with Jürgen Habermas*. London: Verso, 35–56.

Habermas, Jürgen. 1992a. *The Structural Transformation of the Public Sphere: An Inquiry into the Category of Bourgeois Society*. Trans. Thomas Burger. Cambridge: Polity Press.

Habermas, Jürgen. 1992b 'The Horizon of Modernity is Shifting' in *Postmetaphysical Thinking: Philosophical Essays*. Trans. William Mark Hohengarten. Cambridge: MIT Press.

Habermas, Jürgen. 1992c. 'Metaphysics After Kant', *Postmetaphysical Thinking: Philosophical Essays*. Trans. William Mark Hohengarten. Cambridge: MIT Press, 10–27.

Hahnel, Robin. 2005. *Economic Justice and Democracy: From Competition to Cooperation*. New York: Routledge.

Haken, Hermann. 1984. *The Science of Structure: Synergetics*. Trans. Fred Bradley. New York: Van Nostrand Reinhold.

Hallward, Peter. 2001. 'Translator's Introduction'. In: Alain Badiou, *Ethics: An Essay on the Understanding of Evil*, [1998]. Trans. Peter Hallward. London: Verso, vii–xlvii.

Hammermeister, Kai. 2002. *The German Aesthetic Tradition*. Cambridge: Cambridge University Press.

Hanna, Robert. 2001. *Kant and the Foundations of Analytic Philosophy*. Oxford: Clarendon Press.

Hänninen. Sakari. 2015. 'What is the "World in World Politics'. In: Paul-Erik Korvela, Kari Palonen and Anna Björk, eds. *The Politics of World Politics*. University of Jyväskylä: SoPhi, 200–223.

Hansen, James et al. 2013. 'Climate sensitivity, sea level and atmospheric carbon dioxide', *Philosophical Transactions*, A 371, Issue 2001, 16, http://dx.doi.org/10.1098/rsta.2012.0294 [Accessed 8 February 2016].

Hanson, Norwood Russell. 1958. *Patterns of Discovery: An Inquiry into the Conceptual Foundations of Science*. Cambridge: Cambridge University Press.

Harman, P.M. 1998. *The Natural Philosophy of James Clerk Maxwell*. Cambridge: Cambridge University Press.

Harré, Rom. 1970. *The Principles of Scientific Thinking*. Chicago: University of Chicago Press.

Harvey, David. 2000. *Spaces of Hope,* Edinburgh: Edinburgh University Press.

Harvey, David. 2008. 'The Dialectics of Space-Time'. *In:* Bertell Ollman and Tony Smith, eds. 2008. *Dialectics for the New Century.* London: Palgrave.

Hegel, G.W.F. 1975. *Hegel's Logic.* Trans. William Wallace, Third Edition, Oxford: Clarendon Press.

Hegel, G.W.F. 1977a. *Hegel's Phenomenology of Spirit.* Trans. A.V. Miller, Oxford: Clarendon Press.

Hegel, G.W.F. 1977b. *The Difference Between Fichte's and Schelling's System of Philosophy.* Trans. H.S. Harris and Walter Cerf, Albany: SUNY Press.

Hegel, G.W.F. 1990. *Hegel's Science of Logic.* Trans. A.V. Miller. Atlantic Highlands: Humanities Press.

Heidegger, Martin. 1971. *Poetry, Language, Thought.* Trans. Albert Hofstadter. New York: Harper & Row.

Heidegger, Martin. 1977. *The Question Concerning Technology and Other Essays.* Trans. William Lovitt, New York: Harper Torchbooks.

Heijennoort, Jean Van. 1967. 'Logic as Calculus and Logic as Language'. *Synthese*: 324–330.

Held, David. 2004. *Global Covenant: The Social Democratic Alternative to the Washington Consensus.* Cambridge: Polity.

Held, David. 2006. *Models of Democracy,* 3rd ed. Stanford: Stanford University Press.

Henning Brian G. and Adam C. Scarfe, eds. 2013. *Beyond Mechanism: Putting Life Back into Biology.* Lanham: Lexington Books.

Hesse, Mary B. 1966. *Models and Analogies.* Notre Dame: Notre Dame University Press.

Hesse, Mary. 1995. 'Habermas and the Force of Dialectical Argument', *History of European Ideas,* 21(3): 367–378.

Heuser-Kessler, M.L. 1992. 'Schelling's Concept of Self-Organization'. *In:* R. Friedrich and A. Wunderlin, eds. *Evolution of Complex Structures in Complex Systems.* Berlin: Springer-Verlag, 395–415.

Heynen, Nik, Maria Kaika, and Erik Swyngedouw, eds. 2006. *In the Nature of Cities.* London: Routledge.

Higgins, Winton and Geoff Dow. 2013. *Politics Against Pessimism: social democratic possibilities since Ernst Wigforss.* Bern: Peter Lang.

Hintikka, Jaakko. 1974. *Knowledge and the Known: Historical Perspectives in Epistemology.* Dordrecht: Reidel.

Hintikka, Jaakko. 1989. *Language as Calculus VS. Language as Universal Medium.* Dordrecht: Kluwer.

Hintikka, Jaakko. 1996. 'The Place of C.S. Peirce in the History of Logical Theory'. *In:* Jaakko Hintikka, *Lingua Universalis vs. Calculus Ratiocinator.* Dordrecht: Kluwer, 140–161.

Hintikka, Jaakko. 2007. 'The Place of the *a priori* in Epistemology', *In:* Jaakko Hintikka, *Socratic Epistemology: Explorations of Knowledge-seeking by Questioning.* Cambridge: Cambridge University Press, 107–144.

Ho, Mae-Wan and Robert Ulanowicz. 2005. 'Sustainable systems as organisms?' *Biosystems,* 82: 39–51.

Ho, Mae-Wan. 2008. *The Rainbow and the Worm: The Physics of Organisms,* 3rd ed. New Jersey: World Scientific.

Hodgson, Geoffrey M. 1999. *Evolution and Institutions: On Evolutionary Economics and the Evolution of Economics.* Cheltenham: Edward Elgar.

Hodgson, Geoffrey M. 2013. *From Pleasure Machines to Moral Communities: An Evolutionary Economics Without Homo Economicus.* Chicago: University of Chicago Press.

Hoffmeyer, Jesper. 1993. *Signs of Meaning in the Universe*. Trans. Barbara J. Haveland, Bloomington: Indiana University Press.

Hoffmeyer, Jesper, ed. 2008. *The Legacy of Living Systems: Gregory Bateson as Precursor to Living Systems*. Dordrecht: Springer.

Holling, C.S. 2010. 'Resilience and Stability of Ecological Systems'. *In:* Lance H. Gunderson, Craig R. Allen and C.S. Holling, eds. *Foundations of Ecological Resilience,* Washington: Island Press, 19–50.

Hollis, Martin and Edward J. Nell. 1975. *Rational Economic Man: A Philosophical Critique of Neo-Classical Economics*. Cambridge: Cambridge University Press.

Hong, Felix T. 2013. 'The role of pattern recognition in creative problem solving: A case study in search of new mathematics for biology', *Progress in Biophysics and Molecular Biology,* 113: 181–215.

Honneth, Axel and Hans Joas. 1988. *Social Action and Human Nature,* [1980]. Trans. Raymond Meyer, Cambridge: Cambridge University Press.

Honneth, Axel. 1995. 'The Fragmented World of Symbolic Forms: Reflections on Pierre Bourdieu's Sociology of Culture', *In:* Axel Honneth, *The Fragmented World of the Social.* Charles W. Wright, New York: SUNY Press, 184–204.

Honneth, Axel. 1996. *The Struggle for Recognition: The Moral Grammar of Social Conflict*. Trans. Joel Anderson, Cambridge, MA: MIT Press.

Honneth, Axel. 2007. *Disrespect: The Normative Foundations of Critical Theory*. Trans. Joseph Ganahl, Cambridge: Polity Press.

Honneth, Axel. 2010. *The Pathologies of Individual Freedom: Hegel's Social Theory*. Trans. Ladislaus Lös, Princeton: Princeton University Press.

Hooker, Clifford A. 1982. 'Scientific Neutrality versus Normative Learning: The Theoretician's and Politician's Dilemma', *In:* David Oldroyd, ed., *Science and Ethics*. Kensington: New South Wales University Press, 8–33.

Hooker, Cliff A. ed. 2011. *Philosophy of Complex Systems*. Amsterdam: Elsevier.

Hornborg, Alf. 1999. 'Money and the Semiotics of Ecosystem Dissolution', *Journal of Material Culture,* 4(2): 143–162.

Hornborg, Alf. 2001. *The Power of the Machine: Global Inequalities of Economy, Technology, and Environment*. Walnut Creek: Altamira Press.

Hornborg, Alf and Carole Crumley, eds. 2007. *The World System and the Earth System: Global Socioenvironmental Change and Sustainability Since the Neolithic*. Walnut Creek: Left Coast Press.

Hornborg, Alf. 2011. *Global Ecology and Unequal Exchange: Fetishism in a zero-sum world*. Oxford: Routledge.

Hornborg, Alf, Brett Clark, and Kenneth Hermele, eds. 2012. *Ecology and Power: Struggles Over Land and Material Resources in the Past, Present, and Future*. Abingdon: Routledge.

Houdé, Olivier et al. 2011. 'Functional Magnetic Resonance Imaging Study of Piaget's Conservation-of-Number Task in Preschool and School-Age Children: A Piagetian Approach'. *Journal of Experimental Child Psychology,* 110(3): 332–46.

Hudson, Wayne. 1982. *The Marxist Philosophy of Ernst Bloch*. London: Macmillan.

Hymer, Stephen Herbert. 1979. *The Multinational Corporation*. Cambridge: Cambridge University Press.

Israel, Jonathan I. 2002. *The Radical Enlightenment: Philosophy and the Making of Modernity 1650–1750*. Oxford: Oxford University Press.

Jacob, Margaret C. 2003. *The Radical Enlightenment: Pantheists, Freemasons and Republicans,* [1981], 2nd ed. The Temple Publishers.

Jacobs, Jane. 1961. *The Death and Life of Great American Cities*. New York: Vintage.

Jameson, Fredric. 2003. 'Future City', *New Left Review*, 21, May–June: 65–79.

Jaspers, Karl. 1993. *The Great Philosophers, Volume III*. Trans. Edith Ehrlich and Leonard H. Ehrlich, New York: Harcourt Brace.

Joas, Hans. 1997. *G.H. Mead: A Contemporary Re-Examination of His Thought*. Trans. Raymond Meyer, Cambridge: MIT Press.

Johnson, Mark. 1987. *The Body in the Mind: The Bodily Basis of Meaning, Imagination, and Reason*. Chicago: University of Chicago Press.

Johnson, Mark. 2007. *The Meaning of the Body: Aesthetics of Human Understanding*. Chicago: University of Chicago Press.

Johnston, Adrian. 2014. *Adventures in Transcendental Materialism: Dialogues with Contemporary Thinkers*. Edinburgh: Edinburgh University Press.

Josephson, Brian D. 2013. 'Biological Observer-Participation and Wheeler's "Law without Law"'. *In:* Plamen L. Simeonov, Leslie S. Smith and Andrée C. Ehresmann, eds. *Integral Biomathics: Tracing the Road to Reality*. Heidelberg: Springer, 253–258.

Juarrero, Alicia. 2002. *Dynamics in Action: Intentional Behavior as a Complex System*. Cambridge: MIT Press.

Kalecki, Michal. 1943. 'Political Aspects of Full Employment', *Political Quarterly*, 14(4): 322–331.

Kagan, Jerome. 2009. *The Three Cultures: Natural Sciences, Social Sciences, and the Humanities in the 21st Century, Revisiting C.P. Snow*. Cambridge: Cambridge University Press.

Kampis, George and Peter Weibel, eds. 1993. *Endophysics: The World from Within*. Santa Cruz: Aerial.

Kant, Immanuel. 1987. *Critique of Judgment*. Trans. Werner S. Pluhar. Indianapolis: Hackett.

Kant, Immanuel. 1996. *Critique of Pure Reason*. Trans. Werner S. Pluhar. Indianapolis: Hackett.

Kant, Immanuel. 2005. *Introduction to Logic*. Trans. Thomas Kingsmill Abbott, New York: Barnes & Noble.

Kauffman, Stuart A. 1993. *The Origins of Order: Self-Organization and Selection in Evolution*. New York: Oxford University Press.

Kauffman, Stuart. 2000. 'Emergence and Story: Beyond Newton, Einstein and Bohr?' *Investigations*. Oxford: Oxford University Press, 119–140.

Kauffman, Stuart. 2008. *Reinventing the Sacred*. New York: Basic Books.

Kauffman, Stuart and Arran Gare, 2015. 'Beyond Descartes and Newton: Recovering life and humanity', *Progress in Biophysics and Molecular Biology*, 119: 219–244.

Keil, Roger, et al., ed. 1998. *Political Ecology: Global and Local*. London: Routledge.

Keynes, John Maynard. 1933. 'National Self-sufficiency', Yale Review, 22(4) June: 755–769.

Kitcher, Philip. 1984. *The Nature of Mathematical Knowledge*. New York: Oxford University Press.

Kitcher, Philip. 2011. 'Philosophy Inside Out', *Metaphilosophy*, 42(3): 248–260.

Klein, Naomi. 2014. *This Changes Everything: Capitalism vs the Climate*. Harmondsworth: Penguin.

Kolak, Daniel and John Symons. 2004. 'The Results are In: The Scope and Import of Hintikka's Philosophy'. *In:* Daniel Kolak and John Symons, *Quantifiers, Questions and Quantum Physics: Essays on the Philosophy of Jaakko Hintikka*. Dordrecht: Springer.

Kolakowski, Leszek. 1971. 'Marx and the Classical Definition of Truth'. *In:* Leszek Kolakowski. *Marxism and Beyond*. Trans. Jane Zielonko Peel, London: Paladin, 59–87.

Kormondy, Edward J. and Brown, Daniel E. 1988. *Fundamentals of Human Ecology*. New Jersey: Prentice Hall.

Korten, David C. 2000. *The Post-Corporate World*. West Hartford: Kumarian Press.

Kovel, Joel. 1991. *History and Spirit: An Inquiry into the Philosophy of Liberation*. Boston: Beacon Press.

Kovel, Joel. 2007. *The Enemy of Nature: The End of Capitalism or the End of the World?* 2nd ed. London: Zed Books.

Kuhn, Thomas S. 1957. *The Copernican Revolution*. Chicago: University of Chicago Press.

Kuhn, Thomas S.1962. *The Structure of Scientific Revolutions*. Chicago: University of Chicago Press.

Kuhn, Thomas S. 1977. *The Essential Tension*. Chicago: University of Chicago Press.

Kull, Kalevi. 2009. 'Vegetative, Animal, and Cultural Semiosis: The Semiotic Threshold Zones', *Cognitive Semiotics*, 4: 8–27.

Kull, Kalevi. 2010. 'Ecosystems are Made of Semiotic Bonds: Consortia, Umwelten, Biophony and Ecological Codes', *Biosemiotics*, 3: 347–357.

Lakatos, Imre, 1978. *The Methodology of Scientific Research Programmes*. John Worrall and Gregory Currie ed. Cambridge: Cambridge University Press.

Lakatos, Imre. 1986. *Proofs and Refutations: The Logic of Mathematical Discovery*. John Worrall and Elie Zahar, eds. Cambridge: Cambridge University Press.

Lakoff, George. 1987. *Women, Fire, and Dangerous Things: What Categories Reveal about the Mind*. Chicago: University of Chicago Press.

Lakoff, George. 1996. *Moral Politics*. Chicago: University of Chicago Press.

Lakoff, George and Rafael E. Núñez. 2000. *Where Mathematics Comes From: How the Embodied Mind Brings Mathematics into Being*. New York: Basic Books.

Lamprecht, Sterling P. 1946. 'Metaphysics: Its Function, Consequences, and Criteria', *The Journal of Philosophy*, XLIII(15): 393–401.

Langer, Susanne K. *Mind: An Essay on Human Feeling*, 3 volumes. Baltimore: John Hopkins University Press, 1970–1984.

Langbein, Hermann. 2004. *People in Auschwitz*. Trans. Harry Zohn, University of Carolina Press.

Laske, Otto E. 2008. *Measuring Hidden Dimensions of Human Systems*. Medford: Interdevelopmental Institute Press.

Latsis, Spiro. 1976. 'A Research Programme in Economics'. *In:* Spiro Latsis, ed. *Method and Appraisal in Economics*. Cambridge: Cambridge University Press, 1–41.

Lawn, Philip, ed. 2006. *Sustainable Development Indicators in Ecological Economics*. Cheltenham: Edward Elgar.

Lawn, Philip. 2007. *Frontier Issues in Ecological Economics*. Cheltenham: Edward Elgar.

Lawvere, F. William. 1996. 'Grassmann's Dialectics and Category Theory'. *In:* Gert Schubring ed., *Hermann Günther Grassmann (1809–1877): Visionary Mathematician, Scientist and Neohumanist Scholar*. Dordrecht: Kluwer: 255–264.

Lazzarato, Maurizio. 2004. 'From Capital-Labour to Capital-Life', *Ephemera: Theory & Politics in Organization*, 4(3): 187–208.

Lazzarato, Maurizio. 2015. *Governing by Debt*. Trans. Joshua David Jordan, South Pasadena: Semiotext(e).

Leclerc, Ivor. 1972. *The Nature of Physical Existence*. London: George Allen & Unwin.

Leclerc. Ivor. 1986. *The Philosophy of Nature*. Washington: The Catholic University of America Press.

Lecourt, Dominique. 1975. *Marxism and Epistemology: Bachelard, Canguilhem and Foucault*. Trans. Ben Brewster, London: NLB.

Leff, Enrique. 1995. *Green Production: Toward an Environmental Rationality*. New York: Guilford Press.

Lefebvre, Henri. 1991. *The Production of Space*. Trans. D Nicholson-Smith, Oxford: Blackwell.

Lenhard, Johannes and Michael Otte. 2010. 'Two Types of Mathematization', *In:* B. Van Kerkhove, J. De Vuyst and J.P. Van Bendegem, eds. *Philosophical Perspectives on Mathematics,* London: College Publications, Essay 12, 301–339.

Leontief, Wassily. 1982. 'Academic Economics', *Science,* 217: 104–107.

Leopold, Aldo. 1949. *A Sand County Almanac and Sketches Here and There*. London: Oxford University Press.

Levin, Simon. 1999. *Fragile Dominion: Complexity and the Commons.* Cambridge, MA: Perseus.

Levins, Richard and Richard Lewontin. 1985. *The Dialectical Biologist.* Cambridge, MA: Harvard University Press.

Lewontin, Richard and Richard Levins. 2007. *Biology Under the Influence: Dialectical Essays on Ecology, Agriculture, and Health.* New York: Monthly Review Press.

Lévi-Strauss, Claude. 1969. *Totemism.* trans. Rodney Needham, Harmondsworth: Penguin.

Lévi-Strauss, Claude. 1972. *The Savage Mind.* London: Weidenfeld and Nicolson.

Lichtheim, George. 1961. *Marxism.* London: Routledge.

Limnatis, Nectarios G. 2008. *German Idealism and the Problem of Knowledge: Kant, Fichte, Schelling and Hegel.* Dordrecht: Springer.

Limnatis, Nectarios G. ed. 2010. *The Dimensions of Hegel's Dialectic,* London: Continuum.

List, Friedrich. 2010. *National System of Political Economy* [1856]. Trans. G.A. Matile. Ann Arbour: University of Michigan Library.

Livingston, Paul M. 2004. *Philosophical History and the Problem of Consciousness.* Cambridge: Cambridge University Press.

Livingston, Paul M. 2012. *The Politics of Logic: Badiou, Wittgenstein, and the Consequences of Formalism.* New York: Routledge.

Lizardo, Omar. 2004. 'The Cognitive Origins of Bourdieu's *Habitus*', *Journal for the Theory of Social Behaviour,* 34 (4): 375–401.

Louie, A.H. 2009. *More Than Life Itself: A Synthetic Continuation in Relational Biology.* Frankfurt: Ontos Verlag.

Louie, A.H. 2013. *The Reflection of Life: Functional Entailment and Imminence in Relational Biology,* Berlin: Springer.

Loux, Michael J. ed. 1979. *The Possible and the Actual: Readings in the Metaphysics of Modality.* Ithaca: Cornell University Press.

Luft, Sebastian. 2010. 'Reconstruction and Reduction: Natorp and Husserl on Method and the Question of Subjectivity'. *In:* Rudolf A. Makkreel and Sebastian Luft, *Neo-Kantianism in Contemporary Philosophy.* Bloomington: Indiana University Press, 59–91.

Lukács, Georg. 1971. *History and Class Consciousness: Studies in Marxist Dialectics.* Trans. Rodney Livingstone, London: Merlin Press.

Mac Lane, Saunders. 1981. 'Mathematical Models: A Sketch for a Philosophy of Mathematics', *The American Mathematical Monthly,* 88(7) Aug/Sept.: 462–472.

MacArthur, David. 2008. 'Quinean Naturalism in Question'. *Philo,* 11(1): 5–18.

MacIntyre, Alasdair. 1977. 'Epistemological Crises, Dramatic Narrative and the Philosophy of Science', *Monist,* 60: 453–472.

MacIntyre, Alasdair. 1999. *Dependent Rational Animals: Why Human Beings Need the Virtues.* Chicago: Open Court.

MacIntyre, Alasdair. 2006. *Ethics and Politics: Selected Essays, Volume 2.* Cambridge: Cambridge University Press.

MacIntyre, Alasdair. 2007. *After Virtue,* 3rd ed. Notre Dame: University of Notre Dame Press.

Macpherson, C.B. 1964. *The Political Theory of Possessive Individualism: Hobbes to Locke.* Oxford: Oxford University Press.

Makreel, Rudolf A. 1994. *Imagination and Interpretation in Kant.* Chicago: University of Chicago Press.

Mander, W.J. 2011. *British Idealism: A History.* Oxford: Oxford University Press.

Marchart, Oliver. 2007. *Post-Foundational Political Thought,* Edinburgh: Edinburgh University Press.

Martin, Xavier. 2001. *Human Nature and the French Revolution.* New York: Berghahn Books.

Martinez-Alier, Juan. 1987. *Ecological Economics: Energy, Environment and Society.* Oxford: Blackwell.

Marx, Karl and Friedrich Engels. 1962. *Karl Marx and Friedrich Engels: Selected Works in Two Volumes*. Moscow: Foreign Languages Publishing House, Vol.II.

Marx, Karl. 1962. *Capital*, Vol.I. Trans. Samuel Moore and Edward Aveling. Moscow: Progress Publishers.

Marx, Karl. 1970. *A Contribution to the Critique of Political Economy*. Trans. S.W. Ryazanskaya, Moscow: Progress Publishers.

Marx, Karl. 1973. *The Poverty of Philosophy*. Moscow: Progress Publishers.

Marx, Karl. 1978. *The Marx-Engels Reader,* 2nd ed. Robert C. Tucker ed. New York: Norton.

Mason, Paul. 2015. *Postcapitalism: A Guide to Our Future*. London: Allen Lane.

Matavers, Derek and Jon Pike. 2005. *Debates in Contemporary Political Philosophy: An Anthology*. London and New York: Routledge.

Mathews, Freya. 2003. *For Love of Matter: A Contemporary Panpsychism*. Albany. NY: SUNY.

Matthews, Bruce. 2011. *Schelling's Organic Form of Philosophy: Life as the Schema of Freedom*. New York: SUNY Press.

Mayumi, Kozo. 2001. *The Origins of Ecological Economics*. London: Routledge.

McCumber, John. 2001. *Time in the Ditch: American Philosophy and the McCarthy Era*. Evanston: Northwestern University Press.

McDonald, Christine. 2008. *Green, Inc.: An Environmental Insider Reveals How a Good Cause Has Gone Bad*. Guilford: The Lyons Press.

McDonough, William and Michael Braungart. 2002. *Cradle to Cradle: Remaking the Way We Make Things*. New York: North Point Press.

McKinney, Ronald H. 1983. 'The Origins of Modern Dialectics'. *Journal of the History of Ideas*, 44(2): 179–190.

McMullin, Ernan. 1978. *Newton on Matter and Activity*. Notre Dame: Notre Dame University Press.

McNeill, William H. 1980. *The Human Condition: An Ecological and Historical View*. Princeton: Princeton University Press.

Meillassoux, Quentin. 2012. *After Finitude*. Trans. Ray Brassier, London: Bloomsbury.

Merleau-Ponty, Maurice. 1973. *Adventures of the Dialectic*. Trans. Joseph Bien. Evanston: Northwestern University Press.

Merleau-Ponty, Maurice. 2003. *Nature: Course Notes from the College de France*. Trans. Robert Vallier, Evanston: Northwestern University Press.

Mersenne, Marin. 1974. *L'Impiété de deists,* (Paris, 1624), Vol.I, 230f. Trans. and quoted by A.C. Crombie, 'Mersenne', *In*: Charles Coulston Gillispie ed., *Dictionary of Scientific Biography,* 16 vols. New York: Scribner 1970–80, Vol. IX, 317.

Miller, David. 1990. *Market, State and Community: Theoretical Foundations of Market Socialism*. Oxford: Clarendon Press.

Miller, David. 2000. *Citizenship and National Identity*. Oxford: Polity Press.

Miller, David, ed. 2006. *The Liberty Reader*. Boulder: Paradigm Publishers.

Miller, David. 2013. *Justice for Earthlings*. Cambridge: Cambridge University Press.

Minsky, Hyman P. 2008. *Stabilizing an Unstable Economy*. New York: McGraw Hill.

Mirowski, Philip. 1989. *More Heat than Light: Economics as Social Physics, Physics as Nature's Economics*. Cambridge University Press.

Mirowski, Philip and Dieter Plehwe, eds. 2009. *The Road from Mont Pèlerin: The Making of the Neoliberal Thought Collective*. Cambridge, MA: Harvard University Press.

Mirowski, Philip. 2011. *Science-Mart: Privatising American Science*. Cambridge: Harvard University Press.

Mirowski, Philip. 2013. *Never Let a Serious Crisis go to Waste*. London: Verso.

Modak-Truran, Mark. 2008. 'Prolegomena to a Process Theory of Natural Law'. *In:* Michael Weber and Will Desmond, eds. *Handbook of Whiteheadian Process Thought.* Ontos Verlag, 507–519.

Monbiot, George. 2006. *Heat: How to Stop the Planet Burning.* London: Penguin.

Moore, Matthew E. 2010. *New Essays on Peirce's Mathematical Philosophy.* Chicago: Open Court.

Morris, William. 1999. *William Morris on Art and Socialism.* Norman Kelvin, ed. Mineola: Dover.

Mumford, Lewis. 1972. Quote from *The Myth of the Machine. In:* Erich Fromm, Erich. *The Anatomy of Human Destructiveness.* New York: Holt, Rinehart and Winston.

Nell, Edward J. 1984. 'The revival of political economy' in *Growth, Profits, & Property: Essays in the Revival of Political Economy.* Edward J. Nell ed. Cambridge: Cambridge University Press, 19–28.

Nell, Edward. 1996. *Making Sense of a Changing Economy, Technology, Markets and Morals.* London: Routledge.

Nell, Edward J. 1998. *The General Theory of Transformational Growth: Keynes After Sraffa.* Cambridge: Cambridge University Press.

Nietzsche, Friedrich. 1956. 'The Birth of Tragedy'. *In:* Friedrich Nietzsche. *The Birth of Tragedy and The Genealogy of Morals.* Trans. Francis Golffing. New York: Anchor Books.

Nietzsche, Friedrich. 1990. *Twilight of the Idols.* Trans. R.J. Hollingdale, Harmondsworth: Penguin.

Nirenberg, Ricardo L. and David Nirenberg. 2011. 'Badiou's Number: A Critique of Mathematics as Ontology'. *Critical Inquiry,* 37(4): 583–614.

Noorden, Richard Van. 2014. 'Publishers withdraw more than 120 gibberish papers'. *Nature,* 25 February. doi: 10.1038/nature.2014.14763.

Norgaard, Richard B. 1994. *Development Betrayed: The End of Progress and a Coevolutionary Revisioning of the Future.* London: Routledge.

Nove, Alex. 1987. *The Economics of Feasible Socialism.* London: George Allen and Unwin.

O'Connor, James. 1987. *The Meaning of Crisis: A Theoretical Introduction.* Oxford: Blackwell.

O'Connor, James. 1998. *Natural Causes: Essays in Ecological Marxism.* New York: Guilford Press.

Olafson, Frederick A. 2001. *Naturalism and the Human Condition: Against Scientism.* London: Routledge.

Ollman, Bertell. 2008. 'Why Dialectics? Why Now?' *In:* Ollman and Smith, eds. *Dialectics for the New Century.* London: Palgrave, 8–25.

Ollman, Bertell and Tony Smith, eds. 2008. *Dialectics for the New Century.* London: Palgrave.

O'Neill, R.V. et al. 1986. *A Hierarchical Concept of Ecosystems.* Princeton: Princeton University Press.

Orlov, Dmitry. 2013. *The Five Stages of Collapse: Survivor's Toolkit.* Gabriola Island: New Society.

Ormerod, Paul. 1998. *Butterfly Economics.* London: Faber and Faber.

Ostrom, Elinor. 1990. *Governing the Commons: The Evolution of Institutions for Collective Action.* Cambridge: Cambridge University Press.

Ostrom, Elinor et al. eds. 2002. *The Drama of the Commons.* Washington DC: National Academy Press.

Otte, Michael. 2011. 'Justus and Hermann Grassmann: Philosophy and Mathematics', *In:* Hans Joachim Petsche ed. *Herman Grassmann: From Past to Future,* Basel: Springer, 61–70.

Parker, Kelley A. 2004. 'Josiah Royce', *In:* Edward N. Zalta, ed., *Stanford Encyclopedia of Philosophy,* URL = http://plato.stanford.edu/archives/fall2004/entries/royce/

Patomäki, Heikki. 2015. 'Why Do Social Sciences Matter'. *In:* Paul-Erik Korvela, Kari Palonen and Anna Björk, eds. *The Politics of World Politics.* University of Jyväskylä: SoPhi, 200–223.

Pattee, H.H. 1973. 'The Physical Basis and Origin of Hierarchical Control'. *In:* Howard H. Pattee ed., *Hierarchy Theory: The Challenge of Complex Systems,* ed. New York: George Braziller, 71–108.

Pattee, Howard Hunt and Johanna Rączascek-Leonardi. 2012. *Laws, Language and Life: Howard Pattee's classic papers on the physics of symbols with contemporary commentary*, Dordrecht: Springer.

Paulson, Susan and Lias L. Gezon. 2005. *Political Ecology across Spaces, Scales, and Social Groups*. New Brunswick: Rutgers University Press.

Pearson, James. 2011. 'Distinguishing W.V. Quine and Donald Davidson', *Journal of the History of Analytic Philosophy*, 1(1): 1–22.

Peirce, Charles Sanders. 1955. *Philosophical Writings of Peirce*. New York: Dover.

Peirce, C.S. 1958. *Collected Papers of Charles Sanders Peirce*. C. Hartshorne and P. Weiss eds. Cambridge: Harvard University Press.

Peirce, Charles Sanders. 1992. *The Essential Peirce: Selected Philosophical Writings, Vol.1 (1867–1893)*. Nathan Houser and Christian Kloesel, eds. Bloomington: Indiana University Press.

Peirce, Charles Sanders. 1998. *The Essential Peirce, Vol.2 (1893–1913)*. The Peirce Editions Project ed. Bloomington: Indiana University Press.

Peirce, Charles Sanders. 2007. *Pragmatism as a Principle and Method of Right Thinking: The 1903 Harvard Lectures on Pragmatism*. Patricia Ann Turrisi, ed. New York: SUNY Press.

Perkins, John. 2006. *Confessions of an Economic Hit Man*. New York: Plume.

Perelman, Michael. 2007. *The Confiscation of American Prosperity: From Right-Wing Extremism and Economic Ideology to the Next Great Depression*. New York: Palgrave.

Perron, Paul, et al. eds. 2000. *Semiotics as a Bridge Between the Humanities and the Sciences*. New York: Legas.

Peterson, Garry, Craig R. Allen, and C.S. Holling. 2010. 'Ecological Resilience, Biodiversity, and Scale'. *In:* Lance H. Gunderson, Craig R. Allen and C.S. Holling, eds. *Foundations of Ecological Resilience*. Washington: Island Press, 167–193.

Petsche, Hans-Joachim. 2009. *Hermann Grassmann: Biography*. Trans. Mark Minnes. Basel: Birkhäuser.

Pettifor, Ann. 2006. *The Coming First World Debt Crisis*. Houndmills: Palgrave.

Pettit, Philip. 2012. *On the People's Terms: A Republican Theory and Model of Democracy*. Cambridge: Cambridge University Press.

Piaget, Jean. 1971a. *Insight and Illusions of Philosophy*. Trans. Wolfe Mays. Chicago: Meridian.

Piaget, Jean. 1971b. *Biology and Knowledge: An Essay on the Relations between Organic Regulations and Cognitive Processes*. Trans. Beatrix Walsh. Chicago: University of Chicago Press.

Piaget, Jean. 1971c. *Structuralism*. Trans. Chaninah Maschler. London: Routledge and Kegan Paul.

Piaget, Jean 1976. 'A Brief Tribute to Goldmann', *In* Lucian Goldmann, *Cultural Creation in Modern Society*. Trans. Bart Grahl, Saint Louis: Telos, Appendix 1, 125–127.

Piaget, Jean. 1995. *Sociological Studies*. Leslie Smith ed. Trans. Terrance Brown et al. London and New York: Routledge.

Pibram, Karl. 1991. 'The Implicate Brain'. *In:* B.J. Hiley and F. David Peat, eds. *Quantum Implications: Essays in Honour of David Bohm*. London and New York: Routledge, 365–371.

Piketty, Thomas. 2014. *Capital in the Twenty-First Century*. Trans. Arthur Goldhammer, Cambridge, MA: Belknap Press.

Pihlström, Sami. 1998. *Pragmatism and Philosophical Anthropology*. New York: Peter Lang.

Pimentel, David, Laura Westra, and Reed F. Noss, eds. 2000. *Ecological Integrity: Integrating Environment, Conservation, and Health*. Washington: Island Press.

Pitte, Frederick P. Van de, 1971. *Kant as Philosophical Anthropologist*. The Hague: Martinus Nijhoff.

Plehwe, Dieter, Bernard Walpen, and Gisela Neunhöffer, eds. 2006. *Neoliberal Hegemony: A Global Critique*. Abingdon: Routledge.

Pocock, J.G.A. 1975. *The Machiavellian Moment: Florentine Political Thought and the Atlantic Republican Tradition*. Princeton: Princeton University Press.

Polak, Fred. 1973. *The Image of the Future*. Trans. and abridged by Elise Boulding, San Francisco: Josey-Bass.

Polanyi, Karl. 1957. *The Great Transformation*. Boston: Beacon.

Polanyi, Michael. 1958. *Personal Knowledge*. Chicago: University of Chicago Press.

Polanyi, Michael. 1969. *Knowing and Being: Essays by Michael Polanyi*. Marjorie Grene ed. Chicago: University of Chicago Press.

Popper, Karl R. 1969. *Conjectures and Refutations*, 3rd ed. London: Routledge.

Potter, S.J. Vincent G. 1997. *Charles S. Peirce: On Norms & Ideals*. New York: Fordham University Press.

Prigogine, Ilya. 1980. *From Being to Becoming: Time and Complexity in the Physical Sciences*. San Francisco: W.H. Freeman.

Prigogine, Ilya and Isabelle Stengers. 1984. *Order Out of Chaos*. New York: Bantam Books.

Prugh, Thomas, Robert Costanza, and Herman Daly. 2000. *The Local Politics of Global Sustainability*. Washington: Island Press.

Putnam, Hilary. 1990. *Realism with a Human Face*. Cambridge, MA: Harvard University Press.

Putnam, Hilary. 1992. *Renewing Philosophy*. Cambridge, MA: Harvard University Press.

Pylkkänen, Paavo T.I. 2007. *Mind, Matter and the Implicate Order*. Berlin: Springer.

Quiggin, John. 2010. *Zombie Economics: How Dead Ideas Still Walk Amongst Us: A Chilling Tale by John Quiggin*. Princeton: Princeton University Press.

Quine, W.V. 1959. *Methods of Logic*, 2nd ed. Cambridge, MA: Harvard University Press.

Quine, W.V. 1960. *Word & Object*. Cambridge, MA: Harvard University Press.

Quine, W.V. 1961. *From a Logical Point of View: Logico-Philosophical Essays*, 2nd ed. New York: Harper & Row.

Quine, W.V. 1969. *Ontological Relativity and Other Essays*. New York: Columbia University Press.

Quine, W.V. 1981. *Theories and Things*. Cambridge, MA: Harvard University Press.

Radu, Mircea. 2000. 'Justus Grassmann's Contributions to the Foundations of Mathematics: Mathematical and Philosophical Aspects', *Historia Mathematica*, 27: 4–35.

Ráez-Luna, Ernesto R. 2008. 'Third World Inequity, Critical Political Economy, and the Ecosystem'. *In* Approach'. David Waltner-Toews, James J. Kay and Nina-Marie E Lister, eds. *The Ecosystem Approach: Complexity, Uncertainty, and Managing for Sustainability*. New York: Columbia University Press, Ch.18.

Rappaport. R.A. 1990. 'Ecosystems, Populations and People'. *In* E.F. Moran, ed., *The Ecosystem Approach in Anthropology: From Concept to Practice*. Ann Arbor: University of Michigan Press, 41–72.

Redding, Paul. 2009. *Continental Idealism: Leibniz to Nietzsche*. London: Routledge.

Reid, Robert G.B. *Biological Emergences: Evolution by Natural Experiment*. Cambridge: MIT Press, 2007.

Reinert, Erik S. ed. 2004. *Globalization, Economic Development and Inequality: An Alternative Perspective*. Cheltenham: Edgar Elgar.

Reinert, Erik S. 2007. *How Rich Countries Got Rich ... And Why Poor Countries Stay Poor*. New York: Carrol & Graf.

Reinert, Erik S. and Francesca Lidia Viano. 2012. *Thorstein Veblen: Economics for an Age of Crisis*. London: Anthem Press.

Rescher, Nicholas. 1996. *Process Metaphysics: an Introduction to Process Philosophy*. New York: SUNY Press.

Ricoeur, Paul. 1984. *Time and Narrative, Volume I*. Trans. Kathleen McLaughlin and David Pellauer, Chicago: University of Chicago Press.

Ricoeur, Paul. 1986. *Lectures on Ideology and Utopia.* George H. Taylor, ed. New York: Columbia University Press.

Riegel, Klaus F. 1973. Dialectical Operations: The Final Period of Cognitive Development', *Human Development,* 16: 346–370.

Riegel, Klaus F. 1978. *Foundations of Dialectical Psychology.* New York: Academic Press.

Rispoli, Giulia. 2014. 'Between 'Biosphere' and 'Gaia'. Earth as a Living Organism in Soviet Geo-Ecology'. *Cosmos and History,* 10(2): 78–91.

Ritchie, Jack. 2008. *Understanding Naturalism.* Stocksfield: Acumen.

Ritzer, George. 1993. *The McDonaldization of Society.* Thousand Oaks: Pine Forge Press.

Ritzer, George, ed. 2007. *The Blackwell Companion to Gobalization.* Malden, Oxford and Carlton: Blackwell.

Robinson, William I. 2004. *A Theory of Global Capitalism: Production, Class, and State in a Transnational World.* Baltimore: John Hopkins University Press.

Roe, Emery. 1994. *Narrative Policy Analysis: Theory and Practice.* Durham: Duke University Press.

Romanos, George D. 1983. *Quine and Analytic Philosophy.* Cambridge: MIT Press.

Roosevelt, Frank and David Belkin, ed. 1994. *Why Market Socialism?* Armonk, NY: M.E. Sharpe.

Rorty, Richard. 1980. *Philosophy and the Mirror of Nature.* Oxford: Blackwell.

Rosen, Judith, 2012. 'Preface to the Second Edition: The Nature of Life'. *In:* Rosen Rosen, *Anticipatory Systems: Philosophical, Mathematical and Methodological Foundations,* 2nd ed. New York: Springer, xi–xiv.

Rosen, Robert. 1987. 'Some epistemological issues in physics and biology,' *In:* B.J. Hiley and F. David Peat, eds. *Quantum Implications: Essays in Honour of David Bohm.* London: Routledge, 314–327.

Rosen, Robert. 1991. *Life Itself: A Comprehensive Inquiry into the Nature, Origin, and Fabrication of Life.* New York: Columbia University Press.

Rosen, Robert. 2000. 'The Church-Pythagoras Thesis'. *In:* Robert Rosen, *Essays on Life Itself.* New York: Columbia University Press, 63–81.

Rosen, Robert. 2012. *Anticipatory Systems: Philosophical, Mathematical and Methodological Foundations,* 2nd ed. New York: Springer.

Rosen, Steven M. 2008. *The Self-Evolving Cosmos: A Phenomenological Approach to Nature's Unity-in-Diversity.* Singapore: World Scientific.

Rössler, Otto. 1998. *Endophysics: The World as an Interface.* Singapore: World Scientific.

Rota, Gian-Carlo. 1996. *Indiscrete Thoughts.* Boston: Birkhauser.

Rothschild, M. 1990. *Bionomics: Economy as Ecosystem.* New York: Henry Holt and Co.

Rovelli, Carlo 2014. 'Science Is Not About Certainty'. *In:* John Brockman, *The Universe.* New York: Harper Perennial, 214–228.

Royce, Josiah. 1995. *The Philosophy of Loyalty* [1908]. Nashville, Tennessee, Vanderbilt University Press.

Salthe, Stanley N. 1985. *Evolving Hierarchical Systems.* New York: Columba University Press.

Salthe, Stanley N. 1993. *Development and Evolution: Complexity and Change in Biology.* Cambridge, MA: MIT Press.

Salthe, S. 2005. 'The Natural Philosophy of Ecology: Developmental Systems Ecology', *Ecological Complexity,* 2: 1–19.

Salthe, S.N. 2010. 'Maximum Power and Maximum Entropy Production: Finalities in Nature'. *Cosmos and History,* 6(1): 114–121.

Salthe, S. 2012. 'On the Origin of Semiosis'. *Cybernetics and Human Knowing,* 19(3): 53–66.

Sandel, Michael J. 2005. *Public Philosophy.* Cambridge: Harvard University Press.

Sandel, Michael J. 2005. 'The Procedural Republic and the Unencumbered Self'. *Public Philosophy*. Cambridge, MA: Harvard University Press, 156–173.

Sartre, Jean-Paul. 1968. *Search for a Method*. Trans. Hazel E. Barnes. New York: Vintage.

Sartre, Jean-Paul. 1976. *Critique of Dialectical Reason I*. [1960]. Trans. Alan Sheridan-Smith. London: New Left Books.

Sartre, Jean-Paul. 1991. *Critique of Dialectical Reason Volume II (Unfinished)*. Arlette Elkaim-Sartre, ed. Trans. Quentin Hoare. London: Verso.

Schafer, Paul. 2008. *Revolution or Renaissance: Making the Transition form an Economic Age to a Cultural Age*. Ottawa: Ottawa University Press.

Scheler, Max. 1973. *Formalism in Ethics and Non-Formal Ethics of Values*. Evanston: Northwestern University Press.

Schelling, F.W.J. 1856–61. 'Allgemeine Deduktion des dynamischen Prozesses oder der Kategorien der Physik'. *In:* Friedrich Wilhelm Joseph von Schelling, *Sämmtliche Werke*. ed. K.F.A. Schelling I Abtheilung, vols 1–10, I/4: 1–78.

Schelling, F.W.J. 1936. *Schelling: Of Human Freedom*. Trans. James Gutmann. Chicago: Open Court.

Schelling, F.W.J. 1978. *System of Transcendental Idealism (1800)*. Trans. Peter Heath. Charlottesville: University Press of Virginia.

Schelling, F.W.J. 1989. *The Philosophy of Art*. Trans. Douglas W. Stott. Minneapolis: University of Minnesota Press.

Schelling, F.W.J. von. 1994. *On the History of Modern Philosophy*. Trans. Andrew Bowie. Cambridge: Cambridge University Press.

Schelling, F.W.J. 2000. *The Ages of the World, Third Version (c.1815)*, Trans. Jason W. Wirth. New York: State University of New York Press.

Schelling, F.W.J. 2004. *First Outline of a System of the Philosophy of Nature*, [1799]. Trans. Keith R. Peterson. New York: State University of New York.

Schelling, F.W.J. 2007. *The Grounding of Positive Philosophy: The Berlin Lectures*. Albany: SUNY Press.

Schellnhuber, Hans Joachim. 2008. 'Global Warming: Stop Worrying, Start Panicking?' *PNAS*, 105(37), Sept: 14239–14240. doi: 10.1073/pnas.0807331105.

Schilhab, Theresa, Stjernfelt, Frederik and Deacon, Terrence, eds. 2012. *The Symbolic Species Evolved*. Dordrecht: Springer.

Schiller, Friedrich. 1982. *On the Aesthetic Education of Man In a Series of Letters*. Trans. and ed. Elizabeth M. Wilkinson and L.A. Willoughby. Oxford: The Clarendon Press.

Schleiermacher, Friedrich. 1996. *Dialectic or, The Art of Doing Philosophy*. Trans. Terrance N. Tice, Atlanta: Scholars Press.

Schmid, Christian. 2008. 'Henri Lefebvre's Theory of the Production of Space' *In:* Kanishka Goonewardena et. al. eds. *Space, Difference, Everyday Life: Reading Henri Lefebvre*. New York: Routledge, 27–45.

Sebeok, Thomas A. 2000. 'Semiotics as a Bridge Between the Humanities and the Sciences'. *In:* Paul Perron et al. eds. *Semiotics as a Bridge Between the Humanities and the Sciences,* 76–100.

Seers, Dudley. 1983. *The Political Economy of Nationalism*. Oxford: Oxford University Press.

Seibt, Johanna. 2003. *Process Theories: Crossdisciplinary Studies in Dynamic Categories*. Dordrecht: Kluwer.

Sen, Amartya. 1999. *Development as Freedom,* New York: Anchor Books.

Shaw, Devin Zane. 2010. *Freedom and Nature in Schelling's Philosophy of Art*. London: Continuum.

Shellenberger, Michael and Ted Nordhaus. 2004. *The Death of Environmentalism: Global Warming Politics in a Post-Environmental World*. The Breakthrough Institute. http://thebreakthrough.org/archive/the_death_of_environmentalism [Accessed 3 February 2016].

Siebers, Johan. 2002. *The Method of Speculative Philosophy: An Essay on the Foundation of Whitehead's Metaphysics*. Kassell: Kassell University Press.

Simeonov, Plamen L., Smith, Leslie L. and Ehresmann, Andrée C. eds. 2012. *Integral Biomathics: Tracing the Road to Reality*. Springer-Verlag, Berlin.

Simeonov, Plamen L., K. Matsuno, K. and R.S. Root-Bernstein, eds. 2013. 'Focussed Issue: Can Biology Create a Profoundly New Mathematics and Computation?', *Progress in Biophysics & Molecular Biology,* 113 (2), Sept.

Simeonov, Plamen, Arran Gare and Steven Rosen, eds. 2015. 'Focussed Issue: Integral Biomathics: Life Sciences, Mathematics and Phenomenological Philosophy'. *Progress in Biophysics & Molecular Biology.* 119 (3), Dec.

Simhony, Avital and David Weinstein, ed. 2001. *The New Liberalism: Reconciling Liberty and Community*. Cambridge: Cambridge University Press.

Skinner, Quentin. 1998. *Liberty Before Liberalism*. Cambridge: Cambridge University Press.

Skinner, Quentin. 2002. *Visions of Politics Volume III, Hobbes and Civil Society*. Cambridge: Cambridge University Press.

Skinner, Quentin and Bo Stråth, eds. 2003. *States and Citizens: History, Theory, Prospects*. Cambridge: Cambridge University Press.

Skinner, Quentin. 2003. 'States and the freedom of citizens'. *In:* Quentin Skinner and Bo Stråth, eds. *States and Citizens: History, Theory, Prospects*. Cambridge: Cambridge University Press.

Skinner, Quentin. 2008. *Hobbes and Republican Liberty*. Cambridge: Cambridge University Press, 2008.

Sklair, Leslie. 2001. *The Transnational Capitalist Class*. Oxford: Blackwell.

Skolimowski, Henryk. 1983. 'The Structure of Thinking in Technology'. *In:* Carl Mitcham and Robert Mackey, eds. *Philosophy and Technology: Readings in the Philosophical Problems of Technology*. New York: The Free Press, 42–53.

Smolin, Lee. 2007. *The Trouble with Physics,* Boston: Houghton Mifflin. See also Peter Woit, *Not Even Wrong.* London: Vintage.

Smolin, Lee. 2013. *Time Reborn: From the Crisis in Physics to the Future of the Universe.* Boston: Houghton Mifflin Harcourt.

Smolin, Lee. 2014. 'Think About Nature'. *In:* John Brockman, ed. *The Universe.* New York: Harper Perennial, 127–152.

Smolin, Lee. 2015. 'Temporal Naturalism', *Studies in History and Philosophy of Modern Science Part B: Studies in the History and Philosophy of Modern Physics,* 52 November, Part B: 86–102.

Söderbaum, Peter. 2000. *Ecological Economics: A Political Economics Approach to Environment and Development*. London: Earthscan.

Söderbaum, Peter. 2008. *Understanding Sustainability Economics*. London: Earthscan.

Sorokin, Pitirim A. 1947. *Society, Culture, and Personality: Their Structure and Dynamics*. New York: Harper & Brothers.

Stapp, Henry P. 2006. *Mindful Universe: Quantum Mechanics and the Participating Observer,* Dordrecht: Springer.

Stjernfelt, Frederik. 2007. *Diagrammatology: An Investigation on the Borderlines of Phenomenology, Ontology, and Semiotics*. Dordrecht: Springer.

Straume, Ingerid S. and J.F. Humphrey, eds. 2011. *Depoliticization: The Political Imaginary of Global Capitalism,* Malmö: NSU Press.

Strawson, Galen. 2013. 'Real Naturalism v2', *Metodo. International Studies in Phenomenology and Philosophy,* 1(2): 101–125.

Strawson, P.F. 1992. *Analysis and Metaphysics*. Oxford: Oxford University Press.

Sturm, Douglas. *Solidarity and Suffering: Toward a Politics of Relationality*. New York: SUNY Press, 1998.

Supiot, Alain. 2012. 'Under Eastern Eyes', *New Left Review*. 73, Jan–Feb: 29–36.

Suppe, Frederick. 1977. 'The Search for Philosophical Understanding of Scientific Theories. *In:* Frederick Suppe, ed. *The Structure of Scientific Theories*. 2nd ed. Urbana: University of Chicago Press, 3–243.

Tanner, Richard and Anthony G. Athos. 1986. *The Art of Japanese Management*. London: Penguin.

Taylor, Charles. 1989. *Sources of the Self: The Making of the Modern Identity*. Cambridge: Cambridge University Press.

Taylor, George H. 1986. 'Editor's Introduction'. *In:* Paul Ricoeur, *Lectures on Ideology and Utopia*. New York: Columbia University Press, ix–xxxvii.

Taylor, Maria. 2014. *Global warming and climate change: what Australia knew and buried...then framed a new reality for the public*. Canberra, Australian National University Press.

Thellefsen, Torkild Leo. 2001. 'C.S. Peirce's Evolutionary Sign: an Analysis of Depth and Complexity within Peircian Sign Types'. *Semiotics, Evolution, Energy, and Development*. 1(2): Dec.

Thompson, Evan. 2007. *Mind in Life: Biology, Phenomenology, and the Science of Mind*. Cambridge MA: Belknap Press.

Tiles, Mary. 1984. *Bachelard: Science and Objectivity*. Cambridge: Cambridge University Press.

Todorov, Tzvetan. 1984. 'Philosophical Anthropology'. *In:* Tzvetan Todorov. *Mikhail Bakhtin: The Dialogic Principle*. Trans. Wlad Godzich. Manchester: Manchester University Press, 94–112.

Toews, Edward. 1985. *Hegelianism: the Path Toward Dialectical Humanism, 1805–1841*. Cambridge: Cambridge University Press.

Toscano, Alberto. 2004. 'Philosophy and the Experience of Construction'. *In:* Judith Norman and Alisdair Welchman, eds. *The New Schelling*. London: Continuum, 106–127.

Toulmin, Stephen. 1994. *Cosmopolis: The Hidden Agenda of Modernity*. Chicago: Chicago University Press.

Turchin, Peter. 2007. *War and Peace and War: The Rise and Fall of Empires*. New York: Plume.

Tyler, Colin. 2010. *The Liberal Socialism of Thomas Hill Green, Part 1: The Metaphysics of Self-realisation and Freedom*. Exeter: Imprint Academic.

Tyler, Colin. 2012. *The Liberal Socialism of Thomas Hill Green, Part II, Civil Society, Capitalism and the State*. Exeter: Imprint Academic.

Uexküll, Jacob von. 1926. *Theoretical Biology*. Trans. D.L. MacKinnon, London: Kegan Paul, Trench, Trubner.

Ulanowicz, Robert E. 1997. *Ecology: The Ascendent Perspective*. New York: Columbia University Press.

Ulanowicz, Robert. 2000. 'Toward a Measure in Ecological Integrity'. *In:* David Pimentel, Laura Westra and Reed F. Noss, eds. *Ecological Integrity: Integrating Environment, Conservation, and Health*. Washington: Island Press, 99–120.

Ulanowicz, Robert E. 2009. *A Third Window: Natural Life beyond Newton and Darwin*. West Conschohocken: Templeton Foundation Press.

Unger, Roberto Mangabeira. 1983. 'The Critical Legal Studies Movement', *Harvard Law Review*, 96: 561–675.

Unger, Roberto Mangabeira and Lee Smolin. 2015. *The Singular Universe and the Reality of Time*. Cambridge: Cambridge University Press.

Vanheeswijck, Guido. 1998. 'R.G. Collingwood and A.N. Whitehead on Metaphysics, History, and Cosmology', *Process Studies*, 27/3–4: 215–236.

Varoufakis, Yanis, Joseph Halevi and Nicholas J. Theocarakis. 2011. *Modern Political Economics: Making Sense of the Post-2008 World*. London: Routledge.

Varela, Franciso J., Evan Thompson, and Eleanor Rosch. 1993. *The Embodied Mind: Cognitive Science and Human Experience*. Cambridge, MA: MIT Press.

Vatn, Arild. 2005. *Institutions and the Environment*. Cheltenham: Edward Elgar.

Veilahti, Antti. 2 Oct 2015. 'Alain Badiou's Mistake—Two Postulates of Dialectic Materialism'. arXiv:1301.1203v3 [math.CT].

Verene, Donald Phillip. 2009. *Speculative Philosophy*. Lanham: Lexington Books.

Vickers, Geoffrey. 1973. *Making Institutions Work*. New York: Wiley.

Vijver, Gertrudis van de, Stanley N. Salthe, and Manuela Delpos, eds. 1998. *Evolutionary Systems: Biological and Epistemological Perspectives on Selection and Self-Organization*. Dordrecht: Kluwer.

Waddington, C.H. ed. 1968–72. *Towards a Theoretical Biology*, 4 Vols. Edinburgh: Edinburgh University Press.

Waddington, C.H. 2010. 'The Practical Consequences of Metaphysical Beliefs on a Biologist's Work: An Autobiographical Note'. *In:* CH. Waddington ed. *Sketching Theoretical Biology: Towards a Theoretical Biology, Volume 2*, [1969], 2nd ed. New Brunswick: Transaction, 72–81.

Waibel, Violetta L. 2010. '"With Respect to the Antinomies, Fichte had a Remarkable Idea": Their Answers to Kant and Fichte – Hardenberg, Hölderlin, Hegel'. *In:* Daniel Breazeale and Tom Rockmore, eds. *Fichte, German Idealism, and Early Romanticism*, Amsterdam: Rodopi, 300–326.

Waltner-Toews, David, James J. Kay, and Nina Marie E. Lister, eds. 2008. *The Ecosystem Approach: Complexity, Uncertainty, and Managing for Sustainability*. New York: Columbia University Press.

Wang Hui. 2011. *The End of the Revolution: China and the Limits of Modernity*. London: Verso.

Weart, Spencer. *The Discovery of Global Warming*. Available from: https://www.aip.org/history/climate/index.htm [Accessed 18 January 2016].

Weiner, Douglas R. 1988. *Models of Nature: Ecology, Conservation, and Cultural Revolution in Soviet Russia*. Bloomington: Indiana University Press.

Westra, Laura, Klaus Bosselmann, and Richard Westra, eds. 2008. *Reconciling Human Existence with Ecological Integrity*. London: Earthscan.

Westra, Laura, Klaus Bosselmann, and Colin Soskolne, eds. 2011. *Globalisation and Ecological Integrity in Science and International Law*. Newcastle On Tyne: Cambridge Scholars.

Westra, Richard. 2010. *Confronting Global Neoliberalism: Third World Resistance and Development Strategies*. Atlanta: Clarity Press.

Wheeler, Wendy. 2006. *The Whole Creature: Complexity, Biosemiotics and the Evolution of Culture*. London: Lawrence & Wishart.

White, James D. 1996. *Karl Marx and the Origins of Dialectical Materialism*. Houndmills: Macmillan.

Whitehead, Alfred North. 1929. *The Function of Reason*. Princeton: Princeton University Press.

Whitehead, Alfred North. 1932. *Science and the Modern World*. Cambridge: Cambridge University Press.

Whitehead, Alfred North. 1933. *Adventures of Ideas*. New York: The Free Press.

Whitehead, Alfred North. 1938. *Modes of Thought*. New York: The Free Press.

Whitehead, Alfred North. 1955. Quote. *In:* W.W. Sawyer, *Prelude to Mathematics*. London: Penguin, 183.

Whitehead, Alfred North. 1978. *Process and Reality* [1929], corrected edition. David Ray Griffin and Donald W. Sherburne, eds. New York: Free Press.

Whitrow, G.J. 1980. *The Natural Philosophy of Time*. 2nd ed. Oxford: Clarendon Press.

Whitton, Evan. 2005. *Serial Liars: How Lawyers Get the Money and Get the Criminals Off.* Raleigh: Lulu.

Wiener, Norbert. 1993. *Invention: The Care and Feeding of Ideas.* Cambridge: MIT Press.

Wilkinson, Richard and Kate Picket. 2009. *The Spirit Level: Why More Equal Societies Almost Always do Better.* London: Allen Lane.

Williams, Robert R. 1992. *Recognition: Fichte and Hegel on the Other.* New York: SUNY Press.

Williams, Robert R. 1997. *Hegel's Ethics of Recognition.* Berkeley: University of California Press.

Wittbecker, Alan. 2011. *Global Government: Creating a System for Conducting the Planet.* 3rd ed. Sarasota: Clio Press.

Wittgenstein, Ludwig. 1968. *Philosophical Investigations.* Trans. G.E. Anscombe, 3rd ed., Oxford: Basil Blackwell.

Woit, Peter. 2007. *Not Even Wrong.* London: Vintage Books.

Wolin, Sheldon S. 2008. *Democracy Inc.: Managed Democracy and the Spectre of Inverted Totalitarianism.* Princeton: Princeton University Press.

Worster, Donald. 1994. *Nature's Economy: A History of Ecological Ideas.* 2nd ed. Cambridge: Cambridge University Press.

Yi, Guo, Sasa Josifovic, and Auman Lätzer-Lasar, eds. 2013. *Metaphysical Foundations of Knowledge and Ethics in Chinese and European Philosophy.* Paperborn: Wilhelm Fink.

Young, Robert M. 1985. *Darwin's Metaphor: Nature's Place in Victorian Culture.* Cambridge: Cambridge University Press.

Zalamea, Fernando. 2012. *Synthetic Philosophy of Contemporary Mathematics.* Trans. Zachary Luke Fraser, New York: Orchard Street.

Zammito, John. 2002. *Kant, Herder and the Birth of Anthropology.* Chicago: Chicago University Press, 2002.

Zijderveld, Anton C. 1979. *On Clichés: The Supersedure of Meaning by Function in Modernity,* London: Routledge and Kegan Paul.

Index

End of chapter notes are denoted by a letter n between page number and note number.